Our Voices: *Indigeneity and Architecture*

By Rebecca Kiddle, luugigyoo patrick stewart, and Kevin O'Brien

ORO

EDITIONS

EDITIONS

Publishers of Architecture, Art, and Design
Gordon Goff: Publisher

www.oroeditions.com
info@oroeditions.com

Published by ORO Editions

Graphic Design: Gordon Tillotson
ORO Project Coordinator: Kirby Anderson

10 9 8 7 6 5 4 3 2 First Edition

Library of Congress data available upon request. World Rights: Available

ISBN: 978-1-940743-49-3

Color Separations and Printing: ORO Group Ltd.
Printed in China.

International Distribution: www.oroeditions.com/distribution

ORO Editions makes a continuous effort to minimize the overall carbon footprint of its publications. As part of this goal, ORO Editions, in association with Global ReLeaf, arranges to plant trees to replace those used in the manufacturing of the paper produced for its books. Global ReLeaf is an international campaign run by American Forests, one of the world's oldest nonprofit conservation organizations. Global ReLeaf is American Forests' education and action program that helps individuals, organizations, agencies, and corporations improve the local and global environment by planting and caring for trees.

Table of Contents

For Rewi Thompson

Tribute to Rewi Thompson

Nui whetu i te rangi, mau tonu, mau tonu,
Whatu ngarongaro i te whenua,
Ngaro noa, ngaro noa…

Rewi was strapped at primary school, because Neil Armstrong had just landed on the moon, and a young Rewi, beguiled by this, wanted to be an astronaut. I mean who wouldn't?

Rewi Michael Robert Thompson, architect and adjunct professor of architecture, was born in 1953 to Bobby and Mei Thompson. He was one of the first generation of 'urban Māori' who were raised away from their tūrangawaewae and in the city, in his case Wellington, where his father worked as a bus driver. Unlike many other young Māori people living in similar circumstances, Rewi and his older sister, Ngapine, maintained strong connections to their Ngāti Porou and Ngāti Raukawa whānau and marae. These experiences would become formative influences on his conception of architecture as being fundamentally concerned with land and people, and conviction that architecture could return identity and well-being to people suffering from cultural estrangement.

Rewi originally trained as an engineer at Wellington Polytechnic and, for a short time, worked as a structural draughtsperson at Structon Group before leaving to study architecture at the University of Auckland. Fellow students fondly recall him arriving equipped with a set of highlighter pens and wearing jandals. His exceptional talents became immediately apparent to staff and students. David Mitchell, who was one of his earliest design tutors, recalled that one of Rewi's first student projects was the design of "a bach on an exposed bush-clad site. All the students tried to tone their buildings in with the bush, all except for Rewi. He painted his bright pink and, boy, did it look good. It was a signal about the future" (personal communication to Deidre Brown, 2016). David would later include Rewi's Ngāti Poneke Marae student project in his 1984 book *The Elegant Shed* as an

example of how customary concepts could inform large-scale, urban, contemporary building proposals. This work has influenced many Māori architecture students by demonstrating that Māori architecture can be more than just red ochre paint and a pitched roof, in this instance, a glass and steel monolith cascading down into the Wellington harbour.

In 1983, after registration as an architect, Rewi established his own practice. Three years later, his reputation was such that he joined 'esteemed architects' Ian Athfield, John Blair and Roger Walker on a lecture tour of the United States. His highly-expressive formalism was articulated across a number of residential, commercial, and institutional projects during the 'boom' construction period that occurred between the election of the Labour Government 'in 1984 and the building industry's decline following the 1987 Stock Market Crash. They included: the undulating terraced Wiri State Housing precinct, built as an urban papakāinga - (village) (1986 -1989); the abstracted fish canopies that gave a Pacific identity to the otherwise bland Ōtara Town Centre (1987); and the dynamic Capital Discovery Place and City to Sea Bridge that reimagined the creation stories of Te Whanganui-a-Tara, also known today as Wellington (1988, 1990-1994). His diverse practice extended into exhibition design with the innovative waka huia (treasure box) receptacle that he created for the Ko Tawa touring show of taonga Māori (Māori treasures) associated with Gilbert Mair, its curator, Paul Tapsell, described it as "the boldest ever Māori touring exhibition of the 2000s. Small, compact, but powerful in its wakahuia contained message: the living are the object of our ancestry, not the dead" (Tapsell, 2017). Another important, but unrealised, project dealing with the idea of architecture as a taonga was the shortlisted proposal for the new Museum of New Zealand building, undertaken with Ian Athfield and Frank Gehry. In a very telling comment, made in response to misunderstandings about his work, he once said, "if it can't be absorbed or understood in a bicultural sense then it is seen as a resistance or protest" (Thompson in sub.sist, 2009). Yet, for many in the architectural community, Rewi's ability to undermine western assumptions about architecture through his work was one of his greatest strengths.

Rewi's most notable project was his own home in Auckland's Kohimarama (1985) with its distinctive ziggurat form based on the Māori poutama (or stairway to heaven) tukutuku pattern. Bill McKay recalls Thom Mayne, founder of Morphosis, describing it as the only uniquely distinctive building in New Zealand (personal communication to Deidre Brown, 2016). Founding Director of TOA Architects, Nicholas Dalton, remarks of Rewi's house that it is:

An all-powerful statement of mana, located in an affluent and polite suburb, the house is a calm, yet staunch protest executed in the humblest of ways, simple, plywood cladding, with arrow or taiaha slots to the sides, like a modern day pā, no taiapa fencing but symbolically every bit as steadfast as the Ngai Te Rangi Pā that successfully defended the attack from the infamous Ngapuhi musket raids of 1820.

With its recent sale, the future of Rewi's house is uncertain, but whatever eventuates it will forever remain in the hearts and minds of those he touched. Rewi believed that good architecture could, in his words, 'improve' the land through responding to its rhythms, forms, scale, stories and needs, a philosophy that found expression in many of his later residential projects and, perhaps more influentially, through his teaching. For him, the land was not just a surface, nor the sea a boundary, nor the sky a backdrop. It begged to be investigated through architectural investigation, as seen in the layers of land/sky/cloud cladding on the Pukenga Māori Studies building at Unitec (Auckland, 1991), and through excavation, which he once (controversially) described as a form of moko (tattoo) for the 'Ngawha' Northland Regional Corrections Facility site (Northland, 2005).

His consultancy for the Department of Corrections enabled Rewi to realise his belief that architecture could heal the wairua (spirit) and mauri (life force) of people broken by their circumstances. In the Ngawha project, Rewi advocated for porches facing significant landscape features to enable inmates to reconnect with ancestral places of belonging and look ahead to life outside of prison. In the Mason Forensic Mental Health Clinic Extension project (Auckland, 1998), he and others successfully advocated for the inclusion of large, open foyers to accommodate pōwhiri (Māori welcome rituals), kaumātua (elder) rooms and marae as a means to include whānau in the patient inmates' rehabilitation.

Rewi is also acknowledged for his support and aroha for the Ngāi Tahu people as he extended his practice south to tautoko (support) Bill and Perry of Royal Associates Architects after the 2011 Christchurch earthquakes. They worked on a number of projects together with the auspicious task to redefine Christchurch as a reborn post-colonial city, entrenching identity and place into the heart of the large anchor projects.

When practice was quiet, Rewi would pour his energies into another form of architectural expression, studio teaching. He was appointed an adjunct professor at the University of Auckland's School of Architecture and Planning in 2002, teaching design while also developing with colleagues a culturally-responsive curriculum structure called Te Pare (The Threshold).

He developed his pedagogy to respond to the needs of students from all cultural backgrounds who wished to draw on their heritage in their design projects, encouraging them to investigate and understand sites through drawing, painting, and model-making. The land, for him, was a font of great personal and collective truths and the architect's role was to rediscover them. Dalton recalls experiencing a moment where Rewi, uncharacteristically, got fired up in a "hammer of Thor" moment when a member of staff questioned the integrity of his final year work at the University of Auckland. Rewi, out of the blue, said "you tell [them] these three words, 'Treaty of Waitangi,'" knowing Rewi's good humour the people in the room laughed, and whilst we all looked to Rewi for his usual grin, which would light up any room, his grin was still present however this time somewhat downplayed by the growl that followed, "I'm serious, I'm here to protect the Māori students." And that was that, the mic dropped and nothing more was mentioned. He also championed the contribution of female, Māori and Pasifika students as co-tutors and practitioners.

Rewi left us at a time when his professional career was once again blooming. He had recently joined Isthmus Group, where he delighted in practising with others who shared his vision of the centrality of land and people to design. He was regularly receiving invitations to deliver keynote addresses at important industry conferences and to judge competitions. His students and recent graduates were flourishing in their studies and careers. Bringing him the most joy of all was the return of his beloved daughter, Lucy, to Auckland just weeks before he unexpectedly passed away. Rewi Thompson will be remembered as one of New Zealand's leading architects and an internationally-renowned indigenous architect. Although sadly missed, he leaves us a kete (repository) of remarkable buildings, influential graduates, and profound ideas.

With its recent sale to sympathetic owners, the future of Rewi's house seems promising, with the Indigenous design principles it represents likely to remain in the hearts and minds of those he touched.

Moe mai ra e te rangatira.
Apiti hono, tatai hono
Te hunga mate, haere, haere e hoki atu
Hoki mai ki a tatou te hunga ora
Mauriora

Deidre Brown, Nicholas Dalton and Te Aritaua Prendergast

Associate Professor Deidre Brown (Ngā Puhi, Ngāti Kahu) teaches design and history in the School of Architecture at the University of Auckland. Her specialist teaching, supervisory and research interests are in the fields of Māori and Pacific architectural and art history, and the broader discipline of indigenous design.

This tribute is based on an earlier obituary she wrote about Rewi and published in Architecture New Zealand: http:// architecturenow.co.nz/articles/obituary-rewi-thompson/

Nicholas Dalton (Te Arawa) is a registered architect and the founder and director of Tamaki Makaurau Office Architecture Limited, TOA Architects, located in Auckland's downtown Britomart. He has a Bachelor of Architecture with First Class Honours. In 2003, he received the National Award for 'Design Student of the Year' for his project Nga Puna Ora, in Bastion Point, Auckland.

Te Aritaua Prendergast (Te Whanau a Apanui / Ngai Tahu / Ngati Porou) Te Ari also works for TOA Architects and specialises in realising Iwi aspirations for education, housing, and health, delivering authentic and culturally appropriate design outcomes consistent with Iwi and hapū values. He has a Master of Architecture (Prof.), Masters of Applied Sicence (Ecology) and Bachelors of Resource Management.

References

Thompson, Rewi. (2009). in sub.sist: *New Zealand architecture through a different lens.* Thompson House, Kohimarama. Retrieved from https://kaihoahoawhare. wordpress.com/2009/01/01/thompson-house-kohimarama/

Mitchell, David. (1984). *Elegant Shed: New Zealand architecture since 1945.* Auckland: Oxford University Press.

Voice

Dr. Haare Williams

Koro[1]   Swish–sh-sh-swish
Is that a Māori word

Ae[2] – it's the language
Of Sea, Wind and Trees

Say a single word Shine it
Sharpen it And brandish it like
A coiled weapon

Voice Whenever you use it
Is a language too

As a Chisel Is voice To a carver
Land To a farmer

Line Is voice To an architect
As a pen Is To a writer

A scalpel Is voice
To a surgeon

E Hine[3] Never let anyone
Take that away again

Go home now Reclaim
Remember your voice

Was not the word a weapon
In the pages of The Bible

Dr. Haare Williams

*14 September 2009, Matakana Island
(Inaugural Ngā Aho conference)*

---

[1] Grandfather
[2] Yes
[3] Young woman, girl

Foreword

Dr. Haare Williams

I was a kid raised to believe that the mountain behind our whare is the home of a protective spirit. I grew up profoundly different from the kid growing up to believe that a mountain is simply a pile of inert ore waiting to be mined. Whakapapa (geneology) connected me to the mountain.

Whakapapa is a unifying philosophy found in every Māori tribal tradition that links directly to Creation. In this cultural landscape tribal members can never be alone. My meeting house named 'Te Kura o Mahaki' is a name that resonates with tribal narratives.

Aotearoa (The land of the long white cloud) New Zealand is today working towards honouring the Te Tiriti o Waitangi[4] by seeking mutually empowering partnerships with Iwi and developing policies of affirmative action to redress injustices since the treaty was signed in 1840. The Waitangi Tribunal[5] is retelling this nation's story. Getting to know a nation is a gift. Getting to know people is a sign of humility, respect, and leadership that works in building trust.

This publication highlights the rich and organic voices in architecture and design when viewed through a cultural prism that finds spiritual meaning. This is about co-operation not separation, it does not launder the senses as we watch helpless to frightening hacking, fake news, information bubbles and the use of cyberspace by those seeking greater power. Being honest doesn't make us dishonest – it makes us strong. It makes us human.

Māori society faced oblivion in the wake of a carnival of horrors that triggered an apocalypse through legislative confiscations and losses in Rangatiratanga (chiefly leadership), Te Reo (language), and in a spiritual recession that still cuts deep. They lost mana by artifice of state that stripped them off their estates and homes. Today, there's a strong ascendancy among Māori to tell a new story, a story about human worth, mana, and virtue. New Zealand is now facing a peaceful revolution; an education and a treaty revolution. Change has ushered in a new wave of storytellers in architecture and design who now flex their narrative muscle with stories so richly replete with history, music, humanity, and pathos available to everyone here. The struggle is still on for those who want to rid themselves of the lizards of colonisation.

We are seeing a revolution as people step into the unknown, spurning the urgings of their political, academic, and business leaders by taking on the respected people voices of their nations Is this a voters' 'insurrection'? Their youthful world-wide objections for change from within are laudable.

It's encouraging to know that indigenous architects and designers are collaborating across four nations in a singular voice reaching across Aotearoa NZ, Australia, USA, and Canada. The Ngā Aho Network of Māori Designers along with an Indigenous Taskforce in Canada is a watershed movement that will facilitate symposia, study, scholarship and internships which will cement international practice in a whānau (fellowship) of nations.

Indigenous cultures offer numerous solutions, another way that predominant Western conceptualisation of the world based on capital and neoliberal ideology is only one way. Indigenous wisdom tells us that there are other ways for understanding the world we live in, that global destruction isn't inevitable.

Despite the genius of our modern technological era, we stand on the brink of the greatest ecological catastrophe of our age – global warming, increasing violence and the dislocation of immense numbers of people fleeing war, famine, and poverty in biblical numbers. It is neither change nor technology that threatens the integrity of our planet, it is power; the crude face of greed.

Are we talking? We are talking about unity in diversity across nations. We don't have to abandon our convictions, our philosophies, or our separate traditions, nor do we urge anyone to abandon theirs. But neither do we have any intention to be hemmed in by our values.

Mai rāno (since the beginning of time) – Māori have been listening to the stars. Now societies need to listen to its Indigenous voice by returning to the source and begin listening to the trees. Listening is a new sound. Listening is the new sound of hope, justice, and peace.

Dr Haare Williams

---

[5] Te Tiriti o Waitangi is a Treaty signed in Waitangi, NZ in 1840 by representatives of the British Crown and some Māori chiefs. It afforded Māori and the Crown a range of rights. The Māori language and English versions differed ensuring Māori retained sovereignty in New Zealand in the Māori language version as compared with the English version which afforded sovereignty to the British Crown.
[6] A statutory authority to examine breaches of the 1840 Treaty of Waitangi.

The Ethics of Writing and Producing a Book on Indigeneity and Architecture

Rebecca Kiddle, luugigyoo patrick stewart and Kevin O'Brien

This book is an exciting advance in the fields of architecture and design; the first of its kind in fact. It is an unashamedly Indigenous-centric book. *Our Voices: Indigeneity and Architecture*, is a collaboration across four countries, many cultures and between Indigenous editors from Aotearoa New Zealand (NZ), Turtle Island Canada, and Australia. It represents equal amounts of necessity and happy accident, or fate perhaps. The number of Indigenous architects and designers is starting to reach a critical mass in Aotearoa NZ, Australia, and Turtle Island (Canada and the USA). This critical mass has led to the establishment of professional design networks such as New Zealand's Ngā Aho Network of Māori Designers, the Royal Institute of Canadian Architect's Indigenous Taskforce and, with the production of this book the Our Voices Publishing Collective, an Indigenous network of authors writing about Indigeneity and architecture. These networks have instigated symposia and study tours which have cemented international relationships and resulted in the sharing of culture, language, personal stories, and best practice.

A word on a word: Indigenous

Given the impact of colonisation on all Indigenous groups represented in this book, the very terms used to describe us, either by others or ourselves, are underpinned by political sentiment and ideology. This group has experienced similarly enacted colonial projects which have worked to systematically erase Indigeneity from their respective landscapes. We call it genocide. In addition to this erasure, terms such as aboriginal have been used by these colonial powers to 'other' Indigenous peoples in both Australia and Canada in particular. The term Indigenous is one that unites those who author this book and is the most widely accepted term across all nations talked about here.

Each of the countries represented in the book continue to reframe the terms used by others, and the terms we use for ourselves. In Aotearoa, the term 'Native' has been rejected in favour of the term Māori. Native, used by early colonials, suggested primitivity to the Indigenous people of Aotearoa, whereby Māori, meaning 'normal' in the Māori language, served to differentiate the Indigenous group from the colonial settlers. Both prior to colonial contact, and today, many Māori would describe themselves by their specific tribal affiliations to affirm their particular connections to place in Aotearoa. Tribal nations in the USA also refer to a particular tribal nation or name. Official descriptions often use the terms Native American and Alaska Natives to describe the Indigenous collective. The terms Aborigine alongside Torres Strait Islander are still the most widely used terms to describe the Indigenous people of Australia but some question the term's relevancy for the hundreds of diverse tribal and nation groups across Australia. Where possible specific tribal and nation based names are used by some to acknowledge this diversity of cultural histories, languages and geographies. In Canada the term Aboriginal is still used, but only by government and academics. Indigenous Canadians have rejected this in favour of their tribal nation, Indigenous, First Nations, Métis, and/or Inuit. As you will see, authors have used the term most relevant to them, grounding these writings in the cultural context of their specific places.

Combining Indigeneity with architecture presents additional complexities. When thinking of a book title, a number of discussions unfolded over how we might use the term Indigenous. For some of us the term highlighted the unique architectural field which roots its architecture in Indigenous traditions and worldviews. For others of us the term worked to 'other' Indigeneity, making it somehow lesser, a quaint parochial practice which is nice enough, but not 'real' architecture, in a settler sense. To acknowledge that Indigenous architecture is 'normal' and everyday architecture some have deliberately stayed away from the use of the phrase Indigenous architecture. In either case we assert that these writings, being the first compilation, represent some of the best in architecture and design theory and practice full stop/

period (depending on your vernacular). And, what's more, that our writers are Indigenous adding a sophisticated layer of cultural knowledge to their/our design practice and theory building. The word 'Indigenous' has been capitalised throughout, similar to the way some captialise 'Western', to assert the inherent importance of the notion of Indigenous and Indigeneity as a shared identity, related set of knowledges and experiences.

The Ethics of Production

Not only did we want the content of the book to be Indigenous but the process of production to be an Indigenous one. But what did that mean? This seemed to be relatively new territory so we decided to work collectively to exercise tino rangatiratanga (in Māori) or self determination and develop our own Indigenous process. The first decision was to ensure the editorial team represented the breadth of Indigenous voices in the book. Kevin O'Brien, an architect and academic of Torres Strait heritage coordinated the Australian voices, luugigyoo patrick stewart, an architect and academic of the Nisga'a coordinated the Canadian voices, Wanda Dalla Costa, an architect and academic and member of the Saddle Lake First Nation coordinated the USA voices and Rau Hoskins, architect and academic of Ngāti Hau and Ngā Puhi descent and Rebecca Kiddle an urbanist and academic of Ngāti Porou and Ngā Puhi descent coordinated the Aotearoa New Zealand voices. Rebecca, Patrick, and Kevin have taken on the role of primary editors for the book, whilst Rau and Wanda have supported the work by coordinating authors in the case of Wanda and in the case of Rau, securing funding, identifying authors and inputting into decision-making processes on how the book should be produced.

All chapters have been peer-reviewed but in contrast to the common academic practice of blind peer review, we have kept this open. Chubin & Hackett (1990, p84) talk of peer review as being about "a communal trust in the publication decision by creating a unique formal consultation among authors, editors, and reviewers, or 'referees,' about the merits, scope, style, methods, substance, and knowledge claims of a potential article." Whilst we agree that this is important in order to check the significance of the chapter, questions of power and control are also relevant here. Concerns over who reviews chapters were centred in the fact that Indigenous writing has previously been dismissed as irrelevant, needlessly subjective and parochial by those who have privileged western theory and practice and without clear mandate, nor knowledge set to make educated comment.

In support of Indigeneity, we wanted to privilege Indigenous knowledges and research/writing methodologies as being central to our process. Editors did not want to presume to have all knowledge sets needed so developed an Indigenous review process allowing authors to choose, and elicit peer review from those in their communities whom they respected. Alongside this at least two of the editorial team, one of whom originated from the same country as the author, also peer reviewed the chapter from the perspective of those who had the overall structure and function of the book in mind in order to ensure chapters flowed alongside one another in meaningful ways.

This review process was predicated on the work of the National Collaborating Centre on Aboriginal Health (NCCAH) (2007) in Canada who developed an Indigenous peer review framework for a journal publication they had developed. We wish to thank them for this seminal work. They set out a number of goals which were duplicated and taken on board for this publication given their relevance. These assert that this publication will:

- Create a place of respect and safety where Indigenous writing and wisdom is valued and acknowledged;
- Provide a new model of publication that creates access for Indigenous scholars;
- Provide a place of dialogue and sharing;
- Promote Indigenous Peoples academic research and writing;
- Promote and mentor Indigenous talent; and,
- Reclaim our voice;
- Showcase best Indigenous practice; and,
- Encourage cultural competence and congruence through research and making connections to administration, policy and practice (NCCAH:2007).

This in-depth process has led to the inclusion of a rich range of authors including practitioners, academics and policy and community advocates with differing writing styles and diverse perspectives on architecture and design. As you will read, to be Indigenous is to be political.

Structure and Flow

This book is hosted by Aotearoa New Zealand. To this end, the book begins and ends with the voices of the hosts with an afterword by the three editors which hands over the responsibility of hosting the next volume to another nation. Haare Williams, a Te Aitanga-a-Māhaki and Ngāi Tūhoe artist and poet alongside being the kaumata (esteemed elder) for Ngā Aho: Network of Māori Designers begins the book with a foreword and the first chapter and Rau Hoskins, of Ngāti Hau, Ngā Puhi and a founder of Ngā Aho: Network of Māori Designers completes the book with a fitting tribute to Māori architecture of old. The entire book is dedicated to Rewi Thompson, a prominent Māori architect who recently passed away (2016).

Te Wāhanga Tuatahi (Section 1): He Kaupapa Taketake: Our Voice through Architecture begins with voices articulating a set of emblematic and moral concerns related to architectural processes and starting points. Haare Williams' welcomes the reader through a collection of reflections which speak of growing up Māori in Aotearoa New Zealand and the everyday architecture needed to support everyday traditional practice of living and being as Māori. Kevin O'Brien's work brings us into the present exploring the tensions inherent in architecture in a world that commodifies Indigeneity. Kevin laments the wresting of Indigeneity in relation to architecture and design from Indigenous hands to the power and control of non-Indigenous theorists and practitioners. luugigyoo patrick stewart, writing as he talks, completes this section with a voice from Turtle Island that continues to speak against the ongoing colonial project. Despite this, he outlines hopeful and purposeful projects that serve to produce architecture that is 'of this place.'

Te Wāhanga Tuarua (Section 2): They've Always Been Indigenous Places offers a set of chapters that, for the most part comment on the existing condition of place. It begins with a chronological interpretation of placemaking in Aotearoa New Zealand suggesting that the tide is turning, albeit slowly, to acknowledge through built form that towns and cities in Aotearoa have always been Indigenous places by Rebecca Kiddle. Michael Hromek then outlines the political and spatial history of Redfern, a suburb that throughout history has been a significant place of belonging for Aboriginal people in Sydney. Amiria Perez's memoir of her Māori places mimics Haare's earlier work in style but offers an alternate Māori experience; one that's been shaped by colonisation and the convergence of Māori and non-Māori worlds. David Fortin, Jason Surkan and Danielle Kastelein explore Métis place through the interior layout of domestic Métis architecture, comparing both traditional and contemporary architecture and the ability of current housing provision to support traditional practice and social cohesion. Hauauru Rae and Michelle Thompson-Fawcett offer a comparison of the involvement of Indigenous people in post-disaster place building in both Aotearoa New Zealand and Taiwan. Douglas

Cardinal talks through some of the fundamental responsibilities of the architect in sustaining people both now and into the future and finally, Timmah Ball shapes her chapter in the form of a zine – a style often used to showcase the voices of the unheard. In this zine Timmah bemoans the ways in which Aboriginal identity is co-opted by non-Indigenous architects in the city of Melbourne in the name of supporting Aboriginal place identity.

Te Wāhanga Tuatoru (Section 3): Rebuilding the processes of Indigenous placemaking and placekeeping focuses primarily on the processes which build and keep place. Ellen Andersen, discussing the work of the Māori Built Heritage Team at Heritage New Zealand outlines the tensions of classification in relation to Māori built heritage when Indigenous priorities are different to that of the non-Indigenous majority. Daniel Glenn walks us through his personal journey as an Indigenous architect highlighting the consternations of connecting the worlds of architecture and Indigeneity. Fleur Palmer, offers us a methodology for enabling Māori communities to think aspirationally about future development. Michael Laverdure offers us advice from his Elders around how best to interact with Indigenous communities in order to achieve well-loved architecture. Wanda Dalla Costa, drawing on her experiences as an architecture academic puts forward an Indigenous Placekeeping Framework which supports the keeping of Indigenous place identities. The next chapter written by Jefa Greenaway showcases projects and processes in Melbourne that have led to positive outcomes in the city. Jade Kake outlines historic and contemporary possibilities for papakāinga (Māori settlement) design, couching this analysis in the policy and regulatory tools needed to support papakāinga and a commentary from Sarah Lynn Rees suggests an existing knowledge gap amongst non-Indigenous built environment professionals which needs to be filled before Australia can fully celebrate Indigenous identities in its urban form. Lastly Tammy Eagle Bull, drawing on her own community, highlights the ways in which Indigenous design processes lead to successful long-lasting outcomes for Indigenous communities.

Te Wāhanga Tuawha (Section 4): Reclaiming Architectural Sovereignty starts with a commentary from our youngest author Matthew Groom a Māori secondary school student from Porirua, New Zealand whose eloquent essay speaks from the perspective of the whenua (land). This is followed by Linda Kennedy's straight talking critique of a new high rise building in Melbourne allegedly adorned with the face of the deceased William Barak, a local Aboriginal leader, artist and crusader for social justice. Michael Mossman's essay introduces the idea of Third Space as an opportunity to build mutually desirable outcomes which challenge dominant framing systems. Jake Chakasim's work draws on his own art and architectural work which explores the identities and worldviews of the Omuskegekowuk territory; the place where his own identity is rooted. Danièle Hromek's piece deftly weaves together the multiple voices of Aboriginal Elders to explore the question 'What is Indigenous space?' And, finally Rau Hoskins bring us back to Aotearoa New Zealand, the host of this book, offering a description of the generous learning possibilities inherent in restoring traditional Māori architecture.

This book – *Our Voices: Indigeneity and Architecture* – represents a truly rich set of voices from different countries, nations and tribes; different ages and professions and from different sets of experiences around what it means to be Indigenous and how that might relate to the buildings, homes, spaces, territories, towns and cities in which we live.

References

Chubin, D. E., & Hackett, E. J. (1990). Peerless science: Peer review and U.S. science policy. Albany: State University of New York Press.

National Collaborating Centre on Aboriginal Health (NCCAH) (2007). *Developing an Indigenous Peer Review Framework and process for an online child, family and community focused journal,* Retrieved 2017, 12 from https://fncaringsociety.com/sites/default/files/docs/ Developing_Indigenous_Framework_Process_ OnlineJournal_2007.pdf

Chapter 1: Kumara[1] – more than a vegetable

Haare Williams - Te Aitanga-a-Mahaki, Rongowhakaata, Tuhoe

Dr Haare Mahanga Te Wehinga Williams (BA Dip Ed TTC PhD(Edn) QCM JP) was born in Te Karaka in the rural heart of Te Aitanga-a-Mahaki. At two months he became a living gift to his Tuhoe grandparents. He was raised in a whare raupo (earth floor reed house) at Karaka located between Ohiwa and Kutarere. Immersed in the life and practices of another generation, Haare's grans gardened, fished and preserved food according to a Māori calendar. They exposed him to best practices for co-existing with the natural world while he absorbed a diversity of mātauranga (insights). Haare's grandparents' mode of gardening applied the knowledge of Māori. Haare's physical nourishment was matched with the spiritual substance he received through Te Kooti's[1] scriptural based waiata such as The Songs of David and Solomon, Ringatu writings were inspirational texts which grew his love of language, poetry and narrative. His formative years exposed him to the regularity in which Māori history was told which explains a Māori view of New Zealand history according to the values, constraints and changes he has seen. As a writer, his current project in Puakina – Songs of the Living Word comes from ideas that have engaged his imagination since early childhood. In his art he paints, he writes and he narrates a personal experience of faith that is both forward looking and reflective. His visual language gives new significance to values from his upbringing, his spiritual beliefs and personal experiences.

Note from the editors: The following is a collection of memories and reflections of Haare Williams' childhood growing up in a traditional Māori environment. His reflections speak of everyday tasks and the domestic architecture which supported this traditional Māori way of life.

"Ko te kumara i a Rangi
Ko Pekehawani ka noho i a Rehua
Ko Ruhiterangi ka tau kei raro
Te ngahuru tikotiko i a Uru
Ko Poutu te rangi te matahi o te tau
Te Putunga o te hinu e
Tama"

..'exceprt from a ori ori.

(Excerpt from ori ori (lullaby) from Te Aitanga a Mahaki)

Outside in the early chill she starts a fire in the cooking pit. When the flames take hold, she fills a billy with water from the spring under the gnarled ngaio tree. They chat idly awhile in hushed voices of small inconsequential things, one breath warming the others. These are happy moments, moments never to be forgotten. He smiles, "E ma, I love you."

She stands over the open fire, one arm akimbo. I can still smell the bouquet of her cooking. She was the Michael Angelo, the Mozart of gastronomy. Her virtuosity was cooking in a three-legged pewter camp-oven with hot embers piled upon the lid and between its three stubby legs. Herrings. The smell of her gourmet dish of herrings fried to a crunchy-crisp in butter, garnished with a sprinkling of small onions and served up with rewena (Māori bread) and kumara (sweet potato).

I swallow the ample servings, bones and all. I've not since then tasted anything as tantalising. Hunger after all is the best seasoning that makes a dish taste exquisite.

Of all crops in our expansive garden at Karaka, Rimaha and Wairemana valued most the kumara. That isn't surprising since the plant traces whakapapa to Poutini, and to the later migrations of whales and birds. The passage of kumara is a part of the epic journey of Māori across the Pacific to Aotearoa. Precise details of these journeys are held and imparted in whakapapa. Kumara traces its origins to Maui Wharekino and Pani their mating seed begat the essence of kumara.

Whakapapa links all things. Whakapapa (lineage) is the unifying philosophy found in every Māori tribal tradition that tracks directly to Creation. In this cultural landscape we, with other whānau around the harbour can never be alone. It is to know spiritual meaning.

The arrival in Aotearoa of two migratory birds, the shining cuckoo with its distinctive call, were celebrated with songs, prayers and tears of joy. The other is the long tail cuckoo. They paved a direct pathway to a land and back, guided by instinct and buoyed by prevailing currents.

In waiata, the sacred seeds were borne across Te Moananui-a-Kiwa (Pacific ocean) from Parinuitera on the wings of two giant birds, Ngā Manunui a Ruakapanga.

Rimaha and, after Wairemanal knew them as Pa and Ma, Dad and Mum.

Each year, they would scan the sky for the appearance of the star Te Aotahi and Puanga (Canopus and Rigel) and sent prayers to Rehua (Antares) and his two wives, Pekehawani and Ruhiterangi, guardians for the seasons of planting and for the harvest. They offered thanks to these the deities of kumara.

The planting season was marked by ritual, which ushered in the calls of spring and planting. Grans followed the seasons of the moon closely while waiting to read the appearance of Puanga (Rigel) and Matariki (Pleiades) in a mid-winter morning chill. These gave them clues for the beginning of a new season of planting.

Rimaha and Wairemana gardened, fished and preserved food according to a Māori calendar. Māori communities exposed their children to best practices for co-existing with the natural world while they absorbed a diversity of accumulated knowledge. Their mode of gardening applied mātauranga, or Māori knowledge.

Planting and harvesting were measured by lunar nights, which they understood and applied through knowledge honed over centuries of observation, application and success.

They, and their Tuhoe[2] kin, together with Māori communities faced oblivion in the wake of a carnival of horrors that triggered an apocalypse by legislative raupatu (confiscations) which meant the loss of tino rangatiratanga (chiefly authority), te reo (language), and in the spiritual recession that still cuts deep.

They lost their cherished acres by artifice of the state through The Native Land Court (1865) that stripped them of their whenua (estates) and kāinga (villages).

Te Tiriti o Waitangi (The Treaty of Waitangi) signed in 1840 promised the protection of their lands, forestry, fisheries, and all things precious. Today, after one-hundred and seventy-seven years they're still waiting for the queen's promise.

The Gardens

Planting, cultivating, and preserving food was an art with Rimaha and Wairemana. That isn't surprising given that they and their hapū (kinship group) came through a time where mere survival became an imperative. Without the resources they once managed and controlled, their thriving economies and wellbeing in tatters.

Without the tribal resources they once owned and managed, Rimaha and Wairemana made a move and settled on a small piece of marginal land, with their moko (grandchildren) at Karaka on a remote shore of the Ohiwa Harbour.

Kumara became a symbol of survival.

Gardens. Lots of gardens. Extensive gardens for just three people, one a moko who inherited their grief through the power of storytelling.

Squatting down in the dust, Wairemana would move around on her hands and knees from one spot to the next, working from dawn to dusk. They seemed to be a part of those gardens. Their annual yields of kumara, potatoes, kamokamo (a type of squash), watermelons and rock melons, sugar cane, maize, onions, and tobacco. Puha (a green leaf vegetable) seed was scattered around the perimeter of the gardens amongst the kamokamo. The stream, next to our whare, yielded watercress, eels, and cockabullies. These were happy times.

Apart from its seasonal trappings, there was always greater responsibility to ensure the preservation of mauri (life force) in all things that provided for whānau (family) wellness. Planting and harvesting were marked with constraints and rituals through karakia (prayer) and chants. Each seasonal sign, like the appearance of new leaves or the moulting of feathers signalled times for mediation with nature.

"Whakarongo ki ngā rakau ki ngā kīrehe o te rangi, te whenua me te moana. Korero ki ngā whetu," Rimaha can be heard chanting.

I didn't understand what was meant by listening with the trees and to the life in the land, sky and ocean.

---

[1] Kumara is a sweet potato
[2] Tuhoe is a Māori tribal group based in the eastern North Island of Aotearoa New Zealand

Devoutly religious, they were saintly and faithful. They held nature and all life in reverence and, after awe their beliefs my indoctrination leading me into a deep awareness of some of the logic of nature. I learned later, it's called science. They practiced their religious and devout belief in the land to take care of them. I absorbed their piety for all nature, "... so infinite in faculty." They held a belief in the infinite power of Nature to give. Their belief became my belief. Belief.

They were exemplars, models for excellence or perfectionists of a kind, peerless examples as paragons of great strength. By example, they invested their virtue in their Moko.

Mauri

"Kaua e tukinotia te whenua". Wairemana reminds me. "Do not take the land and its natural gifts for granted E Moko."
"No, I won't. E Ma, why?"
"The seeds especially are tapu."
"Sacred?"
"Don't damage the seeds. They must be protected."
"I don't understand."
"You will. You will e Moko. When you're hungry." She smiled.
"Preserve the mauri in all things. Care for it, nurture it."

They held a belief that all things possessed mauri ora (living spirit).

Tapu (sacredness) was accepted as a function of well-balanced health. A breach of tapu could have, and did have, dire consequences over a person. Any wilful wrongdoing is hara (sin). Any indiscretion committed had hampering effects on a person. In breaches of tapu, there was a need for the intervention of a tohunga (priest) for psychological and spiritual purging. I learned that hara could affect persons for life. Hara is like a violation of the spirit or breaching of that which is essential to wellness. The seeds were protected by the principle of tapu.

Rimaha would say, "Through whakapapa with all things, you can never be alone, it is to be without loneliness."

The mauri ora, or the living spirit was embodied in the seeds and in places where food were planted and gathered. In order to maintain the resource, the mauri of the land must always be protected from abuse or over-use. This principle was applied, not only to kumara but all food bearing places such as the source of a stream or a favoured fishing spot. It was a natural way of life for them. Every aspect of life had a spiritual essence, therefore the presence of deities to protect a resource from 'contamination.'

Observing deities became a way of growing up for me.

In the case of kumara, the part that was eaten was accepted for the body (tinana), but mauri, its spiritual substance (wairua) needed protection through karakia.

With such a noble lineage, it's little wonder kumara had a life of its own.

Back breaking work. A shovel was modified into a heavy hoe with the blade bent, and used to break down clumpy, lumpy turf into fine malleable soil.

Weeds. Everywhere. Wairemana was especially attentive to her patch of watermelons and rock melons. She tended the gardens well and occasionally I helped with watering the tender new shoots. She sang lullabies and fondled the plants as friends.

We lived close to nature's luxuries with the bush behind, the harbour in front and the spring and the streams in between. Next to the stream lay large wet-lands with their seasonal offerings of kopururpuru, eels, weka, raupo and flax. On the other side were stretches of mudflats as a source for snapper, sharks, flounders, herrings, cockles and the muddy titiko (periwinkles).

Besides a steady source of medicines, the bush at the back of the whare (house) gave us timber, kiekie (plant used for making mats etc.) and dyes, and as well the delicious harore, a fungus which grew best on rotted logs, teure a pine-apple-sweet fruit found in the centres of the kiekie. Then there was pikopiko, the delicious, tender curly fern fronds. Berries, trapped in the bough of the taraire trees provided a fermented drink that made anyone quite drunk. Then kānga wai or corn left in running water to ferment. Berries in season came readily.

Kei Runga

Kei runga ko Ranginui
Kei raro ko Papatuanuku
Kei mua ko te moana
Kei muri ko te ngahere
Kei tena taha
Ko nga awaawa
Kei tera taha
Ko te puna wai
Ko nga repo
Kei konei
Ko nga momo oranga
Katoa

- Haare Williams, May 2003

Harvest

The heliacal rising of Rehua (Antares) heralded the start of harvest.

Heaps, heaps, and heaps of kumara. Over four days, Rimaha worked single-handedly digging up about a half-acre of kumara.

A warm cloudy day, without direct sunlight was preferred for sorting the piles of kumara spread around the excavations.

And there she sat, sorting and singing and telling stories about the changing seasons, a time to plant, a time to harvest, a reason for every purpose, for the nights of the moon, and a season announced by the arrival of a number of other signs. No ordinary gardening activity was done without consultation with the signs. The land and the plants were fondled as if they were fragile babies.

Kumara

"E moko,"
She said
"Come help me
Dig out our
Kumara."

Her wrinkled hands
Fondling
In the brown earth
Counting sorting
Kumara.

There she sat and smoked
One arm akimbo skirt tucked in
Gathering the first fruits
In the kits of Tāne
Kumara.

"These we eat now
These for the tangi
These are seed …
And these, e Moko are your
Kumara."

- Haare Williams, May 1975

Dug up, resigned now, kumara lay in mounds protected from direct sunlight by their tendrils and soft-green tender bracken fern. I sat in the dust with Wairemana sorting and drying. She was selective about the weather because direct sunshine would blister the soft tubers. The tubers were separated into three different heaps of large, medium, and cut and small tubers. The damaged and smallest were eaten straight away.

"Kao! No we don't eat the big ones now."
"What?"
"No, we first eat the cut and the small ones. That way there's no waste."
"Why?"
"We set aside the large ones for special times like a wedding or a tangi."
"Me penei. Me pēnei, me pēra. Kia āta haere. Kia āta ngawari to whāwhā i te kumara na te mea he tino ngaehe noa tona āhua. Kia tau tou rangimarie ki runga ki te kumara."
"Be kind to them."
"Why?"
I wonder. Do they have feelings like us?

Wairemana showed me. I followed.

"Be kind to them."
I didn't understand.

Turning the tubers over one by one so that any condensation on the underside would slowly seep away was boring and tedious.

Instruction, when I need it was never in the negative.
"Me pēnei…like this."

The turning had to be done at least three times to eliminate any residue before they were placed into large sacks for Rimaha to carry up a steep slope. This was necessary to ensure that when they were placed inside te rua kumara, (kumara pit) moisture would not harm the rest of the cache.

Te Rua Kumara

The kumara pit was carefully planned and dug into the side of a steep, east-facing slope on a site carefully selected for this purpose. The space was flattened out. Located some 200 yards up, the pit was dug down into heavy clay some five feet down tapering to the top opening and spacious at the bottom. The small opening allowed access for a single person. For access, a short ladder made of an old post with stepping notches was lowered to the bottom.

The inside was lined with freshly cut bracken fern with an underlay of mānuka brush to cushion the tubers but as well provided the necessary air conditions for the preservation of the tubers. The lid covering the aperture was made of two single sheets of overlapping corrugated irons, which were also covered with layers of bracken and mānuka brush. A shallow ditch around the edges was dug to drain away rainwater.

I helped Rimaha, where I could carry the sacks up the steep slope but my job was to carefully place each tuber one by one on top of the other.

One by one.

So, when a cook up was called for, I was the mug to go up the slippery slope, open the pit, fill a kit with kumara, close the pit up again carefully, and come back down. Often I lost my footing and sent the kit with its precious contents scattered everywhere. I hated that job because most times it would be wet and cold.

I recall opening the pit and the outflow of air hitting my face – its dry, acrid smell, the rush of air, hot and stinging across a choking rush.

The positioning of the pit captured the heat of the rising sun each day.

The design of the pit was a feat of engineering, design and architecture in which the skill, the genius and know-how of tīpuna (ancestors) were distilled and handed on through time. The inside of the pit, when fully closed up was airtight. This created a vacuum that kept those precious tubers absolutely dry. Before the kumara were laid in their beds, a fire was lit inside the pit to kill off any fungal diseases, and the ashes became a part of the preservation. Then, there was the warmth in the ground captured when the sun came up over the ridge (of course).

The interior of the pit was also covered with layers of bracken. This sealed out the air, a way tested over decades to ensure the preservation of the fragile tubers over winter.

"The big ones here and those smaller ones over to that side. These are the most important because they are next season's seed."

"That's why we place tapu on these, the seeds."

And yes, the larger kumara were already tagged for the hui or a tangi at the Roimata Marae (communal complex related to a tribal group). Or simply to give away.

I watched. I listened and I followed.

Rimaha, practical, hard-working, and a striking figure anywhere as a man of few words.

Rimaha wasn't into teaching, but rather he allowed me to see how it must be done correcting only when it was necessary. His diligence was to show me how to place the kumara tubers one beside the other and one layer upon another. When it came to the placement of the tubers, it had to be right. One mistake could mean a long winter.

I often wondered in later years, when I had worked out the process used in the construction of te rua kumara, how our tīpuna knew about creating an airtight vacuum by using the warmth of the earth within the pit to preserve those precious tubers. Did not the ancient Egyptians use the same principle in the crypts?

Was it accidental? Serendipity perhaps luck? I like to think it was a combination of observation, demonstration, imitation, application and affirmation.

These are taonga (treasures) or wisdom in knowledge and practical skills handed down. Mai rāno (from a long time ago). He taonga tuku iho (treasures handed down through generations), they would say. The taonga of knowledge was safe with them as they passed it into the safe hands of their Moko to pass on.

Rangiatea

"E kore au e ngaro
He kakano i ruia mai
i Rangiatea"

I will never be lost
I am a seed scattered across the Pacific
From my ancient home in Tahiti

I'll never be lost
(Old Maori saying)

What Have I Learnt

I learned that here is a culture that valued the integration of the active and contemplative, the spiritual and the practical sciences in which the mastery of physical skills and the actions of oratory, storytelling, the force of magic, the performance of appropriate chants at the right time, perfect to a word, in short all things that contributed to a person's standing and wellbeing. Along with this was respect for the regenerative performances and the power of observances. I learned that there is a sexual unity between man, land, and tribe through women, childbirth, children, and the generations that follow. Man and fertility were linked to the land in a succession of kinship; Papatūānuku the Earth, the Mother, Ranginui the sky Father were separated by their offspring and the body of mother became their home. Hence the Maori world-view of Whenua, the source of being a 'person of the land' – 'Tangata Whenua.'

Postscript

Funny how things come around again. I was recently (2004) in Te Kuiti at Oparure Marae where I met Te Kanawa whānau who, a few months before came upon and unearthed an old kumara pit where a horse had fallen in. In it, still intact, they told me was its cache of perfectly preserved kumara, big and seed sizes. The find also disclosed that the families who lived on that site moved out in the early 1950s, and so in their summation this pit must have been abandoned but the pit remained untouched since. The tubers were covered in bracken fern and mānuka brush and remained untouched by moisture, sunlight, or air. This information rang a bell. The next day, we shared our experiences with the students of the Unitec Raranga Diploma with Kahu Te Kanawa. The seeds they planted germinated and I was handed a small collection. I tried them in my tiny suburban garden. Yes the horse was okay. And, yes, I still have kumara seeds from that exchange.

Extraordinary!

2017

Chapter 2: Architecture and Consent

Kevin O'Brien – Kaurerg and Meriam peoples of the Torres Straits Islands

Kevin is a practicing architect in Brisbane. He graduated with a Bachelor of Architecture in 1995, and a Master of Philosophy (Architecture) in 2006 from the University of Queensland. In 2006 he established Kevin O'Brien Architects (KOA) in Brisbane and has completed architectural projects throughout Queensland, New South Wales, Victoria, and the Northern Territory. The work of the practice has received national, state and regional awards from the Australian Institute of Architects. KOA recently completed a health facility for the Casino Aboriginal Medical Service in northern New South Wales, and an office facility for the Cape York Partnership in Cairns, Far North Queensland. Both projects relied on careful community consultation to explore courtyard diagrams, use of local materials and skills, and innovative insulation strategies in order to minimize energy use. In 2012 he directed the Finding Country Exhibition as an official Collateral Event of the 13th Venice Architecture Biennale, Venice. The project brought together 44 participants contributing to the making of a large 8x3m drawing of a reconsidered Brisbane where 50% of the city was removed in order to reveal an individual position in relation to the Aboriginal concept of Country. The project sought to render Country as the beginning of the city to refute the current situation where the city attempts to end Country. Kevin has held board appointments with the Cape York Partnerships 2010-2011, Gallang Place Aboriginal and Torres Strait Islander Counselling Services 2008-2013, and Good to Great Schools Australia 2014-2016. He served on the Queensland Government's Aboriginal and Torres Strait Islander Advisory Council from 2008-2010. Kevin is currently Professor of Creative Practice at the University of Sydney. He was previously Professor of Design at the Queensland University of Technology from 2013-2015.

Introduction

This paper is an examination of the relationship between architecture and consent through the works, experiences, and observations of my practice in the Australian context. The grounding position is located in a project titled 'Finding Country' that is concerned with seeing what has been rendered invisible in the Australian city. This position has come to direct a way into my architectural studios at various institutions and my architectural practice. The associated technique is one of revelation through removal in contrast to concealment through addition. Removal of the city, of building, of mass, even land title, in order to reveal a new condition. Each of these academic and built works has required different kinds of consent to proceed, raising the complex question: is it necessary to acquire consent to achieve legitimacy in the execution of any kind of architectural undertaking? Or put more bluntly, is consent and legitimacy connected or even relevant?

In architecture, cultural, professional, and academic obligations often stand in conflict when attempting to engage with Aboriginal contexts in Australia. This paper will outline ways in which these conflicts might possibly be overcome by observing a genuine sense of respect for Aboriginal people. It inevitably leads to a deconstruction of 'Aboriginal Architecture' and its associated connotations.

To do so, we will need to start with one beginning.

Australia

On 22 August 1770 at Possession Island, Lieutenant James Cook claimed on behalf of the British Crown the entire eastern coastline of Australia that he had begun surveying on 19 April earlier that year (Museum of Australian Democracy, 2006). In 1835, General Sir Richard Bourke, Governor of NSW between 1831 and 1837, applied terra nullius by proclaiming that Aboriginal people could not sell or assign land, nor could an individual person acquire it, other than through distribution by the Crown (Migration Heritage Centre, NSW, 2006). In one swift move, a singular state by way of property title was enacted on the Australian continent radically altering its ancient uses as contrary to common law.

Figure 1. Overlaid drawing of multiple Aboriginal countries and Australia as one country. Image courtesy Kevin O'Brien Architects.

Entering the new millennium, what remains a distinct reality is that the Australian city has not yet come to terms with those origins located deep in the Australian continent. It is not unreasonable to suggest that clues can be found by considering the absence of property title as a way of inverting the imposition of the city. This inevitably leads backwards to a time prior to 1770. From one continent of one country, back to one continent of many Aboriginal countries, and away to something else, it can be further argued that there exists numerous, distinct, and unresolved tensions between city and country (refer Figure 1).

Finding Country

In 2012, I directed the Finding Country Exhibition (O'Brien, 2012) that was staged as an official and independent Collateral Event of the 13th Venice Architecture Biennale. Central to the exhibition was a large drawing of the greater city of Brisbane almost eight metres long and three metres high. The drawing was made up of A4 grids with 44 contributors accepting the challenge to empty their grid by 50% and imagine a reduced population in order to reveal the basis for revealing an argument for the presence of 'Country.' In this instance Country means different things to different people. It can be the absence of Torrens title, a ritualized landscape, or even an estate of production managed by fire (Gammage, 2011). Perhaps the one understanding that holds true is that Country is what you belong to. On the opening night, the drawing was burnt (refer Figure 2).

Australian cities reflect a devastating history of European occupation on Country. Few, if any, gestures towards Aboriginal people and concepts of Country exist. Needless to say, it is a position not many wish to hear. 'Aboriginal Art' is one response, but one that can only reach so far and is susceptible to being overloaded with symbolic gestures. So too is architecture. This suggests that the means to thinking about the city and its components is through Country. Country, I would argue, holds the necessary clues for a way into asking new questions of architecture. Though it may affect the way we think about the future, it is not a blueprint for the future; similarly it is not an attempt to reinstate the past.

To consider this idea, one will need to imagine.

Imagine 200 years from now. Imagine Australia where cities have declined (not unreasonable, think Babylon, Pompeii, Woomera, Chernobyl, New Orleans, Rome, Detroit, or Mexico City). Imagine a construct where a citizen's relationship with land, water and sky is critical (even sacred). Imagine a smaller population (50% reduced). Imagine fire as an instrument of management. Just imagine.

Finding Country, initiated in 2005, is an ongoing project about the potency of Country and what can be revealed if one opens their mind to the notion that there is no such thing as an empty landscape in Australia. This notion exists as a pre-cursor to European occupation and underlies each and every urban concentration in this country – be it city, town, or house. The longer it is denied the more our Aboriginal population continues to be marginalised within these urban settings. This has profound effects on not just architecture and urban planning but also that which strikes at the very heart of what it is to be a citizen of Australia.

The ongoing creative works associated with the Finding Country inquiry have led to a set of principles that have come to inform a way to teach architectural design studios and also to think through architectural works in my practice. As studios, the investigations into various capital cities have progressed the thinking from the scale of Country through the scale of the city and into a carefully argued site for architectural interventions mediating the tension at hand. The iterative technique of removal in order to reveal the form of the argument remains. Inherent to this technique is a dialectical tension ensured through the pursuit of the 50% emptying-come-revelation. The ambition is to arrive at a new paradigm that argues for Country as the beginning of the city, thereby countering the current condition of the city as the end of Country.

Figure 2. Burning of drawing at exhibition opening. Image courtesy Dr Phil Crowther.

White Guilt, Victimhood and the Quest for the Radical Centre

In his essay titled "White guilt, victimhood and the quest for a radical centre," Noel Pearson (lawyer and activist) sets out an agenda for the success of Aboriginal people in modern Australia (Pearson, 2007). The contentious ideas reconsider the past, analyse the present and strike clear ambitions for a new path forward in Aboriginal policy.

In Australia, where the two dominant political parties are generally characterised as progressive and conservative, and the popular one party preferred count at each election swings marginally either side of that pendulum, Pearson is dishing up a digestible plate for both sides. The Left aligns with the notion of rights and the Right aligns with the notion of responsibility. It is here that Pearson has tasted measured success in articulating land rights and welfare reform agendas respectively.

Central to this success is the engagement of political forces to negotiate at what Pearson describes as the radical centre. By presenting a compelling explanation of racism, Pearson establishes the basis for an argument that the Far Left and the Far Right are no longer useful vehicles for radical action because they are unable to synthesize a rights and responsibilities agenda for Aboriginal people into useful pragmatic outcomes. Pearson's argument is that the centre of the political spectrum is where negotiated dialogue can occur and precisely why it is radical.

"The 'radical centre' may be defined as the intense resolution of the tensions between opposing principles (in this example, the principles are freedom and social order) – a resolution that produces the synthesis of optimum policy. The radical centre is not to be found in simply splitting the difference between the stark and weak tensions from either side of popularly conceived discourse, but rather where the dialectical tension is most intense and the policy positions much closer and more carefully calibrated than most people imagine" (Pearson, 2007).

Here, Pearson refers to both Aboriginal and non-Aboriginal contributions to racism as a contextualising argument. By way of generalised summary, on the Aboriginal left is victimhood and on the Aboriginal right is separatism. On the non-Aboriginal left is moral vanity and on the non-Aboriginal right is denialism. Each position can deliver limited returns of sorts. Pearson, however, argues that the real gains can only be found when each comes into negotiation around the centre. This means that the radical centre cannot be occupied by any one entity; it is a space and time of tension.

Moral Vanity and Denial

In 2011, I was forcefully approached on three occasions by an academic wishing to incorporate my work on the Finding Country project into an Australian Research Council (ARC) funded book attempting to cover Indigenous architecture and in my opinion occupy the centre. On all three occasions I clearly declined, the last in writing. Nevertheless, in 2013 the publication was launched and against my express wishes included my work on the Finding Country project. Needless to say, without corroborating research with myself (or access to the project archive), the inclusion stands as a poor attempt to understand and contextualise my work. Perhaps more curious is that the academic's actions pass as an acceptable form of research at that institution.

In 2014 I submitted a claim against the academic for research misconduct on the basis that the academic had clearly breached the ethical guidelines set down by the conditions of the Australian Research Council, and also the academic's institution. The ethical guidelines referred to were the "Guidelines for Research in Australian Indigenous Studies" (AIATSIS, 2012). In particular, I cited Principle 6 as the basis of the claim due to the following:

Principle 6 Consultation, negotiation and free, prior and informed consent are the foundations for research with or about Indigenous peoples.

Researchers should understand the meanings of free, prior and informed consent (FPIC), and the steps that must be taken to ensure that the process is followed properly.

Free, prior and informed consent means that agreement must be obtained free of duress or pressure, and ensuring that Indigenous people are fully cognisant of the details and risks of the proposed research. Informed consent of people as a group, as well as individuals within that group, is important.

Applying the principle

Conduct all research on the basis of free, prior and informed consent.

Ensure that Indigenous people are equal participants in the research process.

Ensure appropriate negotiation and consultation about the aims and objectives, and to ensure meaningful negotiation of processes, outcomes and involvement.

Ensure the research project has FPIC informed consent and plain English statement signed by participants (AIATSIS, 2012, p.9).

The institution revised this breach as merely an "unfortunate misunderstanding," and at the time of writing, the matter remains unresolved and open. The academic remains unapologetic and at one point even attempted to include Elders of another nation in defence of the unethical behaviour. In any case, this is

for all intents and purposes an example of moral vanity. The academic asked the question and irrespective of the answer was determined to proceed ultimately undermining the legitimacy of the academic's work and exposing a regrettable personal character. Clearly the academic did not understand the meaning of free, prior or informed consent. Nor that informed consent means that agreement must be obtained. The same academic continues to colonise the Indigenous context raising a broader question about the relevance, or even presence, of ethics in the architectural discipline.

I stand to gain nothing from either the outcome of the research misconduct claim, nor royalties arising from the publication in question. What the situation is seeking to expose is the double speak associated with the claim by the institution, the funding body and the academic that in subscribing to the AIATSIS guidelines it is referring to a substantial and demonstrable ethical or moral compass in undertaking research with or about Aboriginal people. There exists no real means of enforcing or holding accountable unethical behaviour in relation to the AIATSIS guidelines by either the funding body or the institution. In effect these AIATSIS guidelines hold no water, the institution and the funding body would therefore be better off not subscribing to them and avoiding the need to defend the indefensible. AIATSIS has no power to act on research projects it does not directly fund, the ARC funding body refers any research misconduct back to the institution, and the institution is able to investigate itself on the matter of research misconduct. It could be said that a serious matter has turned into comical proceedings (cue the *Monty Python* soundtrack).

Heading over to the Right, early in 2017, I received extensive correspondence detailing a travelling studio a student had attended in a remote Aboriginal community in 2014. The community was and remains a 'dry' community meaning that no alcohol is allowed. Possession or consumption of alcohol is a legal breach and offenders are treated accordingly under the law.

The student alleges that the academic who led the studio not only brought alcohol into the remote Aboriginal community, but also advised students to bring and furthermore, how to conceal, alcohol while in the community. The student promptly reported this behaviour upon return to the institution, whereupon a faculty committee was eventually set up to review the matter with no substantive outcome. In two instances, the matter crossed the direct table of Aboriginal academics in the institution, one at the level of the Pro-Vice-Chancellor's office and the other at the level of the Faculty. Later in 2017 I attempted to confirm the outcome of the matter with one of these contacts and can only say that the level of obfuscation was nothing short of impressive. After unsuccessful attempts to conclude the matter, the student felt intimidated and left the institution in 2016.

By way of comparison, a decade earlier on the 4 March 2004, the Australian Broadcasting Commission (ABC) published a story titled "Qld Govt advisor loses job over alcohol incident" (ABC News, 2004). The story covered a Queensland Government advisor who transported wine into a dry community on a ministerial jet. In contrast to the academic above, the advisor promptly lost her job.

In my opinion, this is an example of denialism. Here, the academic proceeded as the academic saw fit without observation or respect of local law and expected behaviour. This action effectively undermined the legitimacy of the studio and the fortitude of the institution. What should have been processed as a clear legal breach was set adrift through institutional obfuscation.

Despite both preceding examples emanating from the same institution, it would be amiss to claim all other institutions are shining examples. In fact, it would be simply untrue. That, however, is beyond this paper. What needs to be pointed out is the conflict that exists between good intentions and how easily they are disenfranchised through sloppy ethical behaviour.

Aboriginal Architecture, it's a White thing

In November 2002, artist Richard Bell wrote Bell's Theorem (Bell, 2002) outlining a compelling argument that Aboriginal Art is a commodity exploited through non-Aboriginal control. In the essay, Bell clarifies the difference between the "Aboriginal Art Industry" and an industry that caters for "Aboriginal Art." The former being an empty proposition, and the later being the prevalent situation led by expertise in the fields of anthropology and "western art."

Bell considers the 3 June 1992 Mabo decision that overturned the legal fiction of Terra Nullius (empty land) that led to the Native Title Act (Bell, 2002). Specifically, he details the British Government's doctrine of Terra Nullius as the method used to acquire Sovereignty over Australia. Bell claims that under international and British Law at the time of contact there were three methods by which sovereignty could be acquired by a foreign state, namely: conquest, cession or terra nullius. With the overturning of terra nullius in 1992, the Australian High Court decided a new method to enable continued sovereignty, that of "implied cession" as being distinct from "formal cession." Implied cession is "where, although the sovereignty changes, there has been no formal cession of this sovereignty" (Hocking, 1993, p.204).

The interesting idea here is the acrobatic use of the word "implied" to grant legitimacy to what appears prima facia an act of invasion. As an aside, the British and Australian Governments may well have been better served claiming conquest as the preferred method. At the very least, there would be nothing left to deny.

So, what we have here, as Bell correctly summarises, is a series of obstacles that seek to "deprive us of an equitable future" (Bell, 2002). I will now argue that if we replace the term "Aboriginal art" with the term "Aboriginal architecture," it is possible to claim a very similar position to Bell.

"Aboriginal architecture" is a term that has recently been spruiked as being architecture by, for or about Aboriginal people, place and concepts. I utterly reject this notion. After Bell, there is no Aboriginal architecture industry but there is an industry that caters for Aboriginal architecture.

Contrary to the explicit condition that Aboriginal artists are the creators of Aboriginal art, anyone seems able to be nominated as the creator of Aboriginal architecture. This is best demonstrated in the book New Directions in Australian Architecture by Philip Goad (Goad, 2001). As promised in the title, the book is a survey of leading contemporary architectural practices of that time. However, the inclusion of a separate section titled "Defining Aboriginal Architecture" does no more than reinforce stereotypical behaviour in this space whilst removing an opportunity to move beyond it (Goad, 2001). Goad's attempt to grapple with the topic inadvertently confirms the limitation of the category and anoints works by non-Aboriginal academics and architects as leaders, purveyors and creators of Aboriginal architecture. To be fair to Goad at that time of writing in Australia, there were only two architects of Aboriginal heritage in practice. Co-incidentally both worked together in the Merrima Unit of the Government Architect's Office located in the New South Wales (NSW) Department of Public Works and Services. At that time the Merrima Unit had completed several public buildings with Aboriginal communities throughout NSW. Had Goad omitted the "Defining Aboriginal Architecture" section and elevated the recognised and Royal Australian Institute of Architects awarded work of the Merrima Unit alongside the other 14 practices, he would have been one of the first to successfully counter the current recidivism of the category. As a former (and therefore biased) member of the Merrima Unit, the architectural works certainly warranted stand alone inclusion rather than mere footnoting; if even for the simple reason that the Merrima Unit's public buildings work exposed the familiar housing and cultural centre obsessions of those in the industry.

Figure 3. View of street elevation. Image courtesy Kevin O'Brien Architects.

In the same way that painting with traditional Aboriginal motifs is referenced to prove the existence of Aboriginal art, Aboriginal (public) housing is regularly hauled out to substantiate and more dubiously imply the existence of Aboriginal architecture (occasionally the cultural centre typology makes an appearance too, more for matters of fashion than anything else). For mine, this does nothing other than conveniently limit an understanding of Indigeneity and architecture to a domiciliary undertaking. The irony here is that the predominant delivery of public housing (for aboriginal and non-aboriginal people) in Australia typically excludes the use of architects in favour of "streamlined" procurement models that seek to appoint a head contactor. Even more ironically, is that in the general absence of architects (Aboriginal or non-

Aboriginal), it somehow manages to supply an almost endless supply of academic research opportunities. Just visit the staff profile pages of any architecture school in Australia for further proof.

Given Bell's adapted argument and the low architectural expectation inherent to the housing context, the term "Aboriginal architecture" remains a completely compromised idea and becomes even more vacuous when bound to the "by, for or about" (BFA) definition. In this way it exists as nothing more than a commercial category for academic and professional exploitation by Aboriginal and non-Aboriginal persons alike. The one definition of Aboriginal architecture that absolutely avoids this trap and leads to the establishment of a genuine

Figure 4. View of staff courtyard. Image courtesy Kevin O'Brien Architects.

Figure 5. View of sky-lit corridor to consulting rooms. Image courtesy Kevin O'Brien Architects.

"Aboriginal architecture industry" is one where the architect of the project from beginning to end is an Aboriginal person.

Room with a View

In 2016, my practice Kevin O'Brien Architects (in association with AECOM) completed the Casino Aboriginal Medical Service (CAMS) on the land of the Bundjalung people in northern New South Wales. The new building is approximately 600sqm. The idea of the architecture was to find a way to open and close a building to the environment to balance competing experiential and energy use demands.

The relief of medical staff's high stress levels was the central priority, with a strategy around light becoming the enabler. The CAMS with a brick street elevation, entry, and courtyard, is sympathetic yet striking in its contrast with the prevailing typology of the historical buildings of Casino. There is only one brick, only one bond, and only

one special. Within the rule of "one" it has been possible to yield a flat elevation that has depth, and a large wall that has scale and proportion (refer figure 3). The plan is essentially three parts, with the entry and meeting rooms to the street; the consulting rooms to the sky-lit corridor; and the staff offices around the courtyard native garden (refer Figure 4). Cool room panels with a reflective foil externally seal the masonry perimeter of insulated cast-on-site concrete panels and brick. Laminated veneer lumber (LVL) framed double glazed curtain walls to the street, skylight and courtyard provide minimal thermal gains and maximum vision (refer Figure 5).

Of specific importance is that through an in depth series of conversations with members of the community and the CAMS over a period of almost two years trust was established. Information, thoughts and feelings were shared on the back of this established trust that led to design decisions about how staff and community needed to use this building. As is common throughout Australia, the tentacles of the frontier wars linger across

Figure 6. View of local church framed by gun metal reveal. Image courtesy Kevin O'Brien Architects.

Figure 7. View of cut brick detail to street elevation. Image courtesy Kevin O'Brien Architects.

the past two centuries as a charged silence. This was acknowledged by cutting a window with a gun metal reveal perpendicular to the street so as to frame a view of St Mary's Catholic Church down the road (refer Figure 6). Mediating this reconciled relationship was brick sourced from Bundjalung Country, set out as solid elevation with two patterned territories (one for mothers and one for fathers) of diagonally cut bricks either side of the window (refer Figure 7). Over time, each territory will form water stains from rain dripping down the cuts leaving crying stains bearing witness to the power of healing.

Argument

My observation is that over the past decade, the last century's paternalism has eroded and been replaced with the rise of a new maternalism. A "mother knows best" attitude has begun to colonise the subject of Indigeneity and architecture on the non-aboriginal academic and professional fronts. Of further note is the way predominately non-aboriginal female academics are claiming to speak with authority and interpret matters of Indigeneity in relation to architecture. To dwell on this would lead me into a state of victimhood. In reality, the absence of Aboriginal voices contributing to the architectural debate is what has really created the vacuum that non-aboriginal academics and practitioners have begun to colonise in their image.

By way of setting a course forward, I would like to set out three ideas that are as much a part of a larger conversation with Indigenous colleagues from around the world as my own. For that reason, I shall now elevate the national context of the word Aboriginal to acknowledge the international context of the word Indigenous.

Firstly, a rearguard action by academics and practitioners of Indigenous heritage to stand up and lead this publication is a first of its kind and represents a giant leap forward. A shallow reading would conclude this as an act of separatism. However, the reason it is not is because the ambition is to present and share on the international stage a number of voices on the relationship between Indigeneity and architecture from the Indigenous perspective thereby providing some balance to the prevalent non-Indigenous perspective. The role of academics with Indigenous heritage is to shore up the debate and provide leadership in this contested area.

Secondly, the term Indigenous architecture must be understood in its current form as a BFA commercial category before moving to redefine and reassert its proper direction. A category that enables non-aboriginal academics and practitioners to cultivate business opportunities while keeping a tight stereotyped enclosure around what architects of Indigenous heritage may activate is precisely where we are currently stuck and why there is little movement beyond it.

Thirdly, the making of architecture has become ever so much more complicated with the industrialised division of what once were the central roles of the architect. Many consultants contribute to the design and many contractors build the building. In this setting, it is perhaps an act of self preservation to sit in behind the loudest voices at the table. However, architects of Indigenous heritage must lead the architectural strategy and direction. Sitting in behind other commercial practices leading projects is akin to waiting on a table for scraps; or even worse, waiting outside the tent.

In short, to enter the contest, we must stand and speak. And write.

References

ABC News. (2004, March 4). *Qld Govt adviser loses job over alcohol incident.* ABC News, p. 1.

AIATSIS. (2012). AIATSIS. Retrieved 2014, June 30, from AIATSIS website: https://aiatsis.gov.au/research/ethical-rsearch/guidelines-ethical-research-australian-Indigenous-studies

Bell, R. (2002, November). "Bell's Theorem". Retrieved 2017, June 30, from *The Koori History Website Project*: www.kooriweb.org/foley/great/art/bell.html

Gammage, B. (2011). *The Biggest Estate on Earth, How Aborigines made Australia.* Melbourne: Allen & Unwin.

Goad, P. (2001). *New Directions in Australian Architecture.* Sydney: Pesaro Publishing.

Hocking, B. (1993). *Aboriginal Law Does Now Run in Australia, Reflections of the Mabo case: from Cooper v Stuart through Milirrpum to Mabo.* Essays, 67-85.

Migration Heritage Centre, NSW. (2006). "Governor Bourke's 1835 Proclamation of Terra Nullius." Retrieved 2018, November 1 from *Migration Heritage Centre, NSW* web site: http://www.migrationheritage.nsw.gov.au/exhibition/objectsthroughtime/bourketerra/index.html

Museum of Australian Democracy (2006). "James Cook". Retrieved 2017, November 1, from *Museum of Australian Democracy* web site: https://explore.moadoph.gov.au/people/james-cook

O'Brien, K. (2012, September). "Finding Country Exhibition." Retrieved June 30, 2017, from *Finding Country Exhibition* website: http://www.findingcountry.com.au

Pearson, N. (2007). *White guilt, Victimhood and the Quest for a Radical Centre.* Griffith Review - Issue 16, 34-72.

Chapter 3: architecture as indigenous voice   soul and spirit

luugigyoo patrick stewart – Killerwhale House of Daaxan of the Nisga'a Village of Gingolx

Dr Patrick Reid Stewart's traditional Nisga'a name is Luugigyoo which in English translates as, Calm Waters. Patrick was the first Indigenous person to register as an architect and own and operate an architectural firm in British Columbia, Canada. His firm, Patrick R Stewart Architect which he has operated since 1995. He is also the incoming CEO of Lu'ma Development Management Ltd., specializing in social and affordable housing for Indigenous Peoples in Canada. He is the Chair of the Provincial Aboriginal Homelessness Committee in British Columbia and Chair of the Indigenous Task Force for the Royal Architectural Institute of Canada. Most recently he has been an Associate Professor at the McEwen School of Architecture at Laurentian University, Sudbury, Ontario, Canada. Patrick holds a Doctorate in Interdisciplinary Studies from the University of British Columbia. His dissertation is titled, Indigenous architecture through Indigenous knowledge: dim sagalts'apkw nisim. Patrick is also an alumni of Simon Fraser, Dalhousie and McGill Universities. He participated in the award winning film documentary on homelessness, "Something to eat, a place to sleep and someone who gives a damn" and in the award winning architectural film documentary, "Aboriginal Architecture: Living Architecture." Patrick is also a participant on the Canadian entry, UNCEDED, for the 2018 Venice Architectural Biennale.

aam wilaa wilsima[1] (pronounced am/will/a   will/sim/a) [translated: how are you]? simgigat   sigadum haanak (pronounced sim/gig/gat   sig/a/dum   han/ak) [translated: honourable men and honourable women]   luugigyoothl waẏ (pronounced loo/gig/e/o/thl/why) [translated: calm waters] gisk ahaast niiẏ   (pronounced gis/gas/knee) [translated: i am killerwhale] wilp daaxan niiẏ (pronounced will/p/dack/an//knee) [translated: from the house of daaxan]   nisga a niiẏ (pronounced nis/ga/knee) [translated: of the nisga a nation]   git gingolx (pronounced git/gin/goal/th) [translated: from the place of skulls]   luu-am aamhl gagoodim wilgaa sim (pronounced lou/am/th/l/ga/god/dim/will/gaa/a/sim) [translated: i am glad to be here   literally   my heart is glad to be here]

i have come in from lax mo'on (pronounced lak/maw/on) [translated: the ocean] (see figure 1)

and my name luugigyoo situates me close to the village of gingolx (figure 2)

while the wahlingigat (pronounced wall/ing/gi/gat) [ancient nisga a ancestors] keep watch through the pts'aan (pronounced pit/san [house post] in front of the village over the mo on (pronounced maw/on) [ocean] and xsgaak (pronounced sss/gak) [translated: eagle] (figure 3)   over the ha (pronounced ha) [air]

it is with kwhlixoosa'ankw (pronounced quill/oss/anskw) [translated: respect] that i acknowledge the traditional   ancestral territories of the maori peoples on whose land this book is being grounded   i acknowledge that i am visitor on these lands from the west coast of turtle island in a country the settlers called c\a\n\a\d\a[2] and am actively working against the continuing global tide of colonialism

---

[1] a note about my writing style   since i defended my dissertation Indigenous architecture through Indigenous knowledge: (Stewart, 2015)   i have decided to add another layer of meaning to my use of the nisga a language   where i use nisga a   i provide plain english phonetic pronunciation to assist in reading the language   i use plain english because nisga a is not represented by the international phonetic alphabet (ipa) symbols so i am using a phonetic system based on plain english (as a non linguist)   this is a chapter about voice and i am starting to find mine   i am continuing my experimentation with the written form and for that i want to thank my fellow editors   rebecca kiddle and kevin o brien plus rau hoskins and wanda dalla costa in allowing me the latitude though they have requested a small concession   that proper academic referencing be respected   that i can agree to as i did with my dissertation committee when they asked me to respect the formatting of dissertation abstracts international

[2] as in my dissertation i refer to this country in which i live as   c\a\n\a\d\a   the backward slash   considered wrong in grammatical writing   is analogous to the wrongness of this country in its treatment of the Indigenous peoples   and is a daily reminder to me of the injustices in the country within which i live   reminding me i can never stop advocating \ resisting \ protesting on behalf of Indigenous nations worldwide to ensure our voices are heard

figure 1 k alii aks lisims looking west toward lax mo'on (© patrick r stewart architect 2010 reprinted with permission)

as an architect and designer from an Indigenous nation   the time has come for planning and design to be done not for us or without us: jigaxgu guun (pronounced ji/gack/go//goon) [translated: the future is now]   for many generations our voice was silenced the time is now for us to be heard   more than just talking we need to be doing   we need to claim our communities   our land   our languages   as more and more Indigenous peoples are moving into urban areas   we need to claim the new urban spaces and express our cultures   it is our role as architects, academics and writers to speak out   edward said (2005) wrote that within the area of historical restitution or reposition   the experiences of people that do not have a strong enough lobby are met with dismissal or belittlement   he said that experiences of people are met with disfigurement   dismembering and disremembering by those in power   is that not what we face everyday in our countries?   we have to stand and fight for our existence

as i start this adawaak (pronounced a/da/walk) [translated: story/chapter] i want to at this time also acknowledge the writing style which you are reading i have been experimenting with this writing style since my teens when i began to express myself in poetry (and that s another story as i have a book of poetry coming out in 2018 called   *complex intimacies*) at the time i was not successful when i handed in my writing to my high school english teacher   to his credit he did not fail me but i barely passed and he said I had better learn english   funny story   flash forward forty years to my dissertation submission and one of the graduate studies department reviewers wrote me a note a suggested that i hire myself an editor because I obviously did not know how to write in english   there is something innate within me that I have identified as   blood memory   that wants me to write as i speak   it has been a long academic road to come full circle   in the ensuing forty years i did three other degrees using standard academic writing   by the time i began doing my doctoral coursework   it all came back   in this last academic iteration i began experimenting once again in 2010 in my course work and by 2015 when i submitted my dissertation   i was comfortable expressing myself in my writing as i spoke   at my oral defence one of the university examiners   himself an indigenous person from a neighboring nation   acknowledged that as he read my dissertation   he could hear

figure 2 gingolx community hall (© patrick r stewart architect 2010 reprinted with permission)

his grandfather speak in the longhouse   his
words sent a chill down my spine and you could hear
a feather drop in sty wet tan hall (hun'q'umin'um
(pronounced hunk/a/min/um) for spirit of the west wind)
as i mentioned then   i write like i speak   since
i submitted my dissertation   i have submitted four
other book chapters in this style   and with hopefully
more chapters and books to come

        anxious to implement the recommendations
from my dissertation on the use of indigenous
knowledge in architecture   i applied last year
for a teaching position at the mcewen school of
architecture at laurentian university   laurentian
university has a tri cultural mandate (english/french/
indigenous) resulting in a student population of over
one thousand students   the largest Indigenous
student population of any non tribal post secondary
institution in the country   the mcewen school is
the newest school of architecture in c\a\n\a\d\a   its
tri cultural mandate has resulted in an aboriginal[3]
student population of twelve   the largest number of
aboriginal students in a school of architecture in the
country[4]   at the time of this writing there are three
indigenous faculty at the mcewen school making it the
largest cohort of indigenous architectural faculty in the
country   myself being an indigenous architect
teaching in a university with a tri cultural mandate that
annually monitors its indigenous curriculum content is
confirmation of our voice in the academy

        though we may be starting to find our
voice   the context within which we work has a five
hundred year history on turtle island [north america]

translations of indigenous culture have been works/
words of controversy   our voices were stolen
along with our lands   our nations have endured
generations of loss   our languages were taken
our land was taken   our homes were taken   our
spirituality was taken   our children were and
continue to be taken[5]

        it is only this generation of architects   led by
douglas cardinal oc[6]   that has begun to speak back
to the machine of colonialism   and it is an international
phenomenon   architects   artists and designers
have begun a process of speaking up/out/back   we
are finding our voice   we cannot do it alone   we
need all nations to gather   we need allies to support
there are precedents   here in this country there is
a recent move by a nation just east of what are known
as the rocky mountains   wanting to change the
place names on maps from the settler english to their
nakoda language (cbc news, 2017)   internationally
the maori are talking about influencing urban design
in their cities as an affirmation of their cultural identity

---

[3] you will notice my use of the word aboriginal   the use of this word
is an intentional choice acknowledging the ongoing discourse about/
between the definitions/translations of the politically charged words
aboriginal and Indigenous
[4] there are only sixteen registered Indigenous architects in the country
at the time of this writing
[5] it is a well known decade old statistic among Indigenous nations in
c\a\n\a\d\a that there continue to be more Indigenous children taken
into foster care than were taken at the height of the residential school
system
retrieved from http://www.macleans.ca/news/canada/from-foster-care-
to-missing-or-murdered-canadas-other-tragic-pipeline/
[6] order of c\a\n\a\d\a

figure 3 pts'aan watches over mo'on (© patrick r stewart architect 2010 reprinted with permission)

figure 4 xsgaak keeps watch (© patrick r stewart architect 2010 reprinted with permission)

(t'inukuafe, 2017)   this is my vision for our nations on turtle island   we need to "construct fields of coexistence rather than fields of battle" (said, 2005, p.28) as we know what happens when we take on the colonists   our voice is disappeared as in we are forced to the margins

douglas cardinal was the first indigenous person in this country to obtain his license to open up his own practice but he left the country in order to obtain his degree   it was only in 1963 that douglas opened his own office   there would not be another indigenous person licensed to operate their own practice for almost another thirty years   as it turns out   douglas did have a contemporary that no one knew about   etienne gaboury recently disclosed his metis heritage   and he is not the only one   underlining the thirty year old pronouncement by vine deloria (1995) that it is becoming popular/safe to announce an Indigenous heritage   of course it is not as simple as all that   identity is a complex issue and one that impacts the practice of architecture at a most personal and intimate level   i also believe that identity is a social/cultural/political construct used by the settler society to maintain control of the country growing up "indian" in this country was safer to be invisible so people did not volunteer their identity if they could avoid it   denial was the safest bet   unless you were like me and could not avoid being outed

living as an indigenous person in this country creates an unease in many daily circumstances you never forget growing up   the taunting   the teasing   the bullying   the beatings   the crying

the black eye   the broken arm   all because you were not "white[7]"

it does something to your psyche   your resolve your character   you cannot blame people for not "coming out" for fear of the overt discrimination and racism that is the foundation of this country

how else do you explain stolen land   what do you tell your children?   what do you tell "their" children?   we know they tell "their" children   this land is their birthright   nothing in "their" story about the land being stolen   it is this violence that the settler society perpetuates in its education system   in its governance system   in its legal system   in its religious system   it permeates the foundation of architecture in this country   the whole system is founded on lies that they keeping telling themselves as justification for their continued violence of colonialism

what do you say to a non indigenous journalist that is apologetic for not including any building you have designed in her latest article because it does not have "that look" that the non indigenous magazine editors and publishers are looking for   and when you decry the "starchitect" culture that she as a journalist perpetuates   she bites back   leaving you thinking that you have to justify your own existence to her   she represents all that is wrong with architecture   which leads me to ask   why do

---

[7] read: caucasian   cauc/Asian   pam palmeter (2017) used the term "white" in the discourse about the foster care system in canada

figure 5 sto:lo elders lodge (© patrick r stewart architect 2010 reprinted with permission)

people   other than the designers themselves   feel the need to comment   to "critique" architectural projects?   its ironic isn't it that the people who write about architecture do not know as much about what it takes to produce architecture as the people who work as architects?   why do architectural critics exist?   who are they?   what useful function do they provide?   why do they insert themselves into someone else s process?   what is behind the critic s intentions?   lefevre (1992, p. 8) likens the comments by "architectural critics" to potentially threatening translations made with the intention of influencing a culture   this is especially true when the "critic" is non-indigenous and the architecture is Indigenous designed by an Indigenous architect   the critiques are assimilative in nature   they view architecture through their western settler lens   at this point in the discussion i want to acknowledge william mitchell (2008, p. 9) for the use of the following visual when having to think about such egregious concepts   i too cannot imagine these things without the protection of scare quotes   the writer s equivalent of the dog walker s plastic bag   the "critic" is not part of the community and only scratches the surface of the culture   unfortunately for them they think they understand what it is they are looking at and understand the culture   they will never know the depth of meaning that resides in the communities

the design projects in which i participate are approached from my perspective as a nisga a name holder   knowing my place   without ego   with purely a desire to privilege the Indigenous knowledges of first nations communities and organizations   i

say first nations because i have not yet had the privilege of working with either an inuit or metis community or organization   nor have i had the privilege of working on architectural projects outside of this country the settlers call c\a\n\a\d\a   i see myself as a facilitator of community design ideas…i do not claim ownership   as the ideas originate within the community and culture and it would be like settler appropriation/plagiarism for me to claim sole ownership of any resulting designs   i acknowledge that "copyright" as defined by the legal systems of all settler governments is counter to Indigenous knowledge systems and i have struggled over the years to ensure that copyright remains in the hands of the community who are the knowledge holders

in each project i attempt to privilege Indigenous knowledge   knowing that western-european construction knowledge /considerations often overshadow Indigenous knowledge

acknowledging this helps me understand that not every project will contain all knowledges

the design language i use is based in the culture within which i work   i take a long range view in which i understand that my contribution to the Indigenous practice of architecture

both theory and practice   may take decades or even generations before its effects are felt   the effects of which i speak   will have consequences on the language   the culture   the peoples

figure 6 sto:lo elders lodge (© patrick r stewart architect 2010 reprinted with permission)

the community hall for gingolx in figure 2 was designed at the time to have the largest seating capacity in the nisga a nation   historically "indian" affairs and northern development canada

now politically correct   called Indigenous affairs were never supportive of providing a budget to meet the needs of the communities   this translated into a hall design that could never accommodate the growing community population

the community wanted the design for this hall to be based upon a previous hall that sat on that site forty years before   it was originally reminiscent of a longhouse   so too they wanted this new hall to remind them of a longhouse[8]   the site upon which this hall was built was the site of two previous halls that suspiciously burned down   this time a sprinkler system was installed and now the pts aan (pronounced pit/san [house post] figure 3 watches over the hall

the stó:lô (prounced stah/low) elders lodge   figure 5   is an assisted living[9] facility that was three years in conception prior to construction start   there were communites coming together which took more than a year to gain the trust and confidence of the communities   it took another year to attempt

putting ideas down on paper schematic   which required approvals from the elders and the twenty-five stó:lô communities   before a nail was hit   a political split between the twenty-five communities resulted in the formation of the stó:lô tribal council and the stó:lô nation plus six independent communities while the political mashinations were going on

the elders were able to retain the support of all the communities because they had the support of the people   this was one strategy the elders put in place from the beginning of the project

their strategy was always to gain/retain the support of the people   they used to joke that they would dare any politician to go against them on this project because they had the people on their side and what politician would be foolish enough to go against the people on whose votes they counted?

the construction of the elders lodge met a need to bring the elders back to their home territory

---

[8] our longhouses were historically our dwelling places which were destroyed by the missionaries

[9] assisted living is housing   hospitality   hospitality services and personal assistance to adults who can live independently but require regular help with daily activities (senior living magazine 2017)

figure 7 sto:lo sqemel (©patrick r stewart architect 2010 reprinted with permission)

figure 8 chief tetlenitsa theatre (© patrick r stewart architect 2010 reprinted with permission)

prior to the opening of this project the elders of the nation were spread thoughout the province   often in non Indigenous facilities   and if their family members were in an Indigenous facilities it was usually hours away by car   once the elders met to discuss what they wanted there was lots of discussion about how to ensure that the housing was of their own tradition   they wanted their building to reflect traditional built form which in their territory was a single slope longhouse   they also wanted to ensure that the building did not reflect anything having to do with residential school   in the case of this design there was discussion about the construction materials   the massing of the building   and the colours   in all cases if they disagreed   their response was   a memory of residential school   it was this project more than any other of my projects   that convinced me that negative experiences at residential school influenced generations of first nations peoples   the elders said   no brick cladding   no white walls   no second storey   they wanted to live where they could be in touch with mother earth   to that end every unit was given a patio door to the outside   more than simply access to the outdoors   that door represented a permeability   an openness   a feeling of freedom where they could go outside and look up at the sky with the earth beneath their feet   it was this ground upon which the lodge was built that had most meaning to the elders   this site was part of a traditional meeting place since time immemorial   this was also the reason the missionaries built their residential school on this site   in a way they used this sacred site as bait to

the nation   to say "look   we are not bad   we are using your site (without asking) upon which to teach your children"   nevermind that the families had no choice because by 1896 it was against the law to not send their children to a residential school   parents ended up in prison for hiding their kids   and "they" wonder why the completion rates high school are less than fifty percent[10]   the impetus for the elders to select the site was an act of reclamation   before the residential school existed   this site was a place of annual gatherings of many coast salish[11] communities there are many stories of people walking through the mountains coming to and going from this area

it is these personal stories that infuse an architectural process/project with meaning   for the community   the users   the inhabitants   the nation and the designers   there is such satisfaction being able to privilege the knowledge of the elders into built form that supports their lifestyle   their culture and their vision   how does an outsider justify inserting themselves into such a project   and for what? to insert themselves is to appropriate knowledge   for by themselves they would not understand the building the process or the people   there would be those who could justify their involvement by saying that such design knowledge should be shared with the outside

[10] statistics canada (2011).
[11] coast salish are the people of the salish sea   there are many different nations from the pacific northwest of what is now british columbia and washington state in the united states

figure 9 sto:lo resource centre (© patrick r stewart architect 2010 reprinted with permission)

world   this is where history has shown itself to be the teacher   when Indigenous peoples have shared with intruders/settlers   they were taken advantage of stolen from and worse   if you want to learn the teachings   go to the elders

teaching facilities such as the xá:ytem (prounced hay/tem) longhouse interpretive centre were designed with history in mind   they were based on traditional form of the culture in which they were located   their purpose is to convey a sense of history   a continuity of culture   based on the language and protocols

figure 7 conveys the traditional materiality of a sqemi:l / sqemel (pronounced shk/qem/el) in halkomelem [translated: pithouse]   the design research that went into this project included visits to nearby archeological sites   reading the logs from archeological digs on the site and visits to the elders and people who built the sqemels of neighbouring communities   understanding the cultural/

environmental context of traditional semi subterranean construction and the needs of contemporary Indigenous society played an important role in the design of the site   this site also had its own archeological site as this was the location for a 9000 year old village   this is culture and meaning upon which to design   for the nation it was important that the traditional forms be respected and brought back among the living   i say that because the stó:lô believe/d that rocks and mountains are spirit beings in fact on this site   hatzic rock contains the spirits of three chiefs   i cannot say more because it is not my story to tell   there is protocol to be followed   go ask of the nation

the context of traditional construction of sqemels were defined by the nature of burying cedar or spruce logs into the mud and dirt   the buried ends of the logs tended to rot in about ten years   traditionally the people would then move to another site and dig another pit over which they constructed the log superstructure which would then be covered by

figure 10 sto:lo resource centre (© patrick r stewart architect 2010 reprinted with permission)

organics such as smaller logs, tree bark, soils and grasses   the genius of this construction was the indoor environment it created   the interiors were cool in the summer and warm in the winter

when the xá:ytem sqemels were designed in 2009   the site was already an interpretive centre to which over ten thousand public school children visited each year   these modern sqemels had to be engineered   earthquake resistant   water tight and yet remain based in the traditions of the culture the design and constructed was completed through the daily advice of an elder who was knowledgeable about the traditional construction of sqemels   it is unfortunate that since the design and construction of the xá:ytem longhouse interpretive centre   politics have destroyed what Indigenous peoples built xá:ytem is a victim of devolution   at the time of the uncovering of the site it was the federal government that took responsibility for the project

within a few years the federal government offloaded the responsibility to the provincial government and then with an election of the right   they further devolved the site to the nation but of course without the financial resource to maintain and sustain the site while the senior levels of government were involved they allocated resources to it so it remained successful

at this time the nation is wondering how best to maintain this valuable cultural asset   hopefully the time will come when it is once again fulfilling its role as a cultural educator

the design and construction of the chief tetlenitsa theatre in figure 8 has a very personal and yet sad story   the project began as a graduate design thesis project for lynda ursaki   as a member of the first nations community she wanted to express her culture in commemoration of a treaty signing with the government of c\a\n\a\d\a   she was a graduate of the architectural program at the technical university of nova scotia (now dalhousie university) as was i

figure 11 dave pranteau aboriginal children;s village (© patrick r stewart architect 2010 reprinted with permission)

she was a member of the cook s ferry first nation she approached me one day in the office and asked to talk to me about her thesis project   she produced a set of boards and showed me the design and told me how the design is grounded in the traditional form of the sqemel which was the traditional winter dwellings of her nation she asked if the firm would be interested in participating in this project   should construction funding be found

i replied of course i would support her   that set the project in motion and within weeks lynda and i were driving to her home community to meet with the chief and council   we assisted in funding applications and began the process of confirming the site and starting on schematic design   once lynda showed the community her designs they began to get excited and started to participate in the design work and planning for construction

this project was a commemoration of a declaration that was written in 1910 to the then prime minister of c\a\n\a\d\a   sir wilfred laurier by the interior allied tribes of bc   on nlaka'pamux (prounced nla/kap/am) nation territory near spences bridge the declaration gave a history of contact between the nlaka'pamux and the settlers and requested the prime minister to do the honourable thing and uphold the promises of the queen   lynda s idea was to address the past while looking to the future   in an article in a national Indigenous online news service   nationtalk (2010)   the editor wrote at the time of the opening

Lyndas' design, though influenced by traditional structures of our past, embraces technologies of the present to create a place where our past and future can be celebrated. The path of our ancestors spirals out from the fire pit, where we tell the stories of our past, and follows the interpretive ramp towards the top of the platform, the brightest part of the building and our future. From the platform our history surrounds us. The structure is designed to accommodate professional lighting and audio presentations (NationTalk, 2010).

lynda attended the opening of the commemoration structure (it was later named the chief tetlenitsa theatre after a chief who signed the declaration in 1910) but unfortunately she passed away from cancer a year later   i wanted to write about this project to honour lynda and because i am proud that we were able to get this project completed in time for the centenary and that this project was done on the community's terms   and was designed by a community member

the sto:lo resource centre is located on unceded sto:lo traditional territory near chilliwack bc   i say near because this site is a sacred meeting place that predates the intrusion of the settlers and so the settler community has grown up around the sto:lo nation   the resource centre grew out of a need for a keeping place for sacred cultural items   the facility also contains a traditional longhouse type space for interpretive programming that the nation offers to the schools and the public

the project design was based on a historical longhouse

called qoqolaxel "watery eaves" that existed in the early nineteenth century (Carlson, 2007, p. 148)   think of two coast salish single slope longhouse placed back to back and at the center of the inverted gable was a hollowed out log that acted as an eavestrough and the water flowed through the mouth of a carved raven head this was the early design precedent for the resource centre design

participating in a project that goes to ones core as a human being and touches the spirit in a most profound way is the ultimate experience as an architect   the design of the dave pranteau aboriginal children's village is a project that profound   the building is designed to house the families of foster children   the thing that is different in the this project is that the units are allocated to the children

having grown up in care myself   i know the effect of loneliness   detachment and issues of abandonment can have on a child   this was an opportunity to be able to give back   so in this building we designed support spaces for the youth   a games room   an amenity room

figure 12 dave pranteau aboriginal children;s village (© patrick r stewart architect 2010 reprinted with permission)

a youth support worker room and a youth worker program
all within a physical environment with an enhanced sense
of culture

      as i read what i have written i know that the depth
of respect   relevance   reciprocity   redistribution
relationality   reflection and responsibility   that are
imbued in my projects ensure that their meanings will live
on   it is in this role as translator of design vision in
which i participated   that i can write about them and
know that i have said what i could in a good way   and
with that I say   t'ooyaksiy nisim (pronounced toy/yak/see/
niss/im) [translated: thank you all]   All My Relations[12]

---

[12] which reminds us every time we say or hear it   of our responsibility
to respect life and to fulfill our duties to ourselves   our communities
our nations   our cultures   our languages   this also describes
the epistemology of the Indigenous viewoftheplanet   providing us
with the thinking about how we go about gathering information about
the world (stewart 2015, p.48)

References

Big Sisters of BC. "A brief history of first nations colonization and impacts (n.d.)." Retrieved from http://www.bigsisters.bc.ca

Carlson, K.T. (2007). Toward an Indigenous Historiography: Events, Migrations, and the Formation of "Post-Contact" Coast Salish Collective Identities. In, Bruce Granville Miller (ed.). *Be of Good Mind: Essays on the Coast Salish*. Vancouver: UBC Press, 138- 181.

CBC News. (2017). "What's in a name? For Alberta First Nations seeking heritage recognition, plenty: Application made to rename Calgary and other places with traditional Stoney Nakoda words" Retrieved 2017, November 14 from CBC News website http://www.cbc.ca/news/canada/calgary/alberta-calgary-first-nations-stoney-nakodacanmore-place-names-1.4399941

Deloria, Vine (1995). *Red Earth, White Lies*. New York: Scribner.

Lefevre, Andre (Ed.) (1992). *Translation/history/culture: A sourcebook*. London: Routledge.

Editor (2010, June 1). Celebration unveils memorial. Merritt Herald. Retrieved November 2, 2017 from http://www.merrittherald.com/sir-wilfred-memorial-centennial/

Mitchell, William (2008). *World's greatest architect: making, meaning and network culture*. Cambridge: MIT Press.

NationTalk (2010). "Cook's Ferry Indian Band, Nkemcin, Nlaka'pamux Nation Territory, Announces Completion of Memorial to Honor the Interior Allied Tribes of BC 1908 – 1922 and Invitation to June 11, 2010 Celebration." Retrieved 2017, November 13 from *NationTalk* (online). http://nationtalk.ca/story/cooks-ferry-indian-band-nkemcin-nlakapamux-nation-territory-announces-completion-of-memorial-to-honor-the-interior-allied-tribes-of-bc-1908-1922-and-invitation-to-june

Palmater, Pam (2017). "From foster care to missing or murdered: Canada's other tragic pipeline: how the foster care system – which disproportionately affects Indigenous children – shows that Canada hasn't learned from past policies." *Macleans* (online), April 12, 2017. Retrieved November 12, 2017 from http://www.macleans.ca/news/canada/from-foster-care-to-missing-or-murdered-canadas-other-tragic-pipeline/

Said, Edward (2005). "The public role of writers and intellectuals." In, Sandra Berman and Michael Wood (Eds.), *Nation, Language and the Ethics of Translation*. (pp.15-29). Princeton: Princeton University Press.

Editor (2017). "Definitions." *Senior Living Magazine*. Retrieved November 1, 2017 from http://www.seniorlivingmag.com/housingdirectory/definitions

Statistics Canada (2011). National Household Survey. Retrieved from http://www12.statcan. gc.ca/nhs-enm/2011/as-sa/99-012-x/99-012-x2011003_3-eng.cfm

Stewart, Patrick (2015). *Indigenous architecture through Indigenous knowledge: dim sagalts' apkw nisim*. Vancouver, UBC: Doctoral dissertation. Retrieved 2017, November 12 from https://open.library.ubc.ca/cIRcle/collections/ubctheses/24/items/1.0167274

Stewart, Patrick (in press). *complex intimacies*. chilliwack: bedford park press.

T'inukuafe, Rameka Alexander (2017). "Building culture: why good urban design requires a better understanding of Tikanga Maori." *Unicef: idealog,* November 9, 2017. Retrieved 2017, November 14 from http://idealog.co.nz/urban/2017/11/building-culture-why-good-urban-design-requires-better-understanding-tikanga-maori

Chapter 4: Māori Placemaking

Rebecca Kiddle – Ngāti Porou and Ngā Puhi

Rebecca Kiddle is a Senior Lecturer in Environmental Studies at Victoria University of Wellington. She has a PhD and an MA in urban design from Oxford Brookes University, UK and an undergraduate degree in politics and Māori studies. She is the co-chair Pōneke for Ngā Aho Network of Māori Designers and a panel member of the Auckland Urban Design Panel. Her research focuses on Aotearoa New Zealand place identity and placemaking, decolonising cities and the design of educational space.

Introduction

Placemaking is political (McGlynn and Murrain, 1994). In Aotearoa placemaking has been used as an influential form of control throughout pre-colonial and colonial history. For the last 150 years, the politics of placemaking has, for the most part, been one-sided, vesting control in the hands of European settlers and associated Crown representatives. Early settlements utilised plans designed in Britain and overlayed, sometimes awkwardly, on Aotearoa topographies (Brand, 2004; Brand, 2011; Falconer, 2015) (See for example Figure 1 which illustrates the street plan of Martinborough based literally on a Union Jack). Later, with the growth of the suburbs, urban and suburban life supported both patriarchal and nuclear family structures dominant amongst Pākehā.

For the most part, Māori identities, ways of life and cultural practices have been marginalised in Aotearoa urban settlements. Cities represent loss and marginalisation for some Māori communities and individuals, and are seemingly understood by many not to be Indigenous places.

Two critical contexts are evident in Aotearoa cities. The first centres on manawhenua (Māori tribes who have longstanding connections with a particular place and/or a longevity of habitation) groups whose tribal homes have been engulfed by towns and cities (for example Ngāti Whātua in Auckland, Ngāti Kahungungu in Hastings/Napier or Ngāti Toa in Wellington). These groups are usually formally acknowledged by local and national government structures and processes (Lambert, 2013). The second are mātāwaka (non traditional Māori inhabitants) and taurahere (a subset of mātāwaka – non traditional inhabitants that retain connections to hapū/iwi elsewhere)[1] groups who live outside of their tribal homes in the city. Māori urban migration from the late 1950s to the 1970s was rapid with over 80% of Māori now urban dwellers. This migration forever altered the social, cultural and economic structure of Māoridom and, as is the focus of this chapter, led to major challenges for contemporary urban Māori place-making, planning, urbanism, design, and architecture.

This chapter explores the sometimes painful history of placemaking in Aotearoa for Māori alongside more recent successes. It acknowledges that despite the placemaking hegemony of the Pākehā majority, Māori have always planned and made places that exemplify their cultural and personal values. Finally, the chapter discusses the challenges of contemporary placemaking and possible ways forward in the pursuit of decolonised or Māori cities, that provide for diverse Māori realities (Durie, 1995).

Ko wai au? Who am I?

It is perhaps helpful here to clarify the frame from which I write. I am Māori (descending from the tribes of Ngāti Porou and Ngā Puhi) and Pākehā (descending from families from London and the Orkney Isles in the UK) and trained in urban design in the UK so have been influenced by design theory that, for the most part, has been developed in Europe and the US. I've only recently (in 2015) returned home to Aotearoa after spending ten years studying and working in the UK and then China.

Being away illuminated for me what has and has not been achieved in terms of Māori placemaking over the last decade perhaps more starkly than if I had been amongst it, but equally I acknowledge that subtle nuances may be

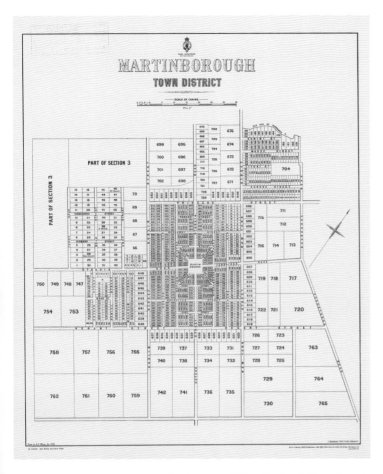

Figure 1. Martinborough town district part of New Zealand. Department of Lands and Survey. Martinborough town district [electronic resource] / drawn by G.P. Wilson ; J. Mackenzie, chief surveyor..
Ref: 832.45951bje 1909. Alexander Turnbull Library, Wellington, New Zealand. /records/31947828

lost on me. Whilst I offer a somewhat emic perspective in terms of my whakapapa (genealogy) and training, my perspective can also only but be etic in that I do not belong to the iwi (tribal) groups that have borne the brunt of urban colonial creation of place and concurrently have been at the forefront of contemporary activities which seek to see their "faces in our urban places" (Matunga, 2016 personal communication).

What is placemaking?

Placemaking as a concept came to prominence in the 1960s when the works of American authors such as Jane Jacobs (1961), William H. Whyte (1980) and Kevin Lynch (1960) promulgated ideas around the social life of the city in response to a perception of the destruction of urbanity through the proliferation of cars and infrastructure for cars. More recently placemaking has been highlighted as a response to the impact of globalisation on cities creating a global sameness stripping out the "place" from urban spaces (Butina Watson & Bentley, 2007).

Placemaking responds, at one end, to the threat of globalisation on distinct places, implicating a neoliberal concern around place as a brand with the ability to attract and foster the tourism industry (Freidmann, 2010; Hultman & Hall, 2012). At the other, placemaking, if done well, embodies democracy, promoting the need for community involvement in making places through which people are inextricably connected with the places around them (Project for Public Spaces, nd.). Potter cautions that "the failings of our cities lie in the increasing homogeneity of their material forms, cultural and economic life, demographics, and the inequities and disenfranchisement that result" (2012, p.137).

A number of urban design scholars, outline frameworks with which to examine existing places. These articulate principles which make 'good place' in order that designers might turn spaces into places, from scratch (Butina Watson & Bentley, 2007; Sepe & Pitt, 2014). These frameworks promote the importance of placemaking processes in the development of 'authentic' place. The Project for Public Spaces, an organisation set up with the central aim of placemaking, asserts that both process and form are equally important here. The involvement in the creation of place by those for whom the place will serve is vital to placemaking success.

> A great public space cannot be measured by its physical attributes alone; it must also serve people as a vital community resource in which function always trumps form. When people of all ages, abilities, and socio-economic backgrounds can not only access and enjoy a place, but also play a key role in its identity, creation, and maintenance, that is when we see genuine placemaking in action. (Project for Public Spaces, nd.)

Placemaking, then, might be defined as spaces which have been created with the people for whom these places hold, or will hold, meaning and connection. These places are holistically understood in that they pay "close attention to the myriad ways in which the physical, social, ecological, cultural, and even spiritual qualities of a place are intimately intertwined" (Project for Public Spaces, nd.).

Pre-colonial Whānau and Hapū Placemaking

Placemaking in pre-colonial times centred on the familial units of whānau (extended family) and hapū (often translated as sub-tribe bßut in essence were larger extended whānau or groups of whānau). Larger still was the political unit, iwi (tribes, generally consisting of

---

[1] See Ryks, Pearson & Waa, 2016 for a fuller explanation of different urban Māori groups.

a number of related hapū). Whānau, hapū and iwi were connected by whakapapa (Brown, 2009). Māori, meaning normal, only became part of common parlance after hapū interacted with early European explorers. Brown notes that this process of viewing this society as a single Indigenous body took approximately two centuries to complete (Brown, 2009, p. 36).

Hapū settlements were seasonal, though permanent, allowing groups to move around from season to season accessing readily available resources as they went. These settlements included temporary and permanent dwellings, some of which were living spaces and others used for food storage and cooking spaces, amongst other uses (Brown, 2009, pp. 27-29).

Pā (fortified villages) developed between AD 1500 and 1800 in response to competition for land amongst a growing Māori population (Brown, 2009, p.35). According to King (2003), the existence of pā, more often than not, signalled a desire to ward off conflict, as opposed to a predilection for conflict. Hapū used these to "make conflict less likely, not more so" (King, 2003, p. 84).

These traditional settlements housed anywhere from individual extended families to large hapū groups of up to 500 people or more (King, 2003, p.84). One of the largest known settlements was Maungakieie (One Tree Hill) held by paramount chief Kiwi Tāmaki of Waihua iwi (tribe) (Ministry of Culture and Heritage, 2016). Maungakieie, located in what is now Auckland, housed thousands of people. In this early 18th Century settlement, Tāmaki housed 4,000 warriors (Ibid.).

However, Brown suggests that pā did not significantly impact on the shape of Māori architectural history as there is little evidence to suggest they were permanently inhabited. Rather, these were, in essence, a form of temporary placemaking which asserted that group's mana (esteem) over a particular place. Brown writes:

> The general role of pā was to indicate the wealth of a user group through the storage and preparation of food, demonstrate defence capabilities and, perhaps, take command of the natural landscape surrounding them. (Brown, 2009, p.35)

This suggests a strategic use of placemaking by pre-colonial Māori communities. Professor of Indigenous Planning, Hirini Matunga asserts that Māori have always planned and did so according to traditional practice that inextricably linked humans to their natural environment. "Indigenous planning has always existed. Indigenous communities pre-date colonialism and were planned according to their own traditions and sets of practices" (Matunga, 2013, p.5). Place-based planning centred around

familial connections with specific places or turangawaewae (a place where one has the right to stand or place where one has rights of residence and belonging through kinship and whakapapa (Moorfield, 2010)).

> The central tenets of Indigenous planning are essentially community/kinship and place-based. It is a form of planning whose roots and traditions are grounded in specific Indigenous peoples' experiences linked to specific places, lands, and resources (Matunga, 2013, p.5).

These hapū places were collectively inhabited familial settlements whereby visitors were invited and welcomed, through the use of pōwhiri (a welcome ritual), to the collective space. Through this the local people would ascertain whether or not the incomers were potential allies or enemies seeking to commandeer resources.

This use of space differs from Western notions of urban form in which public (where anyone is welcome) and private space (which tends to be private to individuals or immediate families) abut each other at a delimited spatial scale – that of the individual house or plot (Falconer, 2015).

Colonial Placemaking

European traders and settlers began to arrive in Aotearoa in large numbers in the early 1800s. Initially, they needed the support of local Māori to survive. Whalers and sealers were often stationed near hapū who enjoyed ready trading opportunities. Enticed by the New Zealand Company's promise of readily available arable land and the promise of home-ownership, something which had been previously out of reach for many working-class Britons, the numbers of settlers arriving grew quickly (Schrader, 2016, p.98). Often land was pre-bought in Britain but on arrival in Aotearoa, settlers were disappointed to find that their land was not yet available, indeed in some cases not even acquired by the agent. They then were confined to existing settlements to wait (King, 2003, p.123) needing to rely on the support and resources offered by local Māori tribes.

As is well documented, the land that these settlers had bought in Britain was acquired from local Māori by oftentimes nefarious means (See for example, Schrader, 2016, pp. 34-36). The swift shift of land from Māori to Pākehā hands soon saw this interdependence between Māori and Pākehā decrease. This coupled with musket based warfare and the introduction of disease that Māori were not immune to, led to the rapid decline in the Māori population and Māori land ownership and urban settlements became primarily Pākehā settlements.

The colonial project focused on the acquisition of land. In placemaking terms, this was the raw material to imprint an identity on the landscape and ideological frame with which to mark territory. Potter writes, "the acquisition of space, or more concretely land and its resources, is, of course, a driving rationale of the colonial project" (Potter, 2012, p.131). Strategies used to restructure and control these landscapes included mapping and land clearances which worked to erase Indigenous placemaking practices (Potter, 2012, p.132). Matunga reiterates the complicit role of planning processes in the colonial project asserting that it has provided the "intellectual, conceptual, and technical skills to facilitate the scorched earth clearance of Indigenous people" (2013, p.9).

As the need for settlements increased, colonial towns and cities grew in number and in size and European ideologies and identities were reinforced by overlaying ready-made grid plans on the Aotearoa landscape. The Dunedin plan is an example of a dogged determination to make the land surrender to this pre-determined grid. City builders used picks and shovels to gouge out the hill in order that the landscape conform to the grid plan (Schrader, 2016, p. 94).

This desire to physically tame these 'new' landscapes and create places, just like back 'home,' was commonplace across the colonial project. Deborah Bird Rose, as elucidated in Potter, talks of the calendar being reset to "year zero" in the colonial frontier whereby "authentic" place only happens post colonisation. Potter asserts that this discourse had political implications, justifying "the rendering of Indigenous sovereignty as past" (2012, p.132).

This taming took place through procedural and legal mechanisms as well. The aim of the settler established Native Land Court (1865) was to convert communally owned Māori land to individual title. Only 10 owners were required to be nominated per block effectively disenfranchising other owners. This both undermined traditional approaches to land ownership and made land easier to sell to settlers (Matunga, 2013, p.7). It was arguably the most effective placemaking tool in the colonial toolbox.

The effect of this, and other tools of land alienation impacted profoundly on Māori placemaking – namely, they lost the land on which to make place and play out their value base. The percentage of land in Māori ownership in the North Island fell from approximately 80% in 1860 to approximately 9% in 1939. In the South Island, all but 1% had been purchased by the Crown by 1865 (Matunga, 2013; Orange, 2004).

This erasure continues in Aotearoa. Political boundaries transgress iwi and hapū boundaries, forcing Māori groups to have to engage with a multitude of local governments and organisations in order to partake in, and influence decision-making processes, and to undertake development on their traditional land. Existing financial instruments make it difficult for Māori to establish housing on Māori land that is communally owned and predominantly in rural areas. And, given mana whenua groups in urban areas have experienced large land losses, most urban land is now privately owned. Current planning regulation does not support the realisation of Māori identities on public or private land.

Urban migration: Mātāwaka placemaking

To provide manpower for industries supporting the World War II effort, Māori, who were initially ineligible to go to war, were encouraged to the cities through accommodation and job based incentives (Ryks et al., 2016; Barcham, 1998; Meredith, 2000; Kukutai, 2014). Following World War II, Māori urban migration was particularly rapid by global accounts (Pool, 1991; Kukutai, 2011). The government's policy at the time was that the economic problems experienced by Māori were a result of the fact that they were geographically isolated leading to a lack of employment opportunities for the growing Māori population in the countryside (Williams, 2015, p. 69). A key solution to this was to encourage Māori, not employed by farming operations, to move to the cities (Ibid.).

Māori whānau set about making place amidst the unfamiliarity of an urban landscape. Williams' book *Panguru and the City: Kāinga Tahi, Kāinga Rua: An Urban Migration History* focuses particularly on the urban migration experience of Māori from Panguru (a small township in rural Northland) though it is likely that the experiences of this group are indicative of the experiences of other Māori migrating to cities. She suggests that these newly established urbanites created place in two key ways: 1) through the retention and maintenance of rurally held values and goals such as "the desire to gain work, to live in better homes and to achieve a higher standard of living, and 2) by upholding cultural norms that identified them as Māori, such as "whakapapa, notions of whānau, rights and obligations and the ties of faith" (Williams, 2015, p.102).

However, Māori access to, and the appropriateness of domestic housing was particularly problematic. Housing did not support the kind of extended family structures that Māori were used to and subtly defined men's and women's spaces in the city. "The ideology of the nuclear

Figure 2. Hangi being prepared in a skip bin on a construction site, Wellington. Dominion post (Newspaper): Photographic negatives and prints of the Evening Post and Dominion newspapers. Ref: EP/1974/7746/8-F. Alexander Turnbull Library, Wellington, New Zealand. http://natlib.govt.nz/records/22825882

family has thus been reproduced in New Zealand's built environment. And architecture has acted as a medium to prescribe patriarchal relations within the family" (Pawson, 1987, 124). Typical three-bedroom state houses did little to support Māori ways of life. The 1950/60s government policy of "pepper-potting" Māori households around the city was enacted in the hope that Māori would assimilate with non-Māori communities. This policy created spatial disconnect leading to the isolation of Māori whānau from one another and social and cultural fragmentation and loss (Kingi, 2005).

Whilst some managed to subvert these structures by using garages as bedrooms, for example, or, in the case of Figure 2, building hangi (traditional Māori earth oven) in skip bins, these physical and cultural structures that surrounded them hastened a loss of culture and identity that would have tremendous implications for following generations. The result of such structures and policy was the "atrophy of traditional Māori social structures such as whānau (extended family) and led to profound degradation of cultural, social and physical living environments" (Rykes, Pearson & Waa, 2016).

Contemporary Placemaking

One of the most significant attempts to adjust to this dislocation for mātāwaka and taurahere groups in the city was the urban marae. Tapsell writes that the genesis of these types of urban marae seems to be "the result of urban migrant Māori wishing to reconstitute their sense of moral community in a foreign environment" (2002, p.152). Tapsell outlines two types of urban marae, the first being pan-tribal (mātāwaka) and the second being maraes for singular tribes (taurahere) built in areas other than the tribe's homelands. These urban marae are not without contention, given their location within the homelands of other tribes. Some see them as symbols of modern-day Indigeneity, whilst others say this model of marae may be counterproductive, disregarding customary values and denying people opportunities to connect with their genealogical heritages (Tapsell, 2002, p.165).

Government responses to urban Māori disconnection include the development of a Māori state housing guideline in 2002. Māori architect Rau Hoskins was commissioned by Housing New Zealand Corporation, New Zealand's central government agency and New Zealand's largest social housing provider, to lead the development of a Māori state housing design guideline Ki te Hau Kāinga: New Perspectives on Māori Housing Solutions (Hoskins et al., 2002). Given the disproportionate numbers of Māori whanau in state housing and earlier concerns around the appropriateness of state housing (Brown, 2009, pp.142-143), the guideline aimed to incorporate into the design of new state housing, Māori ways of living and cultural understandings around how domestic space was used. They assert the need to separate areas considered tapu (e.g. laundries and bathrooms) and noa (e.g. kitchens), to allow space for formal gatherings such as tangihanga and the need to be able to accommodate large and intergenerational whānau to cater to other than nuclear family types (Hoskins et al., 2002; Brown, 2009). Despite the primary focus of these guidelines being on the architecture of state houses, reference is made to the urban context in which these houses sat and suggested a need to consider Māori-centric settlement patterns, in this case papakāinga (housing developments with some communal facilities) in urban and suburban areas (Hoskins et al., 2002, pp. 4-7).

At the scale of settlement design the primary government legislative tools have been the Resource Management Act (1991) and the Local Government Act (2002). These acts devolved planning responsibilities to local government placing some onus on local government to encourage community participation and recognition of the relationship between Māori and the environment (Rae, 2013). The Acts cover both rural and urban contexts but criticisms of both include a lack of shared understanding of the meanings of core concepts in the Acts and their poor performance in dealing with urban growth (Productivity Commission, 2016, p.11). A review of the New Zealand planning system is currently underway.

The inability of the RMA to deal with urban complexities is potentially indicative of the fact that Aotearoa has only relatively recently acknowledged its urbanity. Urban design and placemaking concerns from central and local government are relatively recent, let alone acknowledgement of the importance of Indigeneity within these agendas.

The first machination of this newfound urban concern was that in March 2005 the Ministry of the Environment released the New Zealand Urban Design Protocol. The protocol, seemingly modelled on similar guidance coming out of the UK (see for example the Urban Design

Compendium Volume 1 (Llewelyn-Davies, Yeang, 2000) and Volume 2 (studio | REAL, 2007)) outlined seven essential qualities or the 7 C's: context, character, choice, connections, creativity, custodianship, and collaboration. Unfortunately, the Protocol was developed without consultation with Māori practitioners or communities (Rolleston & Awatere, 2009, p. 2).

In response to this neglect, a group of Māori professionals (architects, landscape architects, planners, engineers, designers, iwi and hapū, educators, artists, local and central government) met in November 2006 to develop a draft National Māori Cultural Landscape Strategy or what would later be called: the Te Aranga Principles. The overarching premise of this strategy was that the:

> Development and articulation of the Māori cultural landscape will contribute to the health and well-being of all who reside in and visit Aotearoa – through realising our unique Aotearoa and Pacific identity (Te Aranga National Steering Group, 2008, p. 5).

In addition, the strategy asserted that mana whenua, as kaitiaki (guardians) have primacy over the lands in their turangawaewae (homeland or literally standing place) both in terms of their own places of cultural significance and all other public and private spaces where the development of these might threaten the health of the broader environment (Te Aranga National Steering Group, 2008, p. 5).

The Te Aranga Principles were then taken around the country and presented to iwi and hapū groups and have since been adopted by a number of different agencies such as Auckland Transport and Tamaki Regeneration Company (a state-owned redevelopment agency). The principles have been used in procurement documents and consultant selection and by education providers in course content. They are also supported and advocated for by the New Zealand Institute of Landscape Architects. Auckland Council has incorporated them into their online design guidance – the Māori Design section of the Auckland Design Manual (Auckland Council, ud.) and, in early 2016, the Council established a Māori focused urban design role – Māori Design Leader: Auckland Design Office.

These principles, though, are understood to provide a base from which individual iwi and hapū might develop a particular hapū based expression of values with respect to urban form. Discussions continue within hapū about how this might be realised.

These principles drew, in part, from the work of Rolleston and Awatere in their work on papakāinga with papakāinga translated to mean sustainable habitation within urban environments (2009, p. 1). The authors set out nine Māori sustainable urban design principles specifically focused on papakāinga development. These

Figure 3. Te Rau Aroha Ki Te Tangata Artwork – Tākaro-ā-poi: Margaret Mahy playground which is a woven pattern design as part of the Ngā Whāriki Manaaki series artworks exemplifying Ngāi Tuāhuriri identity (Matapopore (4)), Image source: Author

are Whānaungatanga (settlement design that supports community and environmental relationships), Kotahitanga (inclusive spaces), Wairuatanga (space design that connects people and environments together), Mauritanga (the mauri or life force of an existing environment must be taken into account in the design), Orangatanga (design should contribute to better cultural, social and environmental outcomes), Manaakitanga (spaces must be places where people are safe and feel included), Kaitiakitanga (designs should provide for the sustainable management of the environment), Rangatiratanga (cultural sites of significance should be protected alongside providing access to other sites to encourage community ownership and responsibility of natural resources found in the community) and Mātauranga (local histories should be reflected in the settlement design) (Ibid.).

In addition to the development of design principles that support Māori urban landscapes, Māori built environment professionals also worked to get "seats at decision-making tables." A consequence of the process of working up the Te Aranga principles was the establishment of Ngā Aho: Māori Designers Network, a "national network of Māori design professionals who come together to support each other to better service the design aspirations of our Māori communities" (Ngā Aho website, ud.). This group continues to grow in terms of size and influence. It has input into a range of decision-making forums such as the recent review into New Zealand urban planning carried out by the Productivity Commission (Whaanga-Schollum et al., 2016). At the time of writing (2016) Ngā Aho is about to sign (early 2017) a Memorandum of Understanding – Te Kawenata o Rata with the New Zealand Institute of Architects (NZIA). This includes provision for a Ngā Aho member to sit on the NZIA council as a voting member.

Māori Landscape Architects have also formed a subgroup of Ngā Aho – Te Tau-a-Nuku. Through this subgroup, the New Zealand Institute of Landscape Architects (NZILA) has now signed a Memorandum of Understanding (MoU) with Ngā Aho to support aims outlined in the NZILA's Bicultural Strategy (2014) (NZILA website ud.).

The Māori planning fraternity have Papa Pounamu which sits under the auspices of the New Zealand Planning Institute (NZPI). Papa Pounamu "focuses on the role of Māori and Pacific peoples in the New Zealand planning framework, and the integration of Māori perspectives in resource management planning and decision-making" (Papa Pounamu website ud.).

Iwi and hapū are working together in many ways to re-make connections with their places and rehabilitate landscapes which have been degraded. This is merely a snapshot of this work. Headway is being made in terms of what 'good' placemaking is and how 'good' placemaking – that is placemaking that reflects Māori identities – should be achieved.

Impact of Treaty Settlements

Alongside the process orientated and theoretical advances outlined above, Treaty of Waitangi settlements have influenced and supported placemaking processes. Treaty settlements have seen the return of some, albeit small amounts of land, and monetary compensation to iwi and hapū around the country in response to historical and contemporary grievances experienced by Māori since the signing of the Treaty of Waitangi in 1840. The Treaty afforded Māori rights to land and resources which, in many cases, were unjustly taken from them.

This post settlement context for many (though a number of iwi and hapū are still in negotiations) has promoted the importance of Māori worldviews with respect to place. In part, this may be because, through the settlement process, a number of iwi and hapū now have resources with which to develop land and housing and to develop capacity to engage with decision-makers at local and central government level. Many iwi and hapū groups have roles within their organisational structures that focus on environmental resource management, or similar. Being able to employ their own environmental advisors has meant that iwi and hapū can push for political power in a way that was not previously possible. Notwithstanding this, Awatere et al.'s (2013) critique still stands – even with these roles, iwi and hapū are stretched in terms of contributing to the many local government committees focused on different environmental issues of interest to Māori.

Related to this is the fact that the Treaty process works to identify discrete groups (iwi and hapū) and the associated lands to which they belong. This is done in order to ascertain the level and type of settlement afforded and to try to ensure that

---

[2] The anchor projects are key projects to be built across Christchurch that are thought to act as catalysts in the regeneration of the city.
[3] Margaret Mahy was a well-known, local and profilic New Zealand children's book author who passed away in 2012.

settlements do not conflict with other iwi and hapū proprietary rights. This increased capacity and clear iwi and hapū boundaries, it could be argued, has forced local government to develop more formalised governance structures that include iwi and hapū. Despite this, iwi and hapū continue to need to push for recognition of their mana whenua status in the landscapes to which they belong.

Impact of Natural Disasters

A further catalyst for the re-creation of Māori identity in urban landscapes were the Christchurch earthquakes of 2010 and 2011. Whilst devastating, the destruction of the central city has offered Cantabrians a unique opportunity to foster a 'new' Christchurch identity.

The post-earthquake recovery took place within the context of a planning system which had, according to Rae, "historically ignored not only the Māori voice, but also community participation in general" (2013, p. 79). Ngāi Tahu, the mana whenua iwi in Christchurch, signed their Treaty settlement agreement with the Crown in 1996 which offered some redress for past losses, a public apology and some opportunities to "exercise greater political power within the system, that is, central and local government, to remediate the political and economic deprivation that Ngāi Tahu were subjected to for nearly 150 years" (Rae, 2013, p. 76).

Through involvement in planning mechanisms since 1996, Ngāi Tāhu and Ngāi Tūāhuriri (the hapū of the area) were well placed and experienced in asserting their rightful place at the Christchurch Earthquake recovery decision-making table. Ngāi Tahu were involved in a range of ways at a number of levels of decision-making (Rae, 2013, p. 93; Kiddle & Kiddle, 2014, p. 222).

In addition to providing exemplary support services to those who were affected by the earthquakes by opening marae for accommodation and providing resources to people across Christchurch who were in need (Rae, 2013; Lambert, 2014), Ngāi Tahu were involved in "multi-level dialogue with the government in reconstructing communities" (Rae, 2103, p. 93). At the central government level, this included being involved at all levels of earthquake recovery decision-making (Rae, 2013, p. 89).

At the level of detailed placemaking decision-making, Ngāi Tūāhuriri and Ngāi Tahu have mandated Matapopore Charitable Trust to provide "cultural advice on Ngāi Tūāhuriri /Ngāi Tahu values, narratives, and aspirations for the anchor projects and any other projects

associated with the regeneration of Ōtautahi/Christchurch (Matapopore website (1) n.d.).[2] Matapopore is a group of environment related professionals including architects, landscape architects, planning professionals, and artists. In addition, they contract in other professional skills where needed but essentially they engage with built and natural environment professionals employed to develop and carry out rebuild projects in Christchurch to ensure that Ngāi Tūāhuriri /Ngāi Tahu values, narratives, and aspirations are incorporated.

To aid this process, Matapopore have developed a unique set of urban design guidelines (Matapopore (2), 2015). Alongside more traditional components found in many urban design guidelines, such as flora and fauna expectations, colour and material palettes, the guidelines are narrative based, telling the stories of places of significance for Ngāi Tahu and Ngāi Tūāhuriri. Underlying the entire ethos of the guidelines is an assertion that engaging stakeholders such as Māori in the design process is critical to good design. "When it comes to working with and for Māori, whether you are Māori or not, if you engage with the people and embrace them as "co-designers" in the process, it can generate stunning outcomes" (Matapopore (2) 2015, 2).

The Tākaro-ā-poi: Margaret Mahy[3] Playground is an example of the guidelines in practice. The outcomes seem to exemplify the willingness for local council, central government and designers to engage with local iwi. The park, opened in December 2015, features Ngāi Tahu "migration and settlement" narratives and references to Ngāi Tahu understandings of natural and spiritual environments (Matapopore (3), (ud.)). These Ngāi Tahu stories are interwoven with snippets from Margaret Mahy's stories and Ngāi Tahu artists have worked to realise these Ngāi Tahu identities in this everyday landscape in central Christchurch.

Contemporary Placemaking Challenges

These successes have relied on the ongoing efforts of a number of Māori design professionals and iwi and hapū members consistently pushing for a "place at the decision-making table" and the right to influence urban form. In the words of Potter, with respect to Australia, but equally relevant to Aotearoa, "place-making post-colonization must always negotiate this context" (Potter 2012, p. 137). Challenges to realise Māori urban places continue.

Today more than 85% of Māori live in urban areas (Statistics New Zealand, 2006; Kukutai, 2014; Ryks, Pearson & Waa, 2016). Maaka states that as of 1991, "80 percent of people identifying as Maori live outside their tribal areas and that some 27.5 percent acknowledge no tribal affiliation" (NZDS 1991 cited in Maaka, 1994, p. 311). Whilst this statistic is now dated, given the growth of urban settlements it is likely that this percentage has only increased in the intervening 26 years.

Of those living in urban settlements over 95 percent of Māori do not live in their turangawaewae (homeland) (Palmer, 2016). This has resulted in complex histories and relationships between the Crown, mana whenua, and mātāwaka (Māori people living in the region another tribe's region). In all of the four largest Aotearoa cities, mana whenua populations are outnumbered by mātāwaka (Ryks, Pearson & Waa, 2016).

A key challenge around this relates to decision-making processes. In some cities such as Christchurch, as outlined above, the local mana whenua have seen recent successes in being involved in placemaking decision-making processes at all levels. For other mana whenua groups with urban settlements in their regions, they are all but excluded from decision-making processes in favour of the inclusion of a general, pan tribal Māori type representation. It should be noted that current legislation supports local and central government agencies engaging with iwi authorities. A number of hapū have set up governance bodies in order to be included in these processes.

Ryks, Pearson and Waa (2016) highlight the complexities around decision-making and note that mātāwaka may be being excluded from representation with respect to urban development and planning "due to a lack of recognition of mātāwaka as a population group" or conversely, "mātāwaka have in some areas had more opportunities for participation in urban development than mana whenua" perhaps due to their high numbers (Ibid., p. 5).

With respect to mana whenua engagement, local government still does not necessarily understand how to engage meaningfully with iwi and hapū and incorporate local Māori perspectives in the physical environment. This lack of understanding is compounded by a lack of iwi and hapū capacity to be able to contribute to placemaking decision-making. Awatere et al. assert that:

> poor understanding by local authorities of Māori values, perspectives and knowledge, and the limited iwi/hapū (tribe/subtribe) capacity are also significant contributing factors to the poor uptake and incorporation of Mātauranga Māori in urban planning. As a consequence there is a lack of direct Māori input into most planning and decision-making processes (2013, p.236).

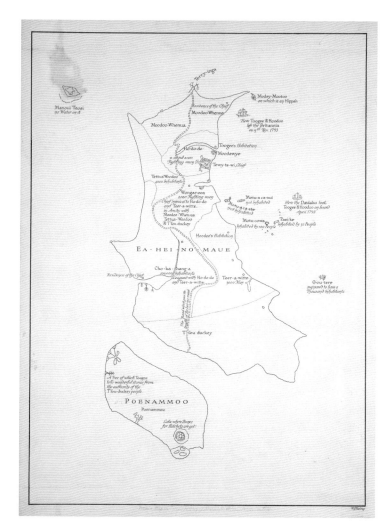

Figure 4. Tuki's Map by Tuki Te Terenui Whare Pira, Milligan, Robert Roy Douglas, 1893-1962. New Zealand Department of Internal Affairs Centennial Publications Branch :Tuki's map [copy of ms map]. [ca.1940]. Originally by Tuki Te Terenui Whare Pirau, b. 1769?. Ref: MapColl-CHA-2/1/9-Acc.36440. Alexander Turnbull Library, Wellington, New Zealand. / records/22866321

Urban placemaking capacity needs to be built amongst both Māori (in terms of numbers able to articulate and contribute to decision-making around these issues) and non-Māori (in terms of understanding Māori values, perspectives and knowledge as it relates to urban settlements).

Added to this, whilst mana whenua identities and mātauranga should have primacy in their regions, if mātāwaka are not included in some way, they risk being excluded from decision-making processes altogether. Engagement processes do not tend to be nuanced enough, engaging with mana whenua (as the kaitiaki (guardians) of the region) and non-Māori (as the other key community stakeholder). Unfortunately, mātāwaka do not tend to be included in these wider community engagement processes leaving mātāwaka groups without explicit representation in placemaking processes.

Despite large urban Indigenous populations, Aotearoa cities today continue to be conceptualised as non-Indigenous spaces. Rural places are the site of Māori authenticity (Walker & Burcham, 2010; Peters, 1996; Porter, 2013). Stereotyping authentic Indigeneity as a rural construct serves to perpetuate Indigenous erasure in urban settings.

This denial of urbanity as Indigenous is problematic. Firstly, it disregards the fact that urban Aotearoa has always been Indigenous space. In addition to land grievances experienced by whānau, hapū and iwi, as land was appropriated or bought to aid the formation of towns and cities, local hapū and iwi were quickly marginalised through the disregard paid to key sites of Indigenous identity (Kiddle and Menzies, 2016).

For both mana whenua and mātāwaka groups, dichotomising urban and rural experiences in this way impacts profoundly on personal subjectivities. For instance, Indigenous urban dwellers are often viewed as being less authentic than rural Indigenous people. "Scholarly research has generally positioned it [urban locales] as incompatible with authentic Indigeneity (which was to be found in rural/non-urban locales). Indeed, "urban" and "Indigenous" are still largely seen as incompatible" (Peters and Andersen, 2013, p.11). This privileging of rurality is mirrored more generally in Aotearoa society (See for example Schrader, 2016).

A further challenge centres on the inherent tension around the promotion of Māori identities in the creation of place and the desire to protect and hold on to place-based mātauranga Māori (Māori knowledge) for fear it will be abused and/or appropriated. For Māori some knowledge is deemed tapu (sacred), only to be held by certain people or groups of people within the tribe and not for general consumption. This tension plays out then as a disregard of all mātauranga Māori relevant to urban landscapes perhaps because either placemaking professionals find it too difficult to engage with such a nuanced process of knowledge gathering or find that time is needed to engage meaningfully so this is bypassed in favour of other placemaking narratives. Alternatively, due to the hegemonic colonial overlays, discussed earlier in the chapter, these same professionals may not even think that there might be histories, as yet unknown to them, that deserve mention. Finally, some built environment professionals may just be at a loss as to how to go about engaging with or translating this mātauranga to a contemporary urban context. Traditional settlements were not particularly large so historical precedent is not easily translated to the larger city context given larger sized settlements create complexities not seen in smaller ones.

This is all, of course, compounded by the fact that most placemaking professionals are non-Māori and therefore less likely to have existing sensibilities around engaging meaningfully with mātauranga Māori in a way that is fundamental to urban placemaking. Who gets to make places matters given that placemaking is an inherently political process. In Aotearoa placemaking processes are, for the most part, instigated and controlled by a range of built environment professionals. These include architects, planners, urban designers, artists and, to some extent, engineers and other professions working with city infrastructure.

With respect to ensuring Māori values and aspirations are evident in the places around them, points of tension abound. Whilst the fact that most built environment professionals are not Indigenous does not necessarily mean that Māori worldviews are not acknowledged in the process, it does require non-Māori professionals to be vigilant in involving Māori stakeholders in the design process.

Relatedly, there is a tendency for design professionals to ignore the politics of placemaking with some designers believing that the act of designing is somehow neutral and value-free. McGlynn and Murrain write, "it is not part of the culture of the environmental professions to be explicit about values…it allows certain things to happen for some people and constrains others" (1994). Potter, with respect to Indigenous communities, outlines the power relations inherent in the relationship between designer and client arguing that the notion of designer as expert is rarely overcome:

> although consultation processes do take place, these are largely formulaic and often rely on discursive techniques that commonly align with dominant western-liberal notions of communication and rarely overcome the power relation embedded in the authority of "architectural expertise" (2012, p. 132).

If professionals are not explicit about their value sets, resting on the laurels of their profession, it is incredibly difficult for Māori, and any other community stakeholder for that matter, to confront these underlying assumptions and suggest alternatives.

In addition, Aotearoa, does not yet have an "as of right" tradition of participatory placemaking due to vague regulatory tools. Urban design level placemaking is understood by some to be "big architecture," a sort of scaling up of more detailed design processes such as housing design which tends to place the emphasis on the architect as expert brought in to create an "original" design. This way of doing things sits in opposition to urban design theory which asserts the importance of stakeholder engagement in the design process. Indeed, some contend that this process of engagement is the very definition of urban design. McGlynn and Murrain assert:

There are many people who can talk extremely coherently and contribute great skill and expertise to the overall design process, but there is a sad lack of people who can translate the values, qualities and objectives derived from that process into a drawing or model with anything like the equivalent skill and precision. This is the unique selling proposition of urban designers: we are concerned with the design of the physical fabric itself via an open and interactive process (1994).

In Aotearoa then, robust placemaking processes would ensure the inclusion of mātauranga Māori, Māori aspirations and values acknowledging that Māori are equally expert in knowing about place.

Finally, for the most part, many Māori perceive cities as negative and in and of themselves tools of colonisation. For many, urbanisation is synonymous with colonisation. People talk with pain and anger about lost connections with "back home." Whilst it's clear that urbanisation has been painful for many, and this is not to be disregarded, this rhetoric tends to imagine the city as not being a Māori place, potentially impeding urban opportunities for us "to see Māori faces in our places." Of interest, Williams (2015) in her analysis of a history of Māori urban migration uses the term urban migration, as opposed to urbanisation to acknowledge the agency with which many Māori migrated to cities.

Ongoing Decolonised Placemaking

So what do we do next? How do we move forward in this quest for Māori urban places? We have had some successes. Māori centred professional networks and groups have formed, in part, to influence design decision-making process but also to share best practice and innovations around Māori design. The Te Aranga Principles and the Urban Design Guidelines developed by Matapopore exemplify forward-looking "new" frameworks, rooted in traditional mātauranga Māori. Tanira Kingi (2010) cited in Walker et al. (2013, pxix) talks of this type of approach as "walking backwards into the future."

Walking backwards into the future can however be problematic for the colonised given many of us have lost and been disconnected from traditional Māori knowledge sets. Historian Aroha Harris, in a recent keynote presentation for the Māori Association of Social Sciences conference (MASS website ud.) drew a metaphorical and literal comparison between Tuki's map (a map drawn by a Northern chief Tuki in 1793 for the Governor of New South Wales) and James Cook's first map of Aotearoa in 1769. Tuki's map was primarily qualitative as opposed to being a representation of land form. The North, his

turangawaewae, looms large and out of scale with the rest of Aotearoa. He makes reference to the location of chiefs, the numbers of fighters available in different places and alludes to everyday practices of the time such as storytelling and collection of resources. In comparison, Cook's map focuses primarily on landform and the potential resource represented by this land. Harris asserts that the history of Aotearoa has been grounded in Cook's cartographic pen lines, not Tuki's, ever since.

As it is, Indigenous efforts to shake off the impacts of colonisation, Harris argues, often continue to be rooted in Cook's map, continuing to work with Cook's conceptualisation of "our place" as the basis for responses. Māori are set up as resistors or collaborators – "these are the only two options." Māori get stuck in combative roles but Harris argues that we need to confidently draw and determine our own maps well removed from this agenda. Harris implored the audience to use Māori maps like Tuki's drawing on Māori histories, both past and present as the basis for self-determination.

This has implications for thinking about contemporary placemaking. Drawing on traditional or contemporary Māori realities to create Māori maps might be seen as a method for realising Māori identity in urban places and has been explored in the field of cultural mapping (Mercier, 2013; Brown and Nicholas, 2012; Walker, 2010).

Relatedly, there may be opportunities to imagine new Māori maps; maps that have never before been imagined or experienced. This development of new mātauranga might rediscover old Māori maps to imagine new ones or try to imagine utopian Māori cities. There is now a strong group of Māori Geospatial Information Systems (GIS) practitioners working on cultural mapping, monitoring, storytelling, and anticipating landscape changes. This group, Te Kahui Manu Hokai: Māori GIS Association holds regular conferences and training workshops for iwi representatives in order to provide technological skills that might aid the mapping of mātauranga Māori (Te Kahui Manu Hokai website, nd.).

One such project that offers up an opportunity to draw new maps is the Imagining Decolonised Cities project that colleagues and I have undertaking with Ngāti Toa (the mana whenua tribe) in Porirua, Wellington (September 2016 – May 2017). The project, funded by New Zealand National Commission for UNESCO, focuses on an urban design competition, open to the wider public, whereby participants submitted utopian ideas for a site in the urban area for which Ngāti Toa are the mana whenua iwi. In addition, colleagues and I with backgrounds in Architecture, Urban Design, Māori Studies, and

Geography worked with a group of high school students from the area to train them in a set of skills useful to developing a submission for entry into the competition.

We focused primarily on working with young people as we felt that this group have much to offer in terms of drawing new and complex maps as the hope is that they are more likely to be unencumbered by colonial processes. In addition, the research team was concerned that young people may not necessarily enter the competition without encouragement. Whilst we included a large group of Ngāti Toa young people we were keen to deliberately also involve non-Māori young people in order that the Treaty partnership is represented in this collaborative process. In addition, non-Māori must also take responsibility for decolonising urban processes, so in this regard, the research team includes Pākehā researchers, whilst being Māori led.

The submissions will be analysed to identify themes from the wider public on what it might mean to decolonise, through physical form, an urban site in Porirua. The underlying method here is that of utopianism (Levitas, 2010; 2013; Ashcroft, 2012). Those entering the competition were asked to think about a utopian vision for the site using either an approach that accepts historic precedent and reimagines possibilities from that starting point, or an approach that imagines a clean slate as if Captain Cook had never arrived. How would the Māori city have developed?

Either approach should be grounded in a set of principles developed with Ngāti Toa, that set out their values and aspirations for their environment. The project highlights possible forward thinking approaches for placemaking. This is by no means the only possibility. We need more projects, more pilots, more methodological testing to push the boundaries of placemaking in Aotearoa cities in ways that privilege Indigeneity.

Conclusion

In Aotearoa pre-colonial history, placemaking was strategic, undertaken at iwi and hapū level. These places provided temporary and permanent homes for families, exemplified as collective space. In addition, these places showcased resources and worked to ward off conflict, in the case of fortified pā.

The colonial project utilised placemaking as a means of control and Indigenous erasure, wresting iwi and hapū identities from the landscape with the acquisition of most of Aotearoa over a short period. In just 25 years 99 percent of the South Island had been acquired by the New Zealand Company and the Crown (New Zealand History, nd.). This land was wrangled and wrestled to create Britain in Aotearoa.

Māori placemaking during and post World War II was deeply influenced by rapid urban migration by Māori into the cities. Māori, in a bid to support the war effort, in search of employment and enticed by government incentives moved to the cities in droves often finding themselves isolated and in housing that did not support their cultural practices. This migration forever changed the cultural, social and economic landscape for Māori communities. To cope with the newfound pressures of city life some Māori communities worked to develop mātāwaka and taurahere urban marae as a means to practice cultural values in this new place. More recently the State has developed Māori housing guidelines as a response to the inappropriate housing in which Māori had found themselves in.

In the last decade, Māori practitioners have sought to broaden the influence of Māori values on towns and cities throughout Aotearoa through the development of the Te Aranga Principles which have been taken up by a number of government agencies. Influential practitioner based groups have formed, namely Ngā Aho: Māori Designers Network, Te Tau a Nuku: New Zealand Institute of Landscape Architects and Papa Pounamu: New Zealand Planning Institute all working to influence the professions they represent.

Alongside this, two key factors have been significant to Māori placemaking in Aotearoa – the Treaty settlement process and the Christchurch earthquakes of 2010 and 2011. Both have resulted in mana whenua groups being able to influence placemaking in ways that Aotearoa had not seen previously due to an increase in iwi held resources. This has led to increased capacity and legislative mandates for iwi involvement and thus wider recognition of the need to engage with iwi.

There remain ongoing tensions, however, which include concern around the promotion of Māori identities and values leading to the appropriation and misuse of Māori knowledge, the continued lack of capacity within mana whenua groups to engage in the myriad of placemaking related issues despite the successes mentioned above and the role of mātāwaka in placemaking decision-making processes.

Placemaking is a fraught process. It is intertwined with broader social norms and expectations. It is, at root, an intensely value laden, political process. In order that good placemaking can occur, these values must be laid bare by those with the power to implement placemaking. Aotearoa New Zealand's post-colonial history has, for the most part, excluded and erased Māori values from our cities, preferring instead to locate rurality as the site of authentic Indigeneity. Yet, it is dangerous to essentialise Māori as being Rather, we belong to and live in diverse spatial realities including urban, suburban, peri-urban, and rural contexts.

Capacity needs to be built and Māori need to be involved in placemaking processes if Aotearoa cities are to flourish as unique places that cater to the diverse realities of Māori. Cities have always been Indigenous places. Hopeful and forward looking placemaking approaches are needed to draw new Māori maps and create new Māori places. These approaches must be centred on participatory, co-design processes whereby Māori are acknowledged as urban experts whose values and aspirations are important for the making of successful places.

Acknowledgements

I would like to thanks Dr. Diane Menzies, Prof. Michelle Thompson-Fawcett, and Prof. Hirini Matunga for their constructive feedback on the chapter.

References

Auckland Council, (2016). *Auckland Design Manual,* Māori Design. Retrieved 2016, October 30 from http://www. aucklanddesignmanual.co.nz/design-thinking/Māori-design.

Awatere et al. (2013). "Kaitiakitanga o Ngā Ngahere Pōhatu – Kaitiakitanga of Urban Settlements" in Walker, R., Natcher, D. and Jojola, T. (Eds.) *Reclaiming Indigenous planning (Vol. 70).* Montreal: McGill-Queen's Press-MQUP.

Barcham, M. (1998). "The challenge of urban Māori: reconciling conceptions of Indigeneity and social change". *Asia Pacific Viewpoint*, 39(3), pp. 303-314.

Ashcroft, B. (2012). *Introduction: Spaces of Utopia, Spaces of Utopia: An Electronic Journal.* 2nd series, no. 1, pp. 1-17.

Brand, D. (2004). "Surveys and sketches: 19th-century approaches to colonial urban design." *Journal of Urban Design*, 9(2), pp.153-175.

Brand, D. (2011). "Crossing the roads: urban diagonals in New Zealand and the nineteenth century Anglo-colonial world." *Planning Perspectives*, 26(3), pp. 423-444.

Brown, D. S., & Nicholas, G. (2012). "Protecting Indigenous cultural property in the age of digital democracy: Institutional and communal responses to Canadian First Nations and Māori heritage concerns." *Journal of Material Culture*, 17 (3), 307-324. 10.1177/1359183512454065

Brown, D.S. (2009). *Māori Architecture: from fale to wharenui and beyond.* Auckland: Raupo Penguin.

Butina-Watson, G. and Bentley, I. (2007). *Identity by design.* London: Routledge.

Durie, M. (1995). *Nga matatini Māori: diverse Māori realities.* A paper prepared for the Ministry of Health. Palmerston North: Massey University.

Falconer, G. (2015). *Living in Paradox: A History of Urban Design*

Across Kainga, Towns and Cities in New Zealand. Auckland: Blue Acres Press.

Hoskins, R. et al. (2002). "Ki te Hau Kainga: New Perspectives on Māori Housing Solutions. A Design Guide Prepared for Housing New Zealand Corporation." Retrieved 2016, September 13 from *Housing New Zealand Corporation* website http://www.hnzc.co.nz/assets/Uploads/ki-te-hau-kainga-new-perspectives-on-Māori-housing-solutions.pdf.

Hultman, J. and Hall, C.M. (2012). "Tourism place-making: Governance of locality in Sweden." *Annals of Tourism Research*, 39(2), pp. 547-570.

Jacobs, J. (1961). *The death and life of great American cities.* New York: Vintage.

Friedmann, J. (2010). "Place and Place-Making in Cities: A Global Perspective", *Planning Theory & Practice*, 11:2, pp. 149-165.

Kiddle, R & Menzies, D. (2016). "Indigenous Places: Contestations of Colonial Landscapes" in *X Section Journal.Issue 6: Divergence, Defining Difference through Design*. http://www. xsectionjournal.com/issue-6. Accessed 21 Jan 2017.

Kiddle, R., & Kiddle, A. (2014). "Place-making and post-quake identity – Creating a unique Otautahi identity." In B. Bennett, J. Dann, E. Johnson, & R. Reynolds (Eds.), *Once in a Lifetime: City-building after Disaster in Christchurch*. New Zealand: Freerange Press.

King, M. (2003). *Penguin History of New Zealand.* UK: Penguin.

Kingi, T. (2005). *Indigeneity and Māori Mental Health*, Copthorne Resort, Waitangi. 25 November. Retrieved 2017, January 21, http://www.massey.ac.nz/massey/fms/Te%20Mata%20O%20 Te%20Tau/Publications%20-%20Te%20Kani/T%20Kingi%20 Indigenety%20and%20Māori%20mental%20health.pdf.

Kukutai T. (2011). "*Māori Demography in Aotearoa New Zealand 50 Years On*", New Zealand Population Review, 37, pp.45-64.

Kukutai T. (2014). "The structure of urban Māori identities." In Peters, E & Andersen, C. (Eds.) *Indigenous in the City: Contemporary Identities and Cultural Innovation.* Vancouver: UBC Press.

Lambert, S. (2014). "Indigenous Peoples and urban disaster: Māori responses to the 2010-12 Christchurch earthquakes." *Australasian Journal of Disaster and Trauma Studies*, 18(1), pp. 39-48.

Levitas, R. (2010). *The concept of utopia (Vol. 3).* Peter Lang.

Levitas, R. (2013). *Utopia as method: The imaginary reconstitution of society. Springer.*

Llewelyn-Davies, Yeang, 2000. *Urban design compendium, First Edition.* English Partnerships/Housing Corporation, London.

Lynch, K. (1960). *The image of the city (Vol. 11).* MIT press.

Maaka, R. (1994). "The new tribe: Conflicts and continuities in the social organization of urban Māori." *The Contemporary Pacific*, 6, 311-36. http://hdl.handle.net/10125/12988. Accessed 20 January 2017.

Matapopore website (1) (nd.). *Home page*, Retrieved 2016, August 24, from http://www.matapopore.co.nz/

Matapopore (2), (2015). *Urban Design Guidelines: Kia Atawhai ki te Iwi, Caring for the People.* Retrieved 2016, August 24 from http://www.matapopore.co.nz/wp-content/uploads/2016/05/

Matapopora-UDG-Finalv3-18Dec2015.pdf

Matapopore (3), (nd.) "A Special Place to Play: Tākaro-ā-poi, Margaret Mahy Playground." Retrieved 2016, August 24 from http://www.matapopore.co.nz/wp-content/uploads/2016/05/1124_CRCL_MP_Ta%CC%84karo_a%CC%84_Poi.pdf

Matapopore (4), (nd.) "Ngā Whāriki Manaaki." Retrieved 2016, August 24 from (http://www.matapopore.co.nz/wp-content/uploads/2016/05/1124_CRCL_MP_Nga-Whariki-Manaaki.pdf

Matunga, H. (2013). "Theorizing Indigenous Planning," pp. 3-32 in Walker, R., Natcher, D. and Jojola, T., 2013. *Reclaiming Indigenous planning (Vol. 70)*. Quebec: McGill-Queen's Press-MQUP.

McGlynn, S. and Murrain, P. (1994). "The politics of urban design." *Planning Practice and Research*, 9(3), pp. 311-319.

Mercier, O. (2013). "Putting Māori history, society and culture on the map." *Freerange, Vol. 7: The Commons*. 7: 28-31.

Meredith, P. (2000, February). "Urban Māori as New Citizens: The Quest for Recognition and Resources". *Revisioning Citizenship in New Zealand conference*, University of Waikato, Hamilton.

Ministry of Culture and Heritage, (2016). "Maungakiekie-One Tree Hill – roadside stories." Retrieved 2016, November 14 from *NZ History website*, http://www.nzhistory.net.nz/media/video/maungakiekie-one-tree-hill-roadside-stories.

Moorfield, J. C. 2010. *Te Aka Māori-English English Māori Dictionary*. Retrieved 2016, October 30 from http://Māoridictionary.co.nz/.

Ministry of Culture and Heritage, (2017). "Māori Land Loss, 1860 – 2000." Retrieved 2017, January 20 from *NZ History website*, https://nzhistory.govt.nz/media/interactive/maori-land-1860-2000

Ngā Aho (nd.) *Ngā Aho website*. Retrieved 2016, August 14 from http://www.ngaaho.maori.nz/.

NZILA website, (nd.) "Cultural Moves." Retrieved 2016, October 23 from *New Zealand Institute of Landscape Architects website* http://www.nzila.co.nz/news-items-roll/news-item-list/cultural-moves.aspx.

Orange, C. (2015). *The Treaty of Waitangi*. Wellington: Bridget Williams Books.

Papa Pounamu (nd.) *Papa Pounamu website*, Retrieved 2016, October 30 from http://www.papapounamu.org/

Pawson, E. (1987). "The social production of urban space." *New Zealand Geographer*, 43(3), pp. 123-129.

Peters, E & C Anderson, eds. 2013. *Indigenous in the city: contemporary identities and cultural innovation*. UBC Press.

Peters, E., 1996. *'Urban' and 'Aboriginal': an impossible contradiction? City lives and city forms: Critical research and Canadian urbanism*, pp. 47-62.

Pool I., 1991. *Te Iwi Māori: A New Zealand Population, Past, Present and Projected*. Auckland: Auckland University Press.

Porter, L., 2013. *Coexistence in Cities: The Challenge of Indigenous Urban Planning in the. Reclaiming Indigenous planning*, 70, p. 283.

Potter, E. 2012 *Introduction: making Indigenous place in the Australian city, Postcolonial Studies*, 15:2 131-142.

Productivity Commission, 2016. "Better urban planning, Draft report – summary version." August 2016. http://www.productivity.govt.nz/sites/default/files/better-urban-planning-draft-report-summary.pdf. Accessed 20 January 2017.

Project for Public Spaces website, nd. "What is placemaking?" http://www.pps.org/reference/what_is_placemaking/. Accessed 10 August 2016.

Rae, H. T., 2013. *Kia tahuri i te riu, kia tika: Indigenous participation in earthquake recovery planning: Insights from Taiwan and Canterbury* (Unpublished masters thesis. Dunedin, New Zealand: University of Otago). http://hdl.handle.net/10523/4147. Accessed 20 January 2017.

Rolleston, S. and Awatere, S., 2009. "Ngā hua papakāinga: Habitation design principles." MAI Review, 2(2), pp. 1-13.

Ryks, J., Pearson, A.L. and Waa, A., 2016. "Mapping urban Māori: A population-based study of Māori heterogeneity." *New Zealand Geographer*, 72(1), pp. 28-40.

Schrader, B. 2016. *The Big Smoke, New Zealand Cities, 1840-1920*, Bridget Williams Books, Wellington.

Sepe, M. and Pitt, M., 2014. "The characters of place in urban design." *Urban Design International*, 19(3), pp. 215-227.

Statistics New Zealand, 2006. Māori Mobility. in/~/media/Statistics/browsecategories/population/migration/Māorimobility-nz/Māori-mobility-in-nz.pdf. Accessed 3 October 2016.

studio | REAL, 2007. *Urban design compendium, Second Edition*. Homes and Communities Agency, London.

Tapsell, P., 2002. "Marae and tribal identity in urban Aotearoa/New Zealand." *Pacific Studies, Vol. 25*, Nos 1/2 March/June, pp. 141-171.

Te Aranga National Steering Group, 28 April 2008. *Te Aranga: Māori cultural landscape strategy, 2nd Edition*. http://www.tearanga.Māori.nz/cms/resources/TeArangaStrategy28Apr08_lr.pdf. Accessed 4 August 2016.

Te Kahui Manu Hokai: Māori GIS Association website n.d http://www.tekahuimanuhokai.org.nz/. Accessed 20 January 2017.

Walker, R. and Barcham, M., 2010. "Indigenous-inclusive citizenship: the city and social housing in Canada, New Zealand, and Australia." *Environment and Planning A*, 42(2), pp. 314-331.

Walker, R., Natcher, D. and Jojola, T., 2013. *Reclaiming Indigenous planning (Vol. 70)*. McGill-Queen's Press-MQUP.

Walker, W., 2010. "Tangata Whenua me te Kāinga Kanohi/Tangata Whenua and the Landscape." In K. Stuart and M. ThompsonFawcett (Eds.) *Tāone Tupu Ora: Indigenous Knowledge and Sustainable Urban Design* (pp. 82-90). Wellington, N.Z: Steele Roberts.

Whaanga-Schollum et al. eds., 2016. Ngā Aho and Papa Pounamu, Better Urban Planning, Report from Māori Built Environment Practitioners Wānanga. 17 June 2016. http://www.productivity.govt.nz/sites/default/files/better-urban-planning-draft-report-wananga.pdf. Accessed 12 November 2016.

Whyte, W.H., 1980. The social life of small urban spaces.

Williams, M.M., 2015. *Panguru and the city: Kāinga tahi, kāinga rua: An urban migration history*. Bridget Williams Books, Wellington.

Chapter 5: The Effect of Redfern's Aboriginal community on local and neighbourhood planning

Michael Hromek - Budawang tribe of the Yuin nation

Michael has a range of specialisations in the broad area of design, theory and architecture. These include the nature of design and its role towards society, and the relationships between theory and practice in planning, society and the city. Michael is currently doing a PhD at the University of Technology Sydney and teaches in the Bachelor of Design in Architecture covering architectural design and history and theory subjects. His thesis focuses on the idea of urban Indigenous community in Redfern and questions, what are the values that constitute this community? How do they differ from what might be considered "traditional" Indigenous values? How have they been altered by inner city processes? How might the proposed future development of The Block contain these values? His other research interests surround the idea of contemporary Indigenous identity and how it might be formalised through built form.

The historic view of an Aboriginal community is often associated with the idea of Country, remoteness, or wilderness, yet approximately 75% of Aboriginal people now live in Australian cities or non-remote areas (Aboriginal population in Australia, n.d. para 6). The effect of this urbanisation has impacted Aboriginal communities in a variety of ways, yet in turn, Aboriginal communities have had a large effect on the city and urbanity. In Redfern in Sydney New South Wales (NSW), the Aboriginal community has had a significant spatial effect on local and neighborhood planning.

Redfern, an inner-city suburb of Sydney, has long been considered an Aboriginal place, not only in contemporary times, but from the early beginnings of colonisation in Australia (with the landing of Captain Cook in 1788), it has always had Aboriginal involvement in one way or another. This chapter will examine the extent of Redfern's Aboriginal involvement – and in particular, a specific location within Redfern known simply as "The Block." I begin with a historic perspective and move to the present context, considering 1) what were the political and social factors that allowed The Block to come about? 2) what effect has Redfern's Aboriginal community had on

local and community planning, and 3) how might this experience inform these disciplines in the future?

The Block's Aboriginal community is unique as it is an urban location that has a strong sense of Aboriginal identity. The Block's Aboriginal community has become a unique focal point for this conversation as it is one of the few urban locations that has this strong sense of Aboriginal identity. This identity is achieved by many things including Aboriginal services, art etc. but the primary catalyst of this identity is The Block's high spatial density, drawing the community together in close proximity. The combination of a strong identity and spatial immediacy has brought strength and empowerment to this particular urban community. As such Redfern has maintained a sense of Indigeneity within the urban landscape even in the face of serious pressures threatening its very existence. These pressures include a declining Aboriginal population in Redfern, rising property prices, gentrification, and splits within the community itself. This resilience to ongoing pressures can be attributed to a very particular set of spatial qualities which embody Redfern's Aboriginal urban community values. These spatial qualities thus have the potential to become a beneficial tool set in terms of thinking about local/community planning that supports Aboriginal communities in the wider national context.

A brief history of Aboriginal Redfern

Redfern in its present context is an inner-city suburb close to Sydney's central business district, however, the local Aboriginal clan, the Gadigal people have had a long-standing history with Redfern which pre-dates white settlement and the development of Redfern as a "mixed" community. In pre-colonial times Redfern was considered a gathering place for many of Sydney's Aboriginal peoples due to its geographical opportunities, such as its adjacency to Shea Creek (the now fully concreted and culverted Alexandria Canal), its nearby wetlands, and its elevated position offering a good view of the surrounding area which would have been important in times of discord, war, or conflict. It remains an important gathering place to this day.

The Gadigal (or Cadigal, or Kadigal) people were salt water people which meant their primary focus was towards the ocean in terms of sourcing food and spirituality. The earliest existing records of the Gadigal people were by the First Fleet settlers in 1788, who described them as "always appear[ing] cheerful and in good humour" and "seemingly enjoying uninterrupted health and live to a great age" (Saunders-Sheehan, 2014, para 7). Additional comments came from Captain Cook himself who famously wrote that the Aboriginal people were,

> far more happier than we Europeans; being wholly unacquainted not only with the superfluous, but the necessary conveniences so much sought after in Europe, they are happy in not knowing the use of them. They live in a tranquillity which is not disturbed by the inequality of condition. The earth and sea of their own accord furnishes them with all things necessary for life… This, in my opinion, argues that they think themselves provided with all the necessaries of life (Saunders-Sheehan, 2014, para 7).

In 1817 the land on which Redfern sits today was granted to surgeon William Redfern by Lachlan Macquarie who was the fifth and final autocratic Governor of New South Wales (Ford, 1967). How this specifically affected and impacted the local Gadigal tribe is unclear, however it is assumed that any Aboriginal community living in the location was moved along as the area was being cultivated and absorbed into the municipality of Sydney.

During the early 20th century, Sydney was connected to the vast rail network across the country and the final stop was Redfern (Department of Infrastructure, Regional Development and Cities, 2007, para 5). These events alongside a general rise in employment in city areas, resulted in a large number of Aboriginal people coming to Redfern to look for work with the nearby Eveleigh Railyards.

From the 1960s onward, significant development and change occurred for Aboriginal Australians (Korff, 2017). This was a busy period where political and civil rights movements aimed at addressing the prejudice and inequalities Aboriginal people faced gained momentum. In 1965 the Freedom Bus ride occurred where a group of nearby Sydney University students formed the Student Actions for Aborigines organisation and went from town to town in a bus with Aboriginal activist and sportsman Charlie Perkins to protest against racial segregation (Korff, 2017).

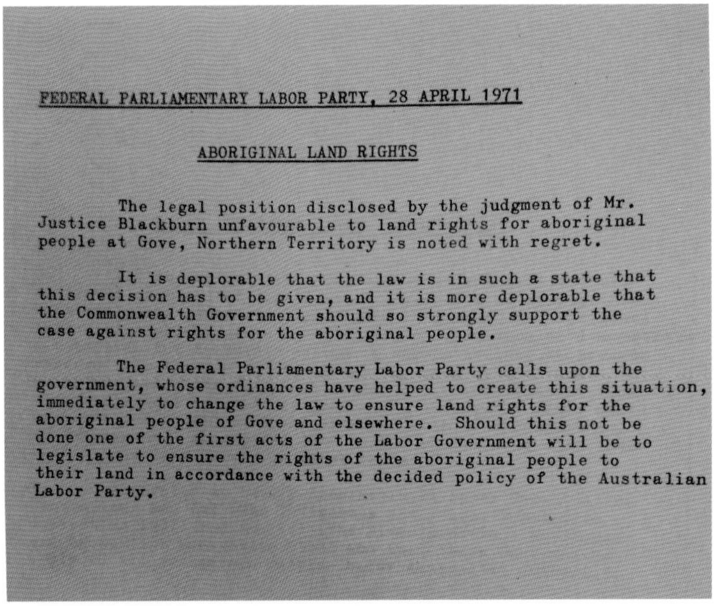

FEDERAL PARLIAMENTARY LABOR PARTY, 28 APRIL 1971

ABORIGINAL LAND RIGHTS

The legal position disclosed by the judgment of Mr. Justice Blackburn unfavourable to land rights for aboriginal people at Gove, Northern Territory is noted with regret.

It is deplorable that the law is in such a state that this decision has to be given, and it is more deplorable that the Commonwealth Government should so strongly support the case against rights for the aboriginal people.

The Federal Parliamentary Labor Party calls upon the government, whose ordinances have helped to create this situation, immediately to change the law to ensure land rights for the aboriginal people of Gove and elsewhere. Should this not be done one of the first acts of the Labor Government will be to legislate to ensure the rights of the aboriginal people to their land in accordance with the decided policy of the Australian Labor Party.

Figure 1. Response from the Labor Government expressing regret over the failed Aboriginal land rights claim in Gove is a good indication as to the party's position on Indigenous issues (1971), Source: Author

Also around this time, Redfern, together with a number of other inner-city Aboriginal suburbs such as Darlington and Waterloo, began to attract much media attention, predominantly negative. The areas were considered slum-like as the houses became rundown and neglected with much focus on the Aboriginal people living there. The dramatic increase in migration to Redfern resulted in serious problems of overcrowding. In addition, and, perhaps most significantly, many Aboriginal people faced discrimination – akin to, but different from the discrimination facing them in their previous "natural" environment – when seeking accommodation.

An investigative report by The Bulletin, 19 September 1964, into Redfern written by Gordon Chesterman described the situation as follows:

> Aboriginal families living in rat-infested, flooded dwellings; of 20 Aborigines living in a two-bedroom dilapidated house; of landlords discrimination against Aborigines forcing them to accept sub-standard dwellings for which exorbitant rentals are charged by landlord sharks (Chesterman, 1964).

Such discrimination culminated in a 1968 campaign to relocate the large Aboriginal population away from inner city areas, with the NSW Department of Housing resettling them to suburbs on the urban fringe such as Mt Druitt and Campbelltown.

The formation of The Block

A key turning point for the Aboriginal community in Redfern, however, was the development of community-controlled services, which included the Aboriginal

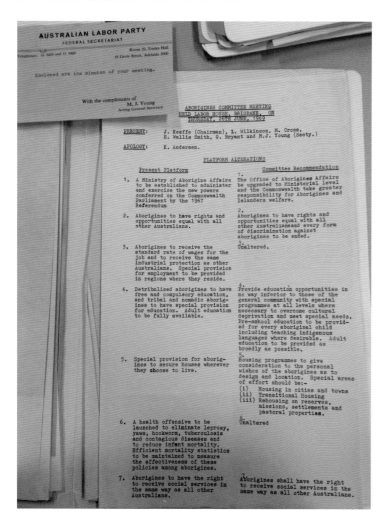

Figure 2. Pg. 1 of the Aborigines Committee Meeting, held at Labor House, Brisbane on Thursday 26th June, 1969

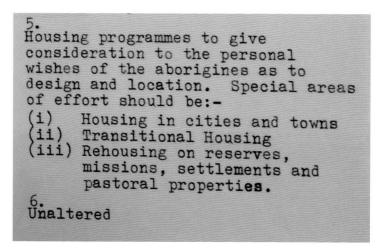

Figure 3. Close up of figure 2 focusing on the effort to house Indigenous people in cities

and then they spread as white families moved out…. The Government may as well give them the block – they just about have it now (Aboriginals Go Alone, 1973).

An article published by *The Daily News*, 16 April 1973 describes the "shock" and "bitter opposition" to the increase in Aboriginal people moving to Redfern (Joy, Anger at Redfern plan, 1973). However, key members of the Aboriginal community were aware of this and rather than take this push-back as antagonistic, they wished to face this issue and come to a resolution. Dick Blair, former Aboriginal boxing champion and founding member of The Block, was particularly vocal about addressing these issues and set up night patrols with several friends in an effort to "keep my own in line" (Uneasy peace, 1973).

The Daily Mirror reports on this by saying,

a handful of…Aboriginals have formed a vigilante group to patrol nightly a block in Redfern which has become notorious in the past few weeks… Ownership of the block bounded by Louis, Vine, Eveleigh and Caroline Street, is sought by the recently-formed Aboriginal Housing Committee so as to develop into a self-contained community (Uneasy peace, 1973).

While the idea of self-governance and developing strong communities through such activities as night patrols are potentially positive, the use of the term "vigilante" is telling highlighting the media bias against the development of Aboriginal community in this urban setting. On this, Blair says that,

I know my people and I know very well they need discipline. But we're not a naturally violent people – our history proves that. City life is bewildering and too fast for those who come from the country, so they escape from it by lifting the elbow at the local and get drunk. And what happens? The police just keep on coming down on us and that doesn't help. I believe in authority – absolutely – but why don't they leave it in our hands, give it to those of us who understand the people. Do

Legal Service, the Aboriginal Medical Service, the Aboriginal Children's Service, and the Aboriginal Black Theatre House. The development of these services provided the Aboriginal community of Redfern with a key foothold in the inner city and was an important moment for a move towards self-determination for many Aboriginal communities nationwide. Most notable of these community-controlled services was the Aboriginal Housing Company (AHC), which, with funding from the Whitlam government in 1972, purchased six terraces on what is today known as The Block. The aim of AHC and its Housing Project was to provide a communal living environment run by Aboriginal people (AHC Timeline, 2017).

Yet the push back by white residents was growing. In one article published by The Daily Mirror on 23 March 1973, the report sensationally talks of the area's last white woman moving out. Mrs. Ethel Ferran, 70, is quoted as saying:

I have to go – I just can't stand the noise any longer… Originally a few Aboriginals moved into a vacant house

Figure 4. Aboriginal activists led by Charles "Chicka" Dixon successfully campaign the Government for funds to start The Block project in Redfern – The Canberra Times, Nov 2 1972

you think we want them fighting each other or the whites when there's so much important work to be done, when right here in this block we're trying to prove something to the world? (Uneasy peace, 1973).

Here, Blair highlights the significance of The Block as a test development to prove, not just to Australia but to the world, that Aboriginal people can live in the city and can fit into existing communities. Yet part of this "fitting in" must come from self-governance. It's clear here that the community wished to deal with these problems in-house, or at the very least, to help address these problems so as to be a part of the solution. This illustrated a strongly held value that personal relations and close social ties are fundamental to addressing local issues and resolving conflict.

Redfern and Politics

This pressure from outside the Aboriginal community led to further activism from within it to try to influence politicians to help deliver a solution to the issue of overcrowding in locations where the community wanted to be. This led to a significant political moment in Australian history with the establishment of the Labor government led by Gough Whitlam from 1972-75, where wide sweeping policy changes were brought in that also included the recognition of Aboriginal property rights and land claims. This included the allocation of a grant by Whitlam to a group of Aboriginal activists, co-founders of The Block Kay and Bob Bellear and Dick Blair among them who campaigned in Canberra for Aboriginal housing in Redfern. This grant was not a land claim by any traditional use of the term, rather it was effectively, an Aboriginal claim on an inner city piece of land. The success of this grant, which allowed for the creation of The Block, was a huge win for the Aboriginal community and spurred further advances in this area.

Before the election of the Whitlam Government in 1972, the Labor Party (not yet in power) were vocal about their position on Aboriginal rights. In a document dated 1971 (see Figure 1), one year before the Party was elected into power, the Party outlined their pro-Aboriginal rights stance through a statement on a failed Aboriginal land right claim in Gove Northern Territory. This document now resides in the Whitlam Collection within the National Archives of Australia.

As seen in the document, the Labor Party took a strong stance on the legal and social rights of Aboriginal people, condemning a legal system that was "unfavourable to land rights for aboriginal people" (Federal Parliamentary Labor Party, 1971), and claiming that if the Party came to power, they would make this a priority issue to address. The Labor Party was elected into power almost one year later in December 1972. The sentiments set out in the document above led to housing policy development and the creation of The Block. The Block enabled the development of this urban Aboriginal community.

1972-75

The Whitlam government were progressive in regards to Aboriginal rights and the role they envisaged Aboriginal Australia should play in the nation. This is illustrated through a document from 1973 from the Standing Committee of Aboriginal Affairs stating that,

With the coming of white people, Aboriginal land was stolen, spiritual links shattered, the tribal economy broken, ritual life ceased and in many cases Aboriginals murdered and tribes separated. Leadership structure and Aboriginal culture was devastated and Aborigines became dependent on white people. Aboriginality no longer meant pride, substance and belonging, it no longer meant a life-long exploration of the joys of the spirit. It came to mean constant denigration and contempt, grinding poverty, fear, helplessness and apathy. All the concepts of the Aboriginal personality were slowly undermined so that Aborigines could only relate to white commercial society with shame and embarrassment...
The election of the Labor Government in 1972 saw the establishment of a Department of Aboriginal Affairs and the appointment of a Minister who had responsibility to attempt to restore land to the Australian indigines and provide compensation for damage inflicted (Standing Committee of Aboriginal Affairs, Labor Party, 1973).

This statement clearly illustrates the Labor Government's intentions for Australia's Aboriginal people, with an aim to "right some of the wrongs" in Australia's history. The Labor government under Whitlam were making a concerted effort to raise the basic living standards of Aboriginal people in Australia, which is further illustrated through the quote below from a report by the Minister for Aboriginal Affairs to Prime Minister Gough Whitlam,

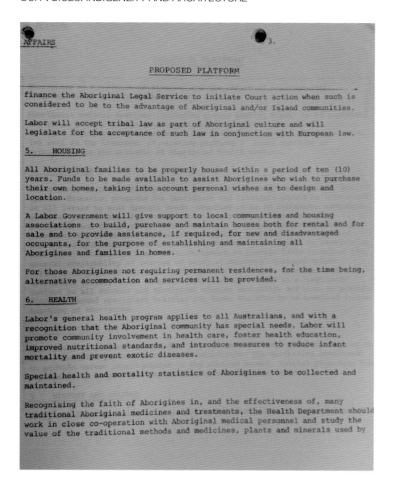

Figure 5. The removal of the word "cities" from the statement of intent for Indigenous housing

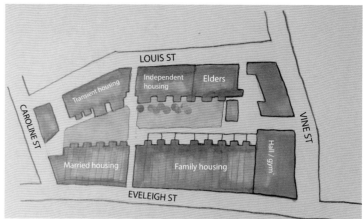

Figure 6. The original plan for The Block – note the central shared space achieved by turning the back yards and a small laneway into a shared zone

This brings me to "White Backlash." Whether we like it or not, it exists and will have to be dealt with. The most unpleasant event on my trip in January was a meeting I had with the "Rights of Territorians" group in Northern Territory. They made it quite clear to me they believed all social service benefits should be taken away from Aboriginal. I was left in no doubt as to their motives – a return to the good old days of plenty of cheap black labour. This sort of "backlash" has its roots in the resentment such people feel that they are somehow being disadvantaged by the Aboriginals emancipation and progress (Bryant, 1972).

The above indicates a progressive outlook by the party in power at the time towards Australia's first peoples which sat, and continues to sit, in stark contrast with Australia's black and white history. Along with the 1967 referendum granting Aboriginal people voting rights, this era brought about changes to the standing of Aboriginal people in Australia and laid the political ground for The Block in Redfern to proceed.

Blacks in the City

This kind of thinking and subsequent policy provided support for places like Redfern and The Block to be created. These policies were reinforced by the recommendations made by the Standing Committee on Aboriginal Affairs who stated that "Funds will be regularly allocated to the Aboriginal Land Fund to allow for the purchase of land for Aboriginal Communities throughout Australia" (Aboriginal Affairs Committee, 1969), with Redfern being a community to receive funding for the allocation of houses on what would eventually become known as The Block.

During the beginning of Whitlam's government sweeping changes were introduced across all aspects of Australian life with the most significant of these being the changes to civil rights and liberties offered to Aboriginal people. These changes included an effort to bring more Aboriginal people into the city. At the Aborigines Committee Meeting of the Labor Party in 1969 specific wording in the Proposed Platform for Aboriginal Affairs sought to bring more Aboriginal people into Australian cities.

5. Housing programs to give consideration to the personal wishes of the aborigines as to design and location. Special areas of effort should be:

(1) Housing in cities and towns
(2) Transitional Housing
(3) Rehousing on reserves, missions, settlements and pastoral properties (Aboriginal Affairs Committee, 1969)

As the document shows there was a specific effort by the Labor Party to bring more Aboriginal people into Australian cities. Yet the location as to where Aboriginal people were to be housed was under constant revision. A subsequent document stated that "Because some Aboriginals have a substantially different lifestyle to the Europeanised life style adopted by the majority of people in this country, design and location of housing should take this difference into account" (Aboriginal Affairs Committee, 1969, p.1).

Figure 7. The Aboriginal tent embassy on The Block protested the Pemulwuy project for 18 months starting in 2014

Figure 8. The Blocks new security fencing erected almost immediately by the Aboriginal Housing Company after the removal of tent embassy in 2016

It was during this time – and with this exact sentiment – that the grant for The Block was approved and allocated. However, this sentiment and policy was not to last. Later documents show a change in the wording removing the word "city" and instead added that "funds will be made available to assist Aborigines who wish to purchase their own homes, taking into account personal wishes as to design and location" (Aboriginal Affairs Committee, 1969, p.1).

The "Proposed Platform" document shown in Figure 5 dated 1972, shows that specific wording related to Australian cities was removed and instead, the emphasis was placed on the more generic wording of "personal wishes as to...location."

The Block was the only urban land grant allocated by the Whitlam (or any other) government. The proposal to build The Block came about due to the happy confluence of supportive policy and change in sentiment. In this sense, The Block was lucky to come about, as only a few years later, specific efforts made to house Aboriginal people in Australia's cities ceased.

While the Whitlam Labor Party was short lived, the policies they implemented continue to make ripples around Australia today. In regards to Aboriginal housing, and to the Liberal Party's credit, some of those policies

implemented during the Whitlam era were carried across to the next government. While the effort to house Aboriginal people in Australian Cities was abandoned by the Labor Party itself, the small gap that opened up during this time directly allowed for the creation of The Block.

Contemporary Redfern

In recent times the Aboriginal community of Redfern has been aggregated, dislocated and pulled apart due to the complete demolition of the housing on The Block in 2011 and the accompanying relocation of the community to other areas. The most recent census in 2016 stated that Redfern's total population is now 13,213 including only 284 Aboriginal people (Australian Bureau of Statistic, 2016). The drop in density and number of Aboriginal people is alarming, yet in many ways Redfern is still no less considered an Aboriginal place.

Given the important role The Block and wider Redfern played in supporting Aboriginal communities, a retrospective analysis of key spatial elements that allowed such an important concentration of urban Aboriginal people to thrive be it due to its potential to enhance or add betterment to other communities, Aboriginal or not is warranted in places like Redfern, Aboriginal people began to be exposed to, and experience, a different way of living as seen through this Western settlement model. The notion of city living – and all that comes with it – is relatively new to Aboriginal people. We as planners, architects, academics and citizens have more to learn in terms of how Aboriginal people live in city areas. Do Aboriginal communities maintain traditional Aboriginal values in these urban locations? What spatial forms come from these Aboriginal communal values? How might this inform the spatial disciplines of planning and architecture? And finally, how does this all relate to Redfern and The Block?

Redfern was a highly articulated and a conspicuous Aboriginal community formed around a single city block. This congregation in a single block was in part due to low rents, nearby employment, and to the fact that the building stock was undesirable and therefore last to let. Yet what spatially about Redfern allowed this Aboriginal community to thrive in its early years? How did the Victorian terrace houses play into this? What modifications, if any, were performed to enhance the community?

The Block: a new model for housing?

The Block has potential to inform new understandings, ideas, and aspects of neighbourhood planning practices. In particular, it offers lessons on the spatial arrangements of housing and the elusive notion of community. Redfern was significant for Aboriginal people as it 1) offered immediate access to the city 2) was a place of their own where they felt comfortable 3) was a place where Aboriginal culture was palpable and allowed those within that culture to indulge in and strongly identify with it, and 4) given the impact of colonisation on the dissipation of Aboriginal culture today, Redfern is a significant example to understand, analyse and potentially reproduce as an urban spatial model that supports Aboriginal communities.

Efforts to modernise Aboriginal living conditions have utilised two modes of Aboriginal housing. The first, and the current dominant approach, is called the "Salt and Pepper" method, where Aboriginal people are distributed and assimilated into existing and predominantly mixed ethnic and cultural background neighbourhoods. The second is what might be considered the "Clump of Pepper" approach where Aboriginal people are housed together in a spatial close or enclosed environment.

The Block, was owned by Aboriginal people and its inhabitants lived in close proximity to one another, partly due to the nature of the Victorian terrace housing typology and partly due to alterations to the back yards, which included the removal of all internal fences to create a common social area within The Block (See Figure 6 noting the "Lawn" section and the nature of social distribution within the urban block).

The original proposal for The Block prompted claims that "The Redfern (Sydney) Aboriginal Community Housing Scheme may well become a hallmark not only for the Black community (especially in towns and cities), but for urban planning as a whole" in an article from The Builder's' Labourers Journal. It went on to describe that "the back fences of most of the houses will be pulled down and the laneway torn up to create a lawn-covered recreation area" (*BLF Newsletter*, 1973, p.33). This created a "meeting place for Aboriginal people," said a former tenant, Cec Bowden, 71. "We'd come from north, south, east and west, and everybody would know everyone" (Khoury, 2010).

Yet not everybody was convinced that allowing Aboriginal people to live together was the best model of living, Aboriginal people included. A prominent member of Redfern's community was Mrs. Shirley Smith – or "Mum Shirl" – who expressed doubt "…about the future of the Redfern community and she talks about the advantages of scattering families through the white suburbs, but friends say this reflects the strain of the past few months. Mum Shirl sees the first need of the Redfern Aborigines as adequate housing" (Forbes,1974).

While there are benefits and drawbacks of any condition, the Salt and Pepper method is raising anxieties around the dissipation of Aboriginal culture. Yet at the same time there exists personal anecdotes about Aboriginal Australians in Redfern and The Block, or the Clump of pepper approach, which perpetuates another kind of anxiety from non-Indigenous people relating to non-Aboriginal people living in or around a majority Aboriginal community. Concerns of after the latter approach focus on personal or property safety, a lack of community cohesion or the devaluation of property prices have been levelled at an approach which seeks to house Aboriginal people alongside their aboriginal communities amidst a mixed neighbourhood. Many of the later anxieties did not manifest, and the prices of nearby property were, on the whole, unaffected.

The Block was also seen as a model for housing not just Aboriginal people, but also non-Aboriginal communities. Gordon Bryant, the Minister of Aboriginal Affairs believed that.

The development was imaginative and highly desirable and could provide a pattern for Aborigines and non-Aborigines alike to follow in inner city areas. It will be a model for inner city communities which wish to preserve their homes and the identity of their areas (Federal Backing for Aboriginal Co-op, 1973).

Mr Bryant, who was involved with the Government effort to revitalise cities in Australia, saw the architectural plan of The Block as a significant mode of housing for enhancing community structures and was "aware of the feelings expressed by many Aborigines that they wanted to develop, not as individuals, but as a community" (Federal Backing for Aboriginal Co-op, 1973).

A major issue affecting communities today is the loss of community through the weakening of social ties due to a lack of proximity with Aboriginal community and the associated anonymity of city life. This is reinforced by author Richard Sennett who claims contemporary society is threatened by passivity and withdrawal (Sennett, 1992). The Block was a test case for not only urban Aboriginal communities, but for the notion of community as a whole. Yet what were the specific spatial aspects behind the idea of the plan that seemed to support strong community?

The shared social space of The Block

While there were many aspects that contributed to the strong sense of community at The Block, for example a critical density of Aboriginal people in one spatially close area and, the presence of Aboriginal services that supported a community, etc. yet one in particular will be discussed here, which is the shared space behind the terrace houses. As seen in figure 6, the back fences of the houses were removed and a shared social space was provided within the urban block. This provided a semi-public / semi-private space for Aboriginal residents to see each other, interact, to get to know each other at a deeper level than if the fences were left up. On this particular aspect, Gordon Bryant in the *Melbourne Sun ($530.000 grant for Aboriginal houses*, said of the scheme "small groups like this give strength to one another without developing a total separate existence" (Bryant,1973), where the design of The Block utilised a particular hierarchy of space (public, to semi-public, to private) to allow for this.

The importance of this hierarchy of space is highlighted by Dmitriy Porphyrios who stresses that architects and planners "emphasize the typological significance of design, to establish hierarchies between public and private realms, and to re-think the constitution of the open spaces of the city" (1989, p.95). This shared space invited residents to interact and to participate with other members of the community. The benefits of the

provision of shared space is reinforced by psychologist Bill Berkowitz (1996, p. 452), who stated that:

> opportunities need to be created to encourage residents to physically see each other, in order to begin to get to know each other through socializing and talking...Safe, attractive public spaces and venues need to be built to encourage community mingling and socializing...the path to community participation begins with seeing, and knowing, liking, trusting, and finally, acting.

The Block's subsequent failures needs further analysis prior to redeploying similar spatial typologies. What could be seen as a failure could be more simply a matter of time and place, a socio-economic conundrum rooted in the 1970s. This, however, is outside the scope of this chapter.

Yet at the same time, The share space of The Block contained specific spatial aspects which allowed for a community to propagate. These aspects were 1) a defined hierarchy of space ranging from public to private, 2) the space allowed for the occupants to be socially engaged and visible to each other promoting social mixing and communication, and 3) the privacy provided a safe space for Aboriginal culture to be practiced away from the external influences of the city, such as non-Aboriginal cultural influences and harassment from others – in particular the police who had a problematic relationship with Redfern's Aboriginal community, etc.

These three aspects are substantiated by Jane Jacobs who said:

> A city street equipped to handle strangers, and to make a safety asset, in itself, out of the presence of strangers, as the streets of successful city neighborhoods always do, must have three main qualities:
>
> First, there must be a clear demarcation between what is public space and what is private space. Public and private spaces cannot ooze into each other as they do typically in suburban settings or in projects.
>
> Second, there must be eyes upon the street, eyes belonging to those we might call the natural proprietors of the street. The buildings on a street equipped to handle strangers and to insure the safety of both residents and strangers, must be oriented to the street. They cannot turn their backs or blank sides on it and leave it blind.
>
> And third, the sidewalk must have users on it fairly continuously, both to add to the number of effective eyes on the street and to induce the people in buildings along the street to watch the sidewalks in sufficient numbers. Nobody enjoys sitting on a stoop or looking out a window at an empty street. Almost nobody does such a thing. Large numbers of people entertain themselves, off and on, by watching street activity (1961, p. 35).

These three spatial aspects as outlined by Jacobs were key to the development of The Block's Aboriginal

Figure 9. A mural of an Aboriginal boxer eluding to the Elouera Mundine Gym on Eveleigh St

Figure 10. A mural of Jenny Munro in Darling Harbour, Sydney, started the Redfern Aboriginal Tent Embassy and a lead activist over the fight for Aboriginal housing at The Block

community. If any were missing, for example were the back fences to stay up, the safety of the interior space would not have been achieved. Or if the community were not socially engaged to watch out for each other, then the building of a strong Aboriginal community in Redfern would have been a more challenging task. It is here that The Block has something to contribute to neighbourhood planning, a clear reminder that these spatial elements that have been established within the profession of city planning must be considered in the design process if a true sense of community is to be achieved and the benefits of it – empowerment, identity, closeness and meaning – be gained by the inhabitants.

Conclusion

The Aboriginal community of Redfern still has a strong sense of identity that is palpable and easy to recognise from the outside looking in. Its tangible sense of community was previously reinforced by

spatial aspects of The Block which is difficult to find the prevailing urban fabric of Australian cities. The idea of togetherness, knowing people in your local area and, not necessarily liking each other at all times is central to supporting Aboriginal culture in the city. There is an agreement or unwritten social contract that allows for the possibility of supporting a community to deal with issues of knowing, supporting, and most importantly, the ability for a community to deal with issues together as a group. The Block was a unique and, in many ways, successful urban spatialisation for Aboriginal people. Despite recent knockbacks, Redfern is still considered to be a significant place for Australia's Aboriginal and even non-Aboriginal peoples. As with many locations within Australia, the centralisation of government and councils means local decisions are increasingly being made at a higher level and usually by those who are not connected to or part of that community. It is a powerful thing when communities have the ability to make their own decisions around issues that directly affect them.

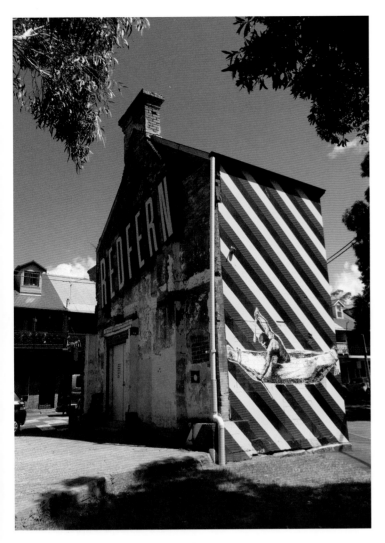

Figure 11. The last remaining Victorian terrace on The Block, now a mural to the Gadigal warrior Pemulwuy, designed by Cracknell and Lonergan Architects

Redfern's Aboriginal community enabled a unique set of urban spatialised values and community attributes that are of benefit when thinking about local planning and community planning more generally. But, in particular these worked to support strong Aboriginal community in what was The Block.

References

"Aboriginal population in Australia," retrieved 16 November 2017. https://www.creativespirits.info/aboriginalculture/people/aboriginal-population-in-australia#ixzz4yaAdRLNY

Aboriginal Affairs Committee, (1969). The Whitlam Collection #M540. Australian National Archives, Western Sydney.

"Aboriginals Go Alone." (1973, March 23) The Daily Mirror.

Australian Bureau of Statistics (2016) 2016 Census. Retrieved 2017, November 17 from http://www.censusdata.abs.gov.au/census_services/getproduct/census/2016/quickstat/SSC13339

AHC Timeline (2017). *Aboriginal Housing Company Timeline* Retrieved 2017, December 11 from http://www.ahc.org.au/about-us/timeline/

BLF Newsletter (1973), The New South Wales builder's Laborer: Official Journal of the N.S.W. Branch of the Builders Laborers' Federation (Aust.), The Branch, Sydney.

Berkowitz, Bill. (1996). Personal and community sustainability. American Journal of Community Psychology 24, 441-459

(1972) *The Whitlam collection, Collection #:M540*, Item #1, Personal communication between Bryant and Whitlam, National Archives, Western Sydney. Pg. 10.

Chesterman, G. (1964, September 19). Aborigines in Rat-infested Squalor in *The Bulletin*.

"Federal Backing for Aboriginal Co-op" (1973) *Adelaide Advertiser*.

Forbes, C. (1974, June). "The Black Enclaves" In *The Age Melbourne*.

Ford, W. (1967). *Australian Dictionary of Biography. Volume 2*.

Department of Infrastructure, Regional Development and Cities (2007) *History of Rail in Australia*, Retrieved 2017, December 12 from https://infrastructure.gov.au/rail/trains/history.aspxhttps://infrastructure.gov.au/rail/trains/history.aspx

Korff, J. (2017). Aboriginal history timeline (1900 – 1969). Retrieved 2017, December 11 from https://www.creativespirits.info/aboriginalculture/history/aboriginal-history-timeline-1900-1969"$530.000 grant for Aboriginal houses" (1973,April 16), *Melbourne Sun*.

Jacobs, J. (1961). *The death and life of great American cities*.

"Joy, Anger at Redfern plan" (1973, April 16), *Daily News*.

Khoury, M. (2010, November 15) "Friday deadline on the Block, but last residents are refusing to go." *The Sydney Morning Herald*.

"Uneasy peace." (1973, April 8) *Sunday Mirror*, Viewed 17 November 2017.

Porphyrios, D. (1982). *The Relevance of Classical Architecture; Classicism is not a style*. St. Martin's Press.

Saunders-Sheehan, T. (2014, June 13). Saltwater Dreaming – Welcme to Cadigal Country, Retrieved 2017, December 1 from http://thebeast.com.au/news/saltwater-dreaming-welcome-cadigal-country/#

Sennett, R. (1992). *The Conscience of the Eye: The Design and Social Life of Cities*. W.W. Norton.

Standing Committee of Aboriginal Affairs, Labor Party, (1973). *The Whitlam Collection*. National Archives Western Sydney

Chapter 6: My Māori Spaces: Women's Spaces

Amiria Perez – Ngāti Porou and Ngā Puhi

Amiria was born in Heretaunga and grew up on an apple orchard, near the Tukituki River. In 1999 she moved to Ruatoria to attend Ngata College for her final year of high school. In 2006 she graduated with a Bachelor of Architecture (Hons) from Victoria University in Wellington and has since worked in cities around Aotearoa New Zealand, as well as spending time traveling in South America and Europe. For the last five years, Amiria has been working in post-earthquake Christchurch, and has also been involved in transitional projects as part of the Festival of Transitional Architecture. Amiria has a particular interest in using a transitional design approach to test how Māori identity can be expressed and celebrated in cities. She also explores the relationship between craft, architecture, and identity.

Nan's House – River Road, Havelock North

My Nan and Grandad lived in an early 1900s villa on the orchard. A typical colonial villa: native timber, weatherboards, sash windows, high ceilings. My parents lived here when I was born. When they first moved there my Pākehā grandad used it as a shed to store stuff. The bank manager offered Dad a loan to fix it, but being the eternal fixer upper, Dad declined the offer. They "did it up" when they could afford to – it took quite a while. When we moved out (down the road, round the corner and down the hill), Nan and Grandad shifted from Hamilton to live in the house.

We knew we could go to Nan's house any time. We'd go most days after school, raid her cupboards looking for lollies (sometimes settling for Quick-Eze), or eat the fried bread or coconut cake she'd made us, and watch cartoons on TV. No invitation needed to climb on her lap when I was smaller, play with her chin skin, which I found comforting. Grandad usually sat, half paralysed by a stroke, in his chair, in the lounge, at the back of the house. The lounge down the long, dark hallway. This room was always dark and cold – big windows on the south, facing the hedge and then the road. Good for

watching TV and for photos. This was where the photos of all my family were. Of me, my brothers and sisters, Mum and Dad, my cousins and aunties and uncles – up on the wall above the fireplace in rows that weren't straight.

Familiarity, comfort and warmth at Nan's house. Everything open and available, spoken about, not rationed. Not one lolly a day. Different from Pākehā spaces.

It was always tidy at her place, but never clinical or bland, never felt like all the life had been wiped away or sucked up by a vacuum cleaner (she swept her carpet with a broom).

Her garden wasn't there for looks (except for the roses, poppies and daffodils). She had proper vegetables and fruit. Always had a huge māra kai. The vegetables I can't remember, (apart from kamokamo because I like the name), but the grapes, boysenberries, grapefruit and persimmons, we pulled off as soon as they were ripe.

My Nan was an extension of Papatūānuku for me; nurturing, no barriers, accepting, harsh sometimes (if you were older than 10), but you mostly figure things out for yourself as you go along – she was just always there.

Aunty Georgie's House – Whakapaurangi Road, Ruatoria

Bossy aunty, who hugs you – it's not a guarded or rigid or bony hug – her hug envelops you. She is a force, so honest, painfully honest and fearless. Shoes off at the door.

There's a horse that comes around now and again to their place– my cousins hop on, bareback, but I'm too young or scared. Cousins home from the army pitch military tents on the immaculate lawn. Diving stuff everywhere and pet cats that used to be strays. My cousins (boys only) go diving with my uncle for kaimoana – they know Moana intimately. We go along and play with the creatures in the rockpools and help mum and my aunty make lunch.

Figure 1. Our first house on River Road, Source: Kiddle Collection

My uncle must have built a room over part of the deck – the walls are different here – rough sawn planks painted dark green, army style. This is where we sleep when we stay. Mattresses on the floor made up into beds. Silky 'Minks' drape lions and tigers over the sleeping surfaces.

A long drop sits across the damp grass. Inside, the pungent smell of fresh and decomposing waste mixed with Ocean Mist air-freshener. The smell of not polluting Awa and Moana. We are mostly too scared to go out to it at night. Māwini! A famous Hiruharama mythical figure – part goat, part man. I hear his clip-clopping some nights, but I'm safe inside, surrounded by my sleeping whānau.

The lounge is long and dark and has lots of photos of relatives around the edges. Only the ones who have died I think. Some were very old; these are the biggest ones in the intricate frames, the beautiful Ngāti Porou princesses.

The kitchen smells like seafood and boil-up mixed together.

Except for the kitchen, the house is dark, even in the daytime. Reminds me of a wharenui. If you want the sun you go out onto the deck. We mixed steam puddings in huge plastic bowls out there once, poured them in plastic bags and then licked the bowl.

The house is rich with texture, smell, and sound. Lots of deep laughing, stories and "atta beis." Naati twang. My Aunty's loud, raspy, warm, voice. Telling someone off, or telling a story about telling someone off – these guys are natural storytellers.

Rāhui Marae – Rangitukia Road, Tikitiki

The old Aunties' high pitched wailing at my Grandad's tangi when we start walking onto the marae ātea. The most beautiful and saddest sound I've heard. Later I lie in the middle of the wharenui with my Nan, beside my Grandad, staring up at the patterns on the high ridge. Crying hysterically while everyone sits around the low edges telling funny stories about him, carved ancestors behind. Could've

Figure 2. Me and my Nan, Havelock North, Hawkes Bay, Source: Kiddle Collection

Figure 3. Auntie Georgie at her home on Whakapaurangi Road, Hiruharama, Ruatoria, Source: Kiddle Collection

been an All Black they say. The stories make me laugh, and then cry even more when I remind myself that he's gone. Eventually Mum tells me to come to her and muffles my crying with a hug and then her blankets – my Aunty has told her to "get that girl." I think we sleep on the visitors' side but I can't remember.

For my Nan's tangi I'm old enough to know I don't know the rules very well – sleeping next to her out on the mahau, with my sister when the sun comes up, being told off because we fell asleep.

The wharekai is like my school's hall with a stage and everything. But this room is just for celebrations and eating – glad-wrapped kai parcels on the tables (mmm "pa pudding," aka steam pudding, with custard and cream). The kitchen is busy and noisy – talking, laughing and stainless steel clattering.

Tawata – Te Araroa Road, Tikitiki

It's down a very long driveway, past Marina's house. The long grass scrapes on the bottom of the car. When you get out, there are sometimes horses, or cows around. Big piles of poo you have to dodge. The urupā sits up on a hill, a white picket fence looking out to the Poroporo River. Plastic flowers and windmills cover the graves – bright colour and sparkles moving with the wind. My Nan and Grandad are buried here in this urupā. So tidy and lovingly cared for by Uncle Jack - pride of place for our whānau. We come to visit Nan and Grandad, and all the other relatives. We feel sad at first but then we start remembering all their stories, start judging who has the best decorations, pick up fallen over

jars and redistribute fresh flowers to replace the faded ones on whanaunga who haven't been visited in a while. Their families probably don't live here either.

You have to wash your hands when you come out – make yourself noa with the water from the milk bottles.

The urupā has always sat beside the house where my Grandad grew up. His siblings who died young were buried in the urupā, and later, stillborn mokopuna. It is filling up quickly now as relatives pass and want to come home.

The tallest orange tree is here with the sweetest oranges, full of pips. We have to jump to get them and knock them with a stick, or climb up the tree. Beside that, the old concrete chimneys from the house where my Granddad grew up. The last visible markers on the landscape which tell of the home that stood here. You can imagine the large house, built by my Great Grandad and where my Great Grandmother raised 17 kids. My Mum remembers the sunken bath as an exotic touch, along with the ornate mirror above the fireplace that stayed in the house long after it was abandoned. You can imagine my Great Grandmother's famous flower gardens here too, the gardens that older relatives still talk about. The beautiful magnolia tree, the mishmash of bright colours, the wisteria that eventually over-ran the place. The once productive orchard with fruit trees grown from cuttings from her whanau, or seeds that germinated after being casually thrown away. A grand plum tree hosted extended whānau Christmas dinners under its shady branches. The huge māra kai needed to feed the kids and to give to her large extended whānau. These Māori/Spanish/Portuguese descendants, who didn't quite fit in. Peti Lima's girls as they are known.

Figure 4. Tawata urupā (graveyard) on my Great Grandparents' land, Source: Kiddle Collection

Figure 5. Remains of my Great Grandparents' house, Tawata, Source: Kiddle Collection

I think Rastafarians burnt the house down. Or someone left the fire going. We don't visit here much since my Aunty moved to Palmerston North.

The Beach House – Airini Road, Waimarama

In the late 1960s my Pākehā grandparents commissioned Māori architect, John Scott, to design a beach house at Waimarama. They built the house themselves off the plans he drew up. It has a high space in the middle. Exposed pine rafters meet here, at the top of a concrete chimney. And then they go down to the low edges. Some of these edges are for sitting or sleeping on mattresses. The carved ancestors are replaced by views to the Pohutukawa, views to Motu-O-Kura, views to Moana and Ranginui and Marama, Tamanui Te Rā. Even though there are nooks and crannies, everyone in the house is connected – there are few doors. You can hear snoring at night, other noises. Most rooms double as sleeping spaces. You just need a mattress on the floor. The beach house is where my grandparents, aunties, uncles, and cousins meet over Christmas, where we spend time together. Whakawhanaungatanga, manaakitanga in a Māori/Pākehā space.

Mum and Dad's House – Te Mata Mangateretere Road, Havelock North

Our second house started as a dray shed with a kitchen and laundry/toilet attached. Built in the 1920s it was later extended to 100sq metres to accommodate Molly's family of nine. Small, but practical. Everything had a use and everything in its place. We always found dates in that

house, written on the back of cupboards; dishwasher 1954, stove 1976, new lino 1963. A stark contrast to the disorganised and perhaps more organic way our family inhabited that place. Despite the fact that Molly died years ago, Mum still thinks of herself as kaitiaki of her plants, taking special care of them. The shed was/is full of wire, bolts, chain, tools, bits of steel – a treasure chest of junk for Dad and us kids.

Growing up in that house, warmth, belonging and cosiness sat alongside episodes of arguing and crockery smashing. A clash of two different upbringings and two different ways of being treated by society. Unrestrained emotion versus restraint and oftentimes, silence.

When Mum moved away for a while, I mourned the loss of her and the pictures that she took with her – my favourite was a big Japanese print of a lady in a kimono with a thick, dark, wooden frame.

When Mum came back to visit over school holidays she was never empty handed, there were always treats – chocolate, chippies and lollies – what a feast! We were in heaven. There was a different feeling in the house when she was there. Always humming and singing made up songs and rhymes about our made up names – Nelly No-knickers, Thomas a Tattamus etc. Although she wasn't hugely affectionate, except with animals, the house always felt warmer when she was there.

When I was older Mum moved back and things became more settled. We changed the house all together. It has

Figure 6. Kiddle Bach, Arini Road, Waimarama, Architect: John Scott, Source: Gavin Scott

Figure 7. Exposed pine rafters, Kiddle Bach, Arini Road, Waimaram, Architect: John Scott, Source Kiddle Collection

a new wairua. A huge photo wall in the middle – all of us and our relations are here in un-straight rows. This photo wall forms the backdrop of the karaoke stage – just like at Rāhui, brought to life at birthdays and New Years, leaving parties, any excuse really.

Bright colours are on the new walls, as bright as the plastic flowers. Wood is everywhere too – Dad had the Macrocarpa tree milled. It held up our swing for all my childhood – now it holds up all the new spaces, absorbing all the life.

Mum's māra kai is flourishing now with everything under the sun – raspberries, strawberries, boysenberries, potatoes, peaches, asparagus, pumpkins, kamokamo, puha, watercress, onions, carrots, cabbages, tomatoes, zucchini, rhubarb, eggplants, etc. Everything multiplying. I always look forward to a batch of seedlings for my growing māra kai – she has something new for me every time I go back.

Epilogue

My current architectural practice draws on lived experiences of Māori space, which all happen to be strongly influenced by women. Warm, creative spaces. I acknowledge that my experience of being Māori differs from others – yet it is still a Māori experience. It's rooted in both the pain of the impact of colonisation and the pleasure of our unique ways of living life and being whānau. Those experiences, coupled with my Pākehā heritage mean that I walk in both Māori and Pākehā worlds. I walk carefully with my senses attuned to the subtleties, nuance and hidden expressions inherent in both worlds.

My practice seeks to be rooted in Māori values and ways of living and being, but continually questions what kind of architecture this results in, given the diversity of Māori realities in the 21st century. I draw on the unique experiences of my Māori spaces. An example is the sensory variety they offer, of both the interior and exterior, contributing to a sense of history, whanaungatanga, manaakitanga and spirituality. This breadth of sensory experience is something I find increasingly lacking in contemporary spaces, where the focus sits squarely with how they look and how they photograph. I seek to create contemporary Indigenous spaces that provide food for all our senses, grounded in Māori-ness – in all its guises – that Māori with diverse realities can connect with alongside Pākehā who acknowledge the unique identity Māoridom offers Aotearoa New Zealand.

Naku te rourou, nau te rourou ka ora ai te iwi.[1]

This chapter is dedicated to my Auntie Georgie – Georgina Mary Parker (nee Grace) who passed away in July this year (2017).

---

[1] Translation: With your basket and my basket the people will live

Figure 8. Mum and Dad's House, designed by Amiria Perez & John Scott, Source: Sarah Horn

Figure 9. Whānau (family) Karaoke, Source: Kiddle Collection

Chapter 7: Métis Domestic Thresholds and the Politics of Imposed Privacy

David Fortin – Métis Nation of Ontario, Jason Surkan – Métis, and Danielle Kastelein – Metis Nation of Ontario

Professor David Fortin was born in Calgary, Alberta and grew up in Prince Albert, Saskatchewan, before pursuing degrees from the University of Saskatchewan (B.A.), the University of Calgary (M.Arch), and the University of Edinburgh, UK (Ph.D). He is a registered architect in the province of Alberta (Architect AAA), a Member of the Royal Architectural Institute of Canada (MRAIC), as well as a member of the Métis Nation of Ontario. He is one of the founding faculty members at the Laurentian University McEwen School of Architecture, the first new school of architecture in Canada in over 40 years. The fledgling program is composed of a unique design-build curriculum that embraces First Nations, Métis, and Inuit cultures to inform how to sustainably design meaningful connections to Northern landscapes and communities through the built environment. He gained professional experience working for McKinley Burkart Architects and GEC Architecture in Calgary, has previously taught architecture at the University of Edinburgh and Montana State University, has been an invited design critic at the University of Calgary, and has lectured publicly on topics related to Métis design, science-fiction, and architecture, designing for climate change, and systems thinking. He is the author of "Architecture and Science Fiction Film."

Jason Surkan was born and raised near Prince Albert, Saskatchewan and holds a Bachelor of Architecture (B.Arch) from Carleton University. He previously studied Commerce at the University of Saskatchewan, Architecture at the University of British Columbia, and is currently in his thesis year of his Masters of Architecture (M.Arch) degree at the University of Manitoba in Winnipeg. He holds a University of Manitoba Graduate Fellowship. He is of mixed Canadian Ancestry – Métis, Scottish, Ukrainian, and Polish. Jason is a member of Fish Lake Metis Local #108, and the Metis Nation of Saskatchewan. He has worked intermittently for Douglas Cardinal Architect since 2014 as well as Oxbow Architecture in Saskatoon. Jason is also an established photographer and has had work published in Canadian Geographic. He also enjoys working at traditional craftwork.

Dani Kastelein is a first year masters student currently enrolled at the University of Waterloo's School of Architecture. She holds a Bachelor of Architectural Studies from Laurentian University in Sudbury. Raised in Burlington Ontario with family ties in both Penetanguishene and Sturgeon Falls, Dani is of Métis francophone heritage holding citizenship status with the Metis Nation of Ontario. An avid painter, knitter, and sketch artist; Dani often draws inspiration from nature and the surrounding landscape. As a part of the design studio courses at Laurentian, Dani has had the opportunity to participate in many design-build projects. Examples of these include designing and building a demountable kiosk structure for the Mill Square Market in Sault Ste. Marie as well as taking part in the construction of an Ice Hut, Sauna and Birch Bark Canoe. This past winter, Dani was selected to participate in the Winter Stations Competition in Toronto.

Introduction

> The growing sense of domestic intimacy was a human invention as much as any technical device. Indeed, it may have been more important, for it affected not only our physical surroundings, but our consciousness as well.

(Rybcynzski, 1987 p. 49)

> You get a home. You get a package. You get a dollar amount that you are going to spend on that home and the building codes dictate…how that building is built and what kind of insulation, what kind of vapour barrier…vents and everything.

(Métis Elder Archie Collins, Elizabeth Settlement)

The blurring of the private and public realms within the Métis[1] home is a concept intrinsic to understanding the historical underpinnings of the culture. It is well documented that one of the defining characteristics of Métis folk homes in 19th century central Saskatchewan was an open interior floor plan (Burley, 2000; Burley & Horsfall, 1989). Not only did this type of design provide flexibility due to its ample interior but it also allowed for expedient construction, "warmth, low building cost, possibilities for expansion," and a crucial means to accommodate various community interactions, with the

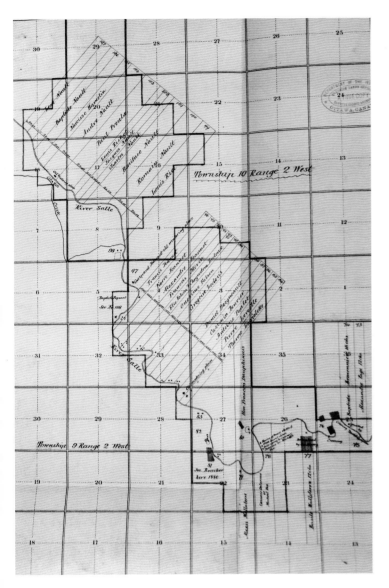

Figure 1. Salle River Staked ClaimsSource: Goulet, Roger. [Map of Salle River Claims, Range 2 West, Townships. 9 &10]. Map Collection, Archives of Manitoba (schedule A0076, accession GR0126), Government of Manitoba, Winnipeg, MB.

home often doubling as a dance hall, a funeral parlor, a social or political gathering space, and a place for daily interaction between immediate family members (City of Winnipeg, 1988, p. 4). For the Métis, partition walls would have impeded the opportunity for such large gatherings, acting as both a physical and metaphorical barrier to the sense of connection and community inherited from their First Nations relatives. As asserted by Diane Payment, the Métis family "valued the primacy of collectivity over the individual" and were "guided by principles of unity" (Payment, 1990, p. 38). Furthermore, David Burley documents the public/private dichotomy within Métis culture, stating that formality and privacy are not encountered within the home but rather there exists a "lack of boundedness" expressed within the range of activities occurring in the space (Burley, 2000, p. 35). It is for these

reasons that crossing the threshold into the Métis domestic interior has been described as closer to the Plains teepee than that of the standard prairie farmhouse (Chandler, 2003).

Yet by the time the government(s) acknowledged their responsibility for providing housing to certain Métis communities across the prairies, a standard and compartmentalized interior quickly became the norm, dissolving the capacity for the Métis home to preserve its role as an inherently social space for communal living. Similar to housing programs imposed on First Nations and Inuit communities with communal domestic social arrangements (the igloo, the teepee, the pit house, the long house, etc.), a critical shift in Métis social relations ensued. This essay will postulate the role of imposed privacy in the breakdown of Métis social systems in the Canadian prairies and how this arguably contributed to an accelerated pace of cultural assimilation during the 20th century.

Imposed Delineation and the Métis

History has repeatedly shown that imposed spatial divisions and Métis values are simply incompatible. For example, from a Canadian colonial perspective, the dividing of land in Manitoba as per the Dominion Grid was a foregone conclusion following the acquisition of Rupert's Land in 1870. Yet the Métis, under the leadership of Louis Riel and others, made one of their first acts of physical resistance not directly against the federal government or the incoming settlers from Ontario, but instead against the surveyors, those hired to re-demarcate the land as per a new imposed spatial system that directly conflicted with the existing Métis river lots along the Red River. Though similarly grounded in the notion of land ownership inherited from the French along the St. Lawrence, the river lots were consistent with Métis values of egalitarianism given that all families would have access to the river and the road, with houses close to each other for a greater sense of community, something the new grid could not provide. Thus, the new system was met with strong resistance, not only because it was perceived as a threat to Métis land ownership, but also because it would disturb Métis

---

[1] The Métis are an Indigenous cultural group originally formed in Canada during the fur trade of the seventeenth and eighteenth centuries mostly from relations between male European settlers and Indigenous women. Over the centuries, this group began intermarrying with each other to form a unique culture with its own political, social, and cultural distinctions in various locations, most prominently the Red River Settlement in present day Manitoba. Various court cases have confirmed that the Métis are considered "Indians" as per the 1763 Royal Proclamation, the 1867 Constitution Act (British North America Act), and the revised 1982 Constitution Act.

Figure 2. Interior of a Metis house on the North West-Mounted Police trek west, 1874. Glenbow Archives NA-47-10.

Figure 3. A Lively Metis dance at Pembina, in an engraving published in Harper's Monthly, 1860. Glenbow Museum. NA 1406-23.

spatial and societal relationships with the land. Emblematic of these tensions, it was a surveyor, Thomas Scott, who was executed at Upper Fort Garry in 1870 by the Riel provisional government. This was followed by the second and final Métis resistance in 1885, also centred on "the nature of land surveys" (Harrison, 1985).

Despite their victory at Batoche in 1885, the Canadian government recognized the Métis were "numerous and potentially dangerous," and thus threatened their plans for federal expansion into western Canada (Taylor, 1983, p. 156). Therefore, Métis land title was officially acknowledged through the controversial scrip system where their land was exchanged for money, or a newly surveyed equivalent, which legally terminated their aboriginal title through a convoluted and imbalanced process ultimately intended to "placate" them (Taylor, 1983, p. 156). However, even after scrips were issued, many Métis still did not see "owning" land being as important as "living on" it, with many continuing to "squat on random lots, not seeing the need to establish a permanent claim to any one place" (Harrison, 1985, p. 74). This supports David Burley's archaeological research into prairie Métis spatial orders in Saskatchewan, which concluded that, even after their shift from communal hunters to settled farmers, the Métis maintained an "organic, informal, unbounded, and open society with strong continuity in the human/nature relationship" (Burley, 2000, p. 32).

Scales of Delineation

The spatial collision of perspectives that initiated in Manitoba was not, however, an isolated one. According to Philip Wolfart, there exist two distinct ideologies governing boundaries and space which became increasingly divided

during the European shift towards the establishment of nation states during the 18th century – the spatial and aspatial (Wolfart, 2012). The spatial sphere is defined by geographically bounded relationships, which involves the formation of social, economic, and political relationships by demarcating the ground and allowing boundaries to form. Conversely, an aspatial is based on a system of social obligations and behaviors that structure daily interactions.

Notions of these concepts exist cross culturally, in which most post-contact societies gradually adopted a more compartmentalized way of perceiving and utilizing space over time. This was the case in Canada towards the end of the eighteenth century which saw the transition into a more delineated world and this continues as the dominant spatial ideology today. This shift can be viewed at multiple scales; from the division of land described above to the organization of the home itself, involving the compartmentalization of space, or placing boundaries on what had been previously "traversable land." Peter Ward discusses this shift in *A History of Domestic Space: Privacy and the Canadian Home regarding the design of interior spaces during the transition into the nineteenth century*, noting that, "Functionally their interior spaces became more spatialized [in houses in English Canada] while the lines between zones of relative privacy became more sharply inscribed" (Ward, 1999, p. 25).

Such privatization of the home had been occurring over the previous centuries throughout Europe, leading to a perception of shared domestic space as being "primitive," or from medieval times when families slept and ate together in the same space before a perceived refinement of lifestyle led to more specialized patterns and spatial divisions to suit (Rybcynzski, 1987). Though the

Figure 4. Interior of a Métis Home at Métis Crossing near Edmonton, AB. (Photograph: Jason Surkan)

Métis have been recognized as having to concede to living within both European and Indigenous spatial perceptions, their domestic space and sociopolitical realms generally followed the latter. For example, Graham Chandler suggests that despite the symmetrical Georgian exterior of the Métis folk house, the open interior was the antithesis of a privatized domestic space and closer to that of the plains teepee (Chandler, 2003). Garnering a sense of community, even within the home, was thus at the forefront of a collective consciousness among the Métis people. Burley characterizes this perception and formation of domestic space as having a "lack of 'boundedness" and this lack of a formally-defined structure within the home's interior undoubtedly influenced the notions surrounding privacy (Burley, 2000).

The Open Interior

Contrasting colonial emphases on physically divided spaces, Indigenous social and spatial organization are often influenced by elements such as kinship, socio-cultural needs, culturally specific behaviors and lifestyle. This results in some significant differences concerning

domesticity between contemporary Indigenous households and their Anglo or Euro-centric counterparts. Similar kinds of spatial relationships can be seen cross culturally from one Indigenous group to another. Examples include observations concerning Cree dwellings and social order by Adrian Tanner, and Paul Memmott's writings on the architectural and social anthropology of Aboriginal Australians. Both Tanner and Memmott argue that these communities developed communal and familial structures that depended on the integration of centralized and flexible group spaces within and surrounding the home (Tanner, 2016). Specifically, Tanner characterizes these societal and spatial structures as "traditional organizations of space" (Tanner, 2016, p. 74).

Furthermore, the open floor plan not only provides increased flexibility, but rather allows for better social surveillance amongst family members. For example, both the 19th century Métis home's central space and a gathering space designed by student-architects enrolled at the Université Laval's School of Architecture, as per the request of their Innu partners, provide a clear view of the main entry threshold (Martin & Casault, 2005). Both

LIVING AREA
KITCHEN
BEDROOM
BATHROOM
STORAGE

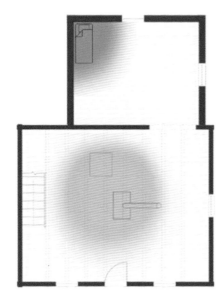

19TH CENTURY MÉTIS LOG HOME   INAC DESIGNED HOME

Figure 5. Architectural plans of a folk home (Left) and of a "Three Bedroom Low Cost House" (Right). The folk home was a single room dwelling that allowed for a flexible use of space. The second home was designed by Indigenous and Northern Affairs Canada (INAC) in 1968. This standardized, compartmentalized plan impeded Métis culture and tradition by disallowing flexible space where cultural and traditional activities could occur within the home. (Drawings: Jason Surkan)

Memmott and Métis Elder Maria Campbell have also commented on increased social surveillance within the context of Métis and Aboriginal Australian homes (Smith & Lommerse & Metcalfe, 2014). As Campbell (2016) recalls, if a grandmother was living in the home it was understood that she would sleep near the door to survey anyone coming or leaving the home. This offers her the ability to view the activities in the house by family members or visitors and brings into focus some stark differences between Indigenous and non-Indigenous ideologies with regards to domestic boundaries and privacy.

Despite colonial attempts to restructure privacy for them, these design preferences for the aspatial continue to permeate Indigenous cultures today. For example, current research by the authors suggest that contemporary Métis self-built home uphold these values (Fortin & Surkan, 2016), as do student design proposals for a communal gathering space within Innu homes (Martin & Casault, 2005). A number of sources further indicate a strong sense of social organization within Indigenous communities which support a more distinct communalistic structure than the more atomistic structure of European settlers (Knafla & Westra, 2010). Therefore this reality has had a considerable

affect on the design of their domestic spaces, focusing on the integration of a flexible gathering area within the home as a way to reinforce their sense of community. This is especially true for the Métis open interiors of self-built homes.

However, it is essential to note that communal values do not eliminate the need for individuality. For example, a report on the mental health of Indigenous peoples cautions that [although] "Aboriginal cultures appear sociocentric in that the self is defined relationally and the well-being of family, band, or community is of central importance...this co-exists with strong support for individual autonomy and independence" (Kirmayer & Macdonald & Brass, 2000, p. 14). As an alternative to building walls to offer privacy, however, the Métis chose to rely on the few pieces of furniture as well as other items of their material culture to define the space. The area which comprised of the kitchen would often include a table placed near the wood burning stove found near the centre of the home where a few chairs might be present (Weinbender, 2003). As for the "bedrooms" or "bedroom," these spaces were defined by a bed tucked in the corner of the space. Thus, while such a domestic space would have been perceived as primitive by

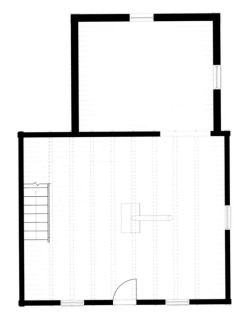
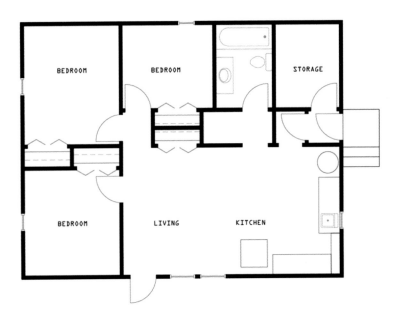

Figure 6. This standardized, compartmentalized plan impeded Métis culture and tradition by disallowing flexible space where cultural and traditional activities could occur within the home. (Drawings: Jason Surkan)

the settlers, it was also imbued with relational meaning. As Rybczynski similarly notes regarding the medieval home, rules about dress and manners, and the scheduling of tasks and events governed the use of the space, and in it, "every object had a meaning and a place in life that was as much a part of its function as its immediate purpose, and these two were inseparable" (Rybczynski, 1986, p. 34). In addition to objects assisting in defining the space, as well as their intended purpose, behavior, social order, and long established cultural conventions were other elements which impressed themselves onto the home (Grøn, 1990). Consequently, changes in the spatial syntax of the Métis home initialized by the subsidized (and compartmentalized) housing initiatives undoubtedly contributed to changes in behaviors in the home, and possibly an increase in domestic forms of abuse and isolation due to this imposed privacy.

Spatial Syntax and Flexibility in the Métis Home

The need for flexibility is essential when discussing how domestic space is viewed by different Indigenous cultures. As previously mentioned, the Métis did not introduce formal barriers or walls to create micro social environments within their homes; in fact, they required this flexibility to allow these moments to occur. For example, as Weinbender writes in Petite Ville "rooms appear to be open and multi-functional" (Weinbender, 2003, p. 144). Thus, for the Métis, the function, flexibility, and efficiency of the home was placed at the utmost priority. At times if additional means of privacy in the form of a physical barrier was required, a sheet or articles of clothing could be hung in order to divide the room (Fleury, 2016). However, it would appear through first and secondhand accounts, particularly having to do with the process of courtship, that the Métis did not require or prefer to rely on this particular method of dividing and allocating space. Instead, cultural methods of organization would be determined through kinship or by the age of the household member. For example, if a home had a second level, the younger children would sleep in the loft while older brothers and sisters, who required more privacy, had their own corner on the main floor along with other members of the family (Fleury, 2016). It is clear that these socio-cultural behaviors would have had an effect on the level of privacy between family members, particularly regarding the notion of increased surveillance.

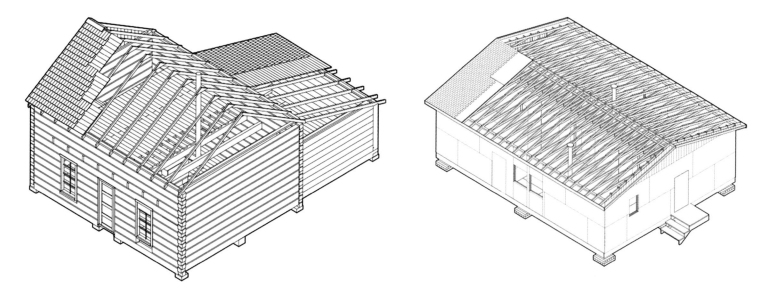

Figure 7. Isometric view of a folk home (Left) and of a "Three Bedroom Low Cost House" (Right). The folk home was constructed of locally sourced logs that were hand hewn and often dovetail notched. The building of these homes was a social event and often many members of a community would lend a helping hand to construct the home. The INAC home was prefabricated of manufactured materials and shipped into communities. Offsite prefabrication often reduces local labour used in the building process and does not allow knowledge around construction and maintenance of homes within the community. (Drawings: Jason Surkan)

In addition, courting behaviors among the Métis provide an excellent example of how specific cultural behaviors affect domestic thresholds as well as the notions of privacy. According to Gordon, courtship for the Métis occurred within the public sphere (Gordon, 2009). Similarly, Weinbender writes that, "The lack of privacy in Métis homes had some interesting effects on the courting" (Weinbender, 2003, p. 10). Due to the open floor plan, privacy was therefore maintained by introducing hushed voices, retreating to a more secluded area of the room, as well as other behaviors that support and protect personal interactions. For example, traditional encounters between couples would occur at the woman's home, the men sharing a dinner, no matter the hour, as well as smoking a pipe, while the women cleared the table (Weinbender, 2003). These acts were most likely carried out to build some rapport between the parents and the male caller in question. The courting couple would then proceed to retreat to the most secluded corner of the room (Weinbender, 2003). Both Irene Gordon and Weinbender mention that the entire family would "suddenly act as though the couple were invisible," allowing them to have a moment to themselves (Gordon, 2009, p. 20). Similarly, the couple would become oblivious to the presence of the family in order to show their affection to each other, seemingly not embarrassed if their conversation was overheard (Robinson, 1879). The couple would take this opportunity to exchange intimate conversation, gifts, or pet names, at times changing the language of some of the words being spoken to avoid "exposure" (Weinbender,

2003). The parents and younger siblings would also do their part in helping the couple create a private moment by participating in loud conversation in another corner of the room or occupying themselves with other tasks (Robinson, 1879).

The History, Effects and Trends of Subsidized Housing

Unfortunately for most communities, political, economic, and social changes have dramatically impacted the Métis way of life, causing rippling effects from one generation to another. For others, however, the housing situation has evolved from a state of dispossession to one of adaptation and resiliency. Individuals once pushed to the fringes of a newly emerging society could safeguard aspects of their culture. Overcrowding and substandard accommodations continue to be a reality for both rural and urban living Métis (Beatch, 1995). These are but some of the many difficulties presently encountered along with the growing shortage of affordable rental housing and increase in poverty (Rivard, 2000). Today, housing programs for both First Nation and Métis communities still exist throughout Alberta, Manitoba, and Saskatchewan.

Subsidized housing programs for Métis communities in northern Saskatchewan were implemented as early as 1960 (Chislett & Milford & Bone, 1987). In lieu of the Métis providing their own living accommodations, designs and funding were procured by the Saskatchewan Housing Corporation and Indigenous and Northern Affairs Canada

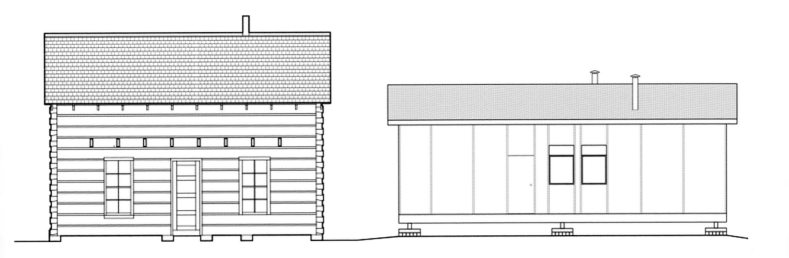

Figure 8. Architectural elevations of a folk home (Left) and of a "Three Bedroom Low Cost House" (Right). The folk home featured a second story loft where families slept in a communal room, heated by a central hearth. The INAC home, features three smaller bedrooms, where personal seclusion was furthered. The main living space is far smaller than that of a folk home and inflexible in nature, which forced settler social practices on Métis families, furthering cultural assimilation. (Drawings: Jason Surkan)

in order to build more affordable housing. Examples of these designs are showcased in the figures found in the next section of this paper. These homes had a number of different effects on Métis communities. Firstly, the design of the homes did not support the particular lifestyle shared amongst this culture. The segmented organization of space has had additional ramifications on the level of wear on the home and how they supported larger families. As a result, overcrowding became a large concern, both within the home and on the land (Rivard, 2000). This put a considerable amount of stain on the home which contributed to higher deterioration rates. Geographic isolation and climatic differences were also a concern when considering the home's' level of durability (Beatch, 1995). Moreover, high cost of material transportation to more remote communities and lack of familiarity with the types of materials used in their construction made it also increasingly difficult to provide adequate maintenance.

Since the 1960s, efforts made by government-funded agencies as well as architects in the Indigenous housing sector continue to provide Indigenous communities with houses designed with an overt Euro-centric mindset. Not equipped to sustain contemporary and traditional Indigenous domiciliary behaviors, these homes quite literally crumble under the pressure. This cannot only be viewed as a direct form of cultural discrimination but a trend which has since threatened Indigenous social sustainability. This indicates that architects and designers should familiarize themselves with the relevant socio-spatial behaviors found

in Indigenous households, thus, providing not only better support and understanding when working with Indigenous communities but also in hopes of raising current standards throughout the entire architectural community.

Conclusion

Homes provided by INAC are emblematic of colonial paternalism, introducing designs which became problematic for families attempting to uphold the communalistic values previously expressed. This is not to say that privacy is less prevalent but instead manifested differently in Métis culture. For many Indigenous cultures as well as the Métis, the lines of privacy are often blurred, implied within a social context rather than in physical built form. Understanding the intricacies surrounding the theme of privacy and social organization of the Métis household much like any other society or culture is often difficult to observe. Therefore, firsthand accounts from Métis people throughout history as well as members of surviving communities are crucial in understanding this dynamic. When considering the dramatic impact, the interior design of INAC homes had on Métis social behaviors and cultural customs, it becomes increasingly evident how the design of the home itself attempted to break down cultural solidarity and egalitarianism through the imposition of physical privacy that was aligned with alienated ideals of liberalism, private space and property, and individual capital acquisition.

References

Beatch, W.T. (1995). *Metis and reserve housing of Northern Saskatchewan a comparison of quality 1981-1991*. Masters Thesis. Saskatoon, SK: University of Saskatchewan. p. 112.

Burley, David V., and Gayel A. Horsfall. (1989). "Vernacular Houses and Farmsteads of the Canadian Metis." *Journal of Cultural Geography 10, no. 1 19-33*.

Burley, David. (2000). *Creolization and late nineteenth century Métis Vernacular Log Architecture on the South Saskatchewan River*. New York, NY.Historical Archaeology 34, no. 3. p. 27-35.

Campbell, Maria. (2016, June 26). Maria Campbell [Personal interview].

City of Winnipeg Historical Buildings Committee. (1988). 3514 Pembina Highway McDougall House. Winnipeg, MB: City of Winnipeg.

Chandler, G. (2003). *The Language of Métis Folk Houses*. Winnipeg, MB: The Beaver. 83:4, pp. 39-41.

Chislett, Katherine., Green, Milford, B., Bone, Robert, M. (1987). "Housing mismatch for Metis in Northern Saskatchewan." *The Canadian Geographer / Le Geographe canadien 31, no. 4*, 341-6. p. 342.

Fortin, David T. and Surkan, Jason L. (2016). "Towards an Architecture of Métis Resistance." *THE SITE MAGAZINE*. June 28, 2017. Retrieved 2017, November 15 from http://www.thesitemagazine.com/read/towards-an-architecture-of-mtis-resistance.

Fleury, Norman. (2016, June 20). Norman Fleury [Personal interview].

Gordon, I.T. (2009). *A People on the Move: The Métis of the Western Plains*. Heritage House Publishing Co.

Grøn, O. (1990). "General spatial behaviour in small dwellings: a preliminary study in ethnoarchaeology and social psychology." *In the Mesolithic in Europe. International Symposium*. 3. pp. 99-105.

Harrison, J. (1985). *Metis: People between Two Worlds*. Vancouver/Toronto: Glenbow Museum.

Kirmayer, Lawrence and Mary Ellen Macdonald, Gregory M. Brass. (2000). Culture & Mental Health Research Unit Report No. 10: The Mental Health of Indigenous Peoples Proceedings of the Advanced Study Institute, The Mental Health of Indigenous Peoples McGill Summer Program in Social & Cultural Psychiatry and the Aboriginal Mental Health Research Team May 29 – May 31, Montréal, Québec.

Knafla, A. Louis and Westra, Haijo. (2010). "Aboriginal Title, and Indigenous Peoples: Canada, Australia, and New Zealand." *Law and Society Series*. Vancouver, BC: University of British Columbia Press. p. 42.

Martin, T. and Casault, A. (2005). "Thinking the Other: Towards cultural diversity in architecture." *Journal of architectural education*, 59(1), p. 7.

Payment, Diane. (1990). The Free People – Otipemisiwak: Batoche, Saskatchewan, 1870-1930. Ottawa: Canadian Parks Service.

Rivard, Ron & Associates. (2000). One Thousand Voices, Métis Homelessness Project-2000. Report Prepared for: The Metis Urban Councils of Prince Albert, Saskatoon, and Regina p. 10.

Robinson, H.M. (1879). *The Great Fur Land, Or, Sketches of Life in the Hudson's Bay Territory (No. 12758)*. GP Putnam's Sons.

Rybczynski, W. (1987). *Home: A Short History of an Idea*. New York, NY: Penguin Books.

Smith, D., Lommerse, M. and Metcalfe, P. eds., (2014). *Perspectives on Social Sustainability and Interior Architecture: Life from the Inside*. Memmott, Paul, Chapter 7: Inside the Remote-Area Aboriginal House, Springer Science & Business. p. 98.

Tanner, Adrian. (2016). T*ogether We Survive: Ethnographic Intuitions, Friendships, and Conversations. (Vol. 79)*. McGill-Queen's Press-MQUP. Chapter 2: Architecture without Rooms: Cree Dwellings and Social Order. p. 82.

Taylor, J. L. (1983). "A Historical Introduction to Metis Claims in Canada." *The Canadian Journal of Nation Studies*, 3/1. p. 156.

Ward, P. (1999). *A History of Domestic Space: Privacy and the Canadian Home*. Vancouver: UBC Press.

Weinbender, Kimberley D. (2003). *Petite Ville: A Spatial Assessment of a Métis Hivernant Site*. Master's Thesis. Saskatoon, Saskatchewan: University of Saskatchewan.

Wolfart, Phillip. (2012). *Contours of a People: Metis Family, Mobility, and History. Edited by Brenda MacDougall, Nichole St-Onge, and Carolyn Podruchny. Vol. 6*. p. 120-133. Norman, OK: University of Oklahoma Press.

Chapter 8: Kia Tahuri i te Riu, Kia Tika: Indigenous Participation in Earthquake Recovery Planning – Insights from Taiwan and Canterbury

Hauauru Rae – Waikato, Ngāpuhi and Michelle Thompson-Fawcett – Ngāti Whātua

Hauauru is a senior policy analyst at the Ministry for the Environment (Manatū Mō Te Taiao). Previously, he was at the Department of Internal Affairs (Te Tari Taiwhenua), working on local government policy. Hauauru has a Bachelor of Arts with Honours in Māori Studies and a Master of Planning from the University of Otago (Te Whare Wānanga o Otāgo). His Master's thesis investigated Indigenous participation in earthquake recovery planning.

Michelle is a professor in Te Iho Whenua (Department of Geography), Te Whare Wānanga o Otāgo (University of Otago), Aotearoa New Zealand. She has a Bachelor of Town Planning and a Master of Planning from the University of Auckland, and a Doctor of Philosophy from the University of Oxford. She has more than ten years' experience as a planning practitioner with city, district and regional councils in the North Island. Michelle's research focuses on power relations and practices of inclusion/exclusion and self-determination in local planning. Her projects with Māori communities investigate processes of urban design, cultural landscape management, cultural impact assessment, and Indigenous resource management and planning. She is co-editor of the book "Tāone Tupu Ora: Indigenous Knowledge and Sustainable Urban Design" (2010) Steele Roberts Aotearoa, and co-author of the book "Māori and Mining" (2013) Te Poutama Māori.

Introduction

Earthquakes are devastating. Post-earthquake recovery is fraught and complex. However, the community that is re-built can be a new being. It is the latter that we focus on in this chapter. In recent years, those involved in urban and rural planning have made increasing efforts to understand disasters and disaster management. Disaster management is commonly understood as comprising four inter-linking stages – mitigation, preparedness, response, and recovery (Berke, Kartez and Wenger, 1993). The least researched of these stages is recovery, although it is currently receiving greater attention as governments begin recognising

their limited knowledge of how to plan appropriately for the restoration of communities following disasters (Peek and Mileti, 2002). National level governments have a key role in facilitating and coordinating recovery efforts, and undertaking institutional reform to empower planning processes that facilitate swiftly addressing the implications of disasters (Berke et al., 1993; Fiorino, 1990). Rosenthal and Kouzmin (1997) argue that the fundamental changes to institutional frameworks in such situations contradict notions of public participation, which leads to what Pearce (2003) describes as a failure by planners to enable participation in recovery planning.

In this chapter, we review the conventional experience of Indigenous groups in post-disaster recovery, then examine the specifics of two case studies, one related to recovery planning in Taiwan and one related to recovery in Christchurch, Aotearoa|New Zealand. We conclude with a discussion of the potential for positive change in Indigenous peoples' engagement in post-disaster processes, derived from the experiences in Taiwan and Christchurch.

Indigenous Peoples and Recovery Planning

It is widely recognised that Indigenous groups have a much weaker influence on environmental management than they would like, and than they were used to pre-colonisation (Hibbard, Lane and Rasmussen, 2008). Many Indigenous groups are identified as politically, economically, and culturally marginalised minorities (Hibbard and Lane, 2004; Sandercock, 1998a; Rewi, 2010). Marginalisation is a concept that is arguably inseparable from the notion of disaster vulnerability. The more marginalised a group is, the more likely they are to be vulnerable to disasters (Gaillard and Cadag, 2012). In addition, it is clear from recent research on post-disaster recovery that Indigenous peoples' input into the recovery of a location, of a city, after a disaster is even weaker than it is normally; that is, the participatory mechanisms involving Indigenous people are less satisfactory than usual (Ritchie and Hamilton, 2004; Gaillard and Cadag, 2012). Most research indicates that in times of an environmental disaster, the type of emergency reconstruction, or recovery processes and institutions set up to undertake such a task, lead to the exacerbation and perpetuation of the political exclusion that Indigenous groups had been facing prior to the environmental disaster (O'Faircheallaigh, 2010). Those emergency, often short-term, post-disaster institutions commonly fail to take adequate account of marginalised groups, including Indigenous groups, and add another barrier to such groups being engaged in decision making processes.

In addition, Indigenous peoples are more likely to be vulnerable to the effects of disasters (through their location and existing inequities) and also less resourced or in a position to manage consequent economic, social and wellbeing impacts (Birkmann, 2006; Bland et al., 1996; Ritchie and Hamilton, 2004). Hsu, Howitt and Chi (2014) depict disasters as being on the same plain – in terms of enormity of effect – as colonisation and hegemonic state power; each resulting in disruption to Indigenous practices, dispossession of resources, and dislocation from traditional territories for Indigenous society, environment and the broader cosmos. This is a portrayal of disaster as yet another major difficulty that builds into an already poorly functioning interaction between Indigenous groups, the coloniser and the national apparatus. Hence, O'Faircheallaigh (2010) argues that disaster management extends and perpetuates political exclusion through new decision-making structures that fail to accommodate and account for marginalised realities. The institutional framework established in recovery planning generally does not demonstrate efforts to avoid political exclusion by enabling ground-level participation (Rosenthal and Kouzmin, 1997). Genuine participation in recovery processes is commonly perceived as inhibiting prompt decision-making and efficient recovery.

Therefore, in the research that we report below, we explore Indigenous engagement mechanisms in recovery planning in Taiwan and Canterbury following major earthquakes. The work is based on analysis of relevant documents and interviews with Indigenous key informants and key informants working for Indigenous organisations (see Figure 1). The aim is to demonstrate evolving Indigenous experiences and underline the potential for enhancing planning processes and empowering Indigenous groups.

Taiwan

The first example that we consider is Taiwan. There is an significant Indigenous presence, particularly notable in the hill country of Taiwan, which was adversely affected in 1999 by a magnitude 7.3 earthquake. On 21 September 1999 at 1:47 am, the strongest earthquake in a century hit the country. Known as the "921 Earthquake," it was the second deadliest in Taiwan's history, killing nearly 2,500 people and injuring over 11,000 more. Ongoing aftershocks damaged buildings and landscapes across the island, particularly in Nántóu and Taichung counties, where the epicentre of the earthquake was located (Shaw, 2000). The earthquake occurred in a relatively low seismic region and, as a result, caught many people off-guard and showed quality of construction to be wanting.

The island of Taiwan (officially part of the Republic of China) had a population of over 21 million in the year 1999. Taiwan's population comprises Hoklo (70 percent) and Hakka (20 percent) peoples who generally identify as Taiwanese, along with Mainlanders, and also Indigenous Taiwanese commonly referred to as "Taiwan Aboriginal Peoples" (Lin et al., 2001; Brown, 2004). In 1999, there were nine recognised Indigenous groups (Tsou, Bunun, Paiwan, Rukai, Atayal, Saisiat, Amo, Puyuma, Yami), numbering over 440,000 – two percent of Taiwan's population (Lin et al., 2001). Centuries of changing colonisers with varied agendas have led to identity and recognition distinctions between different Indigenous groups in Taiwan society and politics. Those groups located down on the plains were initially affected more directly by the changes of multiple colonising forces and eventually faced a diminished recognition of their Indigeneity through assimilation practices; while Indigenous groups in the mountainous locations were increasingly excluded from the emerging political sphere and variously ascribed to reservations (or "preservations" as one key informant called them) and/or moved to lower elevations. In recent decades, the government has not only stipulated how Indigenous peoples participate in planning, if at all, but also determined which ethnic groups within Taiwan can be considered "Indigenous," thereby limiting those who may seek to have their say in decision-making as Indigenous peoples. Communities that seek to be recognised as Indigenous must submit an application to the Council of Indigenous Peoples (Lee and Aberhart, 2007; Sung, 2004). The Council identifies Indigenous peoples on their cultural distinctiveness from Han Chinese. This has proven difficult for those who have been subjected to centuries of assimilation. The issue has been particularly important to plains Indigenous peoples whose claims to being Indigenous have been rejected by the Council because claimants "chose to be assimilated into the society of Han people centuries ago" (Taipei Times, 2009: online). Plains Indigenous groups have, since the 1950s, been denied any capacity to participate in planning as Indigenous

Figure 1. Undertaking research with Indigenous groups in Taiwan.

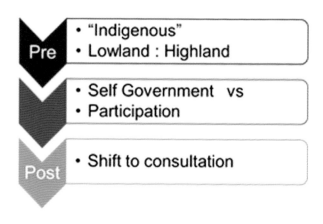

Figure 2. Pre/Post earthquake timeline, Taiwan.

peoples. Indigenous participation in planning is thus dependent on the government's acknowledgement of the need to engage with those who have been able to maintain their cultural distinctiveness despite oppressive regimes that have sought to prevent this. Participation is conceived as a form of privilege granted to those that gain government recognition – a privilege that had been, by 1999, granted to nine ethnic groups.

Cultural ignorance of Indigenous communities has become normalised in mainstream society through a legacy of colonial activity on the island and ongoing policy-based suppression of Indigenous values and aspirations (Huang, 2000; Brown, 2004). One of our key informants stated that there is an assumption in mainstream culture that Indigenous communities are "backward" and "need to change to fit the modern world." Indigenous rights movements have called for greater participation in decision-making to determine informed policies for Indigenous development (Ku, 2005). Indigenous politicians have advocated strongly for Indigenous aspirations, and in particular self-government (Rubinstein, 2015). Political participation is, in addition to self-government, a constitutional right, yet its realisation remains inhibited by inherent cultural subordination. Any discussion of autonomy has largely focussed on Indigenous communities in the mountainous locations, many of which exist within prescribed traditional territories (Rubinstein, 2015). These territories represent reservations established under Japanese rule and maintained by the Kuomintang regime. So, Indigenous participation is a constitutional right that has been gaining steady recognition in recent decades, heralding

a paradigm shift in Taiwan, although it has also been accused of being "little more than political ornament" (Alliance of Taiwan Aborigines, 1993: online). While it is clear that Indigenous influence remains limited, there has been gradual progress in the government's relationship with Indigenous peoples.

Nevertheless, the urgency surrounding a disaster event is quite a test of any positive shifts towards Indigenous sway on decision-making. In 1999, the Taiwanese government mobilised quickly to deal with the 921 post-earthquake recovery. However, the government received extensive criticism related to the effectiveness of the work they undertook, what they accomplished, and how they went about it (Prater et al., 2002; Prater and Wu, 2002). The first thing the government did was set up emergency response institutions to provide immediate relief. But these were under-resourced and not well-equipped, so performance was poor. The central government stepped back in shortly afterwards to coordinate recovery planning in a more systematic and holistic way. Part of what they were trying to achieve by stepping back in was to empower the local community to engage in the process of recovery more effectively than the emergency institutions had achieved. Nevertheless, communities at the local level, including Indigenous communities, were overwhelmed by the complexity of the recovery decision-making processes and structures that were set up and became alienated from the engagement opportunity (Chen, 2002). Predictably, the government was heavily criticised by the international community and Indigenous communities for failing to consider Indigenous views in

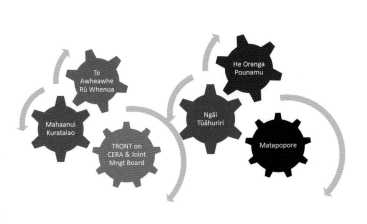

Figure 3. Indigenous voices heard through multiple mechanisms in recovering Ōtautahi|Christchurch

Figure 4. Manu (birds) in Tākaro ā Poi and embedded pepeha along Te Papa Ōtākaro|Avon River

such early recovery efforts (Chen, 2002). The situation is not surprising; Taiwan has a traditionally authoritarian regime so it is not unexpected that community views would have limited traction in a situation of emergency response.

Nonetheless, there was a shift over time in the recovery process that started to improve Indigenous involvement as various tiers of government slowly responded to the criticisms they were facing about Indigenous values not being taken into account. It was not a static situation. It proved to be part of a wider ongoing process of moving forward in terms of how the government was conceiving of Indigenous participation.

In Figure 2 we depict the transition of participatory focus from shortly before to shortly after the 921 Earthquake, based on documents and our discussions with informants in Taiwan. The first point, in the pre-earthquake situation, is that around the world there are quite different understandings of what "Indigeneity" is and there are also different understandings within Taiwan. There are numerous Indigenous groups within the Taiwan context and they have been differentially affected by centuries of colonial activity in terms of their decision-making and participatory influence in the planning and governance arenas. The focus of our research related to the experiences of the highland Indigenous communities who were significantly affected by the 921 Earthquake. Any sense of autonomy for Indigenous groups in Taiwan has largely been focussed on highland Indigenous communities.

The second component of Figure 2 recognises that beyond the debates over who is Indigenous, Indigenous politicians, have advocated fervently for Indigenous aspirations, and in particular for self-government (Rubinstein 2015). The pursuance of Indigenous participation in planning can be well served by implementing self-government because it can deepen the political capacity with which Indigenous peoples negotiate policies for development. In Taiwan, notions of self-government have included territorial autonomy, county self-governance, and joint-management of national parks. The distinction between self-government and political participation becomes somewhat blurred to the extent that both mechanisms seek to ensure the voicing of Indigenous concerns and aspirations.

In the third segment of Figure 2, what we depict – post-earthquake – is a noteworthy shift. It is a move that has come about mainly because of central government's hand in the process of recovering the mountainous areas, as opposed to local government managing the process. The 921 Earthquake recovery was instrumental in setting in motion the development of greater public participation in planning. According to key informants, while recovery at a local level was guided by central government objectives for development, it needed to be informed by local aspirations for restoration because central government neither knew nor understood the needs of local communities. As a result, local communities, many of which were Indigenous, needed to be consulted. This was a welcome shift, as one of our key informants said, Indigenous peoples prefer a "bottom-up approach to policy development, rather than to be told by the authority what to do. Indigenous peoples do not like being told what to do. They want to determine their own future."

The key to this shift in taking account of and being more inclusive of Indigenous groups in the post-disaster recovery period has actually been central government taking the lead – and having the mandate to take that lead – in the local context, over and above local government who should normally play that kind of role. It has not been a radical shift, but it is a positive trajectory for change in the Taiwanese situation. Even so, for many Indigenous communities, particularly those that reside within the most remote areas of the mountains, the government imposed a policy of relocation. Chen (2002) criticises this policy because it demonstrates the government's focus on physical reconstruction, which ignored the social relationship that Indigenous communities share with the land and the significance of the land to their identity. Consultation may have taken place, but the Indigenous voice was not always heard or acted upon. Nevertheless, to a certain extent our key informants indicated that they felt that post-921 they were starting to gain some traction in terms of determining their own future in certain circumstances and certain locations.

What was revealed to us in Taiwan was not what we expected to see. What we expected to see were post-disaster processes that were appreciably worse than usual; engagement, inclusion, decision-making processes that were more exclusionary in terms of Indigenous input. But what we found was that the post-disaster recovery planning process was actually a slight improvement on the norm.

Ōtautahi | Christchurch

In our second case study we reflect on our research in Ōtautahi|Christchurch, Aotearoa|New Zealand. On 22 February 2011, the deadliest earthquake to hit New Zealand in 80 years struck the Canterbury region, centred beneath Christchurch City. Its magnitude, close proximity to the central business district, shallow depth, acceleration and orientation towards the city, and the city's soil composition contributed to the severity of the damage incurred. 185 people died, with infrastructural and physical damage estimated at NZ$15-20 billion, including the collapse of iconic masonry structures, making the post-disaster experience socially, psychologically, culturally and economically devastating for local communities.

The February earthquake occurred subsequent to another major earthquake that struck four months prior, on 4 September 2010. At this time the Government established the Canterbury Earthquake Recovery

Commission, an advisory body consisting of local mayors and other relevant representatives whose role was to advise Ministers on the assignment of funding and resources for the recovery effort. However, the calamity of the 2011 earthquake necessitated a more comprehensive structure to lead and coordinate the Government's response and recovery efforts. Hence the Canterbury Earthquake Recovery Authority|Te Mana Haumanu ki Waitaha (CERA) superseded the Commission at the end of March 2011, establishing an integrated framework aimed at holistic recovery with community involvement at the centre of decision-making. This new arrangement offered an opportunity for reshaping participatory practices during the recovery and rebuild of the city. In particular, the potential for enhanced Indigenous engagement in post-disaster planning was notable.

Again, our research in Ōtautahi|Christchurch focuses on the experience of Indigenous groups in recovery planning. The Canterbury region's ethnic composition is largely constituted by Pākehā (New Zealand European) (77.4 percent) and Māori (7.2 percent), with growing Asian and Pacific populations. New Zealand's planning system has been based on traditional Pākehā environmental ethics and governance ideals, as introduced by the British Parliament in 1852 under the Constitution Act. This system has inevitably failed Māori, who have been an ethnic minority since the end of the 19th century. In response, many Māori have sought some political solace in the establishment of their own institutions to serve their interests in parallel to those of Pākehā institutional arrangements. The establishment of Te Rūnanga o Ngāi Tahu (TRONT) exemplifies such an institution. Ngāi Tahu, as an iwi (tribal) group, covers most of the South Island, including the Ōtautahi|Christchurch area. TRONT was established as Ngāi Tahu's iwi authority and today administers the restoration of the iwi's capacity to "build a stronger economic, social and cultural base for Ngāi Tahu people" (Te Rūnanga o Ngāi Tahu, 1996, online).

Ngāi Tahu's involvement in planning has long been hindered by a legacy of ignorance towards their taha wairua (spiritual wellbeing), mātauranga (knowledges), and counter-colonial interests. This ignorance has been incrementally destabilised through political decentralisation, the introduction of a more minority-conscious electoral system (mixed-member proportional representation), and resource management reforms that have advocated a more community-inclusive approach to planning. The planning processes that Ngāi Tahu now traverse are more open to their interests, both as members of the Canterbury community and as tangata whenua (people of the land). Even so, the forms of participation enabled for Māori have been founded on the democratic reformist ideals of traditional Pākehā governance.

Prior to the earthquakes, in the 20-year period following the enactment of the Resource Management Act 1991, there was an onus on local authorities to consult with Indigenous groups, which was later also reinforced through the Local Government Act, 2002. In addition, there was acknowledgement of the appropriateness of developing the potential of partnership, primarily as a result of the settlement of treaty grievances. For Ngāi Tahu, treaty settlement in 1998 meant that the Crown affirmed the status of Ngāi Tahu as a body with pre-existing planning rights and practices (amongst other things) for which they were now able to seek restitution. That meant Māori principles of environmental management for example, needed to be taken account of by local authority planning activity in a way they had not been before. The post-treaty settlement period led to a new way of Ngāi Tahu engaging with decision-making bodies and local authorities in Ōtautahi|Christchurch.

Since the earthquakes, there has been a period of a multiplicity of forms of community involvement. CERA's framework involved a multi-tiered scaffold – working at regional level, but also working horizontally across agencies, and working within local communities. Although the structure replicated a top-down approach, the power was pragmatically shared between stakeholders, reflecting CERA's facilitative and collaborative role in the recovery. The framework included TRONT as a member of the Recovery Strategy Advisory Committee, the Recovery Strategy Chief Executive Advisory Group, the Recovery Strategy Officials Group, and the Joint Management Board formed to hear resource consent applications for the rebuild of the central city core area. In addition, CERA mobilised a programme for enabling community engagement. This offered an opportunity for Māori to participate in planning as part of the wider Canterbury community in addition to TRONT playing a governance role via CERA. Hence, Ngāi Tahu had a formal place on all the Government derived layers of decision-making activities related to rebuilding the city, and in addition, also utilised a series of tribal and sub-tribal bodies that specifically engaged in areas of recovery where they held particular expertise. This allowed tangata whenua to participate across the tiers of routine tribal activity, following a more traditional bottom-up approach to city redevelopment, in addition to the formal CERA contribution. We have depicted some of the more significant elements in Figure 3.

To consolidate and better communicate their views and interests early on in the recovery, TRONT formed an earthquake recovery group – Te Aweawhe Rū Whenua. Its role comprised providing leadership and a collaborative approach to devising and implementing recovery strategies, maintaining relationships, establishing monitoring mechanisms and distributing resources. The group comprised local representatives of the different hapū (sub-tribes) affected by the earthquake, demonstrating an effort to ensure Ngāi Tahu's traditional bottom-up approach to planning and greater accountability to their respective communities. Te Aweawhe Rū Whenua worked with other Māori organisations, such as Te Puni Kōkiri (the Ministry for Māori Development), Ngāi Tahu's health agency (He Oranga Pounamu), along with Te Rūnanga o Ngā Maata Waka (the Urban Māori Authority for Māori of any tribe in Te Wai Pounamu|the South Island), to respond to the needs of earthquake affected Māori families. Together they established a recovery network dedicated to supporting distressed communities.

Matapopore Charitable Trust was established by Te Ngāi Tūāhuriri Rūnanga (the sub-tribe governance group related to the areas of the city most affected by the earthquake) to ensure meaningful contributions to the design of the city rebuild. It has facilitated Ngāi Tūāhuriri/Ngāi Tahu experts being involved in incorporating significant stories and values relating to natural heritage, mahinga kai (food gardens), te reo Māori (Māori language), and whakapapa (genealogies) into the urban design, art, architecture, and landscape architecture of the new urban environment. Matapopore has played a major role in weaving the presence of tangata whenua into a series of major and anchor projects in the city centre, such as Ngā Whāriki Manaaki (13 welcome mats), embedded pepeha (statements of identity and belonging), and Tākaro ā Poi|Margaret Mahy Playground (Figure 4) all along Te Papa Ōtākaro|Avon River Precinct.

Mahaanui Kurataiao Ltd is a longer-established planning and environmental management agency set up in 2007 by six local rūnanga in Canterbury. It plays a key role in expediting the aspirations of rūnanga (sub-tribal authorities) and advising environmental agencies, local authorities and resource users on cultural values. In this way, the agency is able to ensure a further mechanism for tangata whenua input into the development of plans and projects relating to post-disaster planning for the wider Canterbury region.

All these examples of mechanisms for engagement demonstrate a positive shift in terms of empowering tangata whenua, beyond the levels achieved in conventional planning practice prior to the major earthquakes. Even so, while a range of mechanisms have developed for Indigenous participation in planning around Ōtautahi|Christchurch, CERA demonstrated relatively little effort to engage with non-Ngāi Tahu Māori, that is, mātāwaka:

So Ngāi Tahu have done very well following the earthquake in terms of getting themselves   enacted into legislation, and getting their status as tangata whenua confirmed again. My concern… would be around how non-Ngāi Tahu Māori were led (Māori Key Informant).

This resonates with the experience of Indigenous groups in Taiwan as well – that is, central government, local government, and legislation has been improving in terms of the way local tribal groups - who have maintained their long held heritage in their ancestral location - have rights in the decision-making process, but what about other Indigenous groups? Who is Indigenous – who counts as Indigenous? Understanding the extent of Indigenous participation becomes complicated when deeper consideration is given to Indigenous identity. It is an issue that has been over-simplified in planning by governments who have self-designated an authority to determine who is Indigenous and, therefore, who is entitled to any Indigenous rights, such as participation and, ironically, self-determination. As such, investigating the extent of Indigenous participation remains confined to understanding how those specific ethnic groups that have received government recognition as Indigenous are integrated into recovery planning processes. As a result, the denial of mātāwaka in Aotearoa|New Zealand and plains Indigenous peoples in Taiwan in practice is perpetuated in almost all accounts of Indigenous influence over planning decision-making.

Conclusions

The genuine inclusion of Indigenous voices in planning processes has been a baffling issue for governments in recent decades (Hibbard and Lane, 2004). The added complexity surrounding this issue when confronting recovery from disaster is exacerbated by the sense of urgency required in decision-making processes. In this section, we will conclude by laying out the main messages that emerged from our research.

The first point is that we found that the Indigenous groups involved in the post-disaster recovery context for these two examples had very different ways of participating in the recovery process. They did not participate in a way that they had usually participated in everyday planning processes pre-quakes. They took advantage of new opportunities that came about as a result of new institutional arrangements. Furthermore, in a situation of uncertainty, where the usual processes do not take place, they found other ways to become involved that they had not used in the past.

The second point is that in both cases, the participation had been significantly influenced by central government. Central government, more so than local government, was more attuned to the cutting edge in international thinking about how inclusionary processes might function

for Indigenous groups. In a post-disaster context central government enabled progress in Indigenous engagement in planning processes.

Third, a change in participation practice was related to capacity; that is, both the capacity of government agencies to recognise the implications of Indigenous rights and the capacity of Indigenous groups to engage.

A fourth factor was that participation in recovery was completely different to ordinary participation in environmental management and planning processes. All the terms of engagement change when dealing with emergency situations followed by a recovery period of decades. What existed before, in terms of the inadequacy of the planning process, need not necessarily be repeated as recovery continues.

Finally, there has been a significant growth in the level of respect and understanding, and level of support for bringing about transformation in regard to the knowledge held by Indigenous groups about their area, their environment, and the context in which regeneration is taking place. That is, there has been a growing respect by non-Indigenous groups for Indigenous ways of thinking and Indigenous knowledge.

Our motivation for undertaking this research is that we have transformative hopes. We have hope that decision-makers will grow in their willingness to learn and cherish other ways of knowing; will seek to understand other ways of knowing. We have hope that decision makers will be involved in the capacity building of dominant society to support and understand Indigenous aspirations for cities, landscapes and environments. We have hope that decision makers will be involved in redressing current power imbalances and developing mechanisms that are meaningful for partnership and co-existence of different authorities that live and co-exist in the same place.

So, we want to finish by highlighting the title of our chapter. Turning an old chant on its head, Te Maire Tau suggested at a Christchurch conference some years ago that Indigenous involvement in post-disaster recovery represents an opportunity to turn an upturned waka back to its upright position, that is, to restore society to fulfil community aspirations through partnership: Kia tahuri i te riu kia tika (return the canoe to its upright position). Let us facilitate that ambition by recognising the promise in these incremental improvements to planning practice.

References

Alliance of Taiwan Aborigines (1993). Report of the Alliance of Taiwan Aborigines to the United Nations Working Group on Indigenous Population. Taipei: Alliance of Taiwan Aborigines.

Berke, P. R., Kartez, J. & Wenger, D. (1993). "Recovery after disaster: achieving sustainable development, mitigation and equity." Disasters, 17(2), 93-109.

Birkmann, J. (2006). "Measuring vulnerability to promote disaster-resilient societies: Conceptual frameworks and definitions." In J. Birkmann, *Measuring Vulnerability to Natural Hazards. Towards Disaster Resilient Societies*. (pp. 9-54). New York: United Nations University Press.

Bland, S. H., O'leary, E. S., Farinaro, E., Jossa, F. & Trevisan, M. (1996). "Long-term psychological effects of natural disasters." *Psychosomatic Medicine*, 58(1), 18-24.

Brown, M. J. (2004). Is Taiwan Chinese? *The impact of culture, power, and migration on changing identities*. Berkeley, USA: University of California Press.

Chen, Y. (2002). "The Impacts of the September 21st Earthquake on Indigenous Peoples' Land Rights and the Reconstruction of Place Identity in Taiwan." *Journal of Geographical Science*, 31, 1-15.

Fiorino, D. J. (1990). "Citizen participation and environmental risk: A survey of institutional mechanisms." *Science, Technology & Human Values*, 15(2), 226-243.

Gaillard, J. & Cadag, J. R. D. (2012). "From marginality to further marginalization: Experiences from the victims of the July 2000 Payatas trashslide in the Philippines. Jàmbá." *Journal of Disaster Risk Studies*, 2, 197-215.

Hibbard, M. & Lane, M. B. (2004). "By the seat of your pants: Indigenous action and state response." *Planning Theory & Practice*, 5(1), 97-104.

Hibbard, M., Lane, M. B. & Rasmussen, K. (2008). "The Split Personality of Planning Indigenous Peoples and Planning for Land and Resource Management." *Journal of Planning Literature*, 23(2), 136-151.

Huang, S. (2000). "Language, identity and conflict: A Taiwanese study." *International Journal of the Sociology of Language*, 2000(143), 139-150.

Hsu, M., Howitt, R., & Chi, C. (2014). "The idea of 'Country': Reframing post-disaster recovery in Indigenous Taiwan settings." *Asia Pacific Viewpoint*. 55(3), 370-380.

Ku, K. (2005). "Rights to Recognition: Minority/Indigenous Politics in the Emerging Taiwanese Nationalism." *Social Analysis*, 49(2), 99-121.

Lee, C. & Aberhart, G. 2007. Sakizaya Recognized as Taiwan's 13th Aboriginal People [Online]. Available: http://www.taiwan-panorama.com/en/show_issue. php?id=200739603074e.txt&table=2&h1=Ethnicity%20 and%20Culture&h2=Taiwanese%20Aborigines [Accessed 11 November 2017].

Lin, M., Chu, C., Lee, H., Chang, S., Ohashi, J., Tokunaga, K., Akaza, T. & Juji, T. (2001). "Heterogeneity of Taiwan's Indigenous population: possible relation to prehistoric Mongoloid dispersals." *Tissue Antigens*, 55(1), 1-9.

O'Faircheallaigh, C. (2010). "Public participation and environmental impact assessment: Purposes, implications, and lessons for public policy making." *Environmental Impact Assessment Review*, 30(1), 19-27.

Pearce, L. (2003). "Disaster management and community planning, and public participation: how to achieve sustainable hazard mitigation." *Natural Hazards*, 28(2-3), 211-228.

Peek, L. A. & Mileti, D. S. (2002). "The history and future of disaster research." In R. B. Bechtel & A. Churchman (Eds.), *Handbook of environmental psychology* (pp. 511-524). Hoboken, NJ: John Wiley.

Prater, C. & Wu, J. (2002). "The Politics of Emergency Response and Recovery: Preliminary Observations on Taiwan's 921 Earthquake." *Australian Journal of Emergency Management*, 17(3), 48-59.

Prater, C., Wu, J. Y. & Center, R. (2002). "The politics of emergency response and recovery: Preliminary observations on Taiwan's 921 earthquake." *Australian Journal of Emergency Management*, 17(3), 48-57.

Rewi, P. (2010). Culture: Compromise or perish! In B. Hokowhitu, N. Kermaol, C. Andersen, A. Petersen, M. Reilly, I. Altamirano-Jiménez & P. Rewi (Eds.), *Indigenous identity and resistance: Researching the diversity of knowledge*. (pp. 55-74). Dunedin, New Zealand: Otago University Press.

Ritchie, E. C. M. D. & Hamilton, S. E. P. (2004). Assessing Mental Health Needs Following Disaster. Psychiatric Annals, 34(8), 605-610.

Rosenthal, U. & Kouzmin, A. (1997). "Crises and crisis management: Toward comprehensive government decision making." *Journal of Public Administration Research and Theory*, 7(2), 277-304.

Rubinstein, M. A. (2015). *Taiwan: A new history*, Abingdon, England: Routledge.

Sandercock, L. (1998a). *Making the invisible visible: A multicultural planning history, London, England*. University of California Press.

Sandercock, L. (1998b). *Towards Cosmopolis: Planning for multicultural cities*. Chichester, England: Wiley.

Shaw, D. (2000). "Emergency relief measures and rehabilitation policies in the aftermath of the 921 Chi-Chi (Taiwan) Earthquake." Paper presented at EuroConference on Global Change and Catastrophe Risk Management: Earthquake Risks in Europe, IIASA, Laxenburg, Austria, July 6-9, 2000.

Sung, M. (2004). "When Would The Indigenous Be Indigenous? A Self-Defining, Interest-Isolated, Multiculturalistic Approach to Facilitate Recognition of the Taiwanese Ping-Pu." *Asian-Pacific Law & Policy Journal*, 5(1), 124-154.

Taipei Times. (2009). Pingpu people protest government denial of aboriginal status [Online]. Available: http://www.chinapost.com.tw/taiwan/2009/06/25/213584/Pingpu-people.htm [Accessed 15 December 2012].

Te Rūnanga o Ngāi Tahu. 1996. Mana Recognition [Online]. Available: http://www.ngaitahu.iwi.nz/About-Ngai-Tahu/Settlement/Settlement-Offer/Cultural-Redress/Mana-Recognition.php [Accessed 20 November 2017].

Chapter 9: Cultural Identity and Architecture

Douglas Cardinal – Blackfoot

Born in 1934 in Calgary, Alberta, his architectural studies at The University of British Columbia took him to Austin, Texas, where he achieved his architectural degree and found a life experience in human rights initiatives. Douglas then became a forerunner of philosophies of sustainability, green buildings and ecologically designed community planning. His architecture springs from his observation of Nature and its understanding that everything works seamlessly together. In recognition of such work, Douglas Cardinal has received many national and international awards including: 20 Honorary Doctorates, Gold Medals of Architecture in Canada and Russia, and an award from United Nations Educational Scientific and Cultural organization (UNESCO) for best sustainable village. He was also titled an Officer of the Order of Canada, one of the most prestigious awards given to a Canadian, and he was awarded the declaration of being "World Master of Contemporary Architecture" by the International Association of Architects. Douglas Cardinal is one of the visionaries of a new world; a world where beauty, balance and harmony thrive, where client, architect, and stakeholder build together with a common vision.

Before contact, the Indigenous people of Canada were sovereign nations. As thriving communities living on the land in harmony with the resources they harvested around them, they created very successful communities. The abundance of the resources which they harvested, were balanced with their needs to maintain harmony with each other and with the land. All life was held sacred. They celebrated the gift of their lives, and the lives of all the plants, animals, birds, and fish that enabled the people to flourish. These life givers were honored with ceremonies and prayers.

They evolved a loving and caring society that respected everyone and encouraged each individual to be free and sovereign over themselves, assuming responsibility to serve their clans and their communities. Generosity was admired, and sharing was mandatory. Children were brought up to be in service of others. Each clan regarded themselves to be in service of the other clans.

Governance was conducted in a circle where everyone had a voice. Decisions came from the heart, showing respect for every voice. Decisions were done by consensus. Each voice had to be heard and respected. The majority had to respect the minority voice and decisions were only made when all the voices agreed to take a certain direction.

If any member of the community went against the established rules set by the community, their judicial system was one of restorative justice. It was a process of restoring the person with abhorrent behavior to the group with the help and encouragement of the community. The Elders of the community took a primary role in guiding these governance and judicial systems, reinforcing the concept that the soft power of love is much greater than the hard power of force. These basic principles were reinforced by the grandmothers, who were the matriarchs of the clan system; the foundation of traditional governance.

Many of our Indigenous peoples in Canada are governed by a community of matriarchal clans working in harmony together with the principles of loving, caring and sharing. Many have the women make the decisions in the clan, in the community, and for the nation, while the men implement those decisions and honor the women's decision and direction. Both the Anishinaabe nations and the Haudenosaunee nations are examples of this kind of matriarchal governance.

The British government recognized these nations as sovereign by signing both the *Royal Proclamation of 1763* and nation to nation treaties, recognizing that the people of this land, the Indigenous people, had inherent rights of self-governance according to the British Crown. The clans became the signatories to these treaties. Natural law embraced them and guided their language, their culture, their relationship with their environment, their relationship with each other, their reverence for our mother the Earth, and the mothers on the Earth.

The Indian Act betrays that relationship and the trust between these sovereign nations, and thus dishonors the crown. It is an act of apartheid and genocide and has no place in a society that regards itself as a free democracy, that has aspirations to respect each individual. Indeed, democracies around the world aspire to the concept that everyone has inherent rights guaranteed by the constitution of these free and thriving democracies. The so-called "free world" has been inspired by the democracy and form of government evident in the United States, yet these ideas were adopted from the Haudenosaunee Great Law of Peace. Benjamin Franklin was the Indian agent for the Haudenosaunee people, and he was inspired to use their model of governance as the basis of the American constitution. This, in turn, has inspired many democracies around the world.

Citizens around the world have adopted these inherent rights, defined in the Great Law and the Constitution of the United States as a model for their democracies and the rights of their citizens. The inherent rights defined in this constitution grew out of the Indigenous people, their relationship with the land, and their relationship with their matriarchal clans.

The Great Law that defines the inherent rights of Indigenous people serves as a universal model for a democratic way of life, respecting the inherent rights of the individual. Although it was a form of government respected by the British Crown and ultimately by the United States, by laying a new foundation for their new country, the Indigenous people are governed by a dictatorship defined by the Indian Act, in which they are not allowed to govern themselves.

I believe that architects, engineers, and any other professional team serving First Nations communities should be compelled to honor the inherent rights of every individual in the community they are serving by acknowledging their Indigenous model of self-governance and their traditional way of making decisions.

These communities created a successful model of governance, they are considered sovereign nations, and I believe that every professional that serves these Indigenous nations should treat them accordingly. The nation should be given respect to make all decisions during the evolution of the design, starting from the vision of the project, every detail of the program, and ultimately through every stage of the design, such as schematics, design development, construction documents and tendering. All stages of construction should involve the appointed decision makers in the community, and their corresponding traditional governance systems. Decisions have to be made by the community themselves, not from any other government source.

The problems all professionals who serve communities have is that there is interference in people's rights by the Department of Indian Affairs. It starts from a colonial system imposed on each nation, where the chief and council does not represent the traditional governance and democratic model of each nation. They are a colonial creation of the government in Canada and, as such, they implement with every decision they make, colonization and a program of apartheid and genocide, undermining the sovereignty of the nations and the inherent rights of each individual of each of the nation's they dominate. They make every individual in the community, dependent on the will of each bureaucrat in the department. Because these bureaucrats have taken away the people's lands and resources any income cannot come from their traditional land, but comes from the whims of the department bureaucracy, perpetuating their agenda of colonization and assimilation.

I believe it is the duty of every professional who serves our Indigenous nations that they should support traditional governance systems and take sole direction from the people in the community that follows the traditional customs and governance of each nation. Even the Supreme Court regards the traditional customs as truly representing the will of the people. I believe as professionals we should honor the decisions of the Supreme Court of Canada.

It is also important, as a professional dedicated to serving the public that it is people who feel responsible to our Creator, spiritually, that it is against our principles as honorable human beings to participate in crimes against humanity, such as acts of apartheid and genocide perpetrated on our Indigenous nations. It is unfortunate that the Government of Canada uses our own Indigenous people through the Indian Act to establish colonial systems of Chief and Council, carrying out their policies, undermining the inherent rights of our indigenous citizens. As professional people we should not compromise our integrity by participating in these crimes against humanity.

Canadians expect their professionals to set ideal standards in carrying out their work to the public, and as such we have a responsibility to uphold the public trust. Using the money that comes from the land and resources taken from our Indigenous nations and controlling that money needed for bare necessities for the ongoing existence of our existence of our Indigenous nations continues a colonializing tradition. There's a fraudulent process of power and control using their land and resources, inherent rights, which should belong to the people themselves, used against them to finance the destruction of their sovereignty over their land, and their sovereignty to their inherent rights. It is truly a despicable process. I believe it compromises the integrity of every Canadian citizen.

By requesting that the people are involved in the initial vision of the project and the details of the program, involving the Elders through ceremonies to determine the proper form and symbols that should be expressed in the art and architecture and the environments we create, creates a built environment in our Indigenous communities that shapes their future, because architecture is a very powerful media that truly is a physical manifestation of the culture it represents. Architects have a responsibility to ensure that their architectural statements truly reflect the culture of each community. It is through the bringing together of different architectural voices of Indigeneity that we are able to affect global change for our communities. It is time that colonial nations acknowledge that it is no longer acceptable for design to be done without us or for us, but by us.

Indigenous people have very powerful symbols that have represented their culture for thousands of years. These symbols have marked the earth, been engraved in pictographs or have been formed by nature itself – such as the Sacred Islands and the Great Kettle in the Ottawa River. These symbols have been used in housing, in clothes and implements. Indigenous communities must be represented in the overall layout of the structure and in the details of the building itself. Indigenous people should also choose the materials used for the construction of their buildings, for they should determine the materials that best represents their environment – materials which carry on their culture and traditions and honors their history and the responsibility they have to laying the foundation for the next generations, on the land given back to the people for their survival. Land-use planning should reflect their values and their customs by not only planning for their own people for 7 generations, but also planning for all their life givers for 7 generations, which means planning

for the future of the water, the trees, the wetlands, the plants, the fish, the birds, the herbs and medicines – all of these life-givers ensure the people of the future will have a meaningful existence surrounded by resources they need to survive.

All future developments must be planned in a traditional way, where everyone in the community is mindful of the fact that all of their decisions are grounded in the 7 generations of the past and affect 7 generations in the future, and everyone is mindful of the responsibility they have of truly serving their nation. Our ceremonies remind us that the past, present, and future are all one and that we should have a reverence and respect for all life. We should celebrate the gift of life, of our life, and all life around us. Creation is all good. There's only a good and a crooked good that needs to be straightened out.

There is a need for conversations on these and many issues facing Indigenous peoples around the globe and, as such, the many Indigenous voices contained in this book are a good step forward in bringing to light the global injustices of colonialism.

Chapter 10: Does Blak Design matter or is just a white thing?

Timmah Ball - Ballardong Noongar

Timmah Ball works across urban research and community development. Having completed a Masters in Urban Planning from The University of Melbourne and undergraduate studies in Creative Arts she is interested in looking at creative practice as a way to investigate urban planning problems and address the erasure of Aboriginal voices in the planning system. Her heritage is Ballardong Noongar and she regularly writes about these topics in a range of publications such as "Meanjin," "the Griffith Review," "Assemble Papers," and "Overland."

In 2016 Aboriginal academic Bronwyn Carlson wrote *The politics of Identity: Who Counts as Aboriginal today?* (2016). The text reveals the diverse and layered identities that contemporary Aboriginal people traverse; while also critiquing stereotypes that "the real Aboriginal people" are the ones on the land and urban "white" Aboriginal people are fraudulently passing as Aboriginal. Despite the complexities her book addresses, white Australians often struggle to understand the emerging black middle classes whose needs and aspirations vary. As Stan Grant (2015) wrote in *The Guardian* "it seems many non-Indigenous people find it easier to identify us if we are poor." The changing demographics of Indigenous Australia can also cause tensions within Aboriginal communities themselves. Those of us with new economic, class, and social privileges are often disconnected from others in the wider community who continue to face challenges.

As contemporary Indigenous Australians experience vastly different lifestyles, one thing that unites us is the extreme popularity and growing appetite for our culture by mainstream institutions. In Ellen van Neerven's (2014) novel *Heat and Light*, she imagines an Australian future where "the anthem has been changed to the 2012 Jess Mauboy hit 'Gotcha' and Aboriginal art has almost wiped out all other Australian art – if you're not black forget it" (p. 73). More than ever I am approached by organisations seeking Indigenous perspectives on architecture and urban planning. Everywhere I look somebody wants Aboriginal ideas and knowledge. Van Neerven's fictional words are fast becoming reality.

Last year numerous architecture firms contacted me, seeking advice on research, projects, and design tenders. With a range of lofty visions from Indigenous dreaming gardens; incorporating smoking ceremonies into consultative planning and blending native plant species into the built form; all desperate for approval but no one seemed interested in realistic conversations about their designs. It was becoming clear that this was "black design" by white people, desperate to drive it and take the credit, but unwilling to have the messy conversations and address the crucial question "does this benefit Aboriginal communities?" Although buildings with cultural motifs of the Wurundjeri people would enliven Melbourne's built form, if money, decision making and social capital remained with white architecture firms, would the sudden interest in Aboriginal architecture just be a white thing? As Yuin woman and architecture student Linda Kennedy commented in her blog post *Future Black* "how do we move beyond symbols and gestures. How do we get mob to acknowledge our own aspirations, not those of white people?" (2017).

A boutique architecture firm in Fitzroy contacted me to discuss a design proposal for a gallery in the neighborhood. Over the phone they explained to me that as part of the design we feel that the ongoing history of Aboriginal people should be visible and acknowledged. They asked me what my thoughts were on the idea of a contemporary fire pit/gathering space on the ground floor cafe, a meeting space and yarning circle for all peoples? Caught off guard I meekly replied that it sounded like a good idea but immediately felt uncertain about their suggestion. As Linda Kennedy articulated, the concept was stuck in symbolic gestures. Who was it for? What was the purpose? Or was it just an idea developed by, and for, white people. I wondered.

Figure 1. Aboriginal Placemaking in the City, Source: Author

Aboriginal dreaming or corporate greed?

Blak art used to sell white dreams

OUR POET USED TO SELL APARTMENT BUILDINGS

MARK TUCKEY

LISA BELLEAR

...st up the road Reko Renni reminds us whose land we stand on

REMEMBER ME

Figure 2. Blak art used to sell white dreams. Source: Author

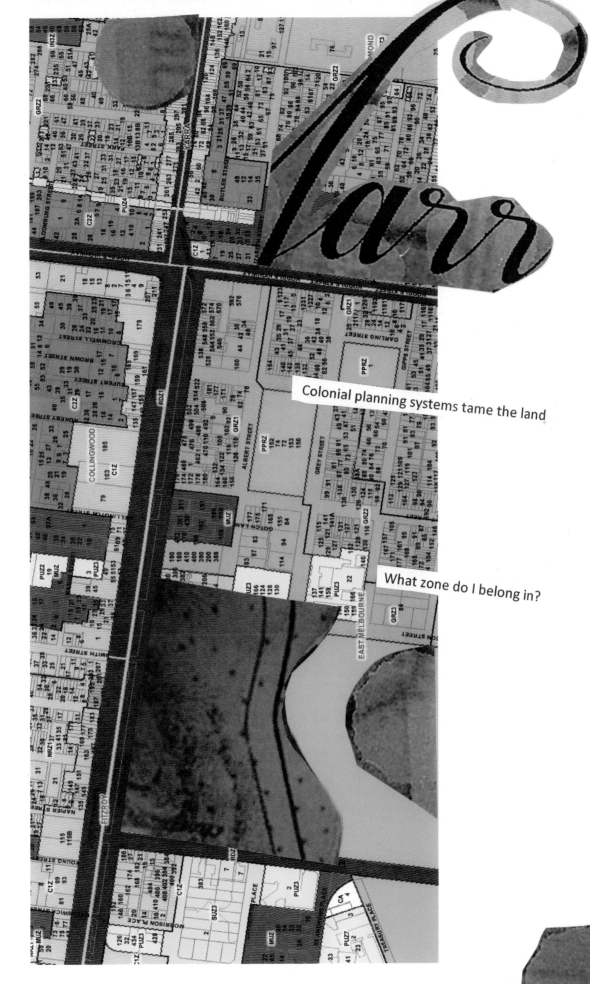

Colonial planning systems tame the land

What zone do I belong in?

Figure 3. Colonial
Planning Systems.
Source: Author

Integrating cultural practices into an industrial chic gallery café, would require sensitivity and the building of strong relationships. The concept of a cultural space as fire pit within an overpriced gallery café jarred. Gathering spaces are vital for community to connect but their vitality also hinges on autonomy, sovereignty and freedom from the white gaze. What then would it bring to the Aboriginal community who lived near the proposed gallery, particularly those experiencing housing stress and job insecurity? And, even more significantly, what was its relevance to the mob sleeping rough with drug and alcohol problems congregating around the corner next to the St. Vinnies soup van? In an essay by Yorta Yorta curator Kimberly Moultan accompanying the powerful exhibition Sovereignty she asks "is Aboriginal art only accepted within the western canon when it suits a capitalist agenda? (Moulton, 2016, p. 29).

Her question lingers uncomfortably whenever architects and planners approach me, quick to develop projects that reference Aboriginal culture. Does "blak" design only matter when it suits their agenda? These incidents leave you feeling that 'blak design is a white thing, with design firms hungry to cash in on a growing trend which benefits their social status, generates revenue and further work. Their interests are met while Aboriginal people continue to struggle, our voices ignored.

As tensions in the design industries play out it is important to recognise the incredible work by Aboriginal artists and designers working in the public realm. Despite concerns around the ethics of white firms, their work persists with autonomy and strength. From Footscray to Oakleigh (two Melbourne suburbs), public art by Maree Clarke and Vikki Couzens pierces the colonial landscape creating tranquil moments to reimagine another existence, even as the traffic blares down the Princess Highway. In inner city Melbourne work by Reko Rennie and Megan Cope reminds us of who we are and that our language continues to thrive even as our country was tamed by maps and western surveying tools. These artists and designers allow us to see ourselves reinserted back into an environment that was changed without our consent, creating important moments for both Aboriginal and non-Indigenous Australians to contemplate a history and cultural identity which is often erased or misunderstood.

Blak design led by Aboriginal people does matter but it should aspire to engage with social justice issues, and empower communities. We need to push the growing interest in Aboriginal design, architecture, and planning and ask how it assists Aboriginal people who continue to experience challenges. As Linda Kennedy proclaims, it's not about incorporating a bit of blak design when it suits the white industry, it's about radically shifting the way the industry operates and empowering Indigenous leadership and sovereignty. She states,

> Rather than being stuck within the institutional frameworks of archi/design and sprinkling on some blackness in the process – how do we move forward to asserting our sovereignty through our work & sprinkling on some archi/ design along the way? How do we flip the power play and stop indulging in the frameworks that continue to oppress and control us? (2017).

This is not a small task and will require all of us working in these industries to consider how our work can incorporate Aboriginal pedagogies rather than following white trajectories which appropriate aspects of blak culture when it suits their agenda. Aboriginal design for Aboriginal people should also move beyond the gestural and aspire to address issues like housing stress, economic disadvantage and access to services which impacts Aboriginal communities. Too often Aboriginal people are the first affected by gentrification, displaced from suburbs like Fitzroy, which have powerful cultural significance to Koori Mob (Indigenous Australians of Victoria). Instead inner city apartments and galleries with cultural motifs designed by non-Indigenous people are emerging but they are not blak design if they do little to assist the traditional owners of this land. As more projects in Melbourne arise we need to stop and think what value will they bring to Aboriginal people, before we indulge in the desires of their white designers.

References

Moulton, Kimberly, (2016). *'Sovereign Art and the Colonial Canon; Are We Lost Until We Are Found?'*, in Sovereignty pp27-33, Retrieved (2018, January 16) from Australian Centre for Contemporary Art website, https://content.acca.melbourne/uploads/2017/03/Sovereignty-Catalogue.pdf

Carlson, Bronwyn (2016) *The Politics of Identity: Who counts as Aboriginal today?* Canberra: Aboriginal Studies Press.

Grant, Stan. (2015, December 14) "The politics of identity: We are trapped in the imaginations of White Australia," *Guardian*.

Kennedy, Linda (2017) "Sovereignty and Spatial Design." Retrieved (2017, December 28) from *Future Blak* http://www.future-black.com/blog/sovereignty

Van Neerven, Ellen (2014). *Heat and Light*. Brisbane, UQP

Chapter 11: Conserving Māori Architecture, Maintaining Traditional Māori Arts

Ellen Andersen, Heritage New Zealand Pouhere Taonga

Ellen Andersen (Ngāti Raukawa ki te Tonga, Ngāti Kapumanawawhiti) has worked for Heritage New Zealand Pouhere Taonga since 2007 with a background in building conservation, having undertaken training in architecture in New Zealand, the United Kingdom, and work in Hawaìi and Australia. Ellen is part of the Māori Built Heritage Team at Heritage New Zealand, which works with Māori communities to conserve, record and restore their heritage places.

Over the past forty years, there has been a small but determined effort from New Zealand's national heritage agency to enable Indigenous-led conservation for historic Māori buildings. The Māori Built Heritage Programme at Heritage New Zealand Pouhere Taonga is an initiative of the organisation's Māori Heritage Council that seeks to promote the conservation and preservation of the Māori architectural heritage of our country.

Our work is primarily focussed on marae; families of buildings that usually consist of a wharenui (meeting house), wharekai (dining hall), and an ablution facility, although there are many other additional buildings and structures that may be included within a marae complex. The individual buildings on a marae will vary in age, but there is a significant number of marae buildings around the country that were constructed between 1880 and 1950, and it is usually these buildings that the Māori Built Heritage Team provide conservation advice and assistance on. The Māori Built Heritage Programme began in the 1970s with one person, and in the early 2000s the team expanded to two, and by the late 2000s to the current three member team. Although most of our work is concerned with marae-based architectural heritage, we also work with Māori communities who want to preserve other architectural taonga, such as historic school buildings, churches, cemeteries, homesteads, monuments, flagpoles, and archaeological sites such as rock art. Many of the places we work are located in rural or remote parts of the country, and there are many more marae located in the North Island than the South Island.

Heritage New Zealand Pouhere Taonga is an autonomous Crown entity, which means it was created by and operates under an Act of Parliament. It is similar to national heritage organisations in many other countries, but a feature that sets it apart from many heritage agencies in other countries with a colonial experience is the responsibilities to New Zealand's Indigenous people's land based cultural and built heritage that are articulated within the Act. The Heritage New Zealand Pouhere Taonga Act 2014 includes a commitment to recognise and respect the Crown's obligations to the Treaty of Waitangi, and one of the key features of the legislation that enables this is the establishment of the Māori Heritage Council. This eight-person advisory body is required to have four members who are Māori, and three members who are held in high regard for their knowledge of Te Ao Māori (Māori world views) and tikanga Māori (Māori protocol and culture). These requirements have meant that since its establishment in 1993, seven of the eight members of the Māori Heritage Council serving at any time have been Māori. The value of having strong Māori leadership at the governance level of the organisation allows for greater opportunities for the strategic direction of programmes to support Māori communities, and that this direction be informed by Indigenous leadership and implemented by Indigenous practitioners.

Heritage New Zealand Pouhere Taonga was originally established with the passing of the Historic Places Act in 1954, and began its work with a ten member Trust Board and one staff member. The work of the National Historic Places Trust (as it was originally known) focused on recording and marking places of significance, and advocating for the retention of important old buildings (MacLean, 2000). The earliest work involving Indigenous heritage places were predominantly archaeological in nature, with special attention given to rock art sites in Rotorua, Murupara, and throughout the South Island. The Trust also established an early relationship with Ngāti Tūwharetoa in the Taupō district in 1958, agreeing to administer and care for Te Pōrere Pā near Tongariro, a site associated with the New Zealand Wars of the 1860s (Christoffel, 2005).

In March 1970, the Classification of Historic Buildings Committee was established with the task of developing a system for classifying all of New Zealand buildings of historical or architectural interest. An additional committee was created in November of that year to look specifically at Māori Meeting houses, extending the reach for Māori Heritage beyond archaeological sites and towards architecture, the main emphasis for the recording work in the wider organisation at the time.

In August 1975 the Trust circulated a list of Māori buildings among universities and other government departments with a view to ranking the importance of these buildings in the same vein that the Trust had been ranking other historical buildings throughout the country (Ritchie, 1977). This process was problematic for both the identification of buildings, and for the approach to attributing significance. The initial list consisted almost exclusively of carved meeting houses built prior to 1900 (Biggs, 1976), and the restrictive nature of the scope of the list made for an inventory with little representation in the south or the far north of the country. The emphasis on carved works meant that the significance attributed to the buildings was not necessarily in line with the way Māori communities saw or valued their architectural heritage.

The issue of classifying and attributing significance for Māori built heritage was dealt with by Apirana Mahuika, who had been appointed as a special advisor on Māori issues in 1975. In a discussion document he outlined to the committee the problematic nature of attempting to rank the importance or attribute a particular level of significance to a marae. Mahuika explained:

> For a Māori on the Māori Buildings Committee or on the Council to enter tribal territory different from his own, and then attempt to classify (A,B,C) their building is asking for trouble and opposition, which would not advance the work of the Trust, or gain the confidence and trust of the Māori people (Mahuika, 1976).

Mahuika used anecdotes from his own iwi, Ngāti Porou of the east coast of the North Island to highlight the various ways by which the aesthetic values of a carved meeting house may not accurately reflect the wider heritage values:

While Porourangi is the most artistic house in Ngāti Porou and indeed the largest, its importance in terms of tribal meetings is overshadowed by Rāhui Marae where

(a)   Ngata always held his important meetings,
(b)   decisions on land issues were made or discussed,
(c)   dignitaries were entertained (Mahuika, 1976).

Mahuika also noted that uncarved houses, such as the Kauwhanganui Māori Parliament Building at Rukumoana, could be just as significant as an elaborately carved wharenui, due to the important historical events associated with the building. This was a critical consideration given some parts of the country had significant Māori architectural heritage, but this significance was not derived from its carving or artistic values.

Subsequently, the decision was made in the late 1970s that Māori architecture, and in particular marae, should not be classified in the way other buildings were, and that the recording of Māori buildings and other important structures would be dealt with in an inventory style approach, where a record was maintained that would remain accessible to each marae, but a ranking of value or importance was not applied. This was seen as a way of more appropriately respecting iwi, hapū and whānau values associated with marae, rather than applying arbitrary criteria to important cultural taonga. Another important aspect to the organisation's approach to marae conservation since the 1970s has also been to "only act if there is a request from the people" (Mahuika, 1978) as this responsive approach to engagement allows for more marae-led collaboration, and recognises tangata whenua as the lead agent in the care and custodianship of marae.

The first significant relationship between Heritage NZ Pouhere Taonga and a marae community began in 1972 with Te Whānau a Kai of Te Aitanga ā Māhaki at Rongopai Marae near Waituhi. Rongopai was built in 1888, but had been largely left untouched and unused since its construction. A ceremony was held to lift the tapu from the house in the late 1960s, and work began by the hapū to restore the whare (building) (Orbell, 1964). The initial work that Heritage New Zealand assisted with was improving the ventilation in the whare, and to commission L. C. Lloyd (Director of the Dunedin Public Art Gallery at the time) to undertake some initial cleaning and restoration of five of the painted panels from Rongopai.

By 1975 the marae trustees were keen to progress further with the restoration of the whare, however the report on restoration work had not been completed by Lloyd, so records associated with the conservation methodology were unavailable to the marae. The marae Trustees requested that a training programme be created to enable members of the marae community to be active in the conservation process, however as a conservator, Lloyd was apprehensive and condescending of the involvement of the marae community, suggesting in a letter to the Director of Heritage New Zealand that:

> The restoration techniques could be given by myself to the local people but it is questionable whether their abilities and dedication to the task could be sustained. I think it is expecting rather much from inexperienced labor to presume they will acquire the expertise in a few hours which has taken the specialist many years to procure (Lloyd, 1976).

As a result of the response from Lloyd, it was suggested by Mahuika to John Daniels (the director of Heritage New Zealand at the time) that Cliff Whiting, of Te Whānau a Apanui, and his colleague Frank Davis from Palmerston North Teacher's College could help supervise the work, and in June 1976 Whiting was approached about involvement in a "training school to prepare local people to participate in the restoration of some houses on the east coast" (Daniels, 1976).

A date of January 1977 was set, and six marae chose to take part in the training school, with representatives from Rongopai at Waituhi, Te Poho o Hinekura at Tuai, Te Poho o Tāmanuhiri at Muriwai, Te Poho o Taharakau and Te Poho o Rukupo at Manutuke, and Porourangi at Waiomatatini. Contact was also made with many members of the Māori art community, including Sandy Adsett and Para Matchitt, and an invitation was extended to John Taiapa and Kuru Waaka of the New Zealand Māori Arts and Crafts Institute at Rotorua. Heritage New Zealand commissioned Pacific Films to create a documentary about the training school, which resulted in the 1978 release of Te Ohaki o Te Po (From Where the Spirit Calls), directed by John Reid.

The success of the training school provided a foundation that guided our continued approach to working with marae, with a focus on transferring skills directly to the marae community, and maintaining a role for the organisation as an advisor to iwi, hapū and whānau for the general process of conservation of marae taonga.

The collaborative relationship of Heritage New Zealand (and the Whiting whānau in particular) with Rongopai marae has continued since this first training school. In the 1980s a workshop for the repair of the woven tukutuku panels of the wharenui took place, and was followed by a comprehensive conservation survey

undertaken by Dean Whiting (son of Cliff, and current manager of the Māori Built Heritage Programme) from 1990 to 1993. In 2002 Dean Whiting provided advice and assistance as the roof was replaced on the wharenui, fire sprinklers installed, and series of training workshops were undertaken for further conservation work on the tukutuku and painted kowhaiwhai artworks of the interior. A further round of conservation planning has been underway since 2016 for the next stage of maintenance and preservation work.

As news of training schools and other services available for the conservation of architectural taonga became more widely known, many marae from around the country have requested assistance from the Māori Built Heritage Programme, and we have visited and provided advice to over 400 marae communities since work began in the 1970s. A common scenario we see is that as a wharenui approaches its centenary, a restoration programme is planned to prepare for its commemoration, which is often a significant celebration for a marae community. This milestone is one where we often seek to take the opportunity to also look one hundred years into the future, and envision what type of planning we can do now, to ensure that it's possible for these important buildings to survive for another hundred years. This kind of planning involves a variety of considerations, including cyclical maintenance planning, training, and sharing knowledge concerning the traditional arts of carving, weaving and building that are associated with the architecture of the marae, and even planning for the plants that will be required for repairing or maintaining the traditional arts in the future. This traditional plant knowledge may include mapping projects to identify the locations of key species within the areas the marae are able to gather from, and may also include the planting of trees or other plants to ensure availability into the future. Access to sufficient natural materials can be problematic for marae, and even within the timeframe that the Māori Built Heritage Programme has been operating there have been instances of the complete loss of traditional materials from some landscapes. Marae communities can find it difficult to provide for their own needs within their immediate region, and we see more frequent need to travel outside of traditional tribal boundaries to access the materials required to maintain the traditional arts within their marae buildings.

It is not only gradual deterioration that results in a need to repair or replace building fabric, but there are also a number of environmental hazards that can cause damage or loss of our Māori architectural heritage. Flooding has been a regular threat to our marae buildings over the years, with many marae located near rivers and other flood prone areas. Fire is a very significant risk to marae, due to remote locations, access to water, and the high costs associated with mechanical fire protection measures. Research covering the period 2005-2010 showed 13 fires on marae over the five-year period, with four marae buildings destroyed, and our experience also suggests that at least one marae building is lost every year to fire (Soja, 2011).

Earthquakes pose a significant risk to buildings and their occupants in New Zealand, however we have no record of any wharenui ever suffering building failure as a result of seismic activity, and many marae have provided shelter to people following significant earthquake events. There are a number of marae around the country that have been designated as civil defence emergency evacuation centres, but this also brings with it additional regulatory issues that can sometimes have a negative impact on historic structures that may not meet current building code requirements.

Volcanic activity is also a hazard that has affected our architectural taonga; most notably with the eruption of Tarawera in 1886. Hinemihi, a carved house that originally stood at Te Wairoa near Mt. Tarawera, famously provided protection to many people during the eruption, including one of its original carvers Tene Waitere. Te Wairoa was subsequently deemed uninhabitable, and in 1893 Hinemihi was purchased and taken to England by Lord Onslow, Governor of New Zealand from 1889 to 1892. Heritage New Zealand has advocated for the return of Hinemihi to New Zealand since the 1970s, and even prior to joining Heritage New Zealand's Māori Built Heritage team, James Schuster (a descendant of Waitere) and his family have been involved in the ongoing conservation of this ancestral house that remains in the United Kingdom at present. The almost total destruction by fire of Clandon House in 2015 whose grounds Hinemihi stands in has provided further impetus for the return of Hinemihi.

Over the forty years that the Māori Built Heritage Programme has evolved, Heritage New Zealand's involvement with Māori communities has greatly expanded, and this increased involvement has largely been the result of a shift in ideology, shown by taking advice from Māori with appropriate expertise, employing Māori staff members, and eventually establishing a Māori governance body. Heritage New Zealand recognises iwi, hapū and marae as the primary kaitiaki of their architectural heritage, but offers expertise from highly trained practitioners to support conservation best practice decision making. Within our team we have backgrounds in conservation science, traditional Māori arts such as carving and weaving, building conservation, historical

research, and decades of combined experience gained from working with marae communities on a wide variety of projects. It is always our intention that we share our knowledge in a way that empowers the custodians of marae to be the key decision makers with regards to their architectural heritage. At times the needs of marae may include the development of new buildings, the upgrading of existing buildings, or even the reinstatement of traditional elements that may have been removed or concealed. There are times where marae may be completely modernised, with no need for conservation assistance, but for the marae communities who wish to retain their historic buildings and continue the traditional arts that make up the fabric of traditional marae buildings, the Māori Built Heritage Team continues to provide a specialist service to iwi, hapū and whānau.

References

Biggs, B. (1976). Letter to J.R.S. Daniels 27/09/1976, Heritage New Zealand Pouhere Taonga Ref. HP 8/17/3, File 29003-001: Māori Heritage Committee – Establishment and Policy, Antrim House, Wellington.

Christoffel, P. (2005). "Genesis: The Origins of The Trust" *Heritage New Zealand* (Winter 2005) no. 97:4-7.

Daniels, J.R.S. (1976). Letter to L.C. Lloyd 07/07/1976, *Heritage New Zealand Pouhere Taonga Ref*. HP 8/17/2, File 29005-001: Māori Buildings Training School, Antrim House, Wellington.

Lloyd, L.C. (1976). Letter to J.R.S. Daniels 24/05/1976, *Heritage New Zealand Pouhere Taonga Ref*. HP 8/17, File 29005-001: Māori Buildings Training School, Antrim House, Wellington.

Mahuika, Apirana (1976). "Classification of Māori Buildings" presented to the Māori Buildings Committee Heritage New Zealand Pouhere Taonga Ref. HP 109/1976, File 29003-001: Māori Heritage Committee Establishment and Policy, Antrim House, Wellington.

Mahuika, Apirana (1978). "Māori Buildings and Advisory Committee" presented to the New Zealand Māori Council by A. T. Mahuika, 16/06/1978. *Heritage New Zealand Pouhere Taonga Ref*. HP 8/17, File 29003-001: Māori Heritage Committee Establishment and Policy, Antrim House, Wellington.

Orbell, M. (1964). "The Painted House at Patutahi" Te Ao Hou (March 1964) no. 46:32-36.

Soja, E (2011) "Sprinklers for community buildings and places of special or historical interest." BRANZ Study Report SR252. BRANZ Ltd, Judgeford, New Zealand:10.

Chapter 12: Finding our voice in our Indigenous homeland

Daniel Glenn – Apsáalooke [Crow] Nation

Daniel J. Glenn (AIA, AICAE) is the Principal Architect of 7 Directions Architects/Planners, a Native American-owned firm based in Seattle, Washington, specializing in culturally and environmentally responsive architecture and planning. Mr. Glenn, a graduate of the MIT School of Architecture and Planning and Montana State University School of Architecture, has more than 30 years of experience in architectural practice and he has taught architectural design at the University of Washington, Arizona State University, Montana State University and the Boston Architectural Center. Mr. Glenn is a nationally recognized expert in design for Native American communities and was selected to be a technical advisor for the HUD (US Housing and Urban Development Department) Sustainable Construction in Indian Country Initiative and is a regularly invited speaker at national and international conferences and universities. His projects include the Skokomish Community Center for the Skokomish Tribe of Washington, designed to be Net Zero, the University of Montana Payne Family Native American Center, a LEED Platinum project, the Place of Hidden Waters for the Puyallup Tribe, the 2012 LEED for Homes Project of the Year, and the Little Big Horn College Campus and buildings in his family's home town of Crow Agency on the Crow Reservation in Montana. Mr. Glenn's work reflects his Apsáalooke (Crow) tribal heritage. He has been featured in the 2005 film, "Indigenous Architecture / Living Architecture," by Mushkeg Media and the book, "Design Re-Imagined: New Architecture on Indigenous Lands" published in 2013 by the University of Minnesota Press. His work was featured in the PBS Natural Heroes episode "Native American Green," in 2016 and he is part of a team of Indigenous architects led by Douglas Cardinal who will be representing First Nations and Native American architects at the 2018 Venice Biennale.

Author's note: The Apsáalooke people are known in English as the Crow Tribe of Montana. Both terms, Apsáalooke and Crow, are used in this chapter.

In 1998 I was living and working in Boston, Massachusetts, 2,200 miles from Apsáalooke (Crow) Country in Montana, where I was born and raised. I had been away from my home and my family's reservation for twelve years. By this time, I had gone to graduate school at the Massachusetts Institute of Technology (MIT) where I had classmates from all over the world, and I had traveled and worked in Boston, Seattle, Mexico City, Nicaragua, India, El Salvador, Ecuador, Puerto Rico and several cities in the US including Houston, Indianapolis and New York City. I had worked with diverse urban and rural communities including Latino, African American, Asian, and Euro-American people on primarily affordable housing design and architectural research, as well as teaching at the University of Washington, the Boston Architectural Center, and the School of Planning and Architecture in New Delhi. Then, in 1998, my father suggested that I come home and apply what I had been learning with our own Apsáalooke people in Montana.

Ink on Mylar: Tribal work under the BIA

Returning to Montana was not something that I had in mind at the time. I had grown up working in my family's company, an Indian-owned engineering, architectural, and construction company owned and operated by my father, the principal engineer, and my mother, the office manager, both members of the Apsáalooke Nation. I started drafting there in the summers and on holidays beginning when I was fourteen years old, and I worked there each summer through high school and college from 1977 to 1984, along with my brother, who also drafted and then worked in the field on our construction projects. Our projects were all on reservations in Montana and the neighboring states of Wyoming and North and South Dakota, as well as in Arizona. The projects were primarily funded by the Bureau of Indian Affairs (BIA), the Indian Health Service (IHS) and the Indian housing division of HUD (Housing and Urban Development) and included housing, schools, office buildings, clinics, and tribal court facilities. The firm also

Figure 1. View of prairies outside of Crow Agency, Crow Reservation, Montana. Photo by Daniel Glenn

did infrastructure projects for reservations, including water and sewer systems, but I worked primarily on the architectural projects.

Adrian Poncho, a Laguna Pueblo tribal member, was our chief draftsman. He taught both my brother and I how to draft, which at that time was ink-on-mylar by hand. My very first project was to assist Adrian in updating reservation maps for the BIA. It was then that I first learned that large swaths of our reservations are largely owned by non-Indians who had purchased allotted lands from tribal members. These non-Indian owners now make up the majority of ranchers and farmers on the Crow Reservation. My own family managed to hold onto our allotted lands in the Pryor District and Lodge Grass Districts of the Crow Reservation. Through our work I learned a lot about the reservation system and its colonial structure within the centralized bureaucracy of the Bureau of Indian Affairs.

The architectural work, in general, was not very exciting or fulfilling. This was government work with low budgets and low expectations. Tribal communities were engaged, at best, marginally in the work that would affect them. Our work was centrally managed by the BIA through the Area Office in Albuquerque, New Mexico. Tribal housing developments were laid out and built using house plans that were largely dictated by the BIA and HUD. There was little or no opportunity for innovation or exploration. For that reason, I never imagined a career in tribal work when I entered architecture school at Montana State University in 1981. Like most young architects in training, I imagined working on significant works like museums, libraries, and extraordinary houses like those by master architects such as Frank Lloyd Wright, Alvar Aalto and I.M. Pei. However, unlike most of my peers, I was also highly politicized and active in social justice issues and causes at the university, fueled by my background on the reservation. I carried with me my father's strong teachings on social justice and my grandfather's work as a district leader on the Crow Tribal Council. As I progressed in my studies, I became more incensed that architecture seemed to be primarily a service to the rich and powerful. I did not have many mentors or heroes in the field of architecture that offered an alternative path.

The architectural projects in the design studios at Montana State University rarely offered opportunities for me to explore either my interests in social justice issues or my tribal heritage. In my third year, I was finally offered my first opportunity by one studio professor, Henry Sorenson. We were tasked with designing a Native American center

Figure. 2 John and Ella Mae Glenn, paternal grandparents of Daniel Glenn, on the Crow Reservation in the 1950's after returning from Washington, D.C. with a delegation of Crow leaders. Glenn family archive

for the university. I was quite excited by this project, and in our studio research I learned about Douglas Cardinal, the First Nations architect of Canada, and his Museum of Civilization in Ottawa. This was my first exposure to the idea of creating culturally significant architecture that reflected and celebrated Indigenous ways of seeing the world, designed by an Indigenous architect. I began to see an alternative path in architecture.

But each summer I returned to my family's office where we worked on much more mundane work, such as "Facilities Improvement and Repair" projects for the BIA. We were tasked with visiting existing housing communities, the nearly identical HUD homes built on reservations across the country, and determining what repairs were needed. I was struck by how poorly these wood frame, three-bedroom houses were built and how quickly they were falling apart. They were often severely overcrowded, and clearly ill-suited to the families they housed. But, like my own relatives' houses and trailers on our reservation, their walls were covered in the photographs of family members and expressions of tribal culture. The families made the best with what they had. Like all tribal communities at that time on reservations, architecture was imposed on them. They were given little or no say in the design of structures on their reservation. No consideration was given to family sizes, the multi-generational make up of families, the varying climates from reservation to reservation, or the cultures of the people who would inhabit them.

In our office, the architects were generally not Indigenous themselves, although my parents sought to hire as many tribal members as they could both in the office and in the field for construction. Our office secretary, for example, was Reno Charrette, a young Crow woman, who would later go on to get graduate degrees in education and eventually became one of the leaders in Montana in Indian education. She is currently the Director of American Indian Outreach at Montana State University.

But the non-Indian architects were tasked with leading the design efforts, and Adrian and I often found ourselves at odds with their design decisions. We had little say as draftsmen. I recall working on a contract to design a series of jails on reservations one summer. We were required to have a maximum of five-inch width glass for security in the cells. The Project Architect sought to use this minimal opening to create thin slits of high windows in each cell, as an architectural gesture. I could only imagine these poor tribal members, trapped in those concrete cells, with no views of the natural world. We advocated to have a foot of glass with a bar in between to increase the natural light and views of the natural world in each cell. It was a very small detail, but I remember it as my first effort to advocate for a more humane environment in my architectural work. I would have preferred not to work on jails at all, and I don't in my current practice, but, I was struck that an architect could think more about an architectural gesture, a supposedly cool looking thin line on a façade, then about the people who had to live with the consequences of that decision.

Travels: Explorations in Community-based Design

In my fourth year of architecture school, I had the opportunity to take a six-month internship in another firm, and I chose one far from home, in Boston, Massachusetts. It was my first experience working on off-reservation projects. But I was committed to continuing to be involved in socially relevant work, so I sought out a firm that focused on designing affordable housing. I enjoyed the work and the firm, but I was disappointed that our housing designs were largely dictated by a for-profit developer. While we were designing housing for communities with diverse cultures and backgrounds, we had very little engagement with the people who would live in the homes we were designing. I began to become disillusioned about the profession and what my place might be in it.

While I was living in Boston in 1985, I became involved in the solidarity movement with the people of Central America. I learned about an organization called TecNica that was providing technical assistance to communities

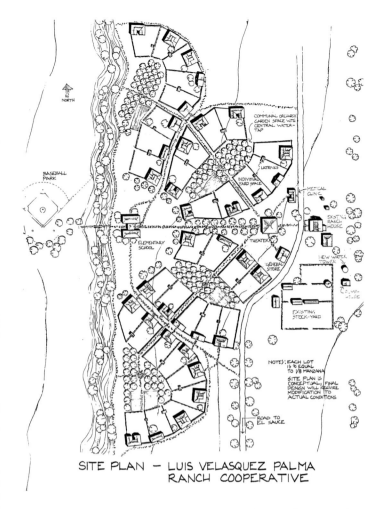

SITE PLAN — LUIS VELASQUEZ PALMA RANCH COOPERATIVE

Figure 3. Site plan for the Luis Velasquez Palma Ranch Cooperate in El Sauce, Nicaragua, 1986, drawing by Daniel Glenn

in Nicaragua. They were looking for an architect to work on a project there. I left my internship in Boston early and flew to Managua to provide volunteer architectural services to a School of Agricultural Mechanization that was expanding and needed planning assistance. This was the sixth year of the revolutionary experiment of the Sandinistas, who had successfully overthrown the 60-year dictatorship of the Somoza family in 1979. They were then under siege by the Contra, a paramilitary counterrevolution heavily supported by the United States government. When I arrived at the school it was surrounded by trenches dug by the students and teachers of the school as they had recently been attacked by members of the Contra militia. In an effort to destroy the gains being made by the Sandinista movement, the Contra routinely attacked any new efforts at social improvement such as schools.

I was one of tens of thousands of international aid volunteers from all over the world who worked in Nicaragua throughout the 1980s. It was an intense and remarkable experience where I felt oddly at home. The landscape of rural Nicaragua where I was working,

with small farms and ranches amidst rolling hills and pine covered mountains, seemed very much like the Crow Reservation in Montana. The significant difference was that the revolution made it feel so full of hope and transformation. A whole people were rising up and demanding a new society with economic and social justice for all. For me it was as if the Indigenous people had taken power and overthrown the colonial government that had put their people on the Rez. I imagined my own people in the process of rebuilding a new society on their Indigenous land. I wanted to be a part of that effort and I began to see a way that I could become a different kind of architect.

I continued my studies and in my fifth year I decided to return to Nicaragua to design my thesis project. I found a newly formed cattle ranch cooperative that needed housing for their community. It was a small microcosm of the larger revolution. The wealthy owner of the former hacienda, a large estate worked by landless campesinos (peasant farmers), had fled to Miami, and the land, the cattle, the corrals and the main ranch house were turned over to the campesinos. These people had lived and toiled away on the ranch for generations, and suddenly found themselves in charge. The stark prairie landscape looked very much like our own allotted lands in the Pryor District of the Crow Reservation where my family are farmers and ranchers. The Nicaraguan campesinos are Indigenous and Mestizo people who had similarly endured centuries of colonial oppression. They lent me a horse, and I rode around the ranch, visiting each of the homes of the campesino families. The big hacienda (ranch house) had been turned into their headquarters, but the families continued to live in rough one room shacks they had built themselves out of available materials in the area. I decided to interview each family (I had studied Spanish in high school) and photographed and sketched their small homes. I asked the families to sketch their own ideas of the kind of house and layout they would like in a new home.

I was inspired by the work of the Egyptian architect, Hassan Fathy, and his book, *Architecture for the Poor*. When he designed the village of New Gourna, he developed plans for the homes by interviewing the residents of a village of squatters and developed contemporary designs based on traditional Egyptian vaulted adobe structures. Like Fathy, I wanted to develop designs with input from the community and using traditional building materials. In Nicaragua, as in Egypt, this was mud brick. I studied local adobe structures, and developed designs using an anti-seismic adobe system for self-help construction that I researched at the University of Managua's School of Architecture.

The Director of the school, Rita DeFranco, became my thesis advisor. My completed thesis laid out the design of the adobe village. It included a village master plan, house designs for 30 homes, an elementary school and a community theater. My thesis document summarized the designs and told the story of the process I went through to develop the design. It is titled: "Machine Guns and Musicians – Architectural Design in Revolutionary Nicaragua," and reflects on the wartime setting of the project and the cultural richness of the community. I felt that through this thesis, I had begun to find effective ways of working as an architect for an Indigenous community.

Before I began my thesis, I came very close to giving up on the field of architecture altogether. I was frustrated by the profession's primary focus on serving privileged sectors of society and wealthy elites. The architectural journals we studied and the architectural history we were taught reinforced this impression. My experience working with tribal communities through the Bureau of Indian Affairs and in affordable housing for private developers only added to my sense that architects were relatively powerless to design work of significance for marginalized communities. Through my thesis project in Nicaragua I started to see a different role for the architect, working directly with empowered communities who are in control of their own land and their resources to create a new vision for their communities.

Developing a Practice of Community-Based, Culturally-Responsive Design

After graduating from Montana State University, I spent twelve years pursuing this kind of work. It began with a return journey to Nicaragua with my former wife and partner, Susan Atkinson Glenn, to provide tools and funding I raised in Boston to help the cooperative build their vision for their community. While living and working in Nicaragua, we worked with another community to create a design/build bamboo house as a demonstration project for the use of locally available resources.

I returned to the United States for graduate school in MIT's Design and Housing Program, one of the few graduate programs in the country that focused on affordable housing for developing nations around the world. I saw parallels to the internal developing nations on reservations in the United States. At MIT I met colleagues from around the world who were searching for ways to improve the built environment for disenfranchised people in their own communities. The program focused on community-based design practice with a strong emphasis on community engagement

processes, building on the work of the planner Kevin Lynch, the schools former director. I gained new mentors there, including the Chinese-American planner, Tunney Lee, the Mexican architect, Jorge Andrade, and the African American community leader, Mel King. In this environment I had the space to further develop my ideas and approach to architecture.

After graduating, I worked on affordable housing and planning projects with Latino communities in Mexico City, rural El Salvador, Puerto Rico, and inner-city Boston, African American communities in Houston, Texas; Indianapolis, Indiana; Detroit, Michigan, and New Haven, Connecticut and diverse communities in Seattle, Washington.

In these years in academia and early professional work, I learned a variety of tools and techniques to directly engage community members from diverse cultures and backgrounds in the design process. I learned the "kit-of-parts" methodology from the affordable housing architect, Michael Pyatok, with whom I co-taught affordable housing design studios at the University of Washington. Pyatok is a master of community engagement in the design of affordable housing communities, and he became a key mentor for me in my teaching and practice.

The "kit-of-parts" methodology is a highly effective method of engaging a community directly in the design process, and it can reveal important cultural preferences. For housing projects, and increasingly in a variety of building types, we engage future residents, community members, and stakeholders in this process, first in relation to the design of the site and building, and then in the design of the unit and interior. The "kits" are created for each project, and include a set of allof the programmatic elements of the project cut out in color coded and labeled pieces, including building uses, walkways, roads, parking areas, trees, etc. We then facilitate small groups with multiple kits to generate a series of design and layout concepts, with the community members laying out different site plan or building plan scenarios using the pieces we have provided. Community members report back to the larger group to explain their design ideas. The process is not intended to yield a single design or approach, instead it brings the knowledge and vision of the community into clear view. It helps them distill their priorities and to build consensus around key design approaches for the project. These are then developed into design options by the design team and presented later to the community for further input and feedback towards the development of a final design option.

Figure 4. Kit-of-parts workshop with the Skokomish Tribe, 2015, photo by Kimberly Deriana, courtesy of 7 Directions Architects/Planners

The "kit-of-parts" method is also a very effective tool to engage people from a variety of other cultures and languages in the design process. This type of convening is an avenue for determining key cultural preferences in the layout of spaces. It has been particularly useful in housing unit designs, where the relationship between the kitchen and other parts of the house varies significantly from culture to culture. In Indianapolis, the "kit-of-parts" method helped us to develop units which reflected a porch and parlor culture that developed in the South for an African American community in the Haughville neighborhood of Indianapolis, Indiana. This translated into unique house plans for a 230-unit affordable housing project called Concord Village/Eagle Creek, a HOPE VI project which was awarded the Boston Society of Architects Housing Design Award. HOPE VI was a federally funded program to redevelop poorly designed and/or deteriorating large-scale public housing projects into revitalized affordable housing communities. I had the opportunity to work with a dozen different communities around the country in the 1990s on these redevelopment efforts, including in Indianapolis, Boston, New York, Houston, New Haven, and many other cities.

Returning Home: Designing the Little Big Horn College Campus

It was when I was nearing the completion of the Concord Village project in Indianapolis in 1998 that my father talked to me about returning to Montana to return to work again with our own Crow people. I had also received an invitation from my undergraduate university, Montana State, to teach in the School of Architecture. I was hesitant to go back to Montana. I was enjoying living in Boston, and working around the country on large-scale affordable housing projects. My father believed that the skills I had been developing could be valuable at home among tribal communities in Montana, and to the work our family firm had been doing. He encouraged me to consider building my own practice as he had done as an engineer there. The teaching position would give me a base to pursue this.

I returned to my homeland to begin teaching at Montana State University. Upon arriving I reconnected with the Crow Tribe and learned that the Little Big Horn College in Crow Agency was needing assistance to develop a new campus plan. Crow Agency is the seat of government of the Crow Nation, and it has been the seat of United States federal power on the Crow Reservation since the agency was established there in the late 19th century. My father, a Crow tribal member, was born and raised

Figure 5. Little Big Horn College campus, view of the arbo, Driftwood Lodges Learning Center, and library/archive. Photo by JK Lawrence Photography, 2008

in Crow Agency. His father, John Glenn, who was also a member of the Crow Nation, lived and worked as a federal employee running the Crow-Cheyenne Flour Mill on the Little Big Horn River in the heart of the small community. The mill provided subsidized flour to tribal members of the two adjacent reservations, the Crow Reservation and the Northern Cheyenne Reservation. My father's mother, Ella Mae Glenn, was a white woman who taught first grade at the Crow Elementary School in Crow Agency.

The Little Big Horn College is a tribal college, one of seven in Montana that was established in the 1970s as part of an effort to bring higher education to reservations during the civil rights movement. Dr. Janine Pease was the founding president of the college in 1980. She invited me to come to the Little Big Horn College in the fall of 1998 to assist with a visioning process to help determine a new campus for the college.

My father and grandfather were well known in the community, and this was very important to my ability to gain the trust of Dr. Pease and the college staff, faculty and board members. My grandfather had become a district leader in the Crow Tribal Council after the flour mill was shut down by the federal government in the 1950s

as part of the Eisenhower Administration's "Termination" policy on reservations. He served on the Council for many years. As a child I would come to Crow Agency with my father and wait for my grandfather to come out of council meetings. He had helped the town build a community gymnasium in the 1960s and it was in that building that the college was established in 1980. This is where I met with Dr. Pease in the fall of 1998 to discuss a new home for the college.

By that time, the students and faculty had themselves expanded and added onto the gymnasium, building classrooms on the perimeter and a second floor with a library. The school was built in a piece meal fashion like this over its first 18 years of operation. As Dr. Pease explained to me, federal funds were not available for capital expenditures for tribal colleges. The US government only provided funding for operations, not growth. So the students and faculty had to make do with a refurbished gymnasium, some portable trailers and their Crow historical archive located in an old house nearby.

Dr. Pease had big dreams for a fully developed college campus with new buildings to house the growing departments and student body. She actively sought funding to transform the school and make her vision a

Figure 6. Interior of the Little Big Horn College library, designed by Daniel Glenn, photo by JK Lawrence Photography, 2008.

reality. But she needed to have plans and drawings to attract funders and gain support from the Tribe and the community at large. I met with Dr. Pease and the college board to discuss an "envisioning process" that would engage faculty, staff, and students in the development of designs for the new campus. This was my first opportunity to apply what I had been learning over the past twelve years to my own community.

As a newly appointed associate professor of Architecture at Montana State University I did not yet have staff or a firm of my own, but I did have fifteen graduate students of architecture in a studio graduate level design studio I was offering that fall. I made the visioning process the subject of the design studio, and harnessed the energy and talents of my students to assist the college. The fifth-year graduate students in my studio had little or no experience or knowledge about tribal communities. The studio became an opportunity for them to become immersed in the Indigenous world of the Crow Reservation.

Montana State University, where the students and I were based, is in Bozeman, Montana, just over the Absoraka Range of the Rocky Mountains from Crow Agency. This mountain range had been the original western edge of the Crow Reservation when it was first established in 1868, and the university is located on land that was part of Crow territory before colonization. Absoraka is actually an anglicization of Apsáalooke, which is the name of the Crow people in our language. The original Crow Agency was in Livingston, Montana, just 26 miles from the university. But the reservation boundary shrank again and again throughout the 19th Century and into the 20th Century, as white settlers demanded more and more Indigenous land. Crow Agency was eventually relocated to a point 180 miles east of the university.

For most of my students, it was a world away. Although there are seven reservations in the state of Montana, and Native Americans represent the largest minority in the state, there is a huge gulf between "Indian Country" and the white world. Throughout that fall semester, I took the students on multiple trips to the Crow Reservation. We began the studio with a tour across the 9,300 square kilometer reservation. We studied the mountain ranges and rivers that are sacred to the Apsáalooke people. Two elders, Dan Old Elk and his brother Walter, hosted a sweat lodge ceremony for the students and me at their home. It was a powerful, spiritual ceremony, marking the beginning of our envisioning process for the College. The students' first task was to create a map of the reservation by sitting down with tribal elders who told stories of the land and its history and marked these on a map. For

me it was all very familiar, but it was also a re-immersion in my family's homeland. It was a strengthening of my connection to my home. Places that I had known as a child took on new meaning as I heard the stories of the elders, the most prominent of whom was Dr. Joseph Medicine Crow.

Learning from our Elders: Dr. Joseph Medicine Crow

At the time we began envisioning a new Crow tribal college Dr. Medicine Crow was 85 years old. He was born in 1913, and he was one of the most esteemed elders of the tribe. He had been a friend of my grandfather, who was a few years older and had passed away by that time. Dr. Medicine Crow had been instrumental, along with Dr. Pease, in founding the Little Big Horn College and he was still an active supporter of its work. It was remarkable for all of us to learn that Dr. Medicine Crow's interest in tribal history began as a boy, when he was told a first-hand account of the Battle of the Little Big Horn. His own grandfather had been a scout in the battle where George Armstrong Custer had met his demise. Medicine Crow went on to get a doctoral degree in history, and was one of the few elders who had both a strong knowledge of the tribe's oral history, and who was also a highly trained academic historian. For some of the traditional Crow elders, his training in western academic history tainted his role as a traditional keeper of knowledge. Traditional oral histories and the academic historian versions did not always align. But Dr. Medicine Crow sought to draw knowledge from both worlds and reconcile them where he could.

Joe Medicine Crow, Dan Old Elk, Walter Old Elk Sr., Barney Old Coyote, Avis Three Irons, and Connie Yellowtail were some of the many elders who told us the stories of the Crow people as part of the envisioning process. The whole faculty and administration of the college, students and many other members of the tribe participated in the process. We held three public design workshops to answer three key questions: What will the new campus be? (Programming), where will the new campus be? (Site Selection), and how will the new campus be designed? (Concept Design). The workshops were held weekly in the gymnasium of the school and led to the selection for four sites for the new campus and initial design concepts. Joe Medicine Crow talked about the campus as a "learning lodge," reflecting on the role of the tepee lodge as the original place of learning for the Apsáalooke people. In the design workshop, we created a "kit-of-parts" of the campus buildings, and explored this concept in small groups facilitated by the

Figure 7. Little Big Horn College Gateway Monument, designed by Daniel Glenn, photo by Daniel Glenn, 2008.

architectural students. One group imagined the campus as both a "learning lodge" and an encampment of lodges. The departments of the college were arrayed in a circle, with a primary entrance to the east, facing the Little Big Horn River. They placed the administration for the college on the western edge of the circle, in the "place of honor" in a tepee lodge.

Another group focused on the Big Horn Medicine Wheel, which is an ancient sacred site in the Big Horn Mountains on the southern end of the reservation. The Big Horn Medicine Wheel is thought to be thousands of years old, and its stone markers create a radial wheel extending outward, with rock cairns marking astronomical events including the summer and winter solstices. The group discussed reflecting the medicine wheel on the campus, with the wheel and its diagonal spokes acting as the organizational pattern for the campus.

The design concepts that came out of the workshop process were developed on four different sites with ongoing input from designated Cultural Advisors from the faculty. At the end of the studio, the design concepts were presented to the college faculty, staff and students, along with a summary document of the process and design outcomes. That document came to be known to the college as the $6 Million Book, because it was utilized by Dr. Pease to help raise the initial funds to begin building the campus. At the closing ceremony for the envisioning process, Joe Medicine Crow presented me with a blanket and sang an Honor Song. Hearing him sing in my honor in the Apsáalooke language was an extraordinary moment I will always remember. He sang about my grandfather, who made bread for our people, and about his grandson, me, bringing this vision of a new campus for our people.

That fall's envisioning process was just the beginning. Over the next ten years, I acted as the campus architect for the college, developing the final campus plan on the selected site, and designing each of the campus's new buildings, including the Driftwood Lodges Classroom Building, the Cultural Learning Lodge, the Library/Archive and Administration Building, the Gateway Monument, and the Dance Arbor. My father participated in the project as well, acting as the contractor for the construction of the Gateway Monument and the new roads and paths for the campus. The Little Big Horn College Gateway Monument, at the entrance to the college, was designed

Figure 8. Opening day at the Payne Family Native American Center, designed by Daniel Glenn. Photo by Todd Goodrich, courtesy of the University of Montana, 2010.

as a monument to the original Apsáalooke territory, which once included most of what is now southeastern Montana. The structure is a four pole structure, based on the four foundation poles of the Apsáalooke tepee lodge, with each pole marking a geographic point that outlined the original Crow territory according to the oral tradition as told to us by the elders including Medicine Crow and Barney Old Coyote. The plaza below the structure is a map of this original territory, and at its center is the current, much reduced, boundaries of the reservation laid out in a granite slab. Over the entrance we placed a quote from Chief Plenty Coups, the last traditional chief of the Apsáalooke Nation. This quote is now the motto of the Little Big Horn College: "Without education, we are the White man's victim, with education, we are his equal."

For the design of that monument, and for each of the buildings for the college campus, I led the students, faculty and staff in a collaborative engagement process with the college. When each structure was completed, a ceremony was held for its opening, and at each of those ceremonies

over those ten years, Dr. Joseph Medicine Crow was there to honor the building with a traditional smudging ceremony of songs and burning sweet grass.

In 2010, Medicine Crow traveled with his son across the state of Montana for the opening of the Payne Family Native American Center at the University of Montana. My work on the Little Big Horn College and its successful implementation had led directly to my being selected to be the Design Architect of a new building to house the University of Montana's Native Studies Department and the American Indian Student Services on a prominent site at the center of the campus. It was the first of its kind in the nation, and the first building to be designed and built off-reservation in the state of Montana that represents the state's Indigenous people. By first gaining the trust and the respect of my own tribe, and creating buildings of significance that strongly reflect and celebrate the culture of the Apsáalooke Nation, I was trusted to develop a building that was intended to reflect and celebrate the culture of all twelve of the state's tribes.

Figure 9. Dr. Joseph Medicine Crow at the University of Montana Payne Family Native American Center beneath his quote etched into the building, opening day, 2010, photo by Daniel Glenn, 2010

In an effort that echoed the work I had done on the Little Big Horn College, I engaged the students and faculty of the Native Studies Program at the University of Montana as well as representatives from all seven tribal colleges in the state in an envisioning process for this new building. It was this process that led to a design that was widely embraced by students and faculty and the state's tribal community.

By the time of the opening of the Payne Family Native American Center, Joe Medicine Crow was 98 years old. His son aided him as he walked around this new LEED Platinum building, which was designed to provide a place of their own for Indigenous students and community. LEED (Leadership in Energy and Environmental Design) is the US Green Building Council's green rating system, and the Platinum rating indicates a building design to the highest standard and indicates a building which uses less than half of the energy of a conventional building. We had asked prominent elders from tribes around the state to offer a quote that we could etch into the building's façade. We walked with Joe and his

son around the building to see his words, which read:

Chichiáxxaa baalúoolak lichikbaaliia huák baaleé íikukkak, baaleé dashdéemmaachik. Héelak Kukkaalaítchee aawáhkuuwoommaachik. Anmaaleeíhehihsheesh libaakoonmaakaawoommaachik.

"We stand side by side in the circle of no beginning and no ending, The First Maker, Creator Of All Things, is in the center. He heard the words of our supplication and blesses us with his infinite love, which is 'Peace' itself."

During the opening ceremony, he once again burned sweet grass in a smudging ceremony to cleanse the building to begin its new life in service of the Native American students. The opening ceremony included representatives from all twelve Tribes of the state of Montana, who marched around the campus oval in full regalia and gathered at the entrance. Joe lifted his feathered war staff and struck it four times on the door. He said he was "counting coup" on the building and then sang, his voice still strong at 98.

It was a powerful moment for the state's tribal people, and for me personally. In addition to Joe Medicine Crow, Reno Charrette, the former secretary in my father's office spoke at the opening. She was there on the stage in her capacity as the Director of American Indian Outreach for the state's universities. The new Payne Family Native American Center was a huge step forward for tribes in their effort to reach out and make the University of Montana a more welcoming place for Native American students. For both of us, we had come a long way from our days in my parents' office working on projects for the Bureau of Indian Affairs.

New Architecture on Indigenous Lands

My tribal work that began anew with the Little Big Horn College in my family's hometown has since extended across the western United States. It has become my life's passion and feeds my spirit. I have had the opportunity and the honor to work with the Navajo Nation and several other tribes in Arizona, the Nez Perce Tribe in Idaho, the Colville, Puyallup, Stillaguamish, Muckleshoot, Skokomish, Lummi, Swinomish Tribes of Washington, the Klamath Tribes of Oregon, and the Tolowa Tribe in Northern California. With each tribe and with each project, I start with the story of who I am and where I come from.

With each project, each new tribe and tribal council, the most important challenge is gaining the trust of the leadership and the community and the voices of the elders. As the architect, we are being entrusted with creating a project that will expend significant financial

BUILDING SITE / ORIENTATION

BUILDING FORM

SPIRIT / GATHERING / DAYLIGHT

MATERIALS / STRUCTURE

PATTERNS / COLORS

CULTURALLY RESPONSIVE DESIGN

7 DIRECTIONS architects / planners

Figure 10. Culturally Responsive Design strategies with tribal works by Daniel Glenn

resources of the tribe, and we are entrusted with developing a design that must provide utility, beauty, sustainability and cultural resilience for the tribe. It must be a true expression of the tribe's culture. We don't consider our work a success unless the tribal members fully embrace the project and recognize it as their own.

With each project we must first design the process, before we can design the building. We need to determine the best way to successfully engage that particular community, and develop an envisioning process and successful engagement tools that can yield a clear consensus vision for the project that is fully embraced by the tribe.

With each tribe, we seek to design for the Seven Generations: three generations of the ancestors, the present generation, and three generations into the future. Through the elders, both those who are still with us and those who have passed, we seek to learn about the traditions, the history and the culture of the people and the place. We

analyze their architectural and design traditions. We seek to carry these traditions into the present and bring them forward into the future as an integral part of the architecture, embedding their beauty and their stories into the patterns and colors and materials and details and artwork of the buildings. Through the Council and the staff, and through workshops and consultations with the community, we work to understand the current culture of the tribe and the needs of the present. It is our responsibility to use the knowledge that is gathered and incorporate it into the building and site programs we develop. We must listen to the youth and plan for the future. We strive to follow the legacy of our ancestors who lived for thousands of years without destroying the environment by building to a high standard of sustainability.

This year our team at 7 Directions Architects/Planners completed the Skokomish Community Center at the southern end of the Puget Sound for the People of the River, the Skokomish Tribe of Indians. The building, which includes a gathering space for the community, a tournament size gymnasium, and elder's Room, community kitchen and fitness center, is on track to be the first Net Zero project on tribal land in the United States. With its photovoltaic system bringing energy from the sun, its air-to-air heat exchangers drawing energy from the air, and its structural insulated panels providing a super insulated building envelope, the building embraces a more sustainable future. And, with a form and materials that reflect the enormous linear cedar plank houses that once lined the coasts of Puget Sound, it celebrates the building tradition of the Skokomish people. Skokomish artists, including carvers and painters, contributed extraordinary designs and artwork to the building. Traditional basket patterns are integrated into acoustic wall panels, stained wood and stained concrete flooring, and tilework. The project seeks to embody the philosophy of "Designing for the Seven Generations."

The Unique Practice of Indigenous Architecture

In 2013, two academic authors, the architect Joy Malnar and her partner, the artist Frank Vodvarka, published the book, *New Architecture on Indigenous Lands*. This book marked the first time that the architectural press acknowledged contemporary Native American architectural design as a recognizable and important genre of architecture. That year, I organized a panel discussion at the University of Washington in Seattle with twelve of the architects from the Pacific Northwest whose work is featured in the book. These architects included both Indigenous and non-Indigenous architects who have designed significant works for tribal communities on tribal land. It was my first opportunity to engage with a number of other architects in this field in a discussion about our work: what makes it unique, what some of our challenges are, and what leads to success.

It also was an opportunity to reflect on what those of us who come from Indigenous communities may bring to our work that is unique. In reviewing the works in Malnar and Vodvarka's book, I think it would be difficult to determine which works were by Indigenous architects and which were not by studying the buildings themselves without speaking to the tribal community. And, because Indigenous and non-Indigenous architects are trained in the same schools and taught the same history and the same methods, I also don't think that being Indigenous necessarily ensures that we will create works that are inherently more Indigenous, without a conscious effort on our part to work in a different way from our non-Indigenous colleagues. I believe that it is primarily the process itself that must be distinct to achieve an outcome that is fully embraced by our clients as distinctly belonging

to them. So what can we bring that others cannot?

Indigenous architects bring an inherent empathy with our tribal clients, a deeper understanding of the issues and the challenges our communities have all faced, and that empathy is critical to a successful process that yields a successful outcome. We have to utilize meaningful engagement methodologies and incorporate Indigenous philosophies into our designs to effectively harness that empathy into transformative architecture for our Indigenous clients. As Indigenous architects, we have a foundation for building trust early on, a trust built on a shared understanding and shared experience. Many of us also bring a sense of a mission to our work. For our firm, we are never just working on another architecture project. We are on a mission, to help undo the years of a building tradition thrust upon us by the cultures that took over our lands. With our work we are part of a larger effort to heal and transform the lives of Indigenous people by creating better homes, better schools, better places. We are working to build cultural resilience for our fellow tribal communities and work toward building projects that are more in tune with and less destructive to the environment, that integrate and celebrate the beauty of the natural world.

The name of my firm, 7 Directions Architects/Planners, reflects an Indigenous worldview that we seek to bring to each project. The Seven Directions in my culture are honored in our smudging ceremonies, with the smoke of sweet grass or sage that is offered to the Seven Directions. These are the four cardinal directions, North, South, East and West, as well as upward to Father Sky, downward to Mother Earth, and the seventh direction is inward, to our hearts. Our elders acknowledge these Seven Directions each time a tepee lodge or a sweat lodge or a Sun Dance Lodge is sited and erected. There is a recognition that a built structure should be a sacred place, not just a shelter or a commodity. We seek to bring this recognition to the contemporary buildings that we design for our Indigenous clients. Because these are the places where they will live out their lives, educate their children, pass on their cultures, honor their elders, and care for their loved ones.

At the recent opening of the Skokomish Community Center a Skokomish elder, Delbert Miller, explained: "When a person walks into this space they take in a deep breath in response to the beauty and awe they feel." That breath is healing for us and each time it happens it gives power to the place. Being in the midst of the patterns, colors, smells, and spaces of a place that is built from the materials and art of their people acknowledges and expresses the value of the culture and can be transformative. It is further removed from the architecture that was imposed by the

Figure 11. A view of the south side of the Skokomish Community Center with its photovoltaic panels. Photograph by Doug Walker Photography, 2017.

Figure 12. Skokomish Community Center interior of the Gathering Space, photo courtesy of 7 Directions Architects/Planners, photo by Doug Walker Photography, 2017.

Figure 13. Apsáalooke Nation Warriors Cemetery overview, Crow Agency, Montana, rendering and design by 7 Directions Architects/Planners 2014

BIA that I worked on as a young man than I ever could have dreamed.

At the end of our panel discussion with architects of tribal projects in 2013, a young woman came up to me and introduced herself as Kimberly Deriana. She reminded me that she was a former student of mine in Bozeman, Montana. She had been one of the students who took part in a summer architecture studio I taught at Montana State University that sought to include Native American high school students. As we talked, I remembered her as one of our stand out students in that summer program. She told me that she had gone on to graduate in architecture at the Savannah College of Art and Design. I hired her later that fall, and she has been working in my office ever since. She has become an indispensable part of my office. She brings a passion to our work with tribes that is deeply rooted in her Mandan-Hidatsa heritage. She too practices architecture with an Indigenous mission and is the next generation developing this unique and important genre.

In April of 2016, Dr. Joseph Medicine Crow, at the formidable age of 102, was laid to rest at the Apsáalooke Warriors Cemetery which overlooks the town of Crow Agency on the Crow Reservation. I had been invited back to Crow to design that cemetery in 2014, and it was completed in 2015. We sought to create a design for the cemetery that honored the Apsáalooke culture. In the Crow way, when a person dies, the elders told me, they go to the "camp on the other side." We designed a gathering place in a circle at the entranceway to the cemetery, and built a low curving stone wall that separates that gathering place from the grave sites. An opening in the wall faces east, with the gravesites to the west on the other side of the wall, representing "the camp on the other side." Dr. Joseph Medicine Crow, a veteran of World War II and the last warrior chief of the Crow Tribe, was the first Apsáalooke veteran to make his way there to the camp on the other side.

Chapter 13: Māori self-determination using dreaming and visualising techniques to build sustainable communities

Fleur Palmer – Te Rarawa, Te Aupouri

Dr. Fleur Palmer is an Architect, Spatial Activist and Associate Professor of Spatial Design in the Faculty of Design & Creative Technologies, Auckland University of Technology. Her research interests are focused on housing Māori communities who have been displaced through the on-going impact of colonisation. Her practice is grounded by consideration of social justice, ethics, sustainability, and kaupapa Māori methodologies.

When I was a child I attended my first Māori Land Court hearing in Panguru, a small town located in the Far North of Aotearoa. It took over a day to travel from Auckland to get to the hearing. As we crossed the Hokianga harbour the skies blackened with clouds. By the time we arrived, Ranginui (sky father) was crying so hard the roads became fiords and our shoes became soaked as we sloshed our way across the marae atea (a sacred open space known as Te Turanga-o-Tu-te-ihiihi, the standing place of Tu Matauenga, the God of War) to the whare hui (meeting house) beyond. Ranginui was sobbing for our people. The hearing was set up as a "benevolent" (Henare, 2014), government initiative to create employment in the region by amalgamating unproductive Māori land into a large-scale forestry plantation leased to a Japanese wood processing company.

In the first part of the 20th century, following a drive to detribalise Māori and enforce dispersed settlement patterns within their communities, the Māori Land Court initiated the first stage of Crown interference by partitioning land in this region into cadastral parcels. The rigid boundaries imposed through the Māori Land Court divisions, was indifferent to the fluid ways Māori traditionally occupied their lands, and did not recognise Māori rights to control their resources. This loss of Māori control over their ancestral land deepened further in the 1970s, when the government amalgamated unproductive Māori land blocks into a large-scale pine plantation. These forestry blocks were leased to Jukken Nishu, (a wood-processing company supported by Japanese interests), in a deal which effectively alienated thousands of shareholders from being able to physically connect to their land. While employment opportunities, albeit limited, emerged through the forestry scheme, it also degraded local ecologies and failed to create wealth and prosperity for the local community (Henare, 2014). Today the North Hokianga has many challenges. The on-going impact of the impact of colonial rule has created a lack of autonomy, disempowerment and loss of social cohesion. This has led to problems associated with violence, drug and alcohol use and a high rate of suicide amongst the younger population (Reti, 2004). People living in this district survive on low level incomes with few alternative employment options outside of forestry and farming, and limited access to educational programmes beyond high school level. Topographically, the terrain is isolated, rugged and vast in scale. It lacks infrastructure, and many houses are substandard. Under planning laws which control how land can be occupied, less than 5% of Māori shareholders who connect to the region through ancestral lineage can build houses in this area (legislation only allows low density housing of one house per 12 hectares). Planning laws are blind to the housing needs of multiple shareholders associated with Māori land, or enabling the development of densely clustered settlements. Through non-sustainable land use practices, such as dairy farming, extraction of native timbers, and the introduction of exotic pests such as possums, stoats, and rats, local ecologies have been extensively degraded.

In order to address these problems in 2012, a series of hui (meetings) were held amongst seven marae (tribal settlements), (Matihetihe, Ngati Manawa, Waipuna, Motuti, Waihou, Ngati Tupoto and Waiperera) to discuss options for future development in the North Hokianga. The community

Figure 1. Envisioning a Future pamphlet cover (Palmer, F., 2016)

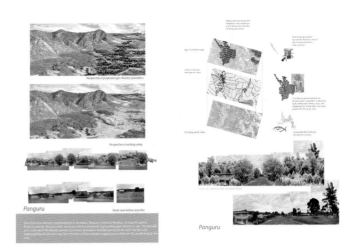

Figure 2. Strategic Thinking

was interested in transforming itself by focusing on the strengths and needs of its people and finding ways to overcome the continuing adverse effects of colonial oppression.

The community wanted to:

- Identify and discuss existing requirements and future initiatives that will elevate health and well-being
- Identify skills and strengths and think of ways to support local initiatives
- Explore the shared visions and values of the community to establish a plan of action
- Ensure that the North Hokianga would have a future – by developing a plan to make the region a sustainable and vibrant place to live in, where children would thrive
- Stop practices that were damaging to social well-being and adversely impacting on the natural environment
- Enable businesses and housing to be developed in the region in a sustainable way

The community was also interested in future development that focused on:

- Health and well-being
- Affordable housing
- Economic development
- Protecting local ecologies

The intension was to find a way to transform the community by focusing on the strengths and needs of its people. The aim was to identify initiatives that would elevate the area, by establishing a united approach

focused on health and well-being. As a means of considering change, a strategic vision was developed based on the aspirations of the community to test ideas and to consider the long-term vision of the community. The aim was to find a way to collectively establish whānau ora (family well-being), to activate the mauri (spiritual life force of the region) by caring for spiritual, physical, social, and environmental health, while also considering employment opportunities, affordable housing and utilising the skills and resources of the wider community (social capital), and collectively working together to make this happen.

To create an aspirational vision for future development for this region, the community had to overcome a legacy of issues associated with negotiating across adjacent and multiple sites owned by individual groups who retained intergenerational tensions after a history of conflict and displacement enforced through processes of colonisation and Māori Land Court partitioning, which had divided collectively occupied land into rigid plots by cadastral boundaries. The impact of colonisation, had also led to loss of control over local resources such as fisheries and the local Rarawara forest which had become seriously degraded. In considering the wider interests of the community, the question was how could a collective vision for the region that supported the hopes and dreams of the people be achieved?

To coordinate the different groups spread across a wide area, and to overcome the residue of internal conflicts associated with Māori Land Court partitioning, the strategy was to synthesise the information collected during the wānanga (meetings) into a pamphlet that visualised aspirations for future development across the whole region. This pamphlet was not only an efficient

Figure 3. Revitalising our streams (Palmer, F., 2016)

way to show potential land use transformation, it also meant that any ideas raised could be widely discussed amongst the different tribal settlements.

In synthesising multiple aspirational perspectives across the region, the ethos behind the pamphlet was based on asserting an overarching role of kaitiaki (guardianship) by proposing alternative ways to use land to activate the mauri (life force) of the region, (Morgan, 2008). In doing this, ideas identified within pamphlet also resonated with the Tū Whare Ora guidelines (Awatere et al., 2008) and the Te Aranga principles (Te Aranga 2008), (a series of Māori centered values developed by practitioners, interested in asserting mātauranga Māori (Māori Knowledge) and Māori values in the design of built environments) as a way to overcome the adverse effects of colonisation.

The aspirational visualisations within the pamphlet affirmed an overarching role of kaitiaki (guardianship) over the region, by removing the barriers and structures of control that had led to the exploitation and devastation of local forestries and fisheries and degradation of Papatūānuku (Earth Mother). To make positive changes, the pamphlet introduced plans to replace exotic pine plantations with a range of Indigenous trees species such as manuka, kanuka, kauri, and totara (proven to maintain soil and water values) (Rosoman, 1994), and plans to actively protect biodiversity by replanting pastoral land areas with mixed tree species to improve productivity, reduce erosion and incorporate timber production with other products such as nuts, fruits, honey, herbs, and fungi. It was argued that the increase in plant species and diversity of land use would, in turn, provide different sources of income, alongside proven benefits in increasing insect and disease resistance (Lin, 2011). Maps identified areas which could be replanted to reduce erosion and flooding and mitigate against sea level rises, boost local ecologies and enhance food security through a broader range of land use practices. The development of a range of industries to boost local economies and

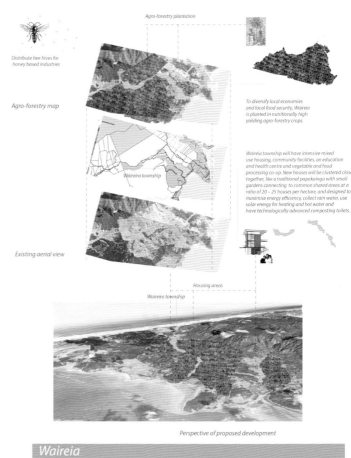

Perspective of proposed development

Figure 4. Panguru

support the wider community were also considered. The existing farming and forestry industries based in the region relied on the extraction of raw materials, but in this instance the interest was in created added value through high end production, like developing pharmaceutical products based on Manuka honey and Green Lipped Mussels. The community also considered benefits associated with developing educational programmes focused on health, sustainable food production, and protecting local ecologies.

To support housing development, parts of the region were rezoned to encourage the development of pockets of intensive mixed use housing settlements located in flood free areas, where families could return to live and work in the region and participate in the education programmes, forestry replanting schemes and create a range of local business to boost local economies. To reduce costs and environmental impact and access to communal shared facilities, areas of proposed mixed use housing areas were clustered close together, like traditional papakāinga (village settlements), with

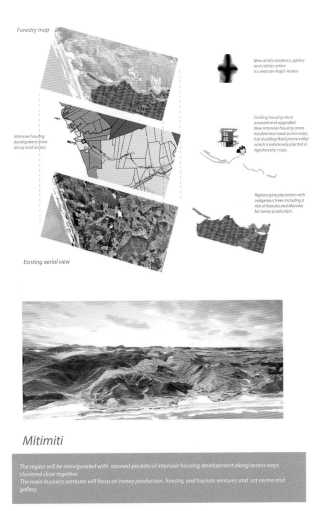

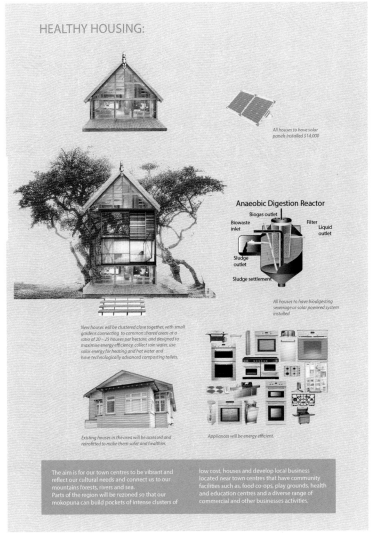

Figure 5. Housing settlements (Palmer, F., 2016)

small gardens connecting to common shared areas at a ratio of 20 – 25 houses per hectare. It was proposed that all new houses would be designed to maximise energy efficiency, collect rain water, use solar energy for heating and hot water and have technologically advanced composting toilets. The development of more intensive settlements would also encourage the emergence of local business, establishment of community facilities such as, food co-ops, play grounds, health and education centres and provide a diverse range of commercial and other businesses activities in the region.

These initiatives took a long-term view of future development in the region, by supporting the creation of a wide range of local businesses in a way that that remained respectful to the rights of Papatūānuku (Earth Mother), strengthening the biodiversity and abundance of the region through non-exploitive land-use practices that revitalised the area, and by creating places where the community could live and be educated in ways that resonated with Māori world views.

With the treaty settlement process, tribal entities are looking for ways for their communities to participate in rebuilding their economic and cultural capacity to support community well-being. The question is how to do this in an effective way? The proposals represented in this pamphlet harnessed the potential of individual as well as collective interests within the North Hokianga region, by acknowledging Māori worldviews, and a connectivity to the environment and reinforcing the community's role as kaitiaki in support of future generations. This process, enabled the wider collective interests of the community to overcome fears associated with individual prejudice, by thinking and looking at wider concerns of this region, such as thinking about where future papakāinga (village settlements) would be developed? How the community might deal with the risk of sea level rise, or stop the destruction of biodiversity and exploitation of local resources? How food security could be better established through more sustainable land use practices and the development of local fisheries? Or, how economic security

Figure 6. Agro-forestry orchard (Palmer, F., 2016)

could be boosted through more sustainable land use practices? This approach enabled the community to focus on aspirations that resonated with Te Ao Māori (Māori world views) to generate something that the community could reflect on and talk about. By showing the region's transformation within this pamphlet, the community could discuss the advantage of making changes without having to invest too much time in imagining how to express these ideas to initiate changes in the first instance. The pamphlet also enabled these ideas to be presented in such a way that the interests of the community could be widely distributed amongst other tribal settlements across this region.

By asserting a shared vision of future prosperity aimed at meeting the needs of its people, the pamphlet was not a definitive blueprint. Instead it imagined a way that the community could move forward, build trust, and think of how to instigate changes to strengthen and enable the region to self-heal. Rather than providing a singular map, the main purpose of this exercise was to create a platform for having a conversation that touched at the heart of a system of values and beliefs already present within this community.

Māori activist Linda Tuhiwai Smith argues that the ability to "imagine a world in which Indigenous peoples become active participants is essential for preparing Māori to strategically plan for any challenges that lie ahead" (Smith, 1999a, p. 124). When new authorities become enforced,

it is difficult for colonised communities to challenge, or make changes to the status quo. The aspirational visualisations of the North Hokianga region outlined in the pamphlet enabled this community to rethink how they might live differently, unbounded by existing regulatory or budgetary constraints, in a way that supports Te Ao Māori (Māori world views). This in turn, allowed the community to reconsider how they might reassert mana whenua (their authority over land) in a way that was more inclusive of their people. While these visualisations do not address how they would achieve their aspirations in reality by asserting their aspirations for an alternative future, the pamphlet serves as a catalyst for challenging non-sustainable land use practices and a hostile regulatory environment to activate change.

References

Awatere, S., Pauling, C., Hoskin, R., & Rolleston, S. (2008). "Tū Whare Ora: Building capacity for Māori driven design in sustainable settlement development." *Research Report, Landcare Research*. Hamilton, New Zealand.

Henare, M. (2014). "The loss to the Ecological Economy of Tai Tokerau, A new look at sustainable forestry of the future." *NZ Journal of Forestry*, February 2014, Vol. 58, No. 4

Lin, B.B. (2011). "Resilience in agriculture through crop diversification: adaptive management for environmental change." *Bioscience* 61:183–193

Morgan, T. (2008). "The value of a hapü perspective to municipal water management practice: Mauri and potential contribution to sustainability decision making in Aotearoa New Zealand" (Unpublished PhD thesis). University of Auckland, Auckland, New Zealand.

Palmer, F., (2016). "Building sustainable papakāinga to support Māori aspirations for self-determination" (Unpublished Doctoral Thesis). AUT University, Auckland, New Zealand

Reti, S.R. (2004). "Assessing The New Zealand Health Strategy in Northland." Masters dissertation. Auckland, New Zealand, University of Auckland.

Rosoman, G. (1994). "The Plantation Effect-an ecoforestry review of the environmental effects of exotic monoculture tree plantation in Aotearoa/New Zealand." *Greenpeace*. New Zealand.

Smith, L. T. (1999a). *Decolonizing methodologies: Research and Indigenous peoples*. Zed books.

Te Aranga. (2008). Te Aranga Māori Cultural Landscape Strategy.

Chapter 14: Everything is a circle

Michael Laverdure – Makwa Doodem, Anishinabe and Turtle Mountain Band of Chippewa

Mike Laverdure, Migisi Migwan (Eagle Feather) comes from the Makwa Doodem (Bear Clan) and is an Anishinabe (People From Whence Lowered), an enrolled member of the Turtle Mountain Band of Chippewa located in North Dakota, USA. Mike is the first member of his Tribe to become a registered architect. He is a partner at DSGW Architects and is president of the Indigenous owned firm, First American Design Studio. Mike is currently serving as president of the American Indian Council of Architects and Engineers and is also a board member and Sequoyah Member of the American Indian Science and Engineering Society. Working with Indigenous nations throughout the USA, Mike has designed a wide variety of projects including schools, community centers, clinics, casinos, multi-family housing, museums and more. Mike also was the principal architect on the first Net Zero school located on tribal lands in North America, located on the Spirit Lake Sioux reservation in North Dakota, USA.

Mike's mother Betty Laverdure, Migizi (Eagle), walked onto the spirit world in 2014. She was a teacher and role model to Mike, influencing his outlook on life and his career in architecture. His father, Andrew Laverdure (deceased) served two tours in World War II, wanted Mike to become an engineer and taught Mike Algebra in the 6th grade.

His mission in life is to promote architecture and engineering as valid and vital STEM career for tribal youth and to have Indigenous architecture create real change in our Tribal communities.

Teachings from my Mother

"Everything is a circle. We are each responsible for our actions. It will come back."

- Betty Laverdure, Migizi (Eagle), from the book *Wisdom's Daughters* by Steve Wall

I remember the day that Steve Wall was at our house in Ipswich, South Dakota. My mom told me a photographer from *National Geographic* was going to be in town to interview her. When he started with his questions, I listened to the stories she told him. I realized, through her stories, she was teaching me how to live a good life. Respect. Humility. Thinking of others before myself. Love. The power of women. The importance of our Elders. Being Indigenous.

We are taught early in life, that everything is a circle. My mother's stories weaved back and forth always coming back to the beginning. She also didn't teach me in a literal sense but through her example and actions. Such as the small comments she would make while we were at the ceremony: "Mike, we are guests here. If you are offered something, you should take it and say thank you." "Mike, you should go help pitch in setting up the tipis over by the arbor." And "Respect your elders when they are speaking. Listen."

We had a large family, and I was the youngest. We are Anishinabe (the People). All of my siblings were grown and away at either college, boarding school, or back home on the Rez (Rez is the name we affectionately term what is commonly known as a Reservation). As a result, it was just Mom and me living in a small town, Aberdeen, South Dakota. In school, I was the only Native kid most of the time. I always had a braid flowing down to my belt line. Being the only Native kid, I was keenly aware of my Indigenous identity. I would get bullied. I would fight. I would cry. My mom would tell me that I would have to learn how to "walk in two worlds" and to "find balance." But, she told me, never forget that I was Indigenous. Those teachings stayed with me. I was both Indigenous and a citizen of a mostly non-Indigenous community and country.

It is interesting, as I come full circle in my career, how my mother's teachings have impacted my perspectives and practice as an Indigenous architect. As I sit here typing this, I'm wearing a shirt from a friend in Canada. It has

Figure 1. Betty Laverdure at Madeline Island, Wisconsin. One of her favorite places for her to be with her family, a sacred place of memory for the Anishinabe people, Source: Author

Figure 2: At the entrance road to the Oceti Sakowin Camp in North Dakota, 2017, Source: Author.

Ojibwe/Cree floral patterns on the cuffs and collar and Abalone buttons. I'm headed to a meeting in downtown St. Paul, Minnesota for a presentation on an Indigenous supportive housing project we are working on. I am meeting with the Metropolitan Council, a local authority having jurisdiction in approving plans and their designs. I have to explain the need to integrate cultural aspects such as a sweat lodge and medicine garden into our project. I continue to live in two worlds every day.

I am a Warrior Architect

At a recent conference, I was participating in a "talking circle." I talked about the many frustrations I had about being an Indigenous architect and trying to work for Tribes. I spoke of the many times I felt rejected. Especially those times where a Tribe had selected a non-Indigenous architect. I could feel the pain in my voice and was glad for the smudge in the room – "I don't understand. Why don't they know that I want to be there to help them?" I spoke words from my heart to those in the circle with my voice beginning to quiver. There was a long moment of silence, and someone across the circle said to me:

"You are a Warrior Architect."

I was stunned. That one statement forced me to look back on my career and service to Indigenous clients. I posted "I am a Warrior Architect" on my social media without any explanation, just a statement. I needed to state it out loud, to reaffirm that foundational piece of my being.

What is a warrior? Merriam-Webster.com defines warrior as, "a person engaged or experienced in warfare; broadly: a person engaged in some struggle or conflict."

Being told that I was a "Warrior Architect" was a Truth. Something which honored my core belief that, as Indigenous architects, we have a moral and ethical as well as a cultural responsibility to our Tribal clients. We have gone to college, as we were told by our elders, gained the technical expertise as professionals and experts, and have returned home to be warriors. We are engaged in a struggle to ensure that the Tribal populations we serve benefit from our services, resulting in an improved quality of life. We also work to address the culturally specific needs and desires of our Tribal clients to realize their dreams for their communities. Sometimes we have to "go to war" on behalf of our Tribal clients with the government, grant, code or funding agencies. Often, we find ourselves advocating the need for a cultural element,

Figure 3. No community meeting is complete without some food. Shown is a meal prepared for a meeting at Fort Belknap Indian Community in Montana. Shown is a dish called "bullets & bangs" (from the slang Metis with a French language base, meaning meatballs and fried bread), Source: Author

Figure 4. Mike is looking out on Gitchi Gami (Lake Superior) on Madeline Island, Wisconsin. Madeline Island is a place of memory for the Anishinabe people, as this is where they found "food growing on the water" (Mahnomen – wild rice), per their prophecies, and could stop the great migration from the east coast, Source: Author.

design or function, such as the need for a sweat lodge and a medicine garden on a supportive housing project.

We are warriors. Indigenous people who go to college and return to work for their Tribal communities are contemporary warriors. Today, we are what our communities need to fight for and with them. If you ask any Indigenous person who has left the reservation to get a degree, they all remember a leader from the Tribe speaking at their High School graduation ceremony, asking them to "go get a degree and come back and help your people." I love the evolution of this concept by Elder Stan Lucero at the 2015 American Indian Science and Engineering Society conference, "It used to be said...go get your education and come back and help your people. It should now be said, go get your education and help humankind and Mother Earth with the ethics and morals of a Native American."

As an Indigenous architect, gaining knowledge and experience to help Tribal peoples, you learn to become a warrior.

Modern. Indigenous. Disconnected.

Modern Indigenous peoples have reached a critical juncture, an identity crisis. Also, architecture in our Tribal communities has become disconnected from the very thing it is supposed to reflect: people and place.

As a practicing architect, I work with communities all along US Highway 2, running east to west along the US/Canadian border from Michigan to Washington State. What I see is a considerable need for projects. But when observing completed projects, there are little, or no culturally sensitive community focused processes, where the community voice and dreams realize the design or development of the architectural concept. We typically see completed projects that do not include the cultural perspective and views of the community and that they are ill-suited for the Tribal population.

> The Peacemaker taught us about the Seven Generations. He said, when you sit in council for the welfare of the people, you must not think of yourself or your family, not even of your generation. He said, make your decisions on behalf of the seven generations coming, so that they may enjoy what you have today. – Oren Lyons (Seneca) Faithkeeper, Onondaga Nation

Metal buildings. Square, stick framed buildings. Many projects are oversized and overpriced, forced through by disingenuous team members. Temporary, modular buildings. Poor quality construction. Energy-poor design. Environmentally conscious degradation. I could keep typing, but I know that for those that are familiar with these types of architectural solutions, my point is clear. Many Tribal facilities are not designed to serve our people. How could this happen? The process of architectural design in Tribal communities needs to honor and respect as well as be inclusive. Going into

Figure 5. Community design meeting to discuss the new Tribal offices & college at Red Lake, MN. Source: DSGW Architects

Figure 6. Chairman Buck Jordain speaking about the Migisi (Eagle) design of the buildings and the cultural significance of what that means to the Anishinabe people of Red Lake, Source: Monte Draper | Bemidji Pioneer

our Tribal communities without a real, collaborative, culturally responsive process is also not Seven Generational thinking, nor Indigenous. It's all about RESPECT.

Architectural design not connected to Indigenous communities through a respectful process that honors them contributes to the systemic failure of healthy communities that last generations. These pre-engineered, poorly planned projects, are usually placed on a site with little or no environmental or cultural consideration. Believe it or not, I've been told to not talk to the community on Tribal projects before, because the public would only complicate the process. Nonetheless, the warrior in me fights back and commits to reaching out to the community, to my people.

"We spend 90% of our time indoors" (Tristan, 2016). Many US architects know this quote very well, but don't realize its origins. It comes from a survey commissioned by the United States Environmental Protection Agency (EPA) about indoor occupancy and potential exposure to pollutants. It's closer to 87%, and it's crucial because architecture, namely buildings, have a central role in examining the cultural practice of communal living in Tribal communities. Proper planning can, and does, improve quality of life when inclusive. Poor design does the opposite.

Why is this important? I want to make the point that virtually every building in Tribal communities lacks

an Indigenous process, an Indigenous architect, an Indigenous heart – yet Indigenous people live 90% of their lives in these buildings. There are many studies on the effects of proper building design improving the lives of the inhabitants. My position is that buildings that use an Indigenous process do something you can't quantify; they create an environment of subsistence and improve the quality of life for Indigenous peoples.

Let's do some math and build a truth.

There are 567 federally recognized Tribes (Wikipedia (2), nd.). Let's hypothesize that almost every Tribe typically has several main facilities: a school, a clinic, Tribal headquarters, a road department, agency buildings, and Tribal housing. Not counting housing, there are potentially 3,000 facilities in the United States located on Tribal land. How many of these had an Indigenous architect as a part of the process? In 2015, the American Institute of Architects (AIA) published some statistics on diversity noting that nationwide, American Indian architects represent less than 1% of all architects. Using this 1% rule of thumb, out of 3,000 base buildings on Tribal lands, only 30 may have been designed by an Indigenous architect.

---

1 Oshkaybewis – Helper in Ojibwemowin. The most prominent example in my people's stories is the Oshkaybewis who helped the young boy learn the Seven Teachings from the Seven Grand Fathers.

I bring this point up because, I feel – no, I know – that my fellow Indigenous architects have a personal interest in providing quality that lasts generations. That, when we are a part of the project, our projects are more connected to people, community, and place. Why? It is because we were brought up by our elders, our mothers, our fathers, and our communities to listen and be respectful. That empathy and the fact that many of us are from a similar cultural background typically results in a project that is successful from a Tribal perspective.

We have a personal, spiritual, cultural, and generational stake in the outcome, especially when we work for our 'home' reservations.

Colonization in Practice

As Indigenous architects, we need to understand that our design process has been colonized and need to work with our communities to reclaim what was once an accurate reflection of our Tribal Nations.

From the first day, we attend a non-Indigenous design program; we study western architecture. We learn about Brunelleschi and the Dome, Pope Sixtus V's new vision for Rome, the Bauhaus, and Frank Lloyd Wright. We never learn about architecture that existed before colonization. In my academic experience, I never learned about the Cahokia mounds (Wikipedia (1), nd.) and how they were the most substantial earthen construction in North America, north of Mexico. I did not learn that a tipi was the perfect structure for Indigenous plains tribes because of its mobility, adaptability to seasonal changes, and why so many different tribes called a tipi home. Even though I was Anishinabe, I never knew about the different types of architecture my people constructed to survive, used as spiritual spaces, utilized as medicinal places, and created for communal living. Every Tribe had its architecture, yet not a single Indigenous archetype was in a lesson plan during my higher education.

During my attendance at North Dakota State University College of Architecture, we did a small study on vernacular architecture. I had done my vignette on a wigwam, a typical structure used by Anishinaabe. We posted our vignettes in a hallway outside of our studio. As I walked down the hall looking at the different projects, I came upon a tipi, a structure used by many Plains tribes. I thought: "oh, cool!" As I began to review the project on the tipi, my heart broke. It noted, "me make um heap big tipi" and "squaw does cooking, brave does hunting" along with other culturally inappropriate statements peppered throughout its theme. I was shocked and angered at its caricature of my culture. I confronted the student, and he

apologized. Was this a result of an academic curriculum lacking in diversity and global education? Or, was it an expression of colonization, suppressing the validity and legitimacy of Indigenous architecture?

Lately, I've enjoyed my engagement in meaningful dialogue with Indigenous design professionals from across the globe. We talk about the colonization of design. What we all understand is that we experienced a colonized education process and we struggle with what the process would have been if we were grounded in an Indigenized educational curriculum.

Decolonization: the removal of colonialism As Indigenous architects, we need to reframe the discussion towards Indigenous beliefs and ideals. Acknowledging colonialism is the first step in reclaiming the process and moving toward a professional practice that reflects a place and a people. The path to Indigeneity.

We are still here. I've heard that phrase many times in recent memory, but I think that Lakota Elder, Albert White Hat says it in a way that makes sense to me.

> It's still here. What was two to three hundred years ago, is still here. The language. The spirituality. The songs are still here. All we have to do is go back and take it. Albert White Hat- from the film Across the Creek by John Cournoyer.

To decolonize the process, you have to look on memory and traditions to live in that spirit let the Creator know what we are doing.

Architecture is about People

What I have come to believe is that architecture is about people. Indigenous architecture is about "a" people in "a" place. Architecture does not belong to me; it belongs to the community.

Removing an architect's ego goes a long way to decolonizing the process. I believe we are here as Oshkaybewis (helper). A real helper, an Oshkaybewis, listens to those they serve and with some wisdom, they guide the process so that the result is a successful project. Successful projects should not be judged by the awards they win or magazines published in. Success should be quantified by a happy community, their view of the project, the measure of success.

> "The Creator gave you two ears and one mouth for a reason." – Betty Laverdure, Migizi.

Many architects like to hear themselves talk. We are trained to promote our abilities and design projects. We learn to think on our feet and to be able to verbalize our thought process and make connections on the fly. I catch myself doing this all the time. I have to remember to listen. To learn from the stories. To practice what my mother told me.

Years ago our company was selected to do a new Tribal Headquarters and Tribal College with the Red Lake Nation in Minnesota. Our first task, as always, was to meet with the community. We adopted the practice of listening. This is the most respectful way to go about any Tribal project. Meet with the community and listen. At this meeting, I heard about how their lakes, Upper and Lower Red Lake, were an essential part of their lives and livelihood. They also told us how fishing was central to their culture and economy. At that time, the walleye population in Red Lake had been "fished out." A five-year moratorium was implemented, which required that the community forego commercial fishing. They worked with the State of Minnesota to restock the lake. The initiative was a success, and the lake became a part of their lives again. More important to them, the Eagles returned to the upper and lower basins of Red Lake, and that gave the people hope.

As we continued to meet, we began to look at site diagrams and aerial photographs along the shores of Red Lake, our proposed site. It was near their traditional Niimiwin[2] (a community dance, gathering) grounds. We gave the community foamcore blocks approximating the size of the programmed and proposed building structures. As we moved these blocks around the site, placing two of the main building components along the shore, as well as located in a radial offset from the Niimiwin grounds, I made the off-hand comment, "Cool! Those look like two eagles around a nest." That was all it took. The Tribal Chairman, Buck Jourdain, from that time forward, proceeded to push us to design the buildings to emulate an Eagle, "Migizi."

As architects, we are trained to infuse cultural elements into our designs subtly. Our architectural firm did not want to be one that designed a project using iconic Native symbolism. We always work towards being sensitive to Tribal cultures. We began to look at the exterior to see how we could start designing some architectural elements to be representational of an Eagle. Our first attempt reminded me of the angular knight on horse sculptures by Antonio Gaudi at the church of the Sagrada Familia. Very angular.

Of course, the Chairman told us, "More Eagle!" We joked internally that this reminded us of the famous Saturday Night Live Skit, "More Cowbell!"[3]

Around that time, I had moved on to other projects, but kept in touch with my business partner, Erik Wedge, who was leading the efforts to finish the design. As he went to more meetings, he would send me renderings of where the concept was going. "Howah[4], more Eagle no doubt!" What

we ended up with was two buildings on the shores of Red Lake, that on the exterior have a detailed representation of a Bald Eagle, made out of fiberglass. The interior remained functional, but the exterior was the result of one focus, the returning of the Migizi to Red Lake. We listened. Again, my partner Erik Wedge understood that his role as an Oshkaybewis was to listen, to provide a project that represented the Tribal collective. To this day, I still see and hear from people who love that building. They like the fact that all of their Tribal government meetings are held there. That their students go to college in a building that affirms who they are as a people. They love the idea that as you walk up to those buildings, you are entering a space that is a physical manifestation of what they know as the spiritual being that carries their prayers to the creator, the Migizi.

Whose building is it anyway? To claim a structure as your own is a colonial mindset. The real success of a Tribal project is twofold: One – Does it serve the Tribal community? Two – Is the Tribal community happy? One may be harder to quantify, but two is easy. There is nothing easier to spot than a happy Indigenous person.

Subsistence

Recently, I had the great pleasure to meet one of my elders and Indigenous hero, architect Douglas Cardinal. During lunch, we were talking about buildings, and he expressed his belief that buildings were female. They nurture, they protect. No other words had to pass between us; I knew what he was talking about from my mother's teachings. If the process is inclusive, it removes the masculinity, the ego, and reclaims it for a different purpose.

I believe that we want our buildings to be Elders and create an environment of subsistence which will help sustain Tribal culture. When I speak of Elders, gender is

---

[2] Niimiwin – Pow Wow in Ojibwemowin. A Pow Wow is a community gathering where Indigenous peoples of North America dance in regalia to songs played on a drum.

[3] "More Cowbell"[a] is a comedy sketch that aired on Saturday Night Live on April 8, 2000. The sketch is presented as an episode of VH1's documentary series "Behind the Music" that fictionalizes the recording of the song "(Don't Fear) The Reaper" by Blue Öyster Cult. The sketch featured guest host Christopher Walken as music producer "The Bruce Dickinson," and regular cast member Will Ferrell, who wrote the sketch with playwright Donnell Campbell, as fictional cowbell player Gene Frenkle, whose overzealous playing annoys his bandmates but pleases producer Dickinson.

[4] Howah – Slang used by many Indigenous peoples in American, expressing surprise or as a verbal pat on the back.

[5] Ogaa – walleye in Ojibwemowin. Walleye are a freshwater fish common to the United States, located in the areas where my people, the Anishinabe, call home.

[6] Asemaa – tobacco in Ojibwemowin. Tobacco is traditionally used in our ceremonial pipes to pray. The smoke carries our prayers.

not the first thing I think of, in fact, the word is genderless to me. Instead, I look to Elders for their wisdom, understanding, and guidance. I think of Elders as a singularity, something to learn from, something to respect. When buildings nurture, protect, teach – they are acting like Elders.

> Elders belong to everyone. We are to instruct our families because they are being destroyed.   We need to strengthen our families, plus our communities and our nations. We must strengthen other nations through the prophecies of our society. We must encourage everyone to be there for everyone. – Betty Laverdure, Migizi, from the book Wisdom's Daughters

Throughout my career and my pursuit of understanding what Indigenous architecture could be about, I've come to a point where I believe it all relates to subsistence. Subsistence is defined as "the act of maintaining oneself at a minimum level." This is something that Indigenous people deal with on a daily basis. It's how they maintain their identity through art, culture, community, gatherings, ceremony, language, storytelling and teaching. This system of preserving and communicating ensures that the people will continue, no matter the hardships encountered.

From walking in two worlds, the Indigenous and non-Indigenous, I have found a distinct difference between how each world approaches the definition of subsistence. To understand how these two distinctly unique groups perceive subsistence, think of the following two examples. A non-Indigenous person may consider subsistence as going out and catching a fish, selling it or eating it. An Indigenous person may approach the same task quite differently. Fishing would be a family or community affair, a teaching opportunity. They would teach the name of the fish, ogaa[5] (walleye) in the traditional language, teach them to offer, Asemaa[6] (tobacco). They would instruct them to catch only the Ogaa they need and to share the abundance with the community and elders. They would share a story, a legend possibly with a teaching that relates to the activity of fishing or the fish itself. The process is generational and last a lifetime.

One of the biggest threats that Indigenous people are facing is the degradation of the "act of maintaining oneself at a minimum level." A lack of subsistence. A few difficulties to living in an environment of subsistence could be – living a modern, digital lifestyle, being away from their Indigenous communities, not using ceremony in everyday activities, the lack of fluent Indigenous speakers, among many other obstacles. That "environment of subsistence" I mention as a keystone to Indigenous survival, is deteriorating.

How can we as Indigenous architects help? How can our interactions with Tribal communities and clients help reinforce the values of subsistence?

Listening to your Elders is an essential element. Listen to the history of your people. Listening is learning. That was the genius of how we educate. Our buildings can reinforce subsistence by learning from the past and architecture can be a reflection of that knowledge. Architecture can enable the power of possibility. It can promote an environment where culture thrives and survives, creating an environment of subsistence.

> "We have to learn through the oral and remember through the memory." – Betty Laverdure, Migizi, from the book Wisdom's Daughters

Indigenized Architecture

Tribes need to take ownership of the design process, utilize Indigenous team members & use Seven Generational thinking in their decision-making process.

> "This is where we come to gather our medicine." – Dr. Twila Baker-Demery, speaking about modern Indigenous peoples at professional and community gatherings.

Every year I get the joy of attending the American Indian Council of Architects and Engineers (AICAE) conference. At the AICAE gathering of Indigenous design professionals, we have been talking about Indigenized architecture. How to decolonize the process. How to come together as a society and create a way forward, helping Indigenous communities reclaim their space so that it genuinely reflects the people and place where they exist.

As Indigenous architects, we discuss ways to create a metric, a method of quantifying the voice, the perspective, the values honored by Tribal clients and communities. A certification. How Indigenous is this project? How do we ensure that our Tribal communities are honored, respected, and provided advocacy in building strongly sustainable infrastructures such as buildings, roads, and water/sewer systems? There should be some technical aspects that are universal. Having an Indigenous architect, engineer or designer involved during the process would be an essential element to the Indigenous certification. Having the first meeting include Tribal stakeholders might need to be a prerequisite for Indigenous certification. Site blessing is something I have always championed instead of the colonial way of painting shovels gold and having a groundbreaking where we bless Aki[7] (Mother Earth), praying for the site and a successful project. Blessing the site and process could be a prerequisite for Indigenous certification.

How do you begin to examine if an Indigenous project supports and protects Tribal communities? Will poorly designed projects that fail or further degrade the infrastructure harm our Tribal communities?

Figure 8. Mike is learning how to make a ceremonial pipe. The pipe will be a gift to a family member. Mike's mom taught Mike what she knew about making of a ceremonial pipe – how to harvest the Sumac, where to get pipestone, how the Creator gave our people the pipe, why Assema (Tobacco) is used and how our prayers are carried to the Creator. A real-life example of Subsistence in action, Source: Elizabeth Laverdure

Figure 9. Three pictures showing the cultural gatherings associated with projects. A blessing for the the Fort Totten Alternative CTE Net Zero school. A song and dance celbrating the Ain Dah Yung Supportive Housing project. A gift to commemorate a name given to the Carl Walking Eagle Wellness Center at the grand opening. Source: DSGW Architects

An excellent example of non-Indigenous architecture that fails our Tribal communities are the housing projects built on my reservation, the Turtle Mountain Band of Chippewa Indian Reservation in North Dakota. Typically, these housing sites are clusters of homes spread out within the boundaries of the reservation. Many of them are quite old and now being torn down. One group of housing has been constructed upon a former dumping site and as a result, has had a history of environmental & human physiological complications. These housing sites, are not based upon our tribal communal living ideals, which would incorporate family and extended family encampments. You sign up for housing and are placed in housing in a different district on a site that is sometimes far away from your family support systems. This mode of housing allocation also worked to assimilate our family systems by providing only single family home structures. This has had a lasting impact on our families and our community. This example is an act of colonization and assimilation. The circle is broken, especially the family circle.

You have noticed that everything an Indian does is in a circle, and that is because the power of the World always works in circles, and everything tries to be round. In the old days when we were a strong and happy people, all our power came to us from the sacred hoop of the nation, and so long as the hoop was unbroken, the people flourished. The flowering tree was the living center of the hoop, and the circle of the four quarters nourished it. The east gave peace and light, and south gave warmth, the west gave rain, and the north with

its cold and mighty wind gave strength and endurance. This knowledge came to us from the outer world with our religion. Everything the Power of the World does is in a circle. The sky is round, and I have heard that the earth is round like a ball, and so are all the stars. The wind, in its greatest power, whirls. Birds make their nests in circles, for theirs is the same religion as ours. The sun comes forth and goes down again in a circle. The moon does the same, and both are round. Even the seasons form a great circle in their changing, and always come back again to where they were. The life of a man is a circle from childhood to childhood, and so it is in everything where power moves. Our tepees were round like the nests of birds, and these were always set in a circle, the nation's hoop, a nest of many nests, where the Great Spirit meant for us to hatch our children. But the Wasichus have put us in these square boxes. Our power is gone, and we are dying, for the power is not in us anymore. We are prisoners of war while we are waiting here. But there is another world. – *Black Elk Speaks* by John Neihardt

How do you incorporate an environment of Indigenous subsistence as an element into a metric? One way is to include the community in the design and construction process. At my firm, we typically design our projects thinking of ways to incorporate building technologies so that local Tribal labor can build them. I first encountered this concept in real life as a young architect, when Nathaniel Corum, another young architect, was at my home reservation on the Turtle Mountains in North Dakota. He was there overseeing and building a straw

---

[7] Aki – Earth in Ojibwemowin

bale project with the Red Feather development group for the Turtle Mountain Community College. I used to visit often during my lunch break to learn the process. A book he authored called *Building a Straw Bale House: The Red Feather Construction Handbook (2005)* used this project as one of its case studies. He writes, "The build offered educational opportunities: the construction process – the heart of the build – served as an open 'classroom' where one could acquire construction-related skills, a deeper understanding of sustainable building techniques, and general confidence boosting." On my home reservation, this community build process is still seen as a success today, and I know many other communities utilize the same strategies.

Here's another real-life example. We are currently designing a community center and gymnasium for the Leech Lake Band of Ojibwe here in Minnesota. We had the choice to utilize either tilt-up pre-cast concrete planks or Insulated Concrete Forms (ICFs). We have chosen to go with the ICFs. Why? Because, here in the United States, most tribes require a percentage of Tribal labor for construction projects unless it is technical and your crews are small – what they term a skilled core crew. Precast concrete is typically produced off-site and then shipped to site, installed by a non-Indigenous core crew from off the reservation. Local Tribal members do not have opportunities to learn skills. Money leaves the reservation; the economy is not sustained. In comparison, ICFs are built

almost entirely by Tribal labor. Skills and money stay local. That's a part of subsistence that many architects, even Indigenous architects don't think of when supporting the local economy and employment systems.

Then there are the cultural aspects of the metric we are discussing. Some concepts that we have begun talking about as Indigenous architects here in the United States have been hard to quantify. We have mentioned things like – Is it recognizable as an Indigenous project? Is it built to last? Did it, and does it still have community support? Is it sited appropriately? Is it culturally and historically accurate? Is it sustainable? Quantifying culture is a complicated concept indeed.

What we are trying to create is a way for Indigenous projects to have some way to quantify and to be recognized for their cultural contributions to Indigenous communities. It will also give the American Indian Council of Architects and Engineers a meaningful way to engage our Indigenous communities and offer real value to everyone involved. We feel this is a 'good way' forward and hope to have a culturally responsive best practice model soon.

Think 7

One of my all-time favorite books written by Edward Benton-Banai is The Mishomis Book. Through it, I've learned about my people, the Anishinaabe and the concept of Seven Generational thinking. Its narrative shaped both my professional and personal perspective about the Seven Grandfathers and the Seven Gifts which are as follows:

1. To cherish knowledge is to know WISDOM.
2. To know LOVE is to know peace.
3. To honor all of the Creation is to have RESPECT.
4. BRAVERY is to face the foe with integrity.
5. HONESTY in facing a situation is to be brave.
6. HUMILITY is to know yourself as a sacred part of the Creation.
7. TRUTH is to know all of these things.

Figure 10. Leech Lake Band of Ojibwe tribal members placing Insulated Concrete Forms for the Onigum Community Center, Onigum, MN, Source: Concrete, Inc.

These are all things I also learned from my mother's stories, her teachings. We have come to utilize this thinking in our firm. We talk about our role in any project as that of Oshkaabewis. It's not about awards, acclaim, or our architectural egos, rather out purpose is to serve our clients with HUMILITY and RESPECT. For the Indigenous communities in which we work, we listen to their needs to drive the budgets, design philosophies, and scope of the project. We have the BRAVERY to envision a new design for our clients. Our expertise and advocacy along with our knowledge and experience give us the WISDOM to design a successful project. Through our belief in subsistence, we show LOVE for the environment by creating buildings as Elders. In building this moment of TRUTH, what we are saying is – does this building look out for the best interests of the Indigenous client we serve?

This is a path forward, Seven Generational thinking or 'Think 7.'[8] I've heard the concept of the Seventh Generation explained in many ways. Oren Lyons talks about the seven generations coming. The Anishinabe Seven Fires prophecy which speaks of the Seventh Fire or Generation states:

> In the time of the Seventh Fire, New People will emerge. They will retrace their steps to find what was left by the trail. Their steps will take them to the Elders who they will ask to guide them on their journey. But many of the Elders will have fallen asleep. They will awaken to this new time with nothing to offer. Some of the Elders will be silent because no one will ask anything of them. The New People will have to be careful in how they approach the Elders. The task of the New People will not be easy.

> If the New People remain strong in their quest, the Water Drum of the Midewiwin Lodge will again sound its voice. There will be a rebirth of the Anishinabe Nation and a rekindling of old flames. The Sacred Fire will again be lit.

> It is this time that the light-skinned race will be given a choice between two roads. One road will be green and lush, and very inviting. The other road will be black and charred, and walking

---

[8] Think 7 – A concept, a model process that I have been working on for several years now. It is based on the Seven Teachings from the Seven Grandfathers and is the basis for the design process that I use.

Figure 11. At a celebration for the Ain Dah Yung (Our Home in Ojibwemowin) supportive housing project. Pictured from left to right: Mike Laverdure, Deb Foster, and Bill Vanderwall. This project will help homeless Indigenous youth get a chance at life by providing a safe place to live and help them reconnect with their culture, Source: DSGW Architects

it will cut their feet. In the prophecy, the people decide to take neither road, but instead to turn back, to remember and reclaim the wisdom of those who came before them. If they choose the right road, then the Seventh Fire will light the Eighth and final Fire, an eternal fire of peace, love brotherhood and sisterhood. If the light skinned race makes the wrong choice of the roads, then the destruction which they brought with them in coming to this country will come back at them and cause much suffering and death to all the Earth's people. – Edward Benton Banai

We are at a crossroads and Indigenous peoples, especially architects, can help show the way to live in a good way.

Seven Generational thinking does not belong to my Tribe alone. Many Indigenous peoples here on Turtle Island have similar beliefs, and their interpretations are all true as well. I like the idea that it is a concept without time or place. It's a concept that follows you. It's the three generations before you, your generation, and the three generations in front of you.

I always tell myself to 'Think 7.'

Giga-waabamin ("We shall see you again" in Ojibwemowin as taught by James Vulkelich. Anishinabe people never say goodbye).

References

Benton-Banai, Edward (2010) The Mishomis Book: the Voice of the Ojibway. University of Minnesota Press.

Corum, Nathaniel. Building a Straw Bale House: The Red Feather Construction Handbook. Princeton Architectural Press, 2005.

Cournoyer, J. (Producer). (2014)Across the Creek [film] Retrieved 2017 December 20 from http://www.pbs.org/video/across-creek-full-episode/ PBS.

Elk, B. & Neihardt, J. G. (1998). Black Elk Speaks: Being the life story of a holy man of the Oglala Sioux. University of Nebraska Press.

Roberts, Tristan (2016). "We Spend 90% of Our Time Indoors. Says Who?" in Building Green, Retrieved 2016, December 15 from www.buildinggreen.com/blog/we-spend-90-our-time-indoors-says-who.

Vulkelich, James. 23 Aug. 2017, Ojibwe Word of the Day, Niimi'idiiwigamig. "a dance hall.' https://www.facebook.com/james.vukelich.7/videos/10213445578989531/

Wall, Steve. (1995) Wisdom's Daughters. Barefoot.

Wikipedia (1) (nd.) "Cahokia," Retrieved 2017, October 25 from https://en.wikipedia.org/wiki/Cahokia .

Wikipedia (2) (nd.) "List of Federally Recognized Tribes." Retrieved 2017, October 8 from en.wikipedia.org/wiki/List_of_federally_recognized_tribes.

Chapter 15: Teaching Indigeneity in Architecture: Indigenous Placekeeping Framework

Wanda Dalla Costa – Saddle Lake First Nation

Wanda Dalla Costa, AIA, LEED A.P. is an Institute Professor and Associate Professor at Arizona State University. She has spent nearly 20 years working with Indigenous communities in North America. Her current work focuses on community engagement, Indigenous Placekeeping and climatic resiliency in regional architectures. Dalla Costa was the first First Nation woman to become an architect in Canada, and is part of a team of Indigenous architects representing Canada at the 2018 Venice Biennale. Her coursework at ASU includes Indigenous Planning, Architecture, and Construction and a multidisciplinary Indigenous Construction Studio, where students work directly with tribal communities. Dalla Costa is active in the following organizations: Executive Advisory Board, Construction in Indian Country (CIIC) at Arizona State University; member, American Indian Council of Architects & Engineers (AICAE); member, Royal Institute of Architecture Canada (RAIC) Indigenous Task Force; chair, Education Subcommittee of RAIC's Indigenous Task Force. Dalla Costa holds a Master of Design Research (City Design) from the Southern California Institute of Architecture (SCI-Arc) and a Master of Architecture from the University of Calgary. Her company, Redquill Architecture (www.RQarc.com) is based in Phoenix, Arizona.

Indigenous people have an interrupted history in North America. The non-Indigenous settlers arrived and bypassed normative systems, including socio-cultural structures embedded as built form. Nowhere is this more evident than in the reservation systems planned by the settler society for the Indigenous people. The grid patterning of the reservation town centers, inspired by economic efficiency and urban typologies, stands in stark contrast to traditional Indigenous environments that embodied lifeways, worldviews, and belief systems.

While the formation of reservations interrupted the connection between the built environment and lifeways of Indigenous people, there were a number of other historical factors that contributed to the disruption of

Indigenous cultures over generations. Persistent and aggressive assimilation plans by government and church bodies, including the legislative outlawing of cultural traditions, and the formation of boarding schools (state run schools designed to educate Indigenous children in western teaching pedagogies), obstructed the retention of cultural norms and practices.

Despite these historical challenges, a number of disciplines are seeing a resurgence of cultural methodologies. This includes natural resource conservation, sustainability, education, governance, health care, and now architecture and planning. Architecture is powerful as a mode of re-operationalization of culture as it coalesces a number of culturally potent subjects such as socio-cultural systems, spatial-cultural meanings, ecology, place-based learning, Indigenous science, artistic expression, cultural regeneration, environmental stewardship, Indigenous epistemology, and community development.

While Indigenous design is becoming an increasingly popular subject of exploration by academic institutions, there are few resources to study. A literature review in Indigenous architecture in North America highlights only three book publications in the last 30 years: *Native American Architecture* (1989), *Contemporary Native American Architecture* (1996), and *New Architecture on Indigenous Lands* (2013). All are written by non-Indigenous practitioners and scholars. While these works serve to highlight historic precedents and the contemporary interpretation of precedents, Indigenous authorship in this field is lacking.

This chapter is viewed as a conversation in Indigenous architectural pedagogy, examining the methodology of a tribal studio at Arizona State University. In the studio, which is led by an Indigenous architect, students work directly with an Indigenous community, providing schematic design and planning services. The studios provide deliverables in the form of schematic design services, while at the same time, provide an opportunity for students to engage Indigenous understandings, ways of knowing (epistemology) and ways of being (ontology).

The studio was initiated in 2016 with a class composed of construction management and construction engineering students. The students, with the exception of one PhD student, were non-Indigenous. The 2017 studio has grown, and now includes students from architecture, planning, American Indian Studies, engineering, and construction. The studio is inquiry-based, given the lack of the literature and scholars in this field and the lack of recognition and adoption of alternative forms of knowing in academia.

The studio process or framework presented here, reflects customs and norms which are common to the practice of Indigenous architecture. The terminology is borrowed from complementary subjects including community based research, community engaged scholarship, place-based learning, Indigenous pedagogy, Indigenous planning, and Indigenous methodology. A recent publication, entitled, *Learning and Teaching Community-Based Research: Linking Pedagogy to Practice* (Etmanski, Hall, and Dawson, 2014) was insightful as it provided a number of essays focusing on Indigenous approaches to community based research. It is anticipated that the approach here, has broader applicability beyond Indigenous architecture. Increasingly complex global challenges, which span topics of economic development, poverty, health, housing, food, and water security, are becoming part of a global practice of global citizenship, and require increasingly holistic, multi-sectoral and multidisciplinary solutions (Etmanski et al. 2014, p. 3).

To structure the conversation, we introduce a process called the Indigenous Placekeeping Framework. The term is inspired from the Indigenous use of the concept keeping place, which I first heard when working with the Blackfoot tribe in Southern Alberta to describe repositories of living cultures. The framework is an investigative endeavor, aimed at initiating dialogue for an under examined subject. With 150 years of settler-Indigenous relations, yet still a disconnect between current built form and traditional built environments, radical thinking is required to move this subject forward. The framework has four parts: community-led (or tribally-led), reciprocity, process-based, and place-based.

While there are limitations in creating research frameworks, specifically compartmentalizing components of holistic knowledge, Indigenous frameworks serve a larger purpose. As Kovach reminds us, the intent of Indigenous research frameworks is "not to be deductive, declaratory, or exhaustive. Rather the aim is to offer a portal so as to study characteristics that the Indigenous research community has cited as being specific to Indigenous inquiry" (Kovach, 2009, p.16). Indigenous architecture, as a subject of study in architectural schools, is a new subject and it deserves to be unpacked, analyzed and reassembled. The subject deserves transparency, in product and process, not only for the students, faculty and practitioners, but to allow the community to be involved in its co-creation. Three studios are described here, followed by four parts of the framework.

2016 Studio: Tribal Housing

In the fall of 2016, the studio investigated housing with two local tribes, Gila River Indian Community (GRIC) and the Tolani Lake Chapter of the Navajo Nation. In the first community, tribal leadership from GRIC identified housing energy efficiency as a priority. They also presented a potential solution: the exploration of traditional adobe construction as a more responsive construction for the hot and arid climate of Arizona. Our task as the research institution was to understand how we could help the community with their explorations of traditional principles of construction. With their guidance, some of the activities we initiated, included: an adobe block making demonstration; a construction studio to compare adobe to other forms of local construction; a sustainable housing survey; a community engagement session; and a prototype adobe and wood shade structure.

Also, forming part of the 2016 studio was the Tolani Lake chapter of the Navajo Nation. The community presented the challenge of affordable single family construction in remote communities. The Tolani Lake chapter, is part of nine communities in the Bennet Freeze area, where land disputes halted home construction from 1966 until 2009. Development was halted on 1.5 million acres of Navajo lands by the federal government, as a means to promote negotiations over a land dispute between Navajo and Hopi. As a result of the 43-year ban, residents suffer some of the worst living conditions in the United States. Tolani Lake's challenge is cost-effective and expedient housing solutions, which includes capacity building opportunities such as training locals in housing construction.

2017 Studio: Equestrian Learning & Education Center

Tuba City, a chapter of Navajo Nation, approached Arizona State University (ASU), to investigate an equestrian education and learning center. The studio was done in collaboration with University of Arizona (U of A) College of Agriculture and Life Sciences. The education center is seen as a means of economic development to counteract the job losses associated with the looming closure of the Navajo Generating Station coal-fired power plant in 2019. Potential layoffs include 430 local workers and another 325 at Peabody's Kayenta Mine 80 miles away. Navajo Nation leadership is working on diversifying economic options for its members, and this studio is part of that investigation. Equine practice remains a strong part of the Navajo Nation culture, horses playing a major role in local creation stories, and tied to stories of survival in this region.

2018 Studio: Urban & Campus Indigenous Design

The 2018 studio to be offered by ASU will investigate urban Indigenous identity, both in campus environments as well as downtown Phoenix, where there is little visual representation of Indigenous culture in the form of architecture, wayfinding, signage, or urban design. With one of the largest urban populations in the country, representing over 500 different nations, Phoenix should be exemplary in urban Indigenous design. The studio will investigate historic locations, sites of meaning and cultural assets, as identified by the local Indigenous community. The studio will bring together Phoenix urban leadership, local knowledge brokers (Indigenous people with insight to local context), as well as faculty and students across ASU including American Indian Studies, architecture and urban design, to define a co-methodology of engagement for the work.

PART 1: Community-Led or Tribally-led

Community- or tribally-led is the base principle of the studio. It recognizes that Indigenous people should take control of problem definition, data collection, research design and dissemination of findings. Community-led research can be situated within participatory research methods such as community based research (CBR), community-based participatory research (CBPR), community-led research, action research, participatory action research (PAR), Indigenous research, feminist PAR, and community-university partnerships (Etmanski et al., 2014, p.6). There are a number of underlying principles that assist in supporting tribally-led research: Indigenous knowledge as complementary to western knowledge, dissolution of research hierarchy and inviting Indigenous knowledge structures.

While advances are being made in combining western and non-western knowledges in a number of fields such as ethno-engineering, ethno-botany, ethno-astrology, and ethno-geology, western approaches to learning continue to dominate university teaching environments (Williams, Tanaka, Leik, and Eiecken, 2014, p. 230). According to Tribal Critical Race Theory, educational institutions should teach students "how to combine Indigenous notions of culture, knowledge, and power with western/ European conceptions in order to actively engage in self-determination and tribal autonomy" (Brayboy 2005, p. 437). Faculty can create the intellectual space in the academy, weaving together Indigenous and western protocols and determining how to create more responsive process and outcome (Jojola, 2013, p.148). Universities can play a critical role, acting as neutral advocates for tribal communities. This role was traditionally provided for by Bureau of Indian Affairs (BIA) but with BIA mired with inefficiency and grossly underfunded (Jojola, 2013, p. 169), the academy can take on the role of advocate.

Another underlying principle is to assist in supporting tribally-led research the dissolution of traditional hierarchical roles of learner, teacher, and researcher. Community members should be able to see an "openness in the university to their ways of knowing and learning" (Williams, Tanaka, Leik, and Eiecken 2014, p.243). This may require overcoming a number of researcher assumptions, including binaries of local and expert knowledge (Ball, 2014, p. 43). Researchers who view themselves as the nucleus of authoritative knowledge production, who bring "field work" back to the center (in other words, the university) for knowledgeable experts to decipher, will be challenged (Davidson-Hunt & O'Flaherty, 2007, p. 303).

PART 2: Reciprocity

Research should be viewed as a mutual exchange. If research provides benefits only to the institution, the project should be rethought in terms of what value it can bring to community. Striving for reciprocity requires considerable investigation to align institutional and community priorities. The following three underlying values are intended to frame the idea of reciprocity in Indigenous design research: usefulness, collective value, and accessibility.

Community based research (CBR) aims to be action-oriented, with researchers committed to supporting the community in improving conditions in some way (Etmanski et al., 2014, p. 8). Similarly, Indigenous scholars have recognized that 'giving back' or helping the community in some way is vital to research (Kovach, 2009; Smith, 2009; Williams,1997). According to Kovach, one of the biggest challenges in community based research is defining what is useful. As Kovach states, "giving back involves knowing what useful means... having a relationship with the community, so that the community can identify what is relevant" (Kovach, 2009, p.82). This challenge, brings up a series of fundamental questions that will not be solved here, but need to be investigated in future research: How is usefulness, or research and architecture, defined in a tribal community? How is usefulness measure in Indigenous architecture? Are there cultural differences in defining the usefulness of architecture?

In Indigenous research, there is an expectation of enhancing the success of the community or improving the well-being of the kinship community over the individual (Brayboy, 2005, p. 439, Matunga, 2013, p. 23). This has been referred to as peoplehood (Deloria, 1975) or kinship (Matunga, 2013). Others have described this as a "bond of kinship through common ancestry" that guides human behavior and enables acts of giving and support (Kingi, Wedderburn and Montes, 2013, p. 343). Addressing the notions of collective value in Indigenous architecture brings up a series of questions: How does collective value change priorities? How is individual artistic authority or expression weighed against collective value?

The final underlying principle in reciprocity, is the notion of accessibility, both of language or technical terms and of information. Architecture is a highly technical field. Moreover, the planning, design and construction of a building is a long-term endeavor which can span a decade or more. Community members who are involved in a project, will be interested to know how their contributions are used and what the next steps are. Effective means of reporting back could include a local website, a poster on a local notice board, or a presentation at a community event: "Inviting the community-at-large to witness, acknowledge, and recognize the work" is good practice (Williams, Tanaka, Leik, and Eiecken, 2014, p. 234). Research written solely for an academic or technically trained audience reinforces western research hierarchies. If the aim is to find solutions together, the work should engender local terminology and communication methods should facilitate mutual understandings.

PART 3: Process Based

Indigenous architecture is process-based. It is about building relationships, defining culturally-appropriate modes of engagement, recognition of differences (in process, catalysts, contextual understandings, protocol and communication methods), and devising methods of co-collaboration. A researcher engaged in community-based work in British Columbia, developed a set of terms, which illuminates the change of thinking required in this field. The terms, though not derived from architectural research, will resonate to those working in the field. The researcher described the process using terms such as: "cwelelep (dissonance, uncertainty and anticipation), watchful listening (beyond familiar knowing), celhcelh (a sense of personal responsibility for learning), and kamucwkalha (recognizing the emergence of group purpose within an environment of trust)" (Tanaka, 2007, p. 3). Inspired by the constructed language of the British Columbia researcher, described below are seven considerations or cautions faced by Indigenous design researchers in prioritizing a process-based practice in Indigenous architecture research: comfort with dissonance, watchful listening, historical research trauma, extended time allowances, periphery knowledge production, responsive methodologies, and boundaries of cultural knowledge.

Accessing the multivalent structures of Indigenous knowledge that emerge during architectural research, requires a certain amount of comfort with dissonance. Researchers accustomed to managing the research process and the outcomes, will be challenged by the uncertainty inherent in Indigenous knowledge production. There is a certain amount of "comfort in unknowing" (Kumashiro, 2008) required for Indigenous community based research. Dismantling researcher expectations at the outset, of what can and should be done in the community, in other words, a reflexive process with open dialogue of researcher expectations will support positive outcomes.

Indigenous pedagogy may challenge a researcher. Often times, there is minimum intervention or instruction in the learning process; learning is transmitted by seeing and doing without asking questions (Battiste, 2002, p. 15). The responsibility of the knowledge transfer in Indigenous learning is placed on the listener. Moreover, questions may be answered indirectly, with a story. It is a mode of learning that is centred on "listening beyond our personal thoughts and assumptions, being aware and conscious of everything around you as you focus on the task at hand" (Williams, Tanaka, Leik, and Eiecken, 2014, p. 240). The process of watchful listening, allows students to apply knowledge beyond the immediate context, preparing them for a variety of circumstances (Battiste, 2002. p. 15).

Next, the design researcher must be prepared to work through residues of historical research trauma. University-based investigators may encounter skepticism from members of Indigenous communities. This is a result of "the long histories of catastrophic interventions by colonial governments that devastated Indigenous lives, and of researchers exploiting knowledge in Indigenous communities and using community members as unpaid, uncredited knowledge providers" (Ball, 2014, p. 36). A rigorous process of best practices and protocols would be beneficial to assist in relationship development.

A further consideration when engaging in Indigenous design research is extended time allowances. Architectural practice narrowly accommodates time needed for community understanding, engagement and approvals. In an institutional setting, where timeframes are limited to 4-month or 8-month increments, and researchers are required to transfer their energies to the next study, this process can be especially challenging. Building relationships with community, maintaining relationships beyond the project or study, informing the university project team of Indigenous ways of being and doing, creating ancillary partnerships to complete the project, understanding and applying local Indigenous protocols, and sourcing flexible funding mechanisms that respond to community driven priorities, takes time. Design research, and the associated engagement should be generous enough to allow the community to affirm their goals and influence the direction of the study, and even factor in time for community members to return with new information: "Much of what happens in a community meeting may take place after the meeting… people discuss the ideas and develop an informal consensus through more personal, face-to-face discussions with each other (Davidson & Hunt, 2007, p. 301).

For researchers, the work with Indigenous communities, may sit on the periphery of traditional academic forms of knowledge production. Institutions set on rewarding faculty in terms of research output may overlook the broad nature of community engaged scholarship (Davidson-Hunt & O'Flaherty, 2007). Changes in policy are necessary to recognize enlarged notions of scholarship to include the obligations associated with non-traditional course offerings and to ensure that faculty are not endangering their careers by engaging in work that does not follow conventional metrics of scholarship (Williams, Tanaka, Leik, and Eiecken, 2014, p. 241).

An additional challenge for Indigenous design researchers is that an approach cannot be designed in advance. The work requires a responsive methodology. As stated by one researcher: "There are no easy protocols or right approaches for outside researchers; rather, in addition to appropriate humility and sensitivity to the politics of place and identity, outside researchers must rely on an intellectual pluralism that accommodates

contingency, instrumental expertise and independent reflections" (Underhill-Sem & Lewis, 2008, p. 315). Moreover, community representatives, community leadership and their priorities may change over time, and researchers may need to readapt the project, as necessary. Creating continuity in a research project by continuous documentation and sharing is helpful in this regard.

A thorough understanding of local policy and protocol with respect to boundaries of cultural knowledge will be helpful. Creating project specific principles based on existing programs such as OCAP, an acronym standing for ownership, control, access and possession (First Nations Information Governance Centre website, nd.) will ensure cultural protections are understood and there is a system in place to guide the work.

PART 4: Place-based

Place is a cultural construct. It is a way of understanding, knowing and learning about the world; it is an embodied location of meaning, developed in response to local cultural histories and moralities (Johnson, 2012, p. 833). According to the CAIRNS website, places hold the highest possible meaning in Indigenous culture: "every location within [each tribe's] original homelands have a multitude of stories that recount the migrations, revelations, and particular historical incidents that cumulatively produced the tribe in its current condition." Community-based research should move away from abstract themes and pan-Indian notions to a preference for the local people and context (CAIRNS website). Two notions are highlighted below, the first as a rationale and the second, as a mechanism, for context-specific work: the human-nature relationship (relational worldview) and knowledge brokers.

Central to contextual understandings of architecture and planning, is the notion of the human-nature relationship. Cajete refers to this as one of the fundamental distinctions between Indigenous and non-Indigenous worldviews (Cajete, 2000). According to Cajete, the relational worldview, where humans co-occupy the universe with other living things, both animate and inanimate, creates two distinct ways of being in the world. Place and affinity for nature, become guiding principles in many works of Indigenous architecture. For instance, in the architecture of the Navajo nation, the largest tribe in the USA, architecture often references the four sacred mountains. To the Navajo tribal members, the mountains are abundant with spiritual, cultural, and scientific meaning. These mountains are connected to song, prayer and creation stories, season and diurnal cycles, and are embedded with meanings which reinforce the values and lifeways of the Navajo people. Architecture of the Navajo requires understanding this relationship.

Local actors or knowledge brokers have knowledge of local conditions and are a mechanism for integrating local understandings (Kopperoinen, Itkonen and Niemelä, 2014; Walker, Jojola and Natcher, 2013). Take for instance the pow wow arbor. To local actors, it is more than a site for a yearly dance competition. Embedded within the pow wow structure are a number of systems. For example, there are spatial-ordering systems, such as the circular directional movement of the dancers; there are social systems, such as the priority seating reserved for Elders or the surrounding circle of tipis, people camping out to partake in the social experience of the dance competition; there are also spiritual systems, embedded into rituals such as the blessing of the arbor site or opening ceremonies. Including knowledge brokers in the process of architecture, guarantees solutions are locally derived, adds credibility, to the solutions and fosters growth in this subject through a process of transparency and dialogue.

Future Research

There are a number of critical priority areas in the field of Indigenous architecture design and pedagogy. First, is the area of urban Indigenous design research. Despite the strong attachment to traditional territories, an increasing proportion of Indigenous people are locating to urban centers. In North America, approximately 50% of the population lives in urban centers (Yellow Bird, 2008, p. 1). The subject of urban identities continues to be negotiated in scholarship, however Indigenous urban architecture remains understudied. A proactive approach to establishing Indigenous identity in the urban realm is found in Auckland New Zealand. Developed by Māori professionals, and published as part of the Auckland Design Manual, the city has incorporated Te Aranga Māori Design Principles (Auckland Design Manual website, nd.). The nine principles are application-based, founded on cultural values, and designed to enhance Māori culture and identity in New Zealand. The principles provide a useful basis or framework for global research in urban Indigenous architecture and design policy.

Second, is to investigate institutional challenges surrounding Indigenous knowledge production and pedagogy. Community based research requires a new frame of reference that must disassemble "layers of resistance to learning in different contexts" (Williams, Tanaka, Leik, and Eiecken, 2014, p. 244). Examining multiple research projects across disciplines, will be helpful to solidify the acceptance of Indigenous knowledge. Once identified, studies can be replicated and refined over time and across locations (Ball 2014, p. 33).

Third, is the value of metric systems to the field of indigenous design research. Could metric systems, such as the Te Aranga Cultural Design principles, serve qualitative indicators in Indigenous design? Furthermore, could metrics have applicability beyond Indigenous urban populations? Moreover, could metric systems increase the accessibility of this subject, for both Indigenous and non-Indigenous faculty, students and practitioners, serving to make the process more transparent?

Fourth is the alignment of institutional and Indigenous priorities. Notions such as usefulness or aesthetic value need to be unpacked and assessed. The need for alignment suggests policy and procedure across institutions may be needed. This could include a central ethics committee, legal duty to consult, or ethical standards for research. It opens the question to cultural competency training or testing as mandatory for those wishing to work with Indigenous communities.

Fifth is regarding the agility of funding mechanisms. Narrowly defined research grants do not assist Indigenous communities in self-defining priorities. Universities should take the lead in creating and supporting proactive funding mechanisms that can respond to Indigenous research priorities.

Conclusion

The Indigenous Placekeeping Framework is an exploration of process in Indigenous architecture. The framework takes collaborative research methodologies and lessons from practice, and initiates a conversation around a framework as seen through an interdisciplinary studio at Arizona State University. The four components presented here – tribally-led, reciprocity, process-based and context-based – are exploratory, intended to act as a living framework for design research between academic institutions and tribal communities. The IPKF advocates a slow methodology, based in building relationships, developing understandings, defining new ways of working, all the while allowing community to direct the work. The studio engages students, researchers and academics, utilizing actual case studies to dialogue and discuss complex global challenges, meanwhile abiding by Indigenous customs and norms, and completing work in service of community. The framework is provided in entirety for reference below.

Community-Led or Tribally-led

1. Indigenous knowledge as complementary to western knowledge
2. Dissolution of research hierarchy
3. Inviting Indigenous knowledge structures

Reciprocity

1. Usefulness
2. Collective value
3. Accessibility

Process-based

1. Comfort with dissonance
2. Watchful listening
3. Historical research trauma

4. Extended time allowances
5. Periphery knowledge production
6. Responsive methodologies
7. Boundaries of cultural knowledge

Place-based

1. Relational worldview
2. Knowledge brokers

References

Auckland Design Manual. Te Aranga Māori Design Principles. http://www.aucklanddesignmanual.co.nz/design-thinking/Māori-design/te_aranga_principles

Ball, Jessica. "On Thin Ice: Managing Risks in Community-University Research Partnerships." *In Learning and Teaching Community-Based Research: Linking Pedagogy to Practice*, edited by Catherine Etmanski, Budd L Hall, and Teresa Dawson, 25-44. Toronto, ON: University of Toronto Press, 2014.

Battiste, Marie. 2002. "Indigenous knowledge and pedagogy in first nations education: A literature review with recommendations." Prepared for the National Working Group on Education and the Minister of Indian and Northern Affairs Canada. Ottawa: Indian and Northern Affairs Canada.

Cajete, Gregory. 2000. *Native science: Natural laws of interdependence*. 1st ed. Santa Fe, N.M.: Santa Fe, N.M. Clear Light Publishers.

Corntassel, Jeff, and Adam Gaudry. 2014. *Insurgent education and Indigenous-centred research: Opening new pathways to community resurgence*." In Learning and Teaching Community-Based Research: Linking Pedagogy to Practice, edited by Catherine Etmanski, Budd L Hall, and Teresa Dawson, 229-252. Toronto, ON: University of Toronto Press, 2014.

Crowshoe, Reg. 2015. "Ethical Spaces: Elder Reg Crowshoe and Elder Willie Ermine." Vimeo. https://vimeo.com/112213678.

Davidson-Hunt, Iain J. and Michael O'Flaherty. 2007. "Researchers, Indigenous peoples, and place-based learning communities." *Society & Natural Resources* 20 (4): 291-305.

Deloria, Vine. 1975. God is red. New York: New York: Dell.

First Nations Information Governance Centre website. http://fnigc.ca/

Friedmann, John. 1987. *Planning in the public domain: From knowledge to action*. Princeton, N.J.: Princeton, N.J.: Princeton University Press.

Catherine Etmanski, Hall, Budd L., and Teresa Dawson. 2014. *Learning and teaching community-based research: Linking pedagogy to practice*. Toronto: University of Toronto Press.

Johnson, Jay T.2012. Place-based learning and knowing: Critical pedagogies grounded in Indigeneity. *Geojournal* 77 (6): 829-36.

Jones Brayboy, Bryan McKinley. 2005. "Toward a tribal critical race theory in education." *Urban Review: Issues and Ideas in Public Education* 37 (5): 425-46.

Jojola, Ted. 2013. "Indigenous Planning Toward a Seven Generations Model." In *Reclaiming Indigenous Planning*, edited by Ryan Walker, Theodore S. Jojola, David C. Natcher. 457-472. Montreal: McGill-Queen's University Press.

Kopperoinen, Leena, Pekka Itkonen, and Jari Niemelä. 2014. "Using expert knowledge in combining green infrastructure and ecosystem services in land use planning: An insight into a new place-based methodology." *Landscape Ecology* 29 (8): 1361-75.

Kovach, Margaret. 2009. *Indigenous methodologies: Characteristics, conversations and contexts*. Toronto: University of Toronto Press.

Kingi, Tanira, Liz Wedderburn and Oscar Montes de Oca. 2013. "Iwi Futures: Integrating Traditional Knowledge Systems and Cultural Values in Land-Use Planning." In *Reclaiming Indigenous Planning*, edited by Ryan Walker, Theodore S. Jojola, David C. Natcher. 339-356. Montreal: McGill-Queen's University Press.

Krinsky, C. (1996). *Contemporary Native American architecture:: Cultural regeneration and creativity*. New York: Oxford University Press.

Kumashiro, K.K. 2008. "Partial movements toward teacher quality and their potential for advancing social justice." In *Handbook of Research on Teacher Education: Enduring Questions in Changing Contexts* (3rd ed.), edited by M. Cochran-Smith, S. Feiman Nemser, D.J. McIntyre, & K.E. Demers. 238–242. New York: Routledge.

Matunga, Hirini. 2013. "Indigenous Planning Toward a Seven Generations Model." In *Reclaiming Indigenous Planning*, edited by Ryan Walker, Theodore S. Jojola, David C. Natcher. 3-34. Montreal: McGill-Queen's University Press.

Malnar, J., & Vodvarka, F. (2013). *New architecture on indigenous lands*.

Nabokov, P., & Easton, R. (1989). *Native American architecture*. New York: Oxford University Press.

Sherry, S. 2013. *Transformative Indigenous community development: Indigenous community psychology in practice*. ProQuest Dissertations Publishing.

Smith, Linda Tuhiwai. 1999. *Decolonizing methodologies: Research and Indigenous peoples*. London; New York: Dunedin: New York: London; New York: Zed Books; Dunedin: University of Otago Press; New York: distributed in the USA exclusively by St Martin's Press.

Tanaka, Michelle. 2007. "Crossing the boundaries into Indigenous teaching and learning: Emerging cross-cultural pedagogy in teacher education." Paper submitted for presentation at AERA Annual conference.

Tanaka, Michelle. 2009. "Transforming Perspectives: The Immersion of Student Teachers in Indigenous Ways of Knowing." Doctoral dissertation, University of Victoria, Victoria, BC.

Underhill-Sem, Yvonne, and Nick Lewis. 2008. "Asset mapping and whanau action research: 'New' subjects negotiating the politics of knowledge in Te Rarawa: Asset-mapping and action research in Te Rarawa." *Asia Pacific Viewpoint* 49 (3): 305-17.

Walker, Ryan, Ted Jojola, and David Natcher. 2013. *Reclaiming Indigenous planning*. Montreal; Kingston; London; Ithaca: MQUP.

Williams, Robert A. 1997. "Vampires anonymous and critical race practice." *Michigan Law Review* 95 (4): 741-65.

Williams, Lorna, Michele Tanaka, Vivian Leik, and Ted Eiecken. "Walking Side by Side: Living indigenous Ways in the Academy." In *Learning and Teaching Community-Based Research: Linking Pedagogy to Practice*, edited by Catherine Etmanski, Budd L Hall, and Teresa Dawson, 229-252. Toronto, ON: University of Toronto Press, 2014.

Yellow Bird, M. 2008. Healthcare and Indigenous Peoples in the United States. Poverty and Race, Vol. 17, No. 6.

Chapter 16: Embracing cultural sensitivities that celebrate First Nations perspectives

Jefa Greenaway – Wailwan, Gamilaraay

Jefa is an award-winning architect, interior designer and lecturer/knowledge broker, focussing on Indigenous curriculum development at the University of Melbourne. Jefa is a director of Greenaway Architects, chair of Indigenous Architecture + Design Victoria (IADV) and is one of a handful registered Indigenous architects in Australia. He seeks to embed cultural connectedness within the built environment for clients including Aboriginal Housing Victoria, the Lowitja Institute, RMIT, the Wilin Centre at the VCA and the Koorie Heritage Trust. He champions design leadership in practice, academia and as a member of the City of Melbourne's Public Art Advisory Panel and recently presented at the World Design Summit and the International Council of Design (ico-D) in Montreal to showcase the value of design advocacy and the use of the recently developed International Indigenous Design Charter.

Sophisticated aquaculture systems that pre-date the pyramids, grooming of the landscape for millennia, holistic understandings of the flora and fauna – these are just some of the many illustrations of the Indigenous knowledge systems that inform a deep connection to place by Aboriginal and Torres Strait Islander relationships to their ancient lands. While such deep knowledge has been communicated over generations within the Indigenous communities of Australia, these valuable insights have rarely been acknowledged, appreciated or deemed to have value today. However, as major cities and town evolve at an ever-alarming rate it could be readily contended, that such understandings have great currency and can provide the impetus for design inspiration and connectedness.

Given this reality, how can Indigenous perspectives, sensibilities and acknowledgement become normalised? And, what role do Indigenous practitioners holds in prosecuting the value proposition that the uniqueness of Indigenous culture is something that is indeed an important national consideration? Further, what are the impediments for the inclusion of Indigenous perspectives within the built environment? And, how can Indigenous design thinking inform the way we embrace our complex histories, hidden narratives, and the opportunity to reframe connections to place?

Within Australia's second largest metropolis, we are building ever skyward, charging through our landscapes to privilege the car and boring through terra firma at a rate of knots. Four projects are emblematic of this surge to transform the city of Melbourne. These include, but are not limited to: 1) Southbank Boulevard Master Plan, which seeks to gain back many hectares worth of public space; 2) the newly reclaimed industrial land which will form the new Fishermans Bend Precinct; 3) the renown Queen Victoria Market precinct which seeks to be modernised and 4) the Melbourne Metro Rail Tunnel. Each project will be built on Aboriginal lands and all will have a strong interface with Indigenous culture despite the challenges and capacities of municipal councils, planners, designers, and the public to adequately grapple with these actualities.

It has puzzled many within the design professions, academia and community as to why built environment practitioners have not embraced, celebrated nor referenced the oldest continuing culture in the world, despite the fortune of proximity to these ancient realities. This conundrum is made evermore stark when considering how Australian Indigenous culture is often seen as shorthand, within an international context, for what Australia authentically is. While we praise Indigenous art, dance and film, our relationship between Indigenous culture and the way we shape our built and landscape environment, has often been conspicuous in its absence.

Thankfully there is an emerging cohort of talented, engaged, and design savvy Indigenous practitioners. More and more are being educated in architecture, interior architecture, landscape architecture and urban design along with other disciplines including transport planning, town planning, archaeology and communication design. The necessity to rely upon non-Indigenous design professionals to deliver projects or specialist

Figure 1. Ngarara Place – RMIT University, Artwork: Aroha Groves, Source: Peter Casamento

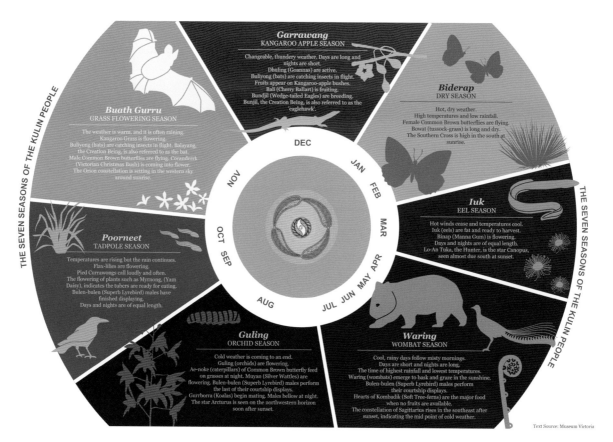

Figure 2. Pedagogical (interpretive) panel – Ngarara Place, RMIT University | Greenaway Architects, Source: Greenaway Architects

design knowledge – by, for, or with Indigenous people, communities or organisations has diminished. With this new reality, the added benefit is that Indigenous sensitivities and world views can be incorporated more readily within the built environment, through these strong Indigenous perspectives.

In the first instance, there has been an evolving trend to explore, capture, and nurture the notions of caring or connecting to Country. This perspective amplifies the desire for Indigenous knowledge systems, ecological strategies and culturally respectful actions to inform how the land in which we share, can be protected, enhanced or revived. Knowledge is what has sustained Indigenous people on this land for hundreds of generations or as Stan Grant well describes "with each discovery a new page is written, dates revised, antiquity measured in millennia. Ten thousand, 30,000, 60,000 years: it tells us what we have already know – we have always been here" (Grant, 2016).

Caring for Country fuses a sense of responsibility as custodians of the land, the seas and the culture to ensure that is protected for those who follow. This spirit of cultural connectedness is explored poetically by Aunty Doreen Garvey-Wandin, when she says "in my lalal's (grandfather's) day, there were no supermarkets. The Birrarung Yaluk (Yarra River) was their 'supermarket' providing the natural resources for the survival of the

Wurunderji (Traditional Owners of what is now Melbourne) gulinya (men). The yaluk (river) is like veins in Biik (Country), winding and turning, bring to life everything it touches, giving our gulinya (men) fresh baan (water), duat (fish) and bundabun (tortoise) to hunt as tucker. We camped close to yaluk (river) for this reason" (Garvey-Wandin, 2014).

Such perspectives convey the depth of meaning in place, the poetics of story, the fusion of history with landscape and the value of language to illicit a cultural resonance, often eluded through the bluntness of translation. However, these very stories are providing impetus and yearning to proudly express one's cultural pride, resilience, and connectedness.

The normalisation of Indigenous perspectives within architecture and the design community starts with the need to build visibility. Too often Indigenous expression, culture, and Community activity is shoehorned within existing built form infrastructure, which is not always fit for purpose. This process disempowers those seeking to fully project one's own identity through the built environment, while remaining a big player in the process of meaningful cultural expression. The subtle expression, often internalised within place, can be aided as we pave the way to what is unseen, by ascribing to a more demonstrative or overt expression, as a way of facilitating and amplifying cultural pride.

Figure 3, Pedagogical (interpretive) panel in context – Ngarara Place, RMIT University | Greenaway Architects, Photo: Greenaway Architects

The technique of making visible distinct perspectives aids accessibility. Given that a large proportion of the mainstream population often indicate that they rarely interface with Indigenous people, culture, or Communities, the capacity to enable cultural and knowledge exchange, can develop a clear means to accessing an understanding and appreciation of the shared cultural connectedness that binds rather than separates the dominant cultures from First Nations perspectives. This approach has much opportunity within architectural expression, particularly where purpose built interventions are favoured over retrofitting often inappropriate places, which have invariably provided a disconnect to place, Community, or culture.

The value of such considerations lies in the ability to acknowledge, celebrate and embrace a bi-cultural experience. This is consistent with what Joe McCullagh, from the Manchester School of Art calls 'bi-visual design' (McCullagh, 2017), or the ability to consider, interpret or appreciate a dual understanding or design literacy that includes one's own design lens as well as those of others, informed by different cultural viewpoints. Such considerations also seek to avoid 'otherisation' or cultural hegemony through humility. This approach embraces impermanence, the unknowable and the unanswerable as a way of falling into the realm of 'designosaurs,' that

is, those who narrow their design understanding to only a blinkered point of cultural access as to resign themselves to design irrelevance (McCullagh 2017). The broadening of education perspectives that infuses Indigenous perspectives into design teaching and eventually design thinking therefore provides a further means to embed many voices and cultural interactions.

There is a strong trend in recent years to Indigenise curricula within architectural and design education. By way of example, the University in which I am engaged (the University of Melbourne) has constructed a new academic role which seeks to embed Indigenous sensibilities, perspectives and knowledge systems by reshaping the design degree in both discrete and potentially more fundamental ways. This degree encompasses twelves design disciplines, within the design faculty. The approach demonstrates that there is a subtle yet significant shift, that sees that benefit of connecting to this place which centres design education upon the foundations of deep history and meaning. Similarly, there are numerous Universities, including the McEwan School of Architecture at Laurentian University (Sudbury, Canada), which has created what Dr. Terrance Galvin titled in his recent presentation at the World Design Summit, "a radical experiment in architectural education" (Galvin, 2017), whereby they have implemented a pedagogical structure that embeds a cumulative Indigenous knowledge experience, with design build studios and Elders-in-residence initiatives.

This reinforces the importance of Indigenous practitioners and design trained Indigenous academics as having a unique and distinct role as critical interlocutors and interpreters. This comes with a responsibility as such contributors become key connectors, facilitators, and enablers as well as being cultural knowledge brokers. These leadership roles move beyond strictly Community, but rather have a broader appeal and relevance. As Wesley Enoch well puts it "we are both a moral authority – gifted to us through our heritage, and the history of injustice and the continued connection to this landscape – and we also have solutions that are based on the concept of putting the arts and our cultural expression in the centre of our society" (Enoch, 2014).

The process of cultural exchange has many layers; it requires a process of listening – deep listening, it requires patience and generosity of spirit, which Indigenous people have in abundance, and it requires an acute attention to protocols and processes that places acknowledgement, authorisation and input from Elders at its centre. Consequently, such important roles act as a cultural bridge or design diplomacy to ensure that we move to

Figure 4, Urban design intervention, Ngarara Place, RMIT University | Greenaway Architects, Photo: Peter Casamento

a space that moves beyond the simplistic or tokenistic, towards a considered approach that captures the rich affinities that reside in Indigenous culture.

Setting aside the deep discourse on the ravages of colonisation, racialized attitudes and deliberate obfuscation towards the motives of those with power, which have undoubtedly impacted on the active Indigenous participation within the built environment, there are a series of quite straight forward and tangible inhibitors, to Indigenous involvement in architecture and design.

Cultural relevance within design education and curriculum is needed across all Australian design schools. Apart from the example above, a cursory review of architectural education in Australia reveals very little obvious engagement with Indigenous culture or specific subjects that build capacity among the design leaders of tomorrow. This cultural amnesia belies the anecdotal interest among staff and students, as well as the emerging trend to meaningfully engage with Indigenous

perspectives, particularly among government and industry bodies over the past 5-10 years in Australia.

The simple solution is to draw upon the cohort of Indigenous practitioners to actively role model and showcase the stories, the journeys and successes that enabled them to have a voice within the professions that shape our environments, our places and our communities. As is clearly known, it is very difficult to aspire to become that which one cannot see. To put a face and a name to those trail blazers who have made a pathway through offers real value. Coupled with design advocacy, from organisations such as Indigenous Architecture and Design Victoria [IADV], a not-for-profit network of design practitioners, graduates and students – new voices can be heard that showcase the projects, experiences and challenges encountered. There are a series of positive initiatives and networks evolving, which endeavour to explore through research, case studies and events a public awareness of those practitioners deeply immersed in the design realm. These include the International Council of Design (ico-D) endorsed

Figure 5, Landscape design, Ngarara Place, RMIT University | Greenaway Architects, Photo: Peter Casamento

International Indigenous Design Network – Indigo, which utilises a series of global design ambassadors to connect, celebrate and engage in design from an Indigenous perspective. Other organisations include the Koorie Heritage Trust in Victoria, which at more than thirty years old, is one of the more established organisations which acts as a tangible and productive bridge between Indigenous people and artistic/design practice and expression. As an Aboriginal run and created institution it has become a key point of contact, a visual expression of cultural identity and a destination that embraces its reference to place as a badge of honour, while eschewing a simplistic view that Aboriginal culture is all the same. The references within its own purpose designed space privileges Kulin Nation culture (representative of the five language groups, that make up the broader Melbourne metropolitan area), to show the distinctness of Aboriginal culture in the South East of Australia.

Where an active and collaborative model within tertiary institutions, which specifically targets the creative talents of prospective Indigenous students are embraced, the design education experience becomes a positive and empowering journey. This however requires a concerted effort to support through lateral pathways of entry, clear wrap around services, which also provide the culturally nuanced scaffolding to assist in the long, intense and depth of engagement to make it through, along with a level of cultural awareness to respond to the specific needs of students often overwhelmed by the cultural shock of a tertiary environment.

This also requires a depth of engagement internal to tertiary institutions among both academic and professional staff. Those directly interacting with Indigenous students or Indigenous content within design teaching require the necessary skills or tool kit to draw upon to ensure a cultural responsiveness that eschews a rudimentary level of engagement. Importantly the next level of engagement seeks to raise the level of cultural competency required to do this in a meaningful way. This becomes pivotal and a means to crossing the rubicon of Indigenous knowledge and sensibilities to authentically contribute to new ways of incorporating distinct

Figure 6. Koorie Heritage Trust | IADV with Lyons, Photo: Peter Bennetts

Figure 7. The 'gathering table', Koorie Heritage Trust | IADV with Lyons, Photo: Peter Bennetts

Figure 8. The Koorie Heritage Trust | IADV with Lyons Photo: Peter Bennetts

Figure 9. The Koorie Heritage Trust | IADV with Lyons Photo: Peter Bennetts

perspectives and deep time knowledge. By engaging with Indigenous voices, one can limit the unavoidable cultural faux pas or the fear of "walking on cultural egg shells" shifting to a productive and informed approach which embeds inclusivity while embracing diverse perspectives.

The value of this manifesto of Indigenous awakening, within the architectural and design disciplines is to embrace Indigenous design thinking as both aspirational and valuable to all. The advantages are threefold; it enables Indigenous led approaches, it facilitates First Nations collaborations, and communicates the values of such thinking predicated on defined systems or protocols to enable best practice.

Further, the use of case studies of exemplar designs by Indigenous practitioners becomes a useful way to unpack the sophisticated, culturally responsive and unique methods used in a project which often straddle culturally complex and challenging political environments. Two examples come to mind, which illustrate well some of the issues encountered through the interface of Indigenous culture and the desire to develop a design solution. The first project was for an urban/landscape/public intervention within a city-based University located in Melbourne. The brief was to create a culturally safe space for the Indigenous unit within RMIT University – known as the Ngarara Wilin Centre. The genesis of the design idea was to celebrate a sense of cultural continuity. This started as an acknowledgement that there was, is and will always be an Indigenous presence, even within a major city like Melbourne.

The design inspiration became the seven seasons of the Kulin Nation (being the five language groups which make up the broader Melbourne metropolitan area). These ideas were explored by breaking down the distinctions between design disciplines in favour of a collaborative model which combined the skills of an Aboriginal design collective including an architect, landscape designer, and artist to showcase a cultural connectedness through an unashamedly contemporary design lens. The design resulted in a space for cultural practice, including for use in the traditional 'welcome to Country' ceremony and provision for traditional dance. The design centred on a sculptural fire pit, with an amphitheatre effect capitalising on the adjacent topography, enabling a place for respite and contemplation with perimeter seating and a landscape incorporating edible and medicinal plants as well as plants which would have been used for weaving – all localised to the specific bio region in which the site was located. The design for "Ngarara Place" demonstrates that cultural reference points, coupled with a purposeful dialogue with the (Indigenous) client, including liaising

with Traditional Owner groups, can result in a place of cultural significance which is both contemporary, draws upon cultural motifs while embracing a connection to history and meaning predicated on strong emphasis on a connection to Country.

The second case study explores how collaboration can utilise the skill of Indigenous contributors to facilitate a partnership embedding a process that guides the evolution of a design proposition to ensure that it remains cultural responsive. This project was the for the relocation of one of Australia's oldest cultural institution or "keeping place," which is the custodian of over 6,000 pieces of art, artefacts and photographs of great cultural significance to Indigenous peoples, particularly from the South East of Australia. A collaboration between IADV and Lyons architects, oversaw the relocation of the Koorie Heritage Trust from the literal and figurative fringes of the city to the cultural heart of Melbourne. This project explored how to weave an Indigenous narrative within the very DNA of the project.

Located adjacent to Birrarung (or the "River of Mists") better known as the Yarra River, the existing building to be internally refurbished, turned its back on the river. These shortcomings were an opportunity to remedy this reality by embedding a journey that evoked connections to water, to landscape, and to stories. The project built over three levels required the ability to pull people up vertically through the building from a plaza level on the ground floor through an intermediate floor not part of the client's tenancy to the upper most level. A carefully calibrated engagement strategy, along with a considered level of cultural advocacy and design input, resulted in a design which referenced traditional artistic practices of Indigenous peoples of the South East, the use of traditional language embedded within the architecture and a palette and materiality that referenced river banks, water and washed river pebbles. Contemporary references to carved trees, shield patterns, traditional canoes, and Indigenous astronomy in ceiling lights sought to evoke a sensory engagement with place and story.

The project showcased culture in a manner which became accessible, visible, and celebratory. It reinforced the importance of connections to the landscape, the value of conversation within a cultural space while encouraging the normalisation of Indigenous perspectives in the conception of a design solution. The use of Indigenous knowledge brokers acted as a conduit between the Indigenous led cultural organisation and the design team, while utilising the transferrable skills of Indigenous design thinking and education to provide a highly evolved layer of cultural meaning into the project.

Where Indigenous agency is facilitated, empowerment and emancipation soon follows. Indigenous practitioners and academics are fast developing and consolidating their skills, knowledge and confidence here in Australia, as they begin to shape the conversation while being actively sought out to contribute to projects, policy and knowledge exchange. However, given that there are still less than about a dozen or so Indigenous design professionals in private practice nationally, there is still much to be learned and much development to happen. This is where international exchange among First Nations practitioners provides real potential for learning, benchmarking and collaboration. Recent developments in Canada, New Zealand and Australia are resulting in coalitions willing to connect, to network and exchange experiences.

The result of such engagement is revealing parallel work around Indigenous determined protocols, processes, and frameworks which seek to guide or codify a methodology that considers Indigenous culture among designers, consumers of design, as well as a focus on the representation of culture in appropriate rather than "appropriating" ways. Such work is endeavouring to safeguard the integrity of cultural considerations, while empowering practitioners (Indigenous and non-Indigenous alike) to implement strategies that are mindful and respectful of Indigenous knowledge and cultural expression.

In recent times, a partnership between Deakin University in Melbourne, the Design Institute of Australia (DIA) and Indigenous Architecture and Design Victoria [IADV] has developed an Australian Indigenous Design Charter, initially focussing on communication design, which has evolved into a broader examination and realisation of the "International Indigenous Design Charter – Protocols for sharing Indigenous knowledge in commercial design practice" (Kennedy, Kelly & Greenaway, 2017). Through a series of international workshops and conversations among First Nations stakeholders, these open source documents encourage, through an iterative process the adaptation, evolution, and development of the charter/s to explicitly relate to local variances and considerations. Such documents, plus a series of other comparable protocols are evolving through various Universities in Australia and will invariably become the means to test appropriate processes and to ensure accountability and best practice methods can be realised.

A broadening of the frame of reference in which architectural and design stakeholders tackle cultural considerations, particularly focussing on placemaking, is predicated on actively prosecuting the value proposition of "alternative" (and invariably complementary) perspectives on place, people, and process. Indigenous knowledge systems, evolved over thousands of generations along with contemporary evolutions of Indigenous identity, cultural expressions, and sustainable practices offer much that can be embraced by the broader design disciplines. With the convergence of design thinking coupled with Indigenous perspectives that focus on a holistic approach to placemaking, a truly collaborative and multi-disciplinary technique, which imbues a silo-less ethos can be realised. The transformative effect of such thinking can begin a new inclusive chapter which can provide a distinct character that is rooted in place, rather than a homogenous globalised construct of design. It is clear that there is now an emerging appetite to avoid the shortcomings of the past, which have often been blinkered to the depth of Indigenous perspectives, as we move towards developing an enhanced spirit of reconciliation while providing an optimistic way ahead.

References

Enoch, W. (2014). "Wesley Enoch on the Strengths of Indigenous Cultural Leadership" *Daily Review*, Retrieved 2017, December 28 from https://dailyreview.com.au/wesley-enoch-on-the-strengths-of-Indigenous-cultural-leadership/11589/

Galvin, T. (2017) "Laurentian Architecture Laurentienne: A radical experiment in architectural education." presentation at the *World Design Summit*, 18 October 2017, Montreal.

Garvey-Wandin, D. (2014) The Durrung of the Yan-yan' in Nyernila – *Listen Continuously: Aboriginal Creation Stories of Victoria*, Southbank, VIC: Arts Victoria

Grant, S. 2016 *Talking to My Country*, p. 11. Sydney, NSW: Harper Collins Publishers

Kennedy, R., Kelly, M and Greenaway, J. (2017) "International Indigenous Design Charter: Protocols for sharing Indigenous knowledge in commercial design practice," (an iterative open source document prepared in collaboration with Indigenous Architecture and Design Victoria, the Design Institute of Australia and Deakin University). Retrieved 2017, December 20 from http://www.indigo-Indigenousdesignnetwork.org.au/design_charter/

McCullagh, J. (2017) "Flux in the UK – focussing on unpredictable design education encounters", presentation at the *International Council of Design Platform Meetings*, 14 October 2017, Montreal.

Chapter 17: Contemporary papakāinga design – principles and applications

Jade Kake – Ngāpuhi (Ngāti Hau me Te Parawhau), Te Whakatōhea, Te Arawa

Jade Kake (BArchDes, GradCertDigDes, MArch(Prof)) is an architectural designer, housing advocate and researcher. She has experience working directly with Māori land trusts and other Māori organisations to realise their aspirations, particularly around papakāinga housing and marae development, and in working with mana whenua groups to express their cultural values and narratives through the design of their physical environments. In her current role as Principal – Programme Design & Strategy for national Māori housing advocate Te Matapihi, Jade works to advance Māori housing outcomes at a national level through systems advocacy, capacity building, research, and policy. Previously, Jade worked as an architectural graduate at designTRIBE Architects. Jade is fortunate to live within her home area of Whangarei, where she is leading several spatial projects to support the re-establishment and development of papakāinga communities.

My interest in papakāinga (Māori settlements / villages) stems from my own (somewhat unique) upbringing and cultural heritage. My Māori mother and Dutch father met in Melbourne, Australia in the late 1970s, and motivated by a shared vision for an environmentally responsible and socially sustainable way of life – and a better future for their children – they sought an alternative lifestyle outside of the city. In 1982, my parents were involved in the establishment of Billen Cliffs, an intentional community in Bundjalung Country (the traditional territory of the Bundjalung people, a large Indigenous Nation consisting of 15 tribal groups, located in the northern coastal areas of New South Wales, Australia) that brought together people who shared a common interest in rural lifestyles, affordable innovative housing and land regeneration.

Although I was born and raised primarily in Australia, I maintained a connection to Aotearoa New Zealand through my close relationship with my grandfather Haki and his siblings, particularly his eldest sister Ruiha, the matriarch of our family. Seeing the poor housing situations of many of our whānau living at home in Aotearoa, and reaching a growing understanding of the complexities surrounding the utilisation of Māori land, sparked an interest in transferring the learnings (both successes and failures) from our community in Australia for the benefit of our people at home in Aotearoa. My growing interest in social and environmental sustainability, and the potential roles for architecture in community building, lead me to pursue a Bachelor of Architectural Design at the University of Queensland.

Despite having mostly positive early experiences, I was confronted with a real sense of unease (and even complicity) participating in Australian settler culture. My interest in Indigenous design was firmly established during my time at the university, which included some interaction with the Aboriginal Environments Research Centre, housed within the architecture school. Although my interactions with the Centre as an undergraduate were limited, my exposure to the work of people such as Paul Memmott, Carroll Go-Sam, Kelly Greenop, and Paul Pholeros was formative. A deepening understanding of the inequities experienced by Indigenous Australians (and the potential of architectural interventions to alleviate these, if only partially) provoked in me a strong desire to forge a stronger connection between my own Indigenous culture and my chosen profession.

Post-graduation, I was encouraged by my Aunty Eliza (Ruiha's eldest daughter) to reach out to our whanaunga (extended family member / member of the same subtribe) Rau Hoskins, a respected leader in the field of Māori architecture (and fellow contributor to this book). In 2012 I moved to Aotearoa, and with Rau's support began my association with Ngā Aho (the society of Māori design professionals) and the wider community of Māori architectural practitioners. I also began to take up more active roles within our marae (a fenced-in complex of buildings and grounds, in this case belonging to our wider Kake family), my hapū (subtribe) of Ngāti Hau, and our Māori land blocks. This was the beginning of a significant journey, personally and professionally, and a body of work centred around community-based practice. In 2013, I enrolled in a Master of Architecture degree at UNITEC

Figure 1. Kawhia Pā – an example of pre-European and early contact settlement patterns, Source: Pegler, E. (1910). Looking over Kawhia Pa toward Kawhia harbour. Ref: 1/2-019363-F. [Photograph]. Wellington, N.Z.: Alexander Turnbull Library. Retrieved from http://natlib.govt.nz/records/22709281.

Institute of Technology; my final year thesis (on which this chapter draws heavily) examined papakāinga as a model for the cultural, social, economic and environmental regeneration of communities in Aotearoa New Zealand and culminated in a design proposal for the establishment of papakāinga on our whānau marae, Pehiāweri.

This chapter is a summary of the Indigenous models of architectural practice I have been developing as applied to papakāinga design, building on the work of other Māori and non-Māori practitioners and drawing on my own experiences as both a practitioner and housing advocate.

Tāhuhu Kōrero – the papakāinga concept

The word "papakāinga" derives from "papa" (referring to Papatūānuku, the ancestral earth mother), and "kāinga" (the village communal living environment). In pre-European times, the kāinga represented the centre of life and were the places where mana whenua (tribal groups with territorial rights and responsibilities over a particular area) lived, worked, and raised their families. Today, the term papakāinga is generally used to refer to a collection of dwellings occupied by Māori, connected by kinship or a common purpose, with dwellings located in reasonable proximity to each other and generally relating to a marae or other communal areas or buildings. The term papakāinga is predominantly used to refer to housing occupied by mana whenua on ancestral land, however in recent times the word has also been used for "papakāinga-style" developments in urban areas.

Pre-European Māori settlements could be divided into two main categories – kāinga (unfortified villages), and pā (fortified villages, usually built on elevated and naturally defensible sites), with seasonal encampments associated with mahinga kai (food gathering areas) constituting a third (Best, 1941). Kāinga (see Figure

1) were the dominant form of settlement pre-contact, and the focal point of economic activities. Kāinga were deliberately sited near significant resources, and were often associated with a fortified pā nearby. Generally, the kāinga were winter settlements, particularly for hapū (subtribes) who moved seasonally to mahinga kai encampments, however some kāinga were inhabited year-round as old people and some children would remain at winter kāinga during the summers. The occupation patterns of pā varied; some were fortified village bases, others were defensible boltholes in times of conflict, or uninhabited storehouses. Both kāinga and pā consisted of dense clusters of dwellings, arranged in family and extended family groups, with communal facilities sited in accordance with tapu (restricted) and noa (unrestricted).

At the time, Te Tiriti o Waitangi (the original Māori language version of an agreement made between Māori and the British Crown, also known as the Treaty of Waitangi) was signed in 1840, most Māori land remained in Māori possession. Through a series of unlawful Crown acquisitions, land sales, and raupatu (land confiscations), Māori land ownership declined dramatically as the settler population grew (Ward 1997). Successive legislative mechanisms were used to facilitate and justify the alienation of Māori people from Māori lands, and included the *Native Lands Act 1862*, the *Suppression of Rebellion Act 1863*, the *New Zealand Settlements Act 1863*, the *Native Schools Act 1867*, the *Tohunga Suppression Act 1907*, and the *Native Health Act 1909*. By 1911, the Māori land base was reduced to just over 7 million acres, or 11% of the Aotearoa New Zealand's landmass (Ward, 1997, p. 381). Today, Māori freehold land comprises a little over 3.5 million acres, or 5.5% of the New Zealand landmass (Māori Land Court, 2017).

Many rural Māori were subsequently forced, either through direct land seizures or coercion, to move into paid employment within settler society, away from family and cultural support. The rural to urban migration formed part of the broader colonial project, intended to systemically break down Indigenous land-based social structures, whilst also providing the growing urban economy with the much-needed Māori labour force. In 1945, the Māori population was largely rural, with only a quarter of Māori living in urban areas, and with Māori home ownership rates at that time exceeding those of the general population (Statistics New Zealand, 2016, p. 17). Post-World War II, the Māori population became increasingly urban, and by the time of the 2013 census 84.4% of Māori lived in urban areas (Statistics New Zealand, 2016, p. 12).

For those shifting to urban areas, housing was mostly provided through Māori Affairs and State Housing loan schemes and employee housing (such as railway and forestry). The passing of the State Owned Enterprises Act 1986 had an impact on urban Māori, with many evicted from forestry and railway homes (Statistics New Zealand, 1988). The subsequent restructuring of State Advances Corporation to Housing New Zealand Corporation also saw the withdrawal of state support for papakāinga housing, presenting significant barriers for those wishing to return to their home communities (Statistics New Zealand, 1990). The cessation of these schemes (and other factors) saw a rapid decline in Māori home ownership rates, and today Māori home ownership sits at 28.2%, well below the national average of close to 50% (Statistics New Zealand, 2013).

Partially in response to this, and as part of a wider cultural and economic resurgence, in the past three decades we have seen the emergence of contemporary papakāinga – the communal village living environment – which generally includes (but is not limited to) housing, occasionally includes communal facilities encompassing economic, environmental and spiritual dimensions. It is usually on ancestral land, and occupied by a wider family or hapū group, although the concept also has increasing relevance for urban Māori communities. It is an environment where our culture and language can thrive, and where we can exercise our whanaungatanga (kinship relationships) and use our social networks to support one another.

In its most holistic sense, papakāinga are much more than just housing, and offer communities the opportunity to become champions of self-production, independence and interdependence, across key areas such as energy, food and transport. It can empower previously disenfranchised communities to respond fully and cooperatively to their own needs, including through communally owned māra kai (food gardens), community-based micro-enterprise, more traditional land-based agriculture, horticulture, silviculture, and other economic activities across diverse sectors such as technology, arts, culture and tourism. It also offers the opportunity to respond to the social needs of the community through innovative culturally-based health and social service provision, activities for children and youth, and high-quality education programmes.

Reoccupying our whenua and living "as Māori" on our papakāinga is inherently political. In the face of ongoing colonialism and institutional racism, Māori communities have overcome many seemingly insurmountable barriers, asserting our right to reoccupy our whenua and live as

Māori. The papakāinga concept is also important because of its huge (and still largely unrealised) potential to disrupt settler political and economic systems. Through rebuilding our kāinga, we have the power to repair our social structures and reinstate our tribal economies, disrupting settler political and economic systems. Papakāinga also offers a real alternative to – and a degree of protection from – free market capitalism. Whilst acknowledging the significance of Treaty of Waitangi settlements in re-establishing a tribal economic base, many iwi (tribes) do not necessarily see the Crown-led settlement process as "the solution" to the social and economic issues faced by their communities, with the re-establishment of papakāinga firmly placing the power of response at a whānau, marae or hapū level, outside of (or parallel to) Crown and iwi political structures.

Design philosophy

As a Māori person (specifically, a Māori woman) working within a Western professional discipline, yet seeking to apply my skills (developed within Western academic institutions and through my professional experiences) to work for and with my own community, my approach to design has been developed through a process of interrogating my own assumptions and ideas regarding the practice of architecture, and considering the role of the architect as an agent of positive social change under a Māori kaupapa (ethos or topic).

The way we interact with our physical environments as Māori has a huge influence on our approach to shaping them as built environment practitioners. We can conceive of architecture as whakapapa (genealogical links) that connects us to our environments, our histories and each other. Our approach and worldview are holistic, emphasising the connectedness of all things, the importance of kaitiakitanga (guardianship or stewardship, particularly over natural resources, that implies a reciprocal relationship) and our responsibility to consider past and future generations. Built interventions can be considered as an indivisible part of our overall cultural landscape, which encompasses our mountains and rivers, our past and present, and constitutes a vital part of our collective identity.

We can also conceive of our buildings as culturally patterned spaces. In Te Ao Māori (the Māori world), the sacred / restricted (tapu) and the everyday / unrestricted (noa), comprise a set of agreed protocols that inform human behaviour and influence the creation and use of space, with the degree of flexibility or rigidity dictated by tapu and noa. The way we use space is therefore in accordance with tīkanga (correct procedure); events and interactions within our spaces are structured through culturally patterned relationships and the application of appropriate cultural protocols.

In seeking to reconcile a Māori way of doing things with architectural modes of practice, a return to a community-based approach has proven both necessary and inevitable. A community-based approach necessarily involves people playing an active role in designing, developing and delivering the projects they want and need for themselves and their communities. In its broadest sense, community-based design responds to a need within a given community (particularly those whose voices and opinions have not typically been valued, such as Indigenous and migrant communities) that is not currently being met through conventional channels.

In community-based processes, a designer or team of designers will work with community members to identify problems and develop solutions to those problems. The designer does not seek to place themselves above the people they are designing with, instead utilising their skillsets in ways that benefits the group. The role of the architect is reframed as skilled facilitator and interpreter rather than artist or author, drawing upon their technical, social, and cultural expertise to empower people to take a pivotal role in the design of their own communities through participatory design processes and consensus decision-making.

Decision-making by consensus was a key facet of pre-European Māori society (Gallagher, 2008), and is well-understood within the Māori world, with decisions made through clearly identified roles and commonly understood protocols. In the wharehui / wharenui (the meeting house / main building of a marae complex where guests are accommodated) – the formal setting where we have maintained our tīkanga and reo to the greatest degree – consensus is still largely the way decisions are made. Given that consensus is a core tenet of decision-making within Māori society, I believe there is significant potential to continue to develop and refine consensus design methods that take the best of Western thinking and reframe and reinterpret it within a kaupapa Māori framework.

Participatory design assumes "users" are the experts of their own domain and should be actively involved in the design process. Participatory design refers not only to the tools and techniques, but also the ways in which these are successfully adapted for use with a specific group of people on a specific project at a specific point in time (Sanoff, 2000). Given that much of participatory

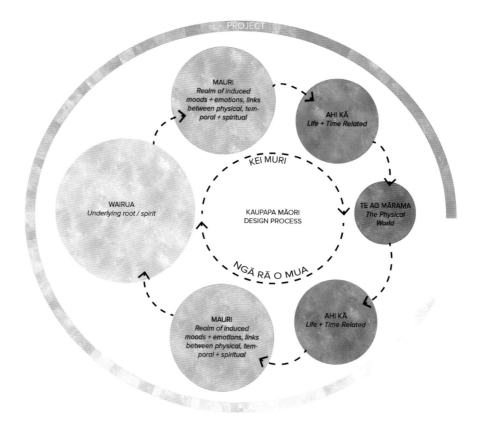

Figure 2. A kaupapa Māori consensus design model

design theory has its origins in North America (Sanoff, 2000), it stands to reason that the ideology or worldview underpinning these techniques does not necessarily prioritise consensus as a desirable or required part of the decision-making process, and as such these techniques need to be viewed and applied critically.

The work of Christopher Day (2003) has been particularly influential in shaping my thinking. His approach to consensus design builds upon Margaret Colquhoun's technique of landscape study, acknowledging physical, spiritual, and temporal elements of our environments. By critically examining our environments and our relationships to these environments (past, present and future), we can develop a deeper understanding of people and place that we can then translate into an enduring design outcome. An attempt to translate this into a working practice model is illustrated in Figure 2.

Design principles and applications

My own practice methods are built on the work of others, and based on a philosophical position that design should reflect the culture, history, and aspirations of the community, and that architecture should be responsive to place, and the people of that place. A typical project development process might begin with outlining korero (narrative, story, conversation) relating to the project site

(the whenua or land), followed by the genealogy and cultural identity of the people of that land (hapū), before moving on to the masterplan and design development process. A summary of this process is outlined in Figure 3.

In the papakāinga design process, wānanga (a term which denotes coming together for the co-creation or transfer of knowledge, and which implies a reciprocal process of learning and teaching) has proven to be a useful technique for facilitating consensus decision-making processes, and for enabling a community to articulate their own values and aspirations. Applied in an architectural context, wānanga can draw on participatory and consensus design methods, whilst adhering to the protocols established through tikanga. In my own projects, I have used several such techniques within a wānanga environment, including the use of consciousness raising tactics to build community awareness and socialise ideas, and the use of site planning kits (models) in facilitated workshops to explore ideas and build community consensus (Figure 4).

In recent years, cultural mapping – which is the process of spatially mapping both intangible and tangible cultural information – has been used as a tool for environmental monitoring and conservation, Treaty of Waitangi claims processes, and managing relationships

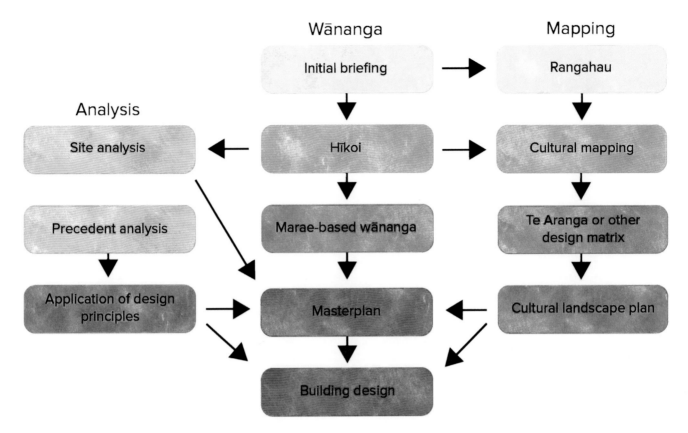

Figure 3. Parallel design processes – a potential approach

between government authorities and tangata whenua. In the design process, cultural mapping can be used to translate cultural values and narratives (collected and interpreted through the narrative interview/oral history process) into design outcomes. Sites of significance are mapped spatially and analysed through the site analysis phase. The locations of sites of significance can then be used to inform the siting of new buildings and landscape elements through the masterplan, and detailed kōrero / cultural narratives are used to inform design strategies at a building level.

The mapping techniques I have utilised over the past few years have been adapted from techniques developed in Canada (Tobias, 2000) and Aotearoa (Harmsworth, 1998). Of particular relevance, is the "diamond method" of data collection outlined by Tobias (2000) – when collecting data, each point, line, or polygon should be considered in terms of data diamonds. The diamond shape, with its four points, refers to the linking of four types of information – a person's name (who), an activity (what), a location (where), and some indication of time period (when). I have adopted (and slightly adapted) the categories developed by Harmsworth (1998), which include: ancestral sites and tribal landmarks (such pā, maunga, awa), cultural and social sites (such as kāinga, marae, and kura), sacred sites (burial grounds, burial sites, ritual places), Indigenous place names (corrective spelling and associated

knowledge), water, geology (significant landforms, mud for weaving, dyes), and animals and vegetation (māhinga kai, māra, plants used for medicine, weaving, carving).

Interviews with elders are an important part of this process. These interviews can be used to record events in living memory (in relation to the whenua), but can also be a way to access collective cultural histories, passed down through oral traditions. Collective cultural information that is passed on intergenerationally, such as whakapapa and cultural narratives, have their own integrity and in-built methods of fact checking and ensuring reliability. Oral history validates Māori knowledge and compliments archival information, such as Māori land court records (which are also oral histories, recorded by the Native Land Court). Interview abstracts and historical research are incorporated into the cultural narrative report, which is a written document that sits alongside the spatial plan, primarily containing detailed kōrero extracted from the map database, but which may also include: transcriptions / abstracts of oral histories, description of methodology, and historical / archival data, such as Māori land court records, newspaper archives and other written sources.

The next step in the papakāinga design process is to translate the cultural narratives into a set of place-based, site-specific applications. The cultural narrative report can be used as the basis for developing a set of text-

Figure 4. Site planning kit in use during a papakāinga planning workshop

based, site-specific urban design strategies, developed by processing cultural information through Te Aranga (a set of seven Māori design principles), or another design principles-based matrix. Mana whenua (tribal groups with territorial rights and responsibilities over a particular area) of Tāmaki Makaurau have begun to develop Te Aranga matrices that utilise the Te Aranga principles, and translate them into place-based cultural landscape strategies, which are used to guide urban development projects in their traditional territory. This tool is increasingly being used by designers (in collaboration with iwi / hapū) to meaningfully integrate culture into planning at an urban or neighbourhood scale. The applicability of Te Aranga principles to papakāinga design is primarily centred on the translation of cultural narratives (captured through the cultural map and cultural narrative report) into design outcomes at an urban scale.

The creative interpretation of the cultural information can then be used to produce a cultural landscape plan in the form of a masterplan overlay. The term "overlay"

derives from the process of laying a sheet of translucent detail (drafting) paper over a physical printed print copy of an aerial photograph of the site, but in practice could include layers in Photoshop, whiteboard projects, markers on laminated maps, etc. Cultural landscape strategies are developed in fulfilment of the architectural brief, developed through wānanga, direct briefing from the community client and in response to the cultural map / narrative report. Strategies developed through the cultural landscape plan are largely interpretive (in that specific meanings / implications for built forms are drawn from cultural narratives) and can be applied at both an urban and architectural level. The final overall masterplan is developed through consideration of the site constraints established through analysis, the incorporation of cultural landscape strategies, and the application of design principles.

In terms of papakāinga design principles, the most comprehensive resource produced to date is Ki te hau Kāinga: New Perspectives on Māori Housing Solutions

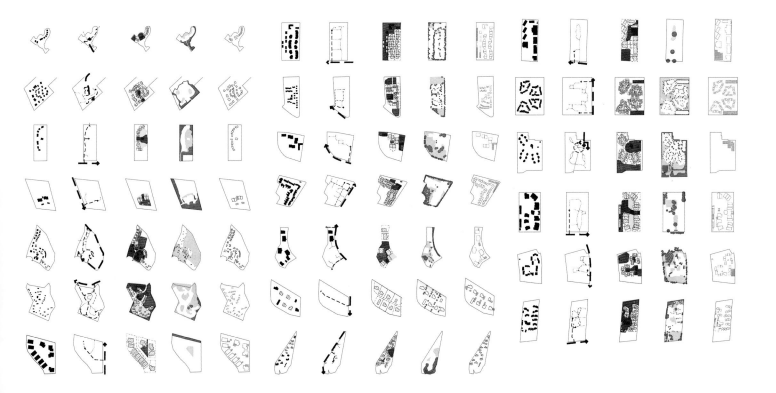

Figure 5. Diagrammatic analysis of papakāinga and cohousing precedents

(Hoskins, Te Nana, Rhodes, Guy, & Sage, 2002). The project was initiated by Rau Hoskins and others in the early 2000s to address the lack of culturally appropriate housing for Māori, and identified the need to develop new housing solutions tailored to the specific needs of Māori communities. The design guide, which was commissioned by Housing New Zealand Corporation, was intended to be used to guide architects, designers, planners and developers as they consider the diverse needs of Māori in planning new housing developments (particularly, state housing projects). A preliminary update was completed by Rau Hoskins and myself in 2014, with a more comprehensive update planned.

The guide includes a set of general masterplanning principles, and guidelines for the design of individual dwellings, alongside conceptual design examples for both papakāinga and individual homes. Some key site planning principles include: no fences between dwellings; areas for food production, including gathering, growing and processing; clustering of dwellings; and the allocation of shared or communal space. Off-grid technologies are considered as both a cultural imperative, and a practical reality given most Māori land is in rural areas that are not well serviced by grid infrastructure. From a cultural perspective, the concepts of tapu and noa are especially significant in determining the arrangement and adjacency

of spaces that are conducive to Māori whānau dynamics and cultural practices.

For the design of individual whare, the floor layout is designed to take advantage of passive solar orientation, and to encourage positive interactions with visitors / guests. Design principles include: a welcoming front entry to the north to allow kitchen, dining and living areas to monitor visitors; rear porch / carport suitable for use as an outdoor food preparation area, particularly for kai moana (seafood / shellfish); a generous main living area, large enough to accommodate whānau gatherings of up to 20 people; kitchens able to accommodate two or more people; location of kitchen and dining room to provide good indoor and outdoor child supervision, with kitchens overlooking outdoor play areas; a second lounge area (mezzanine) where teenagers can retreat during whānau gatherings, or which can be used for marae style sleeping; and two toilets in larger homes to better accommodate large numbers of children as well as visitors / guests.

Providing for universal access for elders and disabled whānau in intergenerational living situations is another key consideration. Design principles include: providing a covered porch on the eastern side off the ground-floor bedroom as a private outdoor space for early-rising kaumātua / kuia; ground floor to Lifemark code (a New

Figure 6. Concept design for Pehiāweri Marae papakāinga – perspective

Zealand design standard and rating system, established to promote universal design) for accessibility for kaumātua / kuia or whānau with disabilities, including at least one bedroom at ground level, wide doors and corridors, wet area disabled access shower, an accessible toilet; and french doors off ground-floor bedrooms (level entry doorways, away from kitchens) to allow for easy fire egress in the event of an emergency.

Sixteen years on, this resource remains relevant, however given the many developments in the papakāinga space during this time, a comprehensive update is now required. A revised design guide could incorporate new case study material, reflect technical and technological advancements, include new and modified principles based spatial analysis and design-based post-occupancy evaluation (some of which is underway through various practice and research projects), and encompass emerging typologies. Some emerging areas for consideration include the design of culturally-based transitional, emergency and supportive

housing, and the development of guidelines for large-scale masterplanned iwi-led urban regeneration projects.

As part of the further development of papakāinga design principles, I have produced a diagrammatic analysis of historic pā, contemporary papakāinga and cohousing projects internationally (Figure 5, commenced as part of my thesis project, which I will be adding to over time). This precedent analysis has revealed several overall site planning principles including the configuration of dwellings, location of communal facilities, placement of roading and pedestrian pathways, and use of landscape design to establish a hierarchy of private, shared and communal space.

Houses are generally stand-alone or duplex, and arranged in smaller groupings or clusters. Overall site coverage approximates a standard suburban subdivision; however, houses are located closer together and more space is given over to communal (rather than private) outdoor space. In the design of individual houses, considerations include intergenerational living, and

accommodating the changing needs of whānau at different life stages. Clusters of dwellings or larger intergenerational homes can be used to accommodate larger whānau and better accommodate changes over time. The communal nature of papakāinga presents the opportunity to provide a variety of dwellings for maximum flexibility, enabling individual whānau units to move around the papakāinga as their needs change over time.

In most of the developments, there is a hierarchy of private space (with most individual dwellings having at least a small private yard or courtyard), shared space (for the use of defined clusters of houses), and common space (for the use of the whole community). This is particularly relevant to larger developments, with the establishment of spatial hierarchies enabling clusters to develop a more intimate sense of community and identity, whilst also retaining opportunities to interact with the wider group. In some developments, communal buildings facilities operate as anchor points, distributed across shared spaces (rather than clustered in one place) to prevent the co-opting of these spaces by one family or cluster group. There is also generally less privacy in modern papakāinga when compared with cohousing, and there are often no fences between dwellings.

Shared communal facilities are essential to papakāinga development and provide opportunities for social cohesion and the realisation of cultural aspirations. Given that most Māori land is located outside traditional employment centres, opportunities for economic development should be provided for and actively encouraged (there are still only limited examples of this in practice), with planning to extend beyond housing provision to include education, recreation and enterprise facilities associated with communal housing as an integral part of the papakāinga. The communal nature of papakāinga provides an opportunity to economise on resources through shared facilities, to promote language and cultural acquisition and retention, and promote economic development through the designation of shared workspaces as a hub for small to medium sized businesses, alongside other more traditional activities such as land-based and cultural production.

In contrast to contemporary papakāinga, cohousing tends to place a greater emphasis on privacy, with cohousing developments more likely to have fences between dwellings. Although there are parallels between the common house, which is a feature of most cohousing developments, and the marae complex, the common house does not carry the same cultural significance, and does not carry the same requirements to accommodate cultural practices. This is particularly significant during tangihanga (funeral, rites for the dead – one of the most important institutions in Māori society, with strong cultural imperatives and protocols). For contemporary papakāinga that are not associated with a marae, the communal buildings may more closely resemble the common house typology.

Circulation is generally a hierarchy of three categories of circulation path – external roadway, main internal roadway (connecting the public access road to the carparking area), and pedestrian paths (connecting the carparking area to private homes, and private homes to the shared spaces). Some developments also contain a fourth category of internal light traffic roading (often in the form of a reinforced, wider-than-usual footpath), which can be used to transport disabled and elderly people to their homes, or in the event of an emergency. Parking is generally located on the periphery of the site, and more often in communal parking lots or covered carparks than in private garages attached to dwellings. The rationale behind this is to enhance the safety for children, to minimise traffic noise within the development, and to encourage people to interact with one other. This also results in a substantial reduction of paved areas (and associated costs).

Pedestrian paths have also been used in some instances to link public pedestrian walkways (alongside the main external roadway) with the main internal pedestrian path, or to link the community with adjacent nature reserves. Overall, vegetation is used (rather than fencing), to articulate boundaries between private/shared/communal zones, and to create areas of defensible space. Defensible space theory argues that an area is safer when people feel a sense of ownership for that piece of the community. This is achieved through design and social acceptance, and includes the application of concepts such territoriality and natural surveillance (Newman, 1972). Many of the developments included a balance between cultivated green space, such as gardens and lawns, and uncultivated green space, such as nature reserves, forested areas, etc. Re-establishing traditional food sources, such as māra kai or food gardens, is an important means of supporting whānau rangatiratanga (sovereignty or independence) in providing for their own needs.

Rangahau mō āpōpō – future research

Some areas for further development (either currently underway or planned) include utilising 3D and digital participatory mapping to incorporate with 3D models produced by drone mapping to produce interactive resources, and the development of geospatial tools to assist with planning and decision-making.

As Te Aranga is still a relatively new and evolving tool, I am also interested in conducting post-occupancy evaluations of projects where Te Aranga has been deliberately applied, to determine to what degree the social reality (of living on the papakāinga / within a housing development, or using / experiencing an urban area or building) matches up with anticipated social outcomes. This evaluation will enable the principles to further develop and evolve over time, particularly as more iwi / hapū adapt and modify the principles to better align to their own values and unique perspectives.

Nationally, there is a growing movement to develop protocols and partnership models that recognise Indigenous data sovereignty, particularly through the work of Te Mana Raraunga, the Māori data sovereignty network. Data sovereignty is an emerging issue for Indigenous communities, both locally and internationally, and is being responded to by these communities in a variety of ways (Kukutai & Taylor, 2016). This is something designers will increasingly need to be sensitive to as they engage in the translation of culturally sensitive material information into design strategies.

Whakaaro whakamutunga – concluding thoughts

What I have described in this chapter is far from definitive. It represents one of any number of possible approaches. There have been, and will continue to be, many variations on these tools, and possible iterations of the design process, engaged by other designers on community projects past, present and into the future. What I have attempted – and will continue – to do, is to work cooperatively to develop and extend Indigenous models of architectural practice, with an emphasis on the formulation of appropriate design methodologies for working within Māori communities (whilst acknowledging the wider post-colonial context within which we operate).

I have been very fortunate through my community-based project work, my close association with Ngā Aho, and my advocacy role with Te Matapihi (the National Māori Housing Advocate), to be exposed to – and be able to influence – changes in policy and practice to support papakāinga development across Aotearoa New Zealand. The connections we have made with our international Indigenous colleagues and friends (which has led to the publication of this book, amongst other initiatives) have been an important development, and fertile ground for shared learnings and advocacy.

In my work so far, I have sought to draw on my lived experiences, my bicultural heritage and the best aspects of my Western education, whilst remembering that my primary accountability is (and always will be) to our Māori communities. I am frequently told by people from our grassroots communities that there is a need for practitioners with the right skills, who understand the complexities of Māori land and our specific cultural context. Moving forward, my priority is to build structures that can effectively respond to this need, aggregate specialist talent and expertise, and create viable career pathways for Māori practitioners so that we may best utilise our professional skills in service of our communities.

References

Best, E. (1941). "The Pā Māori or Fortified Village." *The Māori – Volume 2* (pp. 304-352). Wellington, N.Z.: Polynesian Society.

Day, C. (2003). *Consensus Design*. New York: Architectural Press.

Gallagher, T. (2008). Tikanga Māori Pre-1840. Te Kāhui Kura Māori, 0(1). Retrieved from http://nzetc.victoria.ac.nz.

Harmsworth, G. (1998). "Indigenous values and GIS: a method and a framework." Indigenous knowledge and development monitor 6(3), 3-7.

Hoskins, R., Te Nana, R., Rhodes, P., Guy, P., & Sage, S. (2002). *Ki te Hau Kainga:New Perspectives on Māori Housing Solutions: A Design Guide prepared for Housing New*

Zealand Corporation (second edition, eds. R. Hoskins & J. Kake [2014]). Retrieved from www.tematapihi.org.nz.

Kukutai, T., & Taylor, J. (Eds.). (2016). *Indigenous Data Sovereignty*. Canberra, Australia: ANU Press.

Māori Land Court. (2017). *Māori Land Update 2017*. Retrieved 2017, December 28 from https://www.maorilandcourt.govt.nz.

Newman, O. (1972). *Defensible Space: Crime Prevention Through Urban Design*. New York: Macmillan.

Sanoff, H. (2000). *Community participation methods in design and planning*. New York: Wiley.

Statistics New Zealand. (1988). *New Zealand Official Yearbook 1987-88*. Wellington, N.Z.: Statistics New Zealand.

Statistics New Zealand. (1990). *New Zealand Official Yearbook 1990*. Wellington, N.Z.: Statistics New Zealand.

Statistics New Zealand. (2016). "Changes in home-ownership patterns 1986–2013: Focus on Māori and Pacific people." Retrieved 2017, December 20 from www.stats.govt.nz.

Statistics New Zealand. (2013). "2013 Census QuickStats About Housing." Retrieved 2017, December 20 from http://www.stats.govt.nz.

Tobias, T. (2000). *Chief Kerry's Moose: A Guidebook to Land Use and Occupancy Mapping, Research Design and Data Collection*. Vancouver, B.C.: Union of BC Indian Chiefs and Ecotrust Canada. Retrieved 2017, November 20 from http://archive.ecotrust.org/publications/chiefkerrysmoose.html.

Ward, A. (1997). "National Overview: volume II. Waitangi Tribunal Rangahau Whanui Series." Wellington, N.Z.: *Waitangi Tribunal*. Retrieved 2017, December 20 from https://www.waitangitribunal.govt.nz.

Chapter 18: Closing the [non-Indigenous] gap

Sarah Lynn Rees – Palawa, Plangermaireener

Sarah Lynn Rees is a Palawa woman descending from the Plangermaireener people of northeast Tasmania. She is a Charlie Perkins scholar with an MPhil in Architecture and Urban Design from the University of Cambridge where she produced a thesis on Indigenous housing in remote Australian communities. Sarah also holds a Bachelor of Environments (Architecture) from the University of Melbourne. Sarah has recently returned from London where she worked with Stirling Prize Winner, Will Alsop OBE RA and is currently working as a Graduate of Architecture at Jackson Clements Burrows Architects, a Director of Indigenous Architecture and Design Victoria (IADV), a Sessional Teaching associate for design studio at Monash University, a Research Assistant at the University of Melbourne, an Associate Consultant at Greenshoot Consulting and a Project Manager for MPavilion's 2017 regional program.

"Closing the gap" is an Australian Government initiative established 2007 to address and set targets to improve Indigenous health, education and employment (Gardiner-Garden, 2013, para. 4). These targets highlight "Indigenous disadvantage" (FaHCSIA, 2009) and are predominately focused on providing skills and opportunities to Indigenous people to find success in a western system by western standards. It begs the questions, what would Indigenous led "markers for success" be? Language, culture, Country?[1] The challenge is we can't quantify language, culture and Country into a statistical report. Quantifying the qualitative and intangible is dangerous and could lead to yet another classification system aimed at determining "how Indigenous are you really?" – the oppressing question we are all too often asked in the face of identifying as Indigenous Australians.

If we prioritized, amongst others, culture, language and connection to Country, in the same way we prioritize reading, writing, and arithmetic we would need to dramatically deconstruct our industrial era education system. As it stands, if we applied the Closing the Gap model to the architectural profession it would likely include a measurement of the number of practicing Indigenous Architects. While this is slowly growing, we still only need one hand to make the count. It likely would not include qualitative measures such as connection to Country, placemaking, relationships, and culture.

If we invert the Closing the Gap structure and shift the deficit discourse away from Indigenous people, the question becomes how do we "Close the Non-Indigenous Gap?"

What does this mean for the way we practice and teach architecture? And, how do we empower our non-Indigenous colleagues in order that all architects can operate meaningfully in this space?

Firstly, I will contextualize my perspective through my experience of the architectural profession and my cultural identity. I am a Palawa (Tasmanian Aboriginal) woman descending from the Plangermaireener people in North East Tasmania. I'm also a descendant of convicts and free settlers and undoubtedly many other peoples and cultures. My Aboriginal ancestry is strongly documented and is filled with powerful people such as Mannalargenna, a fierce and cheeky warrior, chief of the Plangermaireener Nation; Woretermoeteyenner, his daughter who survived being sold and abandoned in Mauritius during a sealer expedition eventually making it back to Australia; and, Dolly Dalrymple her daughter, who was adopted into servitude and escaped. She was entrepreneurial and likely the first Aboriginal person to be granted land from the government. I am proud to be related to such resilient and strong people.

I have always known of my Aboriginal Heritage; my childhood home was filled with artefacts and books full of Australian Aboriginal stories and histories. My primary school would arrange for the Indigenous students to engage with our culture through everything from NAIDOC[2] Week events, to cooking mutton bird on the school BBQ, to excursions on Country. From my perspective as a young person there was no shame in being Aboriginal and by virtue of Tasmania's history, all the Aboriginal people I knew had light skin.

Figure 1. Interpretation of the Australian Indigenous Language Map, Source: Author

I'm the first to admit that the colour of my skin has afforded me opportunities that darker skinned Aboriginal people were not. As a child no one ever assumed or labelled me as Aboriginal and I did not have to grow up dealing with the associated oppression. My father worked very hard to give us every opportunity he could and at the same time shielded us from the politics associated with Tasmanian Aboriginality.

My Aboriginal heritage comes from my father's side and when we were kids he made attempts to connect with the community where we lived but was told by an individual that he had to be involved in their political agendas and rallies if he "wanted in." My father isn't very good at being told what to do. He probably would have been on board and engaged if allowed to do so on his own terms but the ultimatum closed that door

for him. He didn't tell me about this until I was an adult, which then made sense of why we, as a family, only talked about our history in relation to who we come from, rather than who we are still related to. I wish my father could have experienced the sense of the community I've been afforded since leaving Tasmania. So much strength comes from community. I hope one day to find my own community in Tasmania and develop my own understanding of the challenges, strength and diversity of Palawa people.

---

[1] Country refers to the physical, linguistic, cultural and ongoing connection to the land occupied by each Indigenous language group.
[2] NAIDOC stands for National Aborigines and Islander Day Observance Committee. NAIDOC week is a celebration of Aboriginal and Torres Strait Islander "history, culture, achievements… and contribution to country and society" (NAIDOC, 2016).

Figure 2. Comparative Non-Indigenous map of Australia's States and Territories, Source: Author

I'm the first person in my family to graduate from university and it wasn't until I was accepted into Cambridge and awarded a Charlie Perkins scholarship that I became publicly impacted by race relations in Australia. I've seen articles written by academics calling out the colour of my skin and the fact that my high school was private and Catholic as criteria for why I don't deserve an Aboriginal scholarship. Others posted my photo with captions like "not black enough." Someone even went up to my brother and claimed the only reason I got into Cambridge was because I am Aboriginal. It was a conflicting time. On the one hand I had people telling me not to react as that only feeds the fire, while another part of me wanted to point out the hypocrisy of at the same time not being black enough, but only getting ahead because I'm "black."

I recognize that what I've been subjected to is nothing compared to the hardships my ancestors faced and that others continue to face today. I have to believe Australia's lack of acknowledgement of its dark history, including

for example "breeding out the blacks,[3]" (Neville, 1947) and events such as the 'black line[4]' (Clements, 2014) in Tasmania are the reason why we still subscribe to the idea that to be a "real" Aboriginal you need to have dark skin and live in poverty.

I have light skin and I have never lived in poverty and I face a constant barrage of questions asking me to justify my Aboriginality. Someone once said to me "If you can't be proud of who you are and where you come from because of the colour of your skin, then the continuation of Tasmanian Aboriginal history, the history of your people dies with you." I take the responsibility embedded in that statement seriously. There are far more important topics to be addressing than the colour of our skin.

Cambridge for me was a crash course in language. I had to learn very quickly how to articulately and concisely discuss my research on Aboriginal Housing in remote communities in a way that could be understood academically but also respected the protocols of the people I was talking about. It was a difficult line to

Figure 3. Attitudes towards land ownership: Non-Indigenous own land vs. the land owns Indigenous people, Source: Author

navigate. Before the fieldwork component of my degree, where I spent six months living in Yuendumu, a remote Aboriginal community in the Northern Territory, I refused to put people in my drawings because I was terrified of perpetuating and committing to ink the media stereotypes I'd grown up watching on the evening news. Navigating the emotional and political landmines associated with each word I chose to use, or the colours in my drawings or even the references I used were exhausting.

Not all of my supervisors understood this and I didn't yet have the skills to articulate it. The responses I received were akin to "use words that other people have written, you don't have to make statements you can shield yourself with other people's research." This is problematic given a lot of early records of Indigenous life are often written by non-Indigenous men within a western academic framework. This kind of patriarchal lens is blind to diversity. It assumes a male power structure which is at odds with the matriarchal stories of Aboriginal communities I had been told. But stories are

not academic peer reviewed papers, they are perceived as qualitative, lacking evidence and fallible to the ego of the author.

There are some resources that are introspective enough to realize the system they are produced in and still find a way to respect the diversity of those they are representing. I relied much on the work of Paul Memmot and the Aboriginal Environments Research Centre, conversations with the late Paul Pholeros and the community of Indigenous built environment practitioners in Australia to find my way through.

I was fortunate to have the support of this community. While my undergraduate degree prepared me well for

---

[3] A strategy to breed Indigenous Australians with white Australians to assimilate and effectively eliminate Indigenous Australians (Neville, 2014).
[4] A line of thousands of soldiers ordered by then Lieutenant-Governor George Author in 1830 to cross Tasmania and capture any remaining Indigenous People (Clements, 2014).

design and communication, there was little Indigenous content or acknowledgement of the lands on which the University stood embedded into the degree. Often in my design studio I would incorporate the continuous Indigenous histories of the sites we were given; however, my tutors weren't able to critically respond in any meaningful way. It was not their fault, they had not been taught and their experience of the profession's limited engagement with Indigenous communities hadn't provided them with a sufficient foundation or authority to comment, guide or criticize. Ultimately, if I as an Indigenous person found it difficult to marry academic structure with Indigenous protocol, I can understand why it felt impossible to my peers.

Now in architectural practice, I asked my non-Indigenous colleagues, both Australian and International about their education and professional experience working with Indigenous communities, whether they would like to work on Indigenous projects and if they had any reservations. Most responded that they knew very little about Indigenous people and culture, few had experience with a specific studio at university or a single project in their professional career and all, except my international colleagues expressed a fear of causing offence, feeling at a loss for where to even start or how to communicate. Interestingly my international colleagues expressed no fears or apprehensions as they had none of the political or social baggage associated with growing up in Australia. They did however express a curiosity and frustration at the lack of conversation and literature they had encountered so far.

This disparity of fear and apprehension was again evidenced when asked how they would approach working with an Indigenous client or stakeholder group. The Australian's predominate response was again a feeling a loss of where to start and how to communicate, whereas the international response was predominately, "I would approach it like any other project." One colleague went on to explain that for him it would be the same if I asked him to design a mosque, he has no understanding of the religion, customs or symbology associated with mosques however his approach would be no different to any other project in that he would take the time to learn and consult with a variety of people that do possess this knowledge and especially those who will use the space.

It is an interesting position to not make any assumptions that your client or stakeholder group shares your frame of reference, aspirations or concept of how one occupies space. We tend to assume most people live the same way we do. After years of architectural education and professional experience we are at risk of adopting a formula based on regulations and standards and rather than making them work for us or challenging them we use them as a fundamental starting point. How then can we break from the formulaic to conceive of something seemingly foreign? Borrowing from the words of neuroscientist Dr. Beau Lotto (2009), "only through uncertainty is there potential for understanding." What we need in this case is to mitigate the fear of the unknown.

To mitigate my colleagues fears we need to start 40,000+ years ago making up for what their education system lacked. We need to explain traditional life, customs, and structures and explore the catastrophic impact of the eras of colonization, protection, assimilation, self-determination and reconciliation. We need to talk about terra nullius, the frontier wars, massacres, martial law, sterilization, eugenics, missions, and the stolen generation. We need to talk about governance, sovereignty, solidarity, resistance, land rights, and treaty. We need to talk about Australia Day, Mabo Day, and NAIDOC week. We need to articulate what it is to be an Indigenous Australian today, how people identify, the fact that Indigenous Australia is not homogenous, what it means to be an Elder, or a Traditional Owner. Explain why it's not okay to ask someone how Aboriginal they are or refer to them as part-Aboriginal. The list goes on. In uncovering the truths of Australia's past we are able to develop a language with which to talk about our present and future. It is from here we can critically debate more contentious questions like "What is Indigenous Architecture?" with a level of grounding and context.

We would need this entire book and probably several more to deconstruct the versions of Australian history my colleagues grew up with. However, changing the education system doesn't serve practicing architects. Their education requires self-driven initiative, collaboration with Indigenous designers, attending conferences that present keynote Indigenous speakers, reading books such as this one or utilizing resources such as the International Indigenous Design Charter. Amongst our community of Indigenous architects and designers we are engaging in ongoing conversations regarding how we define Indigenous Architecture. Some disagree with the classification at all, while others, such as Jefa Greenaway suggest Indigenous architecture is "by," "for," and "with" Indigenous people. My interpretation of Greenaway's definition is the following:

With: Any project claiming relationship with Aboriginal community requires a deep level of engagement to substantiate. The involvement of community needs to be valued as the knowledge they bring is paramount to the success of a project; "valued" in this sense means listening and respecting as well as paying people for their time. A town hall type consultation or a one hour workshop is not sufficient. The protocol of establishing trust takes time and the relationships should continue beyond the life of the project. If you are creating something for community and with community, you are an ongoing part of that project and those people's lives.

For: For and with go hand in hand. You can't create a project for community, without community. It's the make-up of community that changes, based on the project. Sometimes you will work with a community of Traditional Owner groups and Elders, sometimes it will be a community of Indigenous Staff members or students. Recognising whom you are creating a space for, will inform who you work with.

By: In my opinion all architects and built environment practitioners should be capable of engaging in Indigenous projects in a sophisticated and meaningful way because everything that is constructed or deconstructed in Australia is on Aboriginal land. Land ownership systems differ greatly between non-Indigenous and Indigenous Australia. Aboriginal people don't "own" land, they are "owned by it," they are its custodians and are therefore responsible for its health, stories and continuous living histories.

For the most part, our architectural education is lacking the tools to equip future architects with the skills they need, or even a robust acknowledgement and in-depth engagement of the living history and connection to the places their institutions occupy. Consequently, most of the profession is ill-equipped through no initial fault of their own. The reality is that most architects don't then go on to educate themselves because they don't know where to start. In order to start closing the non-Indigenous gap we need to update our education system and embed out architecture degrees with Indigenous content and people who can effectively teach it; we need to have the uncomfortable conversations about Australia's dark history recognizing the context in which we receive this information; and we need to develop resources and form collaborations between Indigenous and non-Indigenous architects. There has been a recent shift to prioritize Indigenous perspectives in architecture and in architectural education with many universities opening the door to this conversation, but we have a long way to go to close the gap.

Valuing Indigenous perspectives in architecture will serve to enrich design projects and practitioner engagement with the land and the first people of Australia. In my opinion all architects should be capable of engaging

with Indigenous people. It will take time to form ongoing relationships and mistakes will be made along the way, but it is better to make those mistakes and learn from them than to be paralyzed by fear and never start at all. First and foremost, making any changes to the way we teach and practice architecture needs to be developed in collaboration with Indigenous Elders, Traditional Owners, and communities and Indigenous built environment practitioners. We need to respect that like land, Indigenous people are custodians of knowledge and therefore cannot transfer its ownership. In this way, I acknowledge the opinions I have expressed in this essay are informed by listening to and sharing with my Elders, the Indigenous architecture community, and the non-Indigenous architecture community. At this point we don't have all the answers and we probably never will, but we are asking questions and engaging in the critical conversations that are necessary to establish alternative and robust forms of practice.

References

Clements, N. (2014). *The Black War: Fear, Sex and Resistance in Tasmania*. University of Queensland Press.

FaCSIA - Department of Families Housing Community Services and Indigenous Affairs (2009). "Closing the gap on Indigenous disadvantage: the challenge for Australia." Canberra: Commonwealth of Australia.

Gardiner-Garden, J. (2013) "Closing the Gap" Retrieved 2017, December 20 from https://www.aph.gov.au/About_Parliament/Parliamentary_Departments/Parliamentary_Library/pubs/BriefingBook44p/ClosingGap.

Lotto, B. (2009) "Optical Illusions show how we see" [Video File]. Retrieved 2017, December 20 from https://www.ted.com/talks/beau_lotto_optical_illusions_show_how_we_see

National NAIDOC Secretariat (2016). NAIDOC Week, Retrieved 2017, December 20from http://www.naidoc.org.au/

Neville, A. O. (1947). *Australia's Coloured Minority: Its Place in the Community*. Sydney: Currawong Publishing.

Chapter 19: Designing to Express Community Values: A new Community School in South Dakota

Tammy Eagle Bull – Oglala Lakota Nation

Tammy Eagle Bull became an architect in fulfillment of a long term family vision. Long before she was born, her grandfather told her father and uncle that one of them should go to architecture school and the other should study law. His reasoning was that someday their Oglala Lakota community in Pine Ridge, South Dakota would need architects and lawyers and it would be best if those professionals came from within. But in the 1950s as the two young men prepared to enter college, racism still impacted career opportunities for Native Americans, and the brothers went into education instead. But a generation later, Tammy fulfilled her grandfather's wish as an architect working with her tribe. Tammy's grandfather was "right on the money" when he predicted that tribal communities would one day need the services of an architect who understands Native American cultures. Tammy is the co-founder of Encompass Architects, p.c., a national firm headquartered in Lincoln, NE. She received a Bachelor of Science in Design – Architectural Studies from Arizona State University and a Master of Architecture from the University of Minnesota-Minneapolis. She is a licensed architect with 30 years of architectural design and project management experience. She is currently licensed in 11 states and is recognized as the first Native American woman to be licensed in the United States. Tammy is an enrolled member of the Oglala Lakota Nation. Her family is from Pine Ridge, SD Encompass Architects is a Native American – Woman owned business offering full service architectural services to clients across the nation.

The communities on the tribal nations in the United States have evolved drastically since the time of settlement by non-natives. For centuries our communities were physical embodiments of our tribe's political systems, social organizations, and unique culture values. Structures were placed in specific locations for specific reasons, built out of local materials and the aesthetics were culturally unique.

The relocation of our people to reservations has had a devastating effect on every aspect of our culture, including the built environment. No longer were the people in control of community planning. A rigid grid system was used to organize our dwellings. No longer were the tribes easily identifiable by the community or structures. Now reservations across the United States have the same look and feel, especially tribal housing developments.

Our traditional structures were a direct response to climate, environment, terrain, and lifestyle. Nomadic people had structures which were easy to move. Sedentary people had more permanent structures. Materials were used which were easily available. The homes were an expression of the people who lived in them.

Now tribal housing in the Pacific Northwest is very similar to that found in the Midwest. No accommodation is made for climate or culture. It is hard to discern that there are completely different tribal nations using the houses. This only adds to the problem of generalizing native people into one common culture. After all these years, Americans are woefully uneducated on the first inhabitants. Many do not understand that the 562 federally recognized tribes in the United States are ethically and culturally diverse, and have distinct languages.

After so many years of destructive policies from the US government trying to terminate, relocate, and assimilate us, our Indigenous cultures have survived and thrived in many ways. We have lost some languages but many others are experiencing a resurgence as our schools have retaken control of the curriculums. Our tribal governments are effectively exerting influence as never before. Many tribes have economic development opportunities which are allowing growth and successful business ventures. Gaming has allowed many to provide much needed services to their members, while allowing a few tribes to not only enrich their members but to become philanthropic and assist other tribes.

It is time to take back our built environment. Our communities need to be unique to each tribe, they need

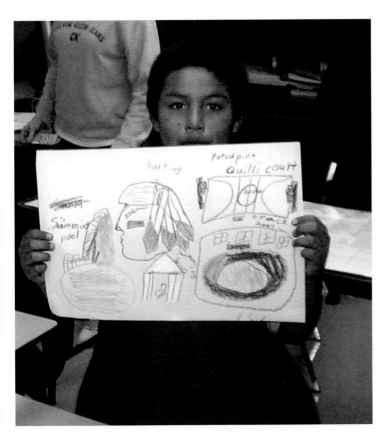

Figure 1. Child with drawing, Source: Encompass Architects

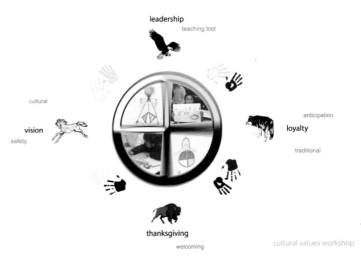

Figure 2. Cultural Values Board, Source: Encompass Architects

to express who we are as a culture. When you drive into a tribal community, you should know that you are in a unique place, a unique nation with unique people. The structures, the organization, the materials used, the aesthetic of the buildings should all tell the story of the people. The story will be distinct to each community, the buildings should be tailored to each function. The architecture should tell a story, not become a Disney interpretation of Native America.

Community is generally defined as a group of people who live in the same area and who share common characteristics. In Indian Country, community is more than that. Community is everything in a tribal nation. We based decisions on how they affected the community, what the community wants, how the community will feel, what's best for the community, for community is family. Tribal communities are made up of several large family trees, thus everyone is related, which is why community is so important. It's not just about neighbors, it's about family.

Among the Lakota the tiospaye is the family, including all extended family members. There is not recognition of "great aunt or second cousin or step dad" or any sort of distant relative. Everyone is a sister, brother, aunt, uncle, cousin or grandparent. It is common to have multiple mothers, fathers, and many grandparents. The

well being of the tiospaye is paramount in our tribe. Decisions are undertaken with the tiospaye in mind.

Thus when a building project is contemplated, it involves the whole community, not just those directly responsible for the specific function of that project. If there is a new office building, not only are the future occupants affected, the whole community is interested and want to be involved. They want to be involved because one of their relatives may work in the building or they feel connected because of its location and potential impact on their daily life in the small community. This is a totally different situation to that in many non-tribal communities. Designing a new office building off reservation does not involve anyone other than the building owner and maybe the occupants. Rarely is the community at large involved unless they are against it for some reason and show up at a public hearing or council meeting.

A new building in a tribal community is a rare occurrence. Funding is so difficult to obtain and is such a long process that when it is awarded to a project, there is always fear that it can be taken away if not spent as soon as possible. This has led to many rushed design phases, or no design phase at all and oftentimes the use of a pre-fabricated or modular building. There is a misconception that using an architect will not only cost more money but will take more time. Many pre-fabricated and modular builders have used this fear to convince tribes to use their product. The result is seen in tribal communities across America. Grocery stores, to office buildings, to schools are located in metal buildings or modular trailers which do nothing to improve the built environment, let alone express the cultural identity of the people.

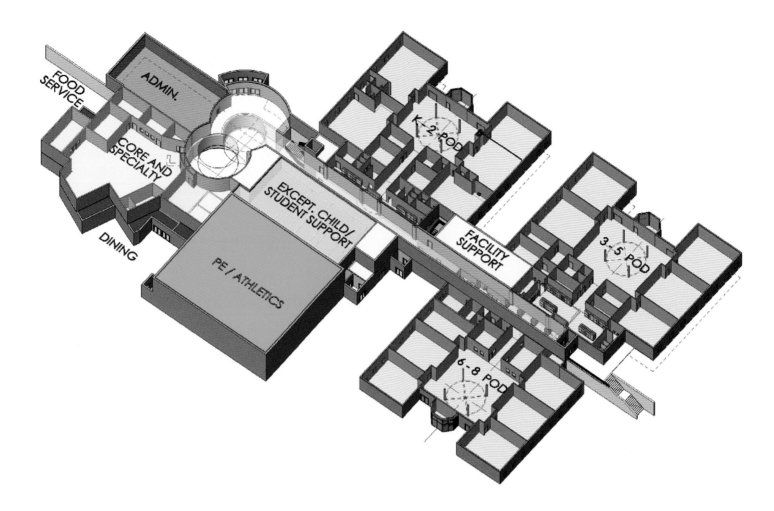

Figure 3. Wóunspe Otipi, Source: Encompass Architects

Funding for community planning or infrastructure planning is largely nonexistent for tribes. Thus when a building is funded, there is usually very little forethought into where it will be placed. Sometimes infrastructure is considered but usually it is an afterthought. There are new tribal buildings that have sat empty for weeks or months because extending the infrastructure was not coordinated or budgeted. This happens very regularly both with architects and without architects involved. Usually the design teams who are involved in these situations are inexperienced in working with tribes and are accustomed to working in non-reservation communities where there are utilities at the property lines and the amount of coordination is minimal and uncomplicated. On tribal land, infrastructure coordination often needs to happen between several federal, state, and local agencies.

When a project is started on a reservation there are many entities to coordinate and involve. A thorough understanding of that tribe's particular situation, organization, and capabilities is necessary. Understanding what questions to ask and whom to ask them of as well as coordinating the various government agencies involvement in the project while maintaining the tribe's sovereignty is a role for which most architects are unprepared. Thankfully, there are a growing number of Native architects who are versed in these challenges and who are successful in working with tribes to rebuild their sense of community.

Tribal buildings often must serve a variety of purposes beyond their initial intended functions. As usable and modern space is at a premium and there are so many unmet needs, spaces need to be designed as multipurpose and multifunctional.

When funding for a new school is received for a tribe, it is often a once in a lifetime experience for tribal members. The existing school is likely to be 50 years old or more and the new one will probably have to last just as long. Schools are often the center of the community, especially small communities. Many activities occur at the school beyond sanctioned school functions.

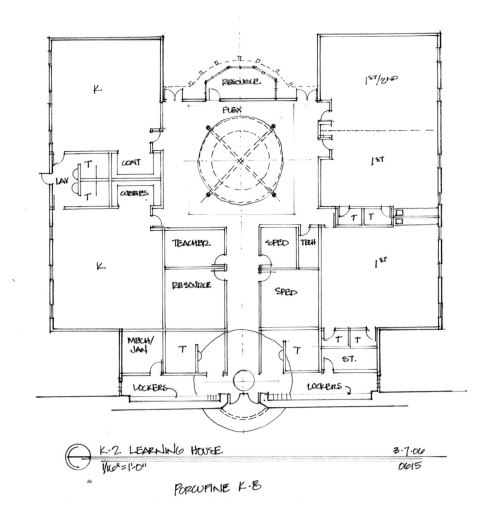

Figure 4. 3d Floor Plan, Source: rendering by Encompass Architects

My family is from the Pine Ridge Indian Reservation in the southwestern corner of South Dakota, near the Black Hills. The Reservation is nearly three million acres, the second largest reservation in the United States. The population statistics for the reservation are difficult to verify as estimates range from 28,000 to 40,000 residents. The reservation is divided into nine distinct districts. My mother's family is from the Porcupine district while my father grew up in Pine Ridge village.

Pine Ridge is in Oglala Lakota County, consistently the first or second poorest county in the country. According to the United States Census Bureau website (n.d.), the mean per-capita income in 2015 was $9,150. Unemployment is near 80% with nearly half the residents below the poverty line. The residents of this community have a much shorter life expectancy and the infant mortality rate is five times the national average (Red Cloud Indian School, webpage). Substandard health care, lack of access to affordable fresh food, inadequate housing, and lack of transportation have led to obesity, diabetes, and heart disease at epidemic proportions.

Addiction, abuse, crime, and poverty are part of daily life for residents including children. Teen suicides are a weekly occurrence with children as young as seven taking their own lives.

Depression and demoralization are pervasive and blatant racism exists in the neighboring non-reservation town of Rapid City. Children are openly harassed and taunted by non-Indian adults, usually for merely existing and being Native. All of this affects how the children feel about themselves and feel about their culture.

Despite all of this, the culture has survived. Children are being taught their language and schools are trying to reinforce cultural pride, to tell children that it is ok to be Lakota, it is nothing to be ashamed of, that racism is wrong. Schools are ground zero for the well being of children. It is often the only place a child receives a hot meal, a kind word or a sense of safety and security and belonging.

I was fortunate to be commissioned to design a new K-8 school for Porcupine. While I was already very familiar

Figure 5. Exterior, Source: Encompass Architects

with the community and its residents, I tried not to have any preconceived notions of what was best for them. This is antithetical to how architects are trained. We are taught to be the expert, to know what is best for our client. We are encouraged to design what we feel is needed, not soliciting opinions from clients. Unfortunately it is this type of traditional architectural thinking that has led to tribal communities being in the state they are now. Tribal clients are hesitant to use architects for fear they will not listen, based on past negative experiences. And, when architects are involved they do not solicit interaction and design what they deem to be appropriate representations of the culture. These buildings with pan-Indian patterns or overt graphics in the shape of animals are strewn across Indian Country, creating an inaccurate and disrespectful identity for our tribal communities.

For this school project, I undertook workshops with the school administration, staff, parents, interested community members, and importantly with the children. I asked them what the school meant to them, what they wanted and needed from the new school, and what their concerns were regarding the new school. The responses ranged

from the practical needs for space to the whimsical desire for amenities beyond the budget. Schools are most often funded by the US Department of the Interior, Bureau of Indian Affairs (BIA) through congressional budget allowance. To say the funding is tight would be a gross understatement. There are strict space allocation guidelines for the program development.

Tribal schools often serve as community centers. At Porcupine, the school is the place where large gatherings have to occur such as political meetings, community meetings, wakes, and funerals. The BIA guidelines do not allow space for these activities. So creative space programming and design are necessary to achieve a floor plan which is flexible and multifunctional.

The children had a very unique perspective on the new school. They were asked to draw or write what they wanted or needed in the new school. Many drew cultural items such as a medicine wheel or dream catcher as a way to explain what they wanted the school to represent them, their culture. Others drew

Figure 6. Star Quilt Floor, Source: Encompass Architects

houses. When asked why they drew a house, the response was they wanted the school to be a safe place and they envisioned safety as a typical house. Not their own house but an ideal house, the square with triangle roof, square four-paned windows and center door. The house that all children draw. Many of these children do not have this house, nor this safe home. They needed the school to fulfil this function. To be their safe place.

After the workshops we compiled the input into a cultural values board. This was a visual representation of the input received and the commonalities and important concepts from the workshops. This board was distributed to the design team and was referenced at each design meeting, to make sure we kept the ideas and concepts in mind.

Using concepts developed by the children we set out to design their school as a safe place, a home – a tipi in Lakota. The teaching staff acknowledged that the new school would be much larger than their current school and worried that it would feel overwhelming to

the students, especially the younger ones. They did not want to lose the sense of school community. To address this, they suggested using learning pods to organize the classes. The Wóunspe Otipi, (learning house) was the safe home for the students.

Each Wóunspe Otipi had three grade levels organized around a central multifunctional classroom space. The progression into the Otipi followed the perceived entry into an ideal house. The children envisioned coming in the door, hanging up coats, washing up, and going to the living room. So upon entry to the Wóunspe Otipi, the students hung up coats and backpacks, went by the restrooms and washed hands and gathered in the central living room. Each morning the house gathers together to pray and start the day. They end the day in the same place – as a family a tioyspaye.

To also address the concern that the larger school would be intimidating from the exterior, each learning house was clad in a different brick color. The youngest children all drew schools with red bricks as they probably saw in their books or imaginations. So we clad the K-2

Figure 7. Star Quilt, Source: Encompass Architects

Figure 8. Media Center, Source: Encompass Architects

Wóunspe Otipi in red brick. The middle house has a yellow brick and the more grown up 6-8 pod has a purple brick. This allows the students to visually connect to their home while they are outside the school, and to know where they will be moving to when they progress to the next pod.

As the school functions as a community center several times a month, the gymnasium, kitchen, and dining area needed to be accessible after hours without compromising the security of the entire school. A Lakota tradition is the wopila, which is a time to give thanks by feeding the community and honoring somebody by the gift of a star quilt. The star quilt is handmade in a distinctive star pattern used by the Lakota. It seemed appropriate to use the star quilt as a pattern in the dining hall as this is where the community (either school or larger) is fed and where thanks are given. The bold pattern can be seen from the upper level through a large circular drum that extends through to the roof.

In working with the children and staff, it became apparent that the media center even in its deteriorated state in the existing space, was a special place for them. In the new school, we wanted the media center to be just as

esteemed, a place they could lose themselves in books. Traditionally the Lakota used the Dreamcatcher to ward off bad dreams. So we used a dreamcatcher motif in the light placement. The media center is officially the place to "dream."

The village of Porcupine is like other tribal communities where vandalism is a problem. Buildings are very susceptible to gangs marking them as territory. In the ten years that Pahin Sinte Owayawa (Porcupine School) has been open, there has not been any significant vandalism. Moreover, the students who were involved in the design process felt a real connection with the school and took pride in caring for it. They would remind each other to pick up trash and to treat it with respect. That feeling has been passed down to the new students and there remains a sense of ownership among the students. They might not have been involved in the design, but just knowing that their predecessors were involved has made all the difference to them. They respect that and thus respect the school.

As the largest building in the village, Pahin Sinte Owayawa defines the community aesthetic. The Lakota culture is woven throughout in subtle ways, a brick pattern on the gymnasium references the porcupine quillwork for which the Lakota are known. The material color palette is taken from the surrounding landscape. As a two-story facility, the school is nestled into the side of a hill, respecting the site, not trying to conquer it by being on top. The 72,000 square foot school fits in the environment, feeling connected to the land. The residents have embraced the school, not only for the children's sake, but because they were involved in the process. They were invited to participate; their ideas were heard. Many of the ideas were not realized but the fact they were able to express them was enough to gain community wide consensus.

References

United States Census Bureau. (n.d.) *QuickFacts Oglala Lakota County, South Dakota*. Retrieved 2017, December 20 from https://www.census.gov/quickfacts/fact/table/oglalalakotacountysouthdakota/POP010210#viewtop

Red Cloud Indian School. (n.d.). *Our Story, Our Success. The Reservation*. Red Cloud School website Retrieved, 2017, December 20 from https://www.redcloudschool.org/reservation

Chapter 20: Decolonising the whenua (land)

Matthew Groom – Ngāti Whakaue

Matthew Groom is a 16 year old from Porirua, New Zealand. He attends Aotea College and is in Year 12. He enjoys graphic design and geography the most out of his subjects. He plays the drums and has done hip-hop dancing for over 10 years. He has 2 sisters and he is of Māori descent on his Mum's side of the family.

A note from the editors

This essay was submitted to the Imagining Decolonised Cities competition held in Porirua, New Zealand in early 2017. Contestants were asked to imagine what a decolonised city would like and feel like using a specific site. Matthew chose the Parai whānau's (family) land which was recently bought back from the government having been taken from the tribe years ago under the Public Works Act which allows for the taking of privately held land for public works such as roads and parks etc. Lots of Māori land was lost using this mechanism. After a long fight with the government the Parai whānau were allowed to buy back their land despite having never received any money from the government for it, when it was taken.

Matthew narrates the essay from the perspective of the whenua (land). Matthew's work won a Highly Commended prize.

The feet that paced above me were those that felt familiar. The voices that trailed down my slopes were those of which I recognised. But the atmosphere was not the same as the last time the feet above had gathered. There was a cold breeze that I had not signed permission for, a panic in the air that was not caused by the restlessness of my limbs while I dozed.

Although I knew the discussion that whirled atop my head was important, that's not what my mind was drawn to. My focus was on the two small feet that had skewed away from the group and were racing down my body. They were the smallest feet of the group and definitely the most curious. They belonged to a young boy whose name I seemed unable to learn as it was usually yelled by his mother when he ran off, each letter carried away in the breeze. The boy's feet pushed down on my soft green hair as did the ball he was rapidly chasing. His mother did not protest this time as there were important things to discuss about the families' land being taken away by a mysterious entity they called the public works act. An idea that was a harsh whisper in my ears and a proposal that I shuddered at the thought of. I was not a piece of stock, I was not an item that could be bought or sold but those above me knew this and would not let me go without a fight. Every footstep from them wasn't just a step it was a hug or a greeting and every object placed was one that I did not mind for it bought them something whether it was sustenance or enjoyment. Their ancestors lay next to me and I honoured them everyday with songs sung by the wind that weaved through my grassy fields and art spread across my canvas painted by the sunlight. I was home. These of course were things the young boy was completely oblivious to and would be for a few years to come but ignorance is bliss they say, at least when it comes to the public works act. The boy finally caught the ball much to his enjoyment but was met with a new form of entertainment; a potential friend. A new soul had entered my vicinity, a soul whose feet, whose body language, whose movements, steps, and rhythms were alien to me. The new soul was too, a young Māori boy that had wandered from down the road, who signalled to the other boy that he wanted to join in. A nod of approval was given and the two boys ran up and down kicking the ball into, tripping over, and dashing around every crevice, slope and chisel in my skin until they were both called back to their families and said their friendly goodbyes, promising to meet up again. I made a note to myself to remember the new boy and the way he moved, the patterns and shapes of his feet and toes and the way they dug in to my soil. Then maybe next time I could go easier on him and he won't trip so much.

Four Years Later

It was a day of many mixed emotions the day the long fight for me was over. It was filled with happiness, grievance, and relief. But, it was over and I was handed back to my family or, much rather, sold back for a price should I say, which ruffled my feathers a bit but I tried to keep the mood light for the honorary celebration. I hoped to make it a sunny day but the land over the hill was feeling quite moody so I made no promises. Luckily the families' victory was louder and the sun broke out from between the clouds.

Discussions ranged from person to person but the looming topic was: now what? There were the two boys who I had come to know as Hemi, the curious boy with the ball and Rawiri, the stranger from down the road who was no longer a stranger and was just as welcome to stroll upon me as the Parai whānau. They sat away from the adults but still looked over the harbour from my highest point and discussed their options for what to do with me. The parents and elders had suggested with a smile that Hemi and Rawiri go for a walk but they were coming in to their pre-teen years according to my guesses and were persistent on staying and helping with the grown-ups.

Over the next month the boys travelled back and forth surveying me for opportunities and jotting down ideas that unfortunately I wasn't in the loop with but I guess I just had to wait. Hemi and Rawiri had never been the serious type so seeing them become so intent on turning me into a paradise for the whānau made me so happy I could've sworn my grass turned a brighter shade of green. The day that made me most excited was the day the boys finished their planning and got so excited to show everyone they left heavy footprints from their, what I would call unique, dance moves in the mud. Then came the night the family all gathered in the evening sun to present their ideas and to celebrate all those who had fought to keep me. Idea after idea was put forward by everyone, from rows of gardens to how to arrange living for everyone. But when the group arrived to Hemi and Rawiri they were not expecting the massive project they had in mind and neither was I if I'm honest with you but they say kids have the most active imaginations, you know.

As the boys began to tell their vision the family fell silent, as did I. There was not a breath of wind, the sun poked its head out to listen and the birds fell quiet too eagerly waiting for the words to tumble out and become real. Hemi and Rawiri began to share and my mind was completely empty allowing enough room for every word they uttered to process. They talked about the sixteen houses for everyone, designed to encompass the style of a marae from the shapes to the designs but they were to stand tall with balconies and big glass windows to give a magnificent view of the harbour from any spot. They were to be arranged in a curve that ran up the hill. Almost like a spine, a backbone that supported everyone but one that was hunched with age. A spine that had been around to see it all, had lived through hardships, struggles and had been through pressure and force but was wiser and stronger for it, each home a disc that held the backbone together. They talked of smooth paths that connected each home and were easily accessible for everyone. They talked of the materials that would be used; wood, which was flexible enough to be moved but strong enough to hold together. Sturdy enough to brace against the impact of strong winds, smooth enough to let the warm sun silk it's way in. For every tree used for wood, another would be planted in its place. The big glass panes that were not just a material but a window in which to view and admire the harbour below and let the bright colours and lights of the outdoors, in. There would be solar panels that would blend in to the roofs and make the small community completely independent and clean. They talked of big vegetable gardens made with golden wooden planks for every house that too followed the curve of the spine, provided sustenance to keep the backbone strong. My favourite part was hearing them talk about their invention describing a pulley system made from two poles and a wire that held a big bucket which could be used to deliver kaimoana between the houses after the young ones had dashed down to the harbour to collect some. Kids got to have some fun things to tinker with, right?

All of this talk of what the future could hold for me made me giddy with excitement but I contained myself as not to disturb the boys. Finally, they talked of trees, trees that didn't follow the curve of the backbone but were scattered all over the place as they were after all backbones of their own, their thick roots holding me together and becoming a part of me, linking with every grain of dirt within me. Trees planted everywhere that could provide cool shade, branches to swing from and climb, and future tyre swings to tie around the tree and swing from. I mean, what else are you supposed to do with old tyres?

It's safe to say the family was very impressed and especially thanked Rawiri for his contribution to the fate of their land. From this point onwards things became chaotic. It took a while to get going but Hemi and Rawiri's idea came to life and the next year or so were filled with construction, developments and a lot more feet than usual walking their paths upon me to the point that I could not trace every footprint but it was worth it for the end result.

The day the project was finished was a day I once again recognised every footprint, every movement, every step and rhythm but this time was not a time of stress, it was a time of elation and the happiness was so powerful it became a physical material that soaked in to my soil. Later that day Rawiri showed up and brought his whānau along and the two boys who I had come to know couldn't have been more proud. Despite this their first thought upon greeting each other was to race to the tree at the top of the hill and climb it. Kids are still kids even when they can put their minds to work and come up with something mindblowing I guess. I made sure to hold the roots of the tree they climbed extra tightly so they would be safe.

A Note from the Author

This piece of writing is about decolonisation because it talks about making the land for the Parai whānau a place that represents their values and makes the land their home and something that reflects their culture, identity and needs. My ideas that I communicated through the boys telling of their idea shows how representing Māori culture through decolonisation isn't just about designs or language it's about ideals and values like providing for oneself and others, family and community. This was shown in how I talked about the boys coming up with the pulley system for kaimoana, helping put the value of what's mine is yours plus the virtue of gathering your own food and living off the land in to a feature in the space. It's also shown in the way the materials are sustainable and clean because in Māori culture people have a great respect and connection to the land so using renewable materials and clean energy helps keep negative impact on the environment low plus this is also something the Parai whānau wanted for their development. A signature of the Parai whānau is having a fun, happy place for children to grow up which is made use of through the fun pulley system for kids to help out with kai and the large amounts of trees for playing on and around.

Decolonisation is also shown in the way the harbour and its use for kaimoana is a strong feature with its own tools built in to the land (like the pulley system) that helps keep that aspect thriving and an easy part of everyday life. The buildings in the development are made with materials that are flexible and long lasting which is important in making sure these homes will be around for a long time to keep the culture and how it's represented in the area alive for years to come. Finally, using the land as the perspective and the narrator ties together that use of the land (without negative impact) is a huge part of the culture and that anything on the land is not just there it has a purpose or a meaning like the design described in my story for the Parai, that sets their space in Porirua for everyone to see. These all tie together to strongly represent Māori culture not just in the way the buildings look in terms of Māori design but in how the space is setup to show the strong connection between whānau and the idea of community, providing for each other, being one, and having a good time.

Chapter 21: Face the Irony

Linda Kennedy – Yuin
First published in 2015 by www.future-black.com

Let's say, in colonial terms, you are an award-winning, successful architect. You are one of nine white, male directors leading a large design practice. You pride yourself on your iconic buildings – there is no doubt that you have had an impact on the built environment in Australia for almost twenty years.

Now, let's say you have a new project, a high-rise residential building, centrally located in a capital city. A city frequented by around 800,000 people each day – Melbourne, say. You have approval to build over 100 metres high, 32 stories of expensive, luxurious apartments. You have an opportunity to do anything you want – to assert your relevance in the "urban fabric" of Melbourne, to prove that you are socially conscious, up with the times, maybe even radical, still. You can do "different," you can do "iconic" – as long as it is of value to a large-scale developer, say, Grocon.

So how about you make a statement? How about you design an enormous face onto the facade of your building? How about a black man's face? How about the face of William Barak?

Indeed, how about that!

Construction of ARM's "portrait building," as it has become known, is complete, with the face unveiled in March, 2015. It is part of a new development precinct, Swanston Square, located on the old Carlton Brewery site in Melbourne's CBD, the land of the Wurundjeri people.

More recently, the location has become known as the "wall-collapse site," where passers-by Marie-Faith Fiawoo, Bridget Jones, and Alexandar Jones died in 2012 when a large brick wall from Grocon's construction site fell onto a public footpath. It's also adjacent to Sean Godsell's Design Hub which "prove[d] a danger" to the public when two glass discs from the facade system "plunged to the pavement" (Gardiner, Herald Sun, 2014). Maybe the portrait building will follow suit, and Barak's face will come crashing down onto the streets of Melbourne?

Consider, that even without tumbling down, the 300+ square metre portrait of William Barak's face causes damage to this nation as a by-product of its existence.

In a previous blog post, Archi-Crime: (in the name of) Reconciliation (Kennedy, 2015), I outlined the need to move beyond visual representations of Aboriginal cultures/histories in architecture, the need to focus on Indigenous ways of knowing/doing as primary design principles, and the need to use these principles/values in design beyond Aboriginal user-groups, for both black and white projects.

The portrait building, in contrast, is a building for mainstream occupants, using design principles/ values from the colonial/invader mindset, with a visual representation of Aboriginal Australia stuck to the front of the building.

It would seem that ARM are trying to achieve some kind of ironic relationship between the war memorial on the south of the Birrarung, and a black man's face on the north of the river. Their website (2014) stated that this relationship "stands to unite the city's modern heritage with its ancient history" – as though Aboriginal people died out long ago, and only traces of our existence still remain. Wake up ARM – we are still here.

Let's face it: the irony in this project is not the juxtaposition of imagery. In itself, this symbol will provoke short-term thought responses from a small portion of the public, it will provide a topic for conversation, some food for critics, and it will add five more minutes to Melbourne's walking tours. It will not create social change.

The true irony of this project is the lack of substance delivered by the misdirected will of an all-white design team. The irony: that this building raises more questions about the relationship between white architects and Aboriginal Australia than it raises about the relationship between white and black Australian history, culture, identity.

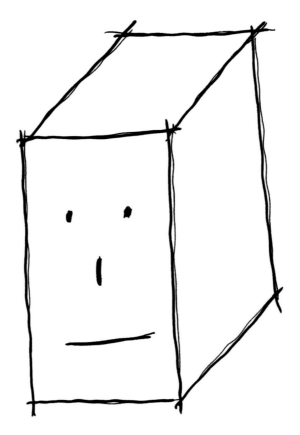

Figure 1. Face the Irony [Source: Hand sketch, Kennedy, L. (2015)]

Yes, this portrait, it tells a history. But it does not live the present. It speaks of our people past as though there is no cultural present, no expected future.

The connection to the war memorial does not hold any significance to me as an Aboriginal woman. I do not need to compare a monstrous stone memorial to an enormous face in order to be able to acknowledge the genocide, to remember the thousands of Aboriginal people who were massacred on this land at the hands of colonial invaders. It is lived and remembered every day.

Of greater value in the archi-sphere is design thinking that chooses to implement change beyond what can be visually seen, and beyond colonial values. Step back and consider the value in Aboriginal ways of knowing/doing – both in historical and contemporary Indigenous cultures. Challenge the nuclear household. Design for adaptation. Understand Country. Engage with community. Build sustainably.

Learn from past mistakes: try something other than statement making. Stop exploiting Aboriginal histories and cultures for designs that are only skin deep.

References

ARM Architecture. (2015). *Barak Building*. Retrieved 2015, February 15 from http://armarchitecture.com.au/projects/barak-building/

Gardiner, G. (2014, October 29). "RMIT Design Hub proves a danger as glass discs fall to ground." *Sun Herald*. Retrieved 2017, December 20 from http://www.heraldsun.com.au/news/victoria/rmit-design-hub-proves-a-danger-as-glass-discs-fall-to-ground/news-story/d368dda9cca47718d8f088fad808ff61

Kennedy, L. (2015, February 15). Archi-Crime: (in the name of) Reconciliation [Blog post]. Retrieved 2017, December 20 from http://www.future-black.com/blog/8/2/2015/archi-crime-in-the-name-of-reconciliation

Chapter 22: Third Space in Architecture

Michael Mossman – Cairns Murri, Descendant of Kuku Yalanji, Warungu and South Sea Islander Heritage

Michael was born in Cairns and lives in Syndey and is currently teaching is currently teaching and researching at the University of Sydney School of Architecture, Design and Planning, where his interest is to situate architecture in the broader Indigenous scholarship environment. As a doctoral candidate, his thesis focuses on the Architecture and the Third Space, an in-between zone of negotiation between Indigenous and Western viewpoints. His thesis aims to promote engagement methods that historicize and politicize worldview commonalities and differences, and strategize future ways of being, knowing, doing, and learning relative to architecture.

Architecture stands as a unique human endeavour: the production of ephemeral or permanent sites and structures to shelter communities and belongings from the elements. The common thread of a temporary dwelling or a permanent building lies in the representation of culture through the project's overall position, the designer's intent, the client's aspiration or the community's narrative.

The communication of position, intent, aspiration and narrative is equally unique in architecture, as the enunciated position of representation is critical to the design and construction qualities of the built form. A community's message to an architect holds transactional significance in the agency of each actor's historic and political experiences to influence the architectural narrative. The message the architect receives from a community holds translational significance for similar reasons. Ideally this process is cyclical and always evolving, allowing contention, negotiation, conflict, resolution, and ongoing contributions to the discussion (Bhabha, 1994).

The binary positions of engaged participants display core "ways" – epistemologies, ontologies and axiologies. The original core worldview positions can remain overall, however it is required to evolve for the specific task at hand. The aim of Third Space is to enable dialogue between cultures of difference: in this case,

the Indigenous "Self" and the Settler Colonising "Other." Third Space situates the enunciated positions of opposed and marginalised, or asymmetrical communities to create temporal, political and culturally-specific sites of negotiation. The resulting confrontation of cultures recognizes localized difference and distinctiveness as a product of social and spatial relations (Bhabha, 2006).

This can lead to the Third Space: How messages are exchanged and how participants interact can influence the levels of comfort for the architectural conversations to occur, the conditions of negotiation for the decisions to be made, and the proactivity of the tasks to be carried out by the stakeholders. Where differences in culture occur, enacting an interstitial Third Space (an in-between space) of robust discussion on cultural difference and cultural productivity can articulate new cultural meaning for a specific application in architecture (Hernandez, 2010).

The enunciation of positions emerge from both sides to affect knowledge previously unknown due to the contextual and temporal setting of the architectural exercise. The Third Space enables opportunities and encouragement to think differently about architecture, its meanings and significance. Expanding a critical spatial consciousness that looks at place, location, locality, landscape, and environment from worldviews of difference can mobilize and evolve historical and political beliefs and sensibilities (Soja, 1996).

The central zone is a liminal place where differences touch, interact, disrupt, unsettle and de-centre pre-existing narratives to produce a structure for marginalized cultures to symbolize themselves to their counterparts (Bhabha, 1994; Mitchell, 1995; Krmpotich, 2016).

While this chapter briefly alludes to the subjects of decolonizing Indigenous methodologies, it primarily focuses on historic drivers of Third Space to identify and critique current debate and indicate potential future investigations. The occupation of a third position advocates a role that aims to synthesize the rights and

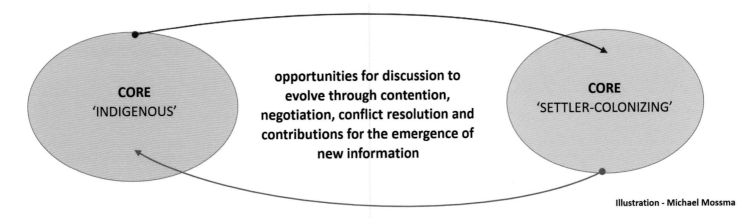

Figure 1. Binaries, Source: Author

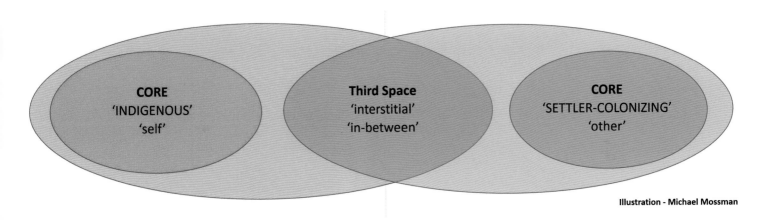

Figure 2. Third Space, Source: Author

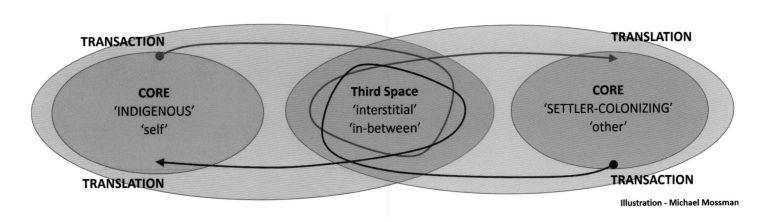

Figure 3. The liminal place, Source: Author

Figure 4. Location of the Gugu Badhun, Kamilaroi and Eora Nations, Source: Author

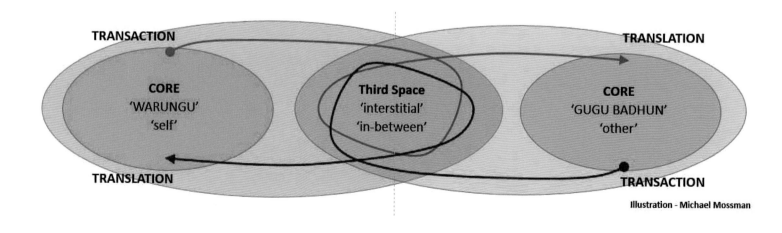

Figure 5. The liminal place, Source: Author

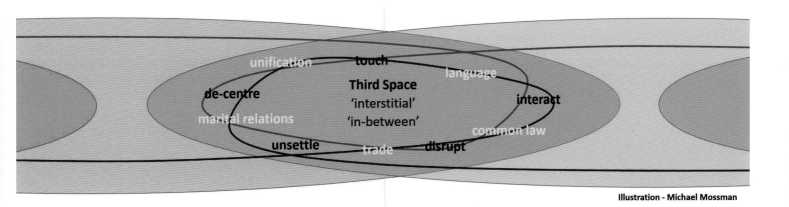

Illustration - Michael Mossman

Figure 6. Negotiation of Third Space, Source: Author

Figure 7. Ngunnawal, Source: Author

responsibilities of communities and their counterparts (Pearson, 2007): a multi-faceted structural engagement process that requires enunciated strategies of self-determined communications for continual negotiation. While knowledge is power, the ability to communicate and share that knowledge base is critical to transformative discourse and practical service delivery. The collaboration of worldviews, both working to shared outcomes that challenge dominant framing systems, can be enabling when played out within the Third Space.

Examples of creative and innovative Third Space dialogue have occurred in my own professional practice experience, where the creation and engagement of local Indigenous reference groups have benefited all participants in a project – from grass roots Indigenous communities to government bureaucracies, designers and contractors. The transactional meanings and idiosyncrasies of Indigenous community communications in design processes overlapping with the translational capabilities of the architect are vital to project outcomes.

It is used to facilitate agency for communication purposes in unbalanced power dynamics. Attention to this notion is drawn from my own existence between two ways: the influences of self and other being critical to my make up within a settler-colonizing society with traditional Indigenous ancestry. As a product of settler-colonization and Indigenous Australian communities that critically challenge its notions, and as a trained professional in mainstream architecture, my role here is to provoke a reconsideration of architecture's past and present narratives in order to envisage more inclusive and productive directions, better suited to the reality of Indigenous world views and practices.

My experiences and interests in the agency of categorized marginalized groups has foregrounded the importance of Third Space, and its integral zones of negotiation, as fundamental issues to be investigated. The architectural application of exchange management relating to Third Space is extensive and apply across all phases of project conception, programming, consultation, design, delivery, management and maintenance of designed and built environments – from civic spaces to landscapes, urban public domains, individual and collective housing, institutional, and infrastructural projects. Architecture delimits space and reduces zones of influence which have historically privileged some and excluded other voices through processes of settler-colonisation.

The structure of this chapter follows a chronology of Australian history relative to Third Space in pre-invasion and settler-colonization contexts, with a brief foreword on contemporary transformations for future investigations. Important to these notions are the qualities of the engagement practices carried out, within the boundaries of traditional custodianship and with settler-colonising practitioners. Critical to this chapter is my own Indigenous standpoint utilising tenets of decolonising Indigenous methodologies and the concept of Third Space to promote conversations between self and other and thus to recast the capacity of architecture and the designed environment to engage more genuinely and productively across Indigenous and non-Indigenous constituencies.

Tradition, Invasion and Settler-Colonization

I propose that the conditions of engagement between Indigenous Australian groups prior to invasion took place within a conceptual and physical Third Space wherein very specific protocols of transaction, translation, access, and movement operated and did so for the ongoing sustainment of communities. Western positivist anthropological and ethnographical research has evidenced that synergistic engagement processes, following complex protocols and laws, were in place within traditional Indigenous communities prior to British invasion. (Kenny, 2012; Gammage, 2011; Smith, 2012; Rigney, 1999) Transactive spatial and territorial practices, both intra and inter-tribal, included land tenure and land management systems.

The spatialized nature of tenure and management utilized zones of negotiation, at times peaceful and other aggressive in nature, to settle ways of existence relative to the conditions of country and generational systems of knowledge. (Mabo, 1992; Gammage, 2011; Prout & Howitt, 2009) Systems of negotiated space between tribal groups were established for spiritual and practical reasons such as the maintenance of cultural and ceremonial practices, the establishment of boundaries and land management responsibilities, the respect for common and different understandings of intellectual knowledge, the framing of trade and relationship protocols and the promotion of shared and distinctive ways of being and knowing.

Specific accounts of the Warungu people of the Gugu Badhun nation west of Cairns, Australia narrate a story that attests to the concepts of Third Space prior to invasion and settler colonization in 1845. Unified relationships between three groups within the Gugu Badhun nation (Warungu and Gugu Badhun and Gatjal) enabled negotiating zones of mutual respect influencing the evolution of culture. Movement within country and externally through adjacent tribal boundaries and afar utilized common language understandings through the present-day Queensland interior, west of Cairns to the New South Wales border (Cadet-James, James, McGinty & McGregor, 2017).

This is significant to Bhabha's linguistic notions of Third Space, which highlight the significance of language as a binding element of cultures to unite with and/or resist external factors of influence (Bhabha, 1994). Research indicates that the maintenance of language and linguistic practices was critical to traditional Indigenous tribal groups' inter-cultural capacity for adaptation, resilience, and survival with the onset of invasion and settler-colonialism. (Edmunds & Carey, 2016) The effective network of protocols and laws were founded in the tight association between language and space, narrative and Country (Norris & Yidumduma, 2014).

Severance of this association was instrumental in the damage done to Indigenous culture: in many cases, the eradication of language accompanied the dispossession of lands. My own access to and experience of language and country has been equally inhibited due to processes of settler-colonization, and the inter-generational erasure and forgetting of such knowledge that was traditionally passed on from one generation to the next. Such knowledge was critical in connecting to and wayfinding within Country and to respectful interaction and travel into and across surrounding nations.

Traditional Indigenous Australian mobility provided daily living security, reinforced geographical connections relating spaces of belonging and identity, and provided opportunities for cultural interactions with communities near and far (Edmunds & Carey, 2016; Prout & Howitt, 2009; Norris & Yidumduma, 2014). Engagement between systems of difference were carried out in Third Space which entailed complex organisation and protocols that regulated how people interacted with each other and with Country. This is evidenced, for example, with gathering sites on Country and involved many surrounding nations. These were gatherings of cultural exchange that could take over a year to organize and negotiate proceedings (Norris & Yidumduma, 2014).

The unified conditions of the Gugu Badhun, Warungu and Gudjal contrasted with relationships to tribal groups to the west and east (coastal), where strict approvals were required when moving across boundaries for trade purposes (Cadet-James et al., 2017). While relationships between traditional Indigenous Australian groups varied, observance of territorial boundaries was critical to law and culture. The boundaries of interaction happened at many different scales and allowed shared knowledge and working relationships to be built over a very long time.

Understanding practices relating to these interactions led to the occupation of an inter-tribal, shared space of knowledge production and innovation. Accommodating different tribal groups meant that particular spatial setups had to be devised and regulated, including access, circulation, location, and distribution of spaces to different groups and families. The fact that such spatial organisations of shared systems and boundaries across communities of difference had been developed and effectively used for 80,000 years at current reckoning is astonishing, given the isolation and vastness of the land. It is likely that inter-tribal interaction resulted in territorial changes, however, the onset of British invasion and settler-colonizing practices forever changed the spatial systems and protocols associated with Country, leading to considerable negative ramifications for First Nations peoples.

British invasion and settler-colonizing practices, including architecture, destroyed social, spiritual and spatial fabrics of traditional Indigenous Australian societies. British lieutenant James Cook declared Crown possession of the east coast of the Australian continent in 1770 after the non-recognition of internationally-agreed treaties due to claims of non-settlement and non-cultivation of land by Indigenous peoples (Edmunds and Carey, 2016; Banivanua Mar, 2010). The claim of terra nullius had far-reaching consequences, not the least of which was justification of land seizure, the establishment of settler-colonies and the imposition of British sovereignty, culture, infrastructure and land management on Indigenous Country (Edmunds and Carey, 2016).

The First Fleet's engagement with local Indigenous peoples of the Eora Nation highlighted radical differences in ways of building, planning, commerce, language, and food procurement (Cunningham, 1827; Troy, 1992). The Western paradigms that framed this engagement did not enable the colonisers to be aware of, let alone appreciate or account for Indigenous Australian systems of land tenure. The wholesale imposition of cadastral division for individual private ownership of territory, with its definitive boundaries and orthogonal Euclidean geometries, effectively disabled any possibility for a Third Space zone of negotiation (Belmessous, 2014; Prout & Howitt, 2009). The introduction of systems of inalienable cartographic boundaries over a pre-existing Indigenous cultural system of complex and overlapping spatial boundaries created a dichotomy that continues to impact Indigenous Australian societies.

Concurrent with these new boundaries were new laws designed to affect a new type of punishment for trespass: entry into private space constituting a breach of British law. While the unjust events of globalized empire building impacted many Indigenous communities, Australia's narrative retains the fact that Indigenous sovereignty of territory has never been ceded through the appropriate legal channels. The illegal basis of British settler-colonizing powers established a cultural binary to systematically exclude Indigenous populations from all forms of sovereignty, human rights and engagement. Socially, the exclusion of Indigenous Australian populations from these imposed systems of freehold and leasehold land, in their own Country, in favour of the settler-colonizing "other," resulted in further degradation of community empowerment. My Indigenous "Self" standpoint laments the lost opportunities had such a Third Space engagement been installed at the outset, together with the richness and diversity that could have resulted from the interactions and collective outcomes that it would have made possible. While the Western spatialized impositions of boundaries did impact Indigenous examples.

Spatialised struggles ensued as a result of colliding settlement ideologies and the lack of treaty declarations with Indigenous societies (Prout & Howitt, 2009). The non-declaration of treaties with Indigenous Australians meant that First Nations peoples were not afforded the same rights as invading settler-colonizing communities, rendering genuine engagement between cultures impossible. Illegitimate possession of sovereign territories occupied and managed by tribal groups prior to invasion produced ravaging effects on Indigenous communities, and its impact continues to the present. Architecture was complicit in empowering colonizing advancements of superiority over societies considered uncivilized. This process irreparably changed the nature of Indigenous peoples' connection with Country. The British settler-colonising state, unable to sustain meaningful engagement with Indigenous Australian societies, and relentlessly engaged in the suppression of resistance, forever impacted pre-existing spatial systems through the imposition of boundary conditions that disturbed, interrupted, or severed generations of Indigenous custodianship of Country.

The processes of settler-colonisation disrupted pre-existing land management/tenure protocols by imposing alien planning and architectural systems and infrastructures such as cadastral boundaries and built forms within individually privatised, "other," concepts of territory. From invasion to the present, the enablement of the built environment empowered settler-colonising sprawl across the Australian continent with infrastructure – police stations, courthouses, hospitals, banks, etc – necessary to support living and commercial ventures. Historical prose on the introduction of disease, frontier warfare and accounts of engaged conflict between settler-colonisers and resistant tribal groups resulted in loss of country, dislocation of communities and sustained acts of cultural genocide (Bownden and Bunbury, 1990; Reynolds, 1982; Newcastle, 2017). As Indigenous Australian connection to land is the basis of life, the appropriation of land favoured the settler-colonising society's narrative of frontier expansion geared to the importation of an ersatz Imperium (Wolfe, 2006; Obert, 2016). The historical and political narratives are vital for application to architectural Third Space to focus specific place contexts into rich conversations for continual negotiation.

Settler-colonialism's use of architecture as a means of territorial and spatial divisiveness estranged spaces through subjection and subversion (Vidler, 1992): subjection from the imposition of the architectural formalities of British "otherness" and subversion through the invasion of social orders associated with such formalities. The devastation to Indigenous communities relative to settler-colonization was immense (Bownden and Bunbury, 1990; Reynolds, 1982; Markus, 1990). Said (1993) quotes "Crosby":

> Wherever they went Europeans immediately began to change the local habitat; their conscious aim was to transform territories into images of what they had left behind. This process was never-ending, as a huge number of plants, animals, and crops as well as building methods gradually turned the colony into a new place, complete with new diseases, environmental imbalances, and traumatic dislocations for the overpowered natives.

The impact of settler-colonizing architecture transformed space into uncannily foreign places for the original custodians (Obert, 2016) driving some Indigenous societies to the edge of existence. The invasion of the Countries of Eora Nation is an example of the devastation and transformation, significantly impacted by the introduction of settler-colonizing architecture.

By contrast, the Warungu, Gugu Badhun oral histories tell a different story—one of engagement between the tribal groups and the non-Indigenous frontier families. My interest lies in the terms of negotiation that took place from first contact in such hostile frontier environments. Crown establishment of privatized leasehold land enabled pastoral station infrastructures. While traditional Indigenous populations rejected settler-colonizing invasion of territories, Indigenous peoples, as manual and house labour, were vital to its commercial viability. Furthermore, with forced transformation of community ways, Indigenous societies retained connections to country and even created bonds with the settler-colonising 'Other' (Cadet-James et al, 2017; Kenny, 2012; Davis, 2004). There was a negotiated Third Space at work here, in which intellectual and practical knowledge of country was enunciated through transactional means and translated to the shared benefit of station operators in exchange for survival, shelter and in harsh frontier conditions.

This brief theorized account of specific Indigenous group engagement with Third Space concepts relates to tradition and settler-colonizing spatial and temporal paradigms. Its aim is to engender an appreciation of fundamental factors when considering engagement in architecture with marginalized communities. History is important to the narrative and current predicaments of communities, and provides lessons relative to the territoriality of Country. The spatiality of the "other" through cadastral land division and the built environment was and continues to be imposed on Country, with formal inclusion a continual advocated negotiation.

Evolving and Contemporary Transformations of Architecture

My investigations of Indigenous methodologies uncovered the concept of Third Space, developed out of linguistics, politics, pedagogy, and geography (Bhabha, 1994) (Soja, 1996), but not yet adapted into architecture or the built environment disciplines such as planning, landscape architecture or urban design in an Indigenous context. I currently observe parallels of Third Space within an architectural dialogical context through the political concept of a central space, such as the "radical centre'." (Pearson, 2009) These can be activated by decolonizing methodological frameworks (Smith, 1999) to interrogate negotiation capabilities of both sides of a binary condition.

A spatialized equivalent are common dichotomous relationships that exist in the built environment: architecture and landscape, figure and ground, inside and out, new and old. (Thompson, 2001) The conditions of such dichotomous notions relating to the transactional and translational are inherently separate from each other, allowing no negotiable Third Space. In a universalized traditional Indigenous sense, the negotiation of such is evolving and at most times co-existent. The occupation of territories to enable life is an environmentally specific, mobile relationship with Country, rather than a commerce-focused, static imposition on Country. Third Space not only recognizes the commonalities

and tensions involved with communities of difference, but extends a zone of continuous negotiation between binary positions, now open to new emergent possibilities.

Narratives of 20th Century enlightenment against imperial domination mobilized people in the colonial world to articulate positions of socio-political agency and new narratives relative to the colonizing experience. This mobilization invokes a Third Space zone between binary oppositions to reclaim capacity, relinquish aspects of power, negotiate perspectives that may overlap and critically exchange imaginations beyond the ways of the epistemological and ontological norms. (Soja, 1996; Bhabha, 1994) The architectural typology of the embassy disrupted, unsettled and de-centred pre-existing narratives to engage the Australian population with Indigenous specific issues. On Ngunnawal Country, the establishment of a place such as the tent embassy enunciated the subjugated cultural position of Indigenous Australia through a powerful architectural act of symbolism. The Third Space occurs when the exclaimed transaction of oppression is translated by a government with cultural constructions representative of a foreign Crown.

The Aboriginal Embassy's architectural Third Space may lie in its beginnings as a seemingly temporary camp with beach umbrellas on the lawn in Australia's zone of imperial Westminster spatiality, the Parliamentary Triangle. (Robinson, 2014) This imposition act on sovereign Crown land used the methods of settler-colonization to reclaim negotiating a Third Space. The Embassy's spatialized act dispossessed the Crown of territory to historical and political effect as the reclamation of this negotiating zone, through architecture, highlighted sovereignty and land rights to Country. It also brought communities of difference together to transact and translate issues of Indigenous oppression and alienation within their own lands.

Paradoxically, the semi permanency of the current structure is more akin to the static conditions of settler-colonial infrastructure and less relevant to the mobile ways of traditional engagement with Country. Rising to express a critical change in society is required and this can be achieved through learning about, and situating oneself in a geography of identities, peoples, and cultures of difference. Despite differences that arise, there are opportunities to overlap through un-hierarchical influence, incorporation, and conflict (Said, 1993). It is because situations such as the Aboriginal Embassy that the negotiation zones of Third Space continue to the present and inform future strategies.

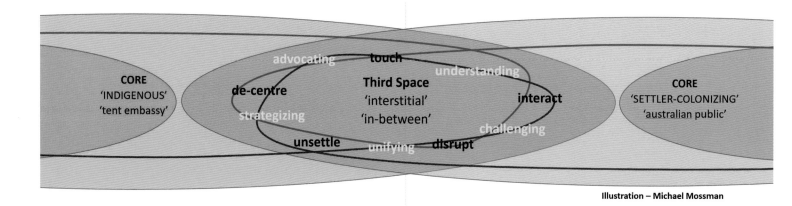

Illustration – Michael Mossman

Figure 8. Negotiation of Third Space, Source: Author

Architecture's role in invasion and settler-colonizing practices requires further specific investigations to initiate an expanded vocabulary of Third Space examples throughout Australian history. It is in this very recent history that the ways of architecture have broadened to promote practices that engage with communities and environments of Indigenous self in meaningful diverse ways. However, in the attempt to facilitate agency for Indigenous communities in the form of built infrastructure, these projects are routinely designed by non-Indigenous architects (Potter, 2012), where lack of contextual understandings produce less desirable to community. While there are small steps to alleviate this concern through Indigenous professional and academic engagement, continuing settler-colonising practices through architectural service procurement predominantly indicates a lack of agency in addressing disparity.

Svirsky relays Deleuze and Guattari by offering an account of the nature of collaborative alliances in cultures of difference whereby "relations is between acting subjects and their productions, rather than on the identity of the subject" (Svirsky, 2014). The potential discourse on offer is rich with experiences of difference to negotiate, synthesize and disseminate in an architectural context. My experiences as an Indigenous architect is vast, where the products of my professional and academic practice have contributed to architectural innovations. I have shared my knowledge, listened to others and built relationships at national and international levels to foster the agency of Indigeneity in the built environment.

Worldviews of difference open new possibilities, new dialogues and discourses to impart wisdom unforeseen and exciting at once. An example within the University of Sydney is eloquently articulated by Shane Houston (2016) in the introduction to the 2016 Charles Perkins Annual Oration:

> It's an important thing we do to acknowledge country and traditional owners, and it's important to see in everything around us that part that reflects Aboriginal and Torres Strait Islander peoples and our culture and the 62,000 years that we have been on this land.

> This marble floor was quarried from Gandangara country to the south west of Sydney. Those sandstone walls were quarried from Wangal and Gadigal country down near Pyrmont. And those magnificent timber beams up there were taken from Bundjalung country on the north coast of New South Wales. So we're never too far from the memory and the life of Aboriginal and Torres Strait Islander people wherever we are.

Describing the University of Sydney's Great Hall in this way – one of the most imposing buildings in the Colony from the 1850s – Houston turns the space and our perception and understanding of it on its head. The insight recognizes that the materiality of space is embedded in its historic connection to country, far and wide; but it also advances the discourse of colonization into another Third Space, this time an intellectual third space that challenges us to think differently and to expand our spatial, geographical and architectural imagination beyond current cultural limits (Soja, 1996). These are "in-between": spaces of negotiation that paint a picture of collaboration with communities and cultures (Burgess, 2004). Shifts in perceptions of architecture

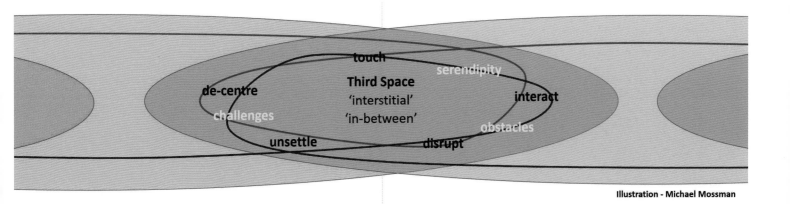

Illustration - Michael Mossman

Figure 9. Negotiation of Third Space, Source: Author

– from the oppressiveness of classicism; to the hegemony of the International style; to the opening of attitudes to allow for spatially diverse socio-cultural encounters in the built environment – can inform strengthened agendas for the marginalized and continue to facilitate alliances across cultural worldviews of difference.

It has been almost three decades since Australia's first Indigenous architecture graduate completed a University recognized degree. Very few have followed with estimates up to 10 graduates in total. As a representative of this under-represented professional group, I am cognisant of architecture's role as an agent of invasion and settler-colonising practices, geared to the imposition of sovereignty over self; but I also consider my practice to be an emancipatory act, working with communities, advocacy groups and "others" to provide architectural agency to the aspirations of Indigenous Australians, and to strengthen the struggle for liberation from oppression. The stories of commonality and tension in the engaged cultures of difference contract and stretch to enable spatialized qualities of the resulting built environment tangible and intangible qualities.

The architectural qualities of a suburban house deck extension in Brisbane Queensland and articulated by O'Brien (2015), the binary conditions of settler-colonial and contemporary engage is generous negotiation. The settler-colonial element is refurbished, with the contemporary representative of universalized Indigeneity concepts. The inside outside and the resulting functionality means if it's hot, one removes the wall; if it's cool, one reinstates the wall. The text and images of the project present a continual negotiation of thought provoking qualities of Third Space. There are many stakeholders involved in architecture with many different worldviews of varying qualities. The Third Space promotes opportunities, challenges, serendipitous moments and obstacles, where it enacts an environment between contending and contradictory positions, it is a space of continuous negotiation (Bhabha, 1994).

My reflections of this topic focuses on real community narratives, situated in processes that overlap and negotiate Indigenous and Western knowledge systems in historical and political acknowledgements, and appreciation of strategic directions. The historic narratives portrayed situations of dispossession and domination, along with political narratives which portrayed situations of inequity and exclusion. Strategic narratives can portray situations of reclamation, re-appropriating power imbalances, inclusion, and collaboration. The role of architecture and the built environment can enunciate a contextualized cultural position from its many participants and communities of difference within a negotiated Third Space.

Conclusion

An analysis and critique of the Third Space has a significant role to play in broader Indigenous/non-Indigenous discourses on architecture. Strategizing systems of engagement and privileging voices is critical from project conception and requires careful management of methodological frameworks, actual methods and ways of disseminating knowledge. The intention of this chapter was to analyse architecture's historical and political narratives relative to invasion and settler-colonising practices; to scope the underlying qualities of Third Space – its interpretations of engagement between binary positions; and to seek new dialogue that can strategize architectural narratives inclusive of all communities. In a built environment context, third space is a transdisciplinary process for critical investigation throughout all phases of a project's life. This allows conversations promoting cross-fertilisation of ideas and considered appreciations of difference. Appropriate Third Space considerations of history, politics and strategy can deliver rich, layered, multidimensional qualities to the project narrative. Importantly, the chapter is written from my Indigenous standpoint as a conscious decision to navigate topics from an Indigenous "self" perspective and my perceptions and experiences of "otherness." Transformative strategies such as third space engagement is another way of exploring a journey of impactful, conciliatory engagement. In paying my respects to those before me who have fought to open doors of opportunity, my own position establishes an Indigenous space that is presently empowered to deeply engage with others who share a willingness to continually negotiate in the Third Space.

References

Banivanua Mar, T. (2010) "Carving Wilderness: Queensland's National Parks and the Unsettling of Emptied." 1890–1910 Making Settler Colonial Space Perspectives on Race, Place and Identity. Palgrave Macmillan, London.

Belmessous, S (2014) "The Tradition of Treaty Making in Australian History in Empire by Treaty: Negotiating European Expansion." 1600-1900. Oxford, Oxford Scholarship Online.

Bhabha, H. (1994) Location of Culture, Routledge, London.

Bhabha, H. (2006) "Cultural diversity and cultural differences in Ashcroft." B., Griffiths, G. & Tiffin, H. (Eds.). The post-colonial studies reader Routledge. New York. p. 155-157.

Bownden, R. and Bunbury, B. (1990). "Being Aboriginal: Comments, observations and stories from Aboriginal Australians." Sydney: ABC Enterprises.

Burgess, G. (2004). Royal Australia Institute of Architects Gold Medal – AS Hook Address.

Cadet-James, Y., James, R., McGinty, S. & McGregor, R. (2017). *Gugu Badhun People of the Valley of Lagoons*. Canberra, AIATSIS Aboriginal Studies Press.

Krmpotich, C. (2016) *Public Humanities as Third Space: Memory, Meaning-Making and Collection and the Enunciation of "We" in Research in University of Toronto Quarterly*, Vol. 85 No. 4, Fall 2016, p. 82-92, University of Toronto Press.

Cunningham, Peter. (1827). *Two Years in New South Wales* (2nd ed. Vol. 2).

Davis, R. (2004). *Aboriginal Managers as Blackfellas or Whitefellas? Aspects of Australian Aboriginal Cattle Ownership in the Kimberley in Anthropological Form*. 14:1. p. 23-42.

Edmunds, P. and Carey, J. (2016). "Australian Settler Colonialism over the long nineteenth century." *The Routledge Handbook of the History of Settler Colonialism*. Cavanagh, E. and Veracini, L. Taylor and Francis Online.

Gammage, B. (2011). *The Biggest Estate on Earth How Aborigines Made Australia*. Sydney: Allen & Unwin.

Hernandez, F. (2010) Bhabha for Architects, Routledge, New York

Kenny, A. (2012). "The 'Society' at Bora Ceremonies A Manifestation of a Body of Traditional Law and Custom in Aboriginal Australia relevant to Native Title Case Law in Oceania." Vol. 82 No. 2.

Mabo v Queensland (No 2) 1992.

Marcus, A. (1990) Governing Savages. Allen & Unwin, Sydney.

Mitchell, W.J.T. (1995) "Translator translated." *Artforum* 33.7, 80-84.

Newcastle, University of. (2017). Mapping the massacres of Australia's colonial frontier from https://www.newcastle.edu.au/newsroom/featured-news/mapping-the-massacres-of-australias-colonial-frontier.

Norris, R. & Yidumduma Harvey, B. (2014) Songlines and Navigation In Wardaman and other Aboriginal Cultures in CSIRO Astronomy and Space Science.

O'Brien, K. (2015) Elemental living: Taringa Pavilion in Houses, April 2015: Issue 103 from https://architectureau.com/articles/taringa-pavilion/

Obert, J. (2016). The Architectural Uncanny in Interventions, 18(1), 86-106.

Pearson, N. (2007) "Hunt for the Radical Centre." *The Australia.*, 21 April 2007

Pearson, N. (2009) "White Guilt, Victimhood and the Quest for a Radical Centre." *Up from the Mission*. Melbourne.

Potter, E. (2012). "Introduction: making Indigenous place in the Australian city in Postcolonial Studies." 15(2), 131-142.

Prout, S. & Howitt, R. (2009) *Frontier imaginings and subversive Indigenous spatialities in Journal of Rural Studies*. Vol. 25: Issue 4: 396-403.

Reynolds, H. (1982). *The Other Side of the Frontier: Aboriginal Resistance to the European Invasion of Australia*. Ringwood: Penguin.

Rigney, L. (1999). Internationalization of an Indigenous Anticolonial Cultural Critique of Research Methodologies: A Guide to Indigenist Research Methodology and its Principles. In Wicazo Sa Review Vol. 14, No.2, Emergent Ideas in Native American Studies (Autumn, 1999): 109-121.

Robinson, S. (2014) The Aboriginal Embassy: an account of the protests of 1972 in The Aboriginal Tent Embassy Sovereignty, Black Power, Land Rights and the State. Ed: Gary Foley, Andrew Schaap and Edwina Howell, Routledge, Milton Park.

Said, E. (1993). *Culture and Imperialism*. First Vintage Books. A Division of Random House, Inc. New York.

Smith. L.T. (2012) *Decolonizing methodologies: research and Indigenous peoples*. Zed Books, London.

Soja, E. (1996). *Thirdspace: journeys to Los Angeles and other real-and-imagined places*. Cambridge, Mass: Blackwell.

Svirsky, M. (2014). On the Study of Collaborative Struggles in Settler Societies. Settler Colonial Studies, 4(4), 434-449.

Thompson, K. (2001) Gradient Architectures in Architecture Australia Vol.90 No.3, Archmedia.

Troy, J. (1992) The Sydney Language Notebooks and responses to language contact in early colonial NSW in Australian Journal of Linguistics 12, p. 145-170.

Vidler, A. (1992). "The Architectural Uncanny in Essays in the Modern Unhomely." MIT, Boston.

Wolfe, P. (2006). Settler colonialism and the elimination of the native in Journal of Genocide Research, 8(4), 387-409.

Chapter 23: Weypiskosiweywin: the people have been displaced

K. Jake Chakasim – Attawapiskat First Nation

Jake is a past recipient of the Architectural Research Centers Consortium (ARCC) Jonathan King Medal for 2010-11, an award that acknowledges innovation, integrity and scholarship in architectural and environmental design research. The basis of his award addressed the absence of an Indigenous epistemology throughout Canadian Schools of Architecture. His design work explores both traditional and contemporary uses of wood as an innovative and culturally sustainable building material – an embodied approach the not only aims to re-contextualize Indigenous traditions but brings into focus 'form determinants' specific to Indigenous art, architecture and planning practices. Trained in the disciplines of architecture and civil engineering, Jake is currently pursuing his PhD in Regional Planning at the University of British Columbia.

Introduction

I want to begin by stating that the Western James Bay Cree, the Indigenous people of Omushkegowuk[1], have a "landscape" informed by the "subtleties of place" – subtleties that evoke a deep sense of awareness, activating one's historical, temporal, and social relationship to place. Despite being categorized as a European term, the word landscape is widely used throughout the world today, even amongst the Cree people of James Bay whose swampy (mushkeg) homelands have been, and continue to be, occupied by Europeans; and, as expected, where the English language remains the dominant discourse. As such, one can immediately see and understand the global power imbalance, the continued ripple effect that has occurred where Indigenous people and their language have been severed from their land and increasingly, Indigenous people have been severed from their instinctive imagination. As Smith (2012, p.40) suggests,

Part and parcel of research is the recovering of our own stories of the past. This is inextricably bound to a recovery of our language and epistemological foundation from which our imagination, when employed as a sociological tool, is a way

of seeing and understanding the world. It provides a way of understanding how people either construct the world or are constructed by the world.

Although it is easy to listen to Indigenous stories it may be near impossible to make sense out of them, especially when the effects of residential school trauma have harvested a different kind of mind-body relationship to place and material objects. Appropriately enough, Smith's notion of language and epistemological foundation from which our imagination grows brings me back to a traditional hunting-harvesting story of walking, listening and observing the Indigenous landscape with my Mooshim[2]. This deeply ingrained memory of place amidst the northern landscape continues to shape and reshape my architectural wonderment as I try to imagine myself in the place of the old ones, elders and ancestors who once were there and to grasp how they might have experienced the Omushkegowuk (swampy) landscape. If my memory serves me correctly, then the embodied knowledge received from my Mooshim has surely set my imagination free, all the while liberating him from his childhood pain – *even if for a fleeting moment.*

Amidst the Hudson Bay Lowlands, on the edge of the grassy mudflats where the tidal banks meet the ebb and flow of the Moose River, we walked. Rifle in one hand and Indigenous knowledge in the other, skillfully, Mooshim would point out a variety of willow and tree samplings to choose from. Tamarack twigs for decoys, Labrador leaves for tea but most of his bundle served to restore and shelter the Indigenous mind-body relationship to place. Playfully Mooshim assembled a hunting blind[3] in what seemed to me like the middle of nowhere. Little did my adolescent mind know this Indigenous landscape. The Mushkegowuk swamp akin to a sponge would be the cultivating ground for my architectural imagination in the years to come.

---

[1] The Anglo term for Omushkegowuk is Swampy Cree and roughly translates to the "people from the muskeg lands."
[2] Cree for grandfather.
[3] A hunting blind is a cover device for hunters, exceedingly simple to construct hunting blinds are designed to reduce the chance of detection from game.

Figure. 1 The James Bay Treaty signing party at Fort Albany. Seated on the right, Duncan Campbell Scott, August 1905. Photographer Unknown. Image source: Archives of Ontario.

Upon being positioned with my back facing the frigid northwesterly winds sweeping over a thinning boreal tree line, I was instructed to face due south and observe the sun that seemed to bend across the sky east-to-west, meanwhile, to listen carefully for the sound of migrating niska (geese) that juxtaposed the natural cycles shaping place around me. "Observe and listen" said Mooshim, "this place may seem like the middle of nowhere to you now but it will soon be everything you will be in search of later in life. It's who we are."

It's important to note, my story is not one of direct victimhood but rather one step removed in the form of intergenerational trauma, primarily a result of government policies that targeted and affected a whole generation of Canadian Indigenous people and their families. As expressed by CBC radio-journalist Deerchild (2015), "For some readers the term 'intergenerational survivor' may not be a familiar one. That's because it's a relatively new way to describe the after-effects of a horrific chapter of Canadian history. The children and grandchildren of residential school survivors often bear the brunt of what previous generations suffered through." It is this after-effect that many Canadian Indigenous architects

find themselves entangled in. Thus "relational context" is key to understanding how the term "grandfathered into" architecture is being applied throughout this article. More importantly, the term "grandfathered into" provides a way for me to unravel the intergenerational effects imposed upon us.

From that day forward, out on the muskeg, is how I have come to untangle it. That is, how I imagine the playful innocence of the child within my Mooshim – unraveled, untouched, and, once again, uninterrupted – out on the land years away from the ideological burden of residential schools. Mooshim's story is not a distant memory. In fact, I carry it every day. It genuinely speaks to the experience of being grandfathered into an architecture of truth and reconciliation informed by a deep reverence for place. Since then, it has morphed into the making of a renewed typology informed by the spatiality, sociology and historicality of the Cree people across the Lower James Bay region. As Antrop (2005, p.21) states, "Landscapes always change because they are the expression of dynamic processes or symbiotic interactions between natural and cultural forces in the environment." As a result, Indigenous landscape values change over time and are typically influenced by the people who have a direct interest, concern or relationship with the land, moreover, are more likely to be expressed by cultural actions involving useful objects, such as a hunting blind that informs the Indigenous mind-body relationship to a northern setting and the architectural imagination that emerges from within.

As RDK Herman (2013, p.69) suggests in Intersections in Space, Time and Becoming:

> It is a dynamic story of how layers of cultural landscape work together and transform one's sense of place and being in those places. As with any indigenous place, we have the opportunity to extend our senses, our imagination, and our personal experiences of Being onto a level deeper than the non-indigenous mind can afford – the space of Indigeneity from which we are transformed through an alchemy of indigenous knowledge, language and place.

This method of narrating temporal knowledge from the vantage point of the lived experience provides an expressive and affective tool that evokes and provokes the Indigenous landscape at the same time, empowering the 21st century Indigenous designer with a renewed sense of purpose, resurgence and ability to reclaim our place of territoriality, and, hopefully, the means to explore a contemporary Indigenous praxis. It is for this reason Indigenous knowledge and its creative ways offer the potential for both an academic and practice-based critiques that are very much at the center of Our Voices: Indigeneity and Architecture.

Weypiskosiweywin – the people have been displaced

To the Indigenous person, language, and land are experienced as immediate relations that can only be understood in terms of local interactions between individuals and place. Herman (2013, p.68) further states, "in language there are words to designate different kinds of places, different use areas, and all the categories and taxonomies of place that make up the cultural landscape in the terminology of the community itself." Without access to the language, one misses out on the richness of expression about place. As Dei, Hall and Rosenberg (2000, p.19) state in Indigenous Knowledges in a Global Context,

> By situating the process of Indigenous knowledge creation in local systems of thought and language, in human feelings and actions, including institutional practices, and in narrative and discursive accounts, we signify the power of both individual and collective agency for change. The search for definitions and boundaries of Indigenous knowledge reveals that these forms of knowledge are linked to human understanding

of both the social and material environment and are also connected to the axes of social difference.

Add to this understanding Ward's perspective (1996, p.55), in *The Suppression of the Social in Design*, "Difference, in fact, is one of the central elements in the marking of social and cultural boundaries, and, as such, is inseparably tied to place and cultural identity." In such a concept of difference, the cultural and social identity of groups whose autonomous existence is already under threat is erased, colluding with the tendency of the dominant culture toward cultural imperialism, visiting not upon remote "natives" but upon disempowered and invisible minorities within our society who have an equal, if not, greater stake at the definition of key conceptual terms (hereinafter, an architecture of reconciliation). Furthermore, this vacuous formalist notion of difference is often used as a justification for the expression of a post-colonial state of schizophrenia in which "stable categories of lived experiences are blurred, where distinctions dissolve, and meaning (cultural identity) itself seems to float, unanchored, adrift and very often, uncertain."

Immediacy and Difference. Experienced from this perspective, a series of structural installations were created in an effort to foreground an architectural binary that deals with the issue of Indigenous displacement and relocation. Specifically, the human after-effects associated with the relinquishment of land be they historical Treaties signed with the Crown (Figure 1), unresolved dispute interests over land development and, of late, the youthful up-rise of socio-political resistance movements in response to extractive resource development infringing on the human rights of North America's Indigenous peoples in the geo-political space of their UNCEDED territories.

As part of an emerging body of design-based research, Weypiskosiweywin I, II and III reinforces a confronting duality associated with Canadian Indigenous art and architecture; on the one hand, there is the localization of global culture, and, on the other, the globalization of local knowledge (Figure 2). As such, *Weypiskosiweywin* aims to rethink the idea of a "northern reformation" within the proximity of a transformational rubric called pan-Indianism. According to James H. Howard (1996, p.75), "One can legitimately define pan-Indianism as the expression of a new identity and the institutions and symbols which are both an expression of that new identity and a fostering of it." Despite the pros, cons, and semantics informing the pan-Indianism debate, sometimes called pan-Aboriginal or some variation thereof, the ambiguity set within this schism is enough to foster both a critical and creative approach to resolving complex social, economic and environmental problems throughout the Indigenous landscape.

On this note, as a design-based researcher what I find appealing is the opportunity to explore this transformational rubric through Indigenous representation; a temporal point process eliciting a call and response action-reaction aimed to provoke observers to experience the political conundrum informing *Weypiskosiweywi*n. Is the integration of Indigenous knowledge as important as separating it from other global knowledges? And, how do the voices informing Indigenous architecture critically and creatively negotiate the dichotomy central to displacement and relocation, or migration and dwelling? Again, informed by the "language of place" and the occupation of large-scale infrastructure disrupting traditional homelands, territories and ways of life *Weypiskosiweywin* speak to the making of a new typology in the geo-political space of Omushkegowuk territory; moreover, reveals "what may be possible" that is deeply rooted in the heterogeneity of the Indigenous lived-experience and emerging Indigenous diasporic identities. As suggested by James (2001, p.70) in *Varieties of Indigenous Experience*, "in everyday practices that deal with mobility and dwelling, the line separating the diasporic from the Indigenous thickens; as a result, a complex northern borderland opens up."

By investigating the set relationships held between art and architectural processes – *the immediate distance, tension and visual dialectic* – offered is both a theoretical point of departure and secular response to the idea of place and displacement, simultaneously. As I have experienced with other creative installations, the act of making *(technè)* coupled with the concept of *"poiesis"* speak to the most abstract level yet are intellectually informed by the boundaries of site (place), that is, of the self's symbolic expression and presencing. As Frampton (1987, p.382) quotes Heidegger in his seminal essay *Building, Dwelling, Thinking*, "the boundary is not the line at which something stops, but, rather, the contour within which something begins its presencing." Add to this response Christine Elsey's view (2013, p.58) in *The Poetics of Land & Identity* from which she states, "poiesis speaks to many thematic representations that express the enfoldment of body and world as they are encoded in the narratives, or storyscapes, and inform and perpetuate the experience of the extended self as a cultural level." In other words, a means to enhance the human experience, and, that, to me, is where the critical dimension informing contemporary Indigenous art and architecture not only gets politically contentious, but, rather, quite necessary if we are to reinterpret and represent them time and time again. Contextually, this would include Indigenous people and their localized understanding of place be it the city, reservation or one with nature.

In hindsight, not only does this view "potentially" problematize the authority and authenticity of the Indigenous artist or architect but it also raises a type of rootlessness – a decentering or displacement of the Indigenous mind. It is, then, the paradox informing *Weypiskosiweywin*, which becomes internally contested, having to move from one geopolitical place to another. As a more personal response, this entailed transferring my understanding of Cree material culture and its embodied relational values from Omushkegowuk Territory to visiting neighboring Indigenous territories which, requires having to "shift from one psychological state to the other"– from the temporal to the oral, the oral to tactile and the tactile to the visual.

In addition, it brings forward the space of insurgent citizenship that constitutes new formations of the social not yet liquidated by or absorbed into the old (Holsten, 1998). As such, *Weypiskosiweywin* embodies a possible alternative future informed by a sense rootedness and rootlessness, shifting or mixed identities and is something that I feel is required in order to re-contextualize, rethink and reimagine the notion of sovereignty within the creative realm of a Cree worldview. Moreover, *Weypiskosiweywin* has allowed me as an Indigenous design-based researcher (trained in architecture) to connect on a socio-political level with non-Indigenous people about a variety of concurrent issues including the notion of a domestic diaspora and how that comes to be represented through form, materiality and embodied movement. Again, it's all about putting Indigenous knowledge into practice. Within Indigenous processes, human actions are carried out simultaneously in relation to the language of the people, the language of their homeland, including the language of objects which, in some cases, might include the need to deliberately objectify a given site-body relationship to place – both present as an object; and, present as a subject.

Wapimisow – to see a reflection of oneself

As an act of reflexivity, first, as an Omushkegowuk person, and, second, as a person trained in architectural studies, I would consider my contribution to *Our Voices: Indigeneity and Architecture* as an emerging cultural practice. The cultural term applied, "wapimisow", is an Omushkegowuk Cree term used to describe the ability to see a reflection of oneself physically, mentally and/or in a premeditated form. In fact, according to Gerald McMaster (2005, p.141), "this type of critical and cultural insight is key to the issue of reconstructing indigenous identities and its ensuing paradoxical art pieces. In order to take part in modern civilization, most Indigenous

weypiskosiweywin I - nibissing first nation

·▽ ·∧ᒡ ᗬ ᒋ ·▽ ·∆ᵃ

...in everyday practices that deal with mobility and dwelling the line separating the diasporic from the indigenous thickens. As a result, a complex northern borderland opens up.

weypiskosiweywin II - tkaronto

weypiskosiweywin III - anishinaabe territory

Figure 2. Weypiskosiweywin I, II, and III – A trilogy of objects emphasizing a northern sensibility while offering a heightened sense of 'situational awareness' when it comes to reclaiming, reimagining and re-contextualizing Indigenous principles of Cree design. Source: Author.

peoples tend to root themselves in the soil of the past while at the same time, striving to find a balance between scientific, technical and political rationality. In the process of this struggle, a dilemma is developed: the double bind of *recognition and practice*. Whether the Indigenous person is inside or outside their society (or societies), they are continuously seeking recognition in the arts mainstream while having to re-examine other centers of activity. Many are coming to realize that some of these older centers, once considered marginal to others, are the new cultural centers once again. These sites of interest, once considered the solution to Duncan Campbell Scott's so called *'Indian problem'* are Indian Reservations and to some contemporary artists, are perceived as sites of rediscovery full of forgotten potential."

For, you see, not only did Duncan Campbell Scott, Deputy of Minister of Indian Affairs from 1913-1932, set in motion the political idea of "getting rid of the Indian problem until there was not a single Indian in Canada that has not been absorbed into the body politic" but

also, inadvertently, suspended in time a First Nation art renaissance that would free itself in the form of political resistance in the latter half of the 20th century, only to reaffirm itself in the Canadian psyche well into 21st century with the recent Supreme Court ruling *Tsilhqot'in Nation v. British Columbia, 2014* (Supreme Court of Canada, SCC 44) over what having Aboriginal title means and how it will affect future resource development projects. Indeed, not a single Indian but ALL First Nations now occupy the Canadian body politic – problem solved, D.C Scott.

Returning to the realm of Indigenous thought, whether it is an isolated First Nation reserve or urban Aboriginal setting, I believe all Indigenous artists, including architects, at some point in time, are faced with the challenge of having to 'bend' back on themselves – ideally, pressured into feeling the tension and compression of their artistic creation that results in newly established identities and/or narratives. As an Indigenous response, Weypiskosiweywin can be looked upon as a catalyst for investigating issues specific to displacement and relocation. Wapimisow can be looked upon as a reflexive strategy. Both embody an Indigenous response born out of the awareness of time that draws our attention back to the northern landscape, and then forward in the direction of the metropolis only to repeat itself from generation-to-generation and place-to-place. The result, being the merging of old world typologies with a contemporary understanding to form new world meanings, especially for myself, a Cree designer who has attempted to emulate the skills of his grandfather, drawing on situational awareness to redefine my understanding of the so-called Indian problem on *my own terms* with the use of my Indigenous language.

As mentioned earlier, as a response to the globalization of local culture, *Weypiskosiweywin* conjures up the idea of arriving on the world stage coupled with the ramifications of displacement. Whether historically misunderstood or virtually connected by 21st century proliferations that predominantly occupy our current time and place, *Weypiskosiweywin* brings forth many interrelated issues that pertain to Indigeneity and diaspora across political borders – even if these imaginary "domestic" borders have become emotive constructs of the Indigenous mind. As lived experiences, arriving and displacing are incommensurable to the idea of Indigeneity and diaspora. If Indigeneity is associated with occurring naturally (as in a particular place) and/or dwelling in place, diaspora is conversely imagined in terms of displacement and movement.

As we have witnessed over the last 40 years, development induced displacement and relocation (DIDR) projects continue to affect many Northern Ontario First Nation communities. As a descriptor, DIDR projects entail small-scale infrastructure, mining projects, including major hydro development projects, which inform a subset of forced migration issues. Take for instance the James Bay hydroelectric power dams constructed across Northern Quebec; the socio-economic imbalance of open-pit mining (diamond exploration) affecting the Attawapiskat First Nation; and the soon to be Ring of Fire (a massively planned mineral chromite extraction) that will undoubtedly continue to disrupt multiple levels of social, cultural, and political organization across the James Bay Lowlands (Treaty 9), which, in turn, foreground the opportunity for the emergence of a "reflexive modernization."

Coined by authors Beck, Giddens, and Lash (1995), the term reflexive modernization is used to describe a scenario (or situation) in which a society may no longer be rooted in their traditions (or place of traditions). As a result, they are forced to bend back on to themselves. All the while confronted with a set of dualities: modern

vs. traditional, technical vs. temporal, or extraction vs. preservation. This brings forward interrelated ideas pertaining to larger diasporic issues that will form new building blocks of Indigenous identity in the postmodern/postcolonial world. The next generation of place makers will call into question newly formed identity pieces, thereby compelling a constant refinement of the design and material process itself.

Taken together, *Weypiskosiweywin* and *Wapimisow* are the making of a Cree duality that not only heightens one's sense of immediacy before misunderstanding and misrepresentation occur, but, also, involuntarily raises issues of cultural survival; of being rootless; living between two worlds; somewhere between a disappearing past and aware of a non-integrated future for everyone. But mainly, bringing one's search for Indigenous understanding to a global audience in *Our Voices: Indigeneity and Architecture*, at the same time, adopting and adapting to a global conversation about what it means to be an Indigenous architect.

Conclusion – enfoldment

This chapter aimed to address the relationship between memory and place while asking, How do Omushkegowuk material objects register as spaces where one can reclaim, reconcile, and re-contextualize stories of the past while forging newer futures? And, how can one represent a Cree worldview in terms of etymology of design? These are the types of questions I am confronted with as my family charters toward new physical, mental, or emotional spaces while desperately trying to untangle the intergenerational after-effects of residential schools in the 21st century. In as much as I would have liked to probe deeper into the historical fallout between the State and Turtle Island's Indigenous peoples, it is well beyond the scope of this chapter, yet, I am certain the horrific chapter of Canadian Residential School history will remain an undertone informing many Indigenous practices in the years to come, including my own.

Unfortunately, though, we are in a time where contemporary non-Indigenous architectural practices and practitioners have decided to vehemently highjack the term "reconciliation" as a space-making business model. For many of us, the excruciating trauma informing Canada's Truth & Reconciliation efforts is very much real, and, quite sadly, raises cause for concern for intergenerational health and wellbeing. Accordingly, these efforts call into question the professional ethics informing the practitioner, either Indigenous or non-Indigenous, to acknowledge the detrimental effects of Indigenous knowledge appropriation, or, in other words, adopting blanket reconciliation strategies and methods of design that undermine traditional forms in and around Canada's boreal forest regions. Without pointing out specific projects and practitioners, I'd like to highlight the need for Indigenous designers of the past, present and future, including professional architects, engineers and planners, even research academics, to not only challenge the status quo, but to strategize ways to maintain and defend Indigenous ways of knowing, doing and making across these design related fields. This would, therefore, ensure proper recognition of emerging practices, including insurgent forms of Indigenous expressionism that sustain cultural identity, while taking into consideration the appropriation of Indigenous knowledge that undermines our Indigenous communities from external non-Indigenous architectural forces.

Suffice to say, it is more than just place-making practices, but, rather, the need to uphold the resurgence of an Indigenous body politic that defines the very nature of Indigenous architecture on Indigenous lands, wherever that may be. It's also fair to say that many, if not all, Canadian universities with a school of design, be it fine arts, architecture, engineering or planning are recalibrating their curriculums to be more inclusive of Indigenous ways of knowing, doing and making. Not because it's in the better interest of Indigenous communities, but, rather, because Indigenous people and their communities, including sovereign nations, will be key to transforming the landscape and the imagination of newer landscapes. And, as much as Canadian institutes with northern research agendas continue to occupy the northern landscape with the incentive to gain a firmer grasp on the Indigenous mind, societies like the Omushkegowuk people now find themselves caught between the extremities of Indigenous knowledge extraction, climate change induced displacement and the forced relocation of their communities.

And whether we are mapping future minds, relying on older bodies of wisdom, or seeking out the spirit of place, the idea that we are all Indigenous architects in some capacity – some of us aspiring to be one, others seasoned elders – we must continue to actively organize ourselves, challenge the existing hegemonic worldview, select a pathway and commit to seeing it through in the interest of future generations and overall cultural sustainability. By connecting architecture with other disciplines, such as art and sociology, this article put forward the idea that a conversation about Indigenous architecture is not exclusively about formal buildings in isolation, but, instead, must be broadened as spatialized visualizations and experienced as a deeper sense of place or as Smith (2012, p.40) simply states, "the need to recover one's epistemological foundation."

In closing, *Our Voices: Indigeneity and Architecture* is not only an exciting advance in the field of global Indigenous architecture and design, but, also, an opportunity upon which a new and forceful generation of Indigenous thinkers can offer specific Indigenous perspectives on architecture with a sense of renewal, purpose and pride, from which new questions will arise, such as, "What happens when we leave our homelands for newer places? Or, what happens when that person or place no longer exists? Then what?" As Lee Maracle (2014, p.21) states in *Memory Serves*,

> There is a multiplicity of ways to remember wherein each individual brings their own gift to the banquet of remembering. There are no standard ways to remember. No single methodology. Our remembering is connected to our emotionality, our physicality, our spirituality and our mentality that we dare not standardize the process for fear of leaving someone's excellence out of the mix.

It's safe to presume the stories and creative works shared within this anthology will inspire the next generation to revisit their homelands to add and create sacred bundles they may have envisioned, dreamed of or simply, were instructed to do. As my Mooshim did, I accept the fact I can only guide my Cree twin boys so far – Tapwewin (speaks truth) and Pawaken (totem) – and hope they too will find their voice, their way and hopefully, sense of who they can become. As Marlene Castellano (2000, p.34) states in Updating Aboriginal Traditions of Knowledge, "the knowledge that will support their survival in the future will not be an artifact of the past. It will be a living fire, rekindled from surviving embers and fueled with the materials of the twenty-first century." Chi-Miigwetch for listening.

References

Antrop, M. (2005). Why landscapes of the past are important for the future. Landscape and Urban Planning, 70, 21–34.

Beck, U., Giddens, A. & Lash, S. (1994). Reflexive Modernization: Politics, Tradition and Aesthetics in the Modern Social Order. Cambridge: Polity Press.

Castellano, M. (2000). Updating Aboriginal Traditions of Knowledge. Dei, G., Hall, J. & Rosenberg, D. (Ed.). Indigenous Knowledges in a Global Context: Multiple Readings of Our World. Toronto, OISE – University of Toronto Press, 21-36

Deerchild, R. (2015). Intergenerational Impacts of Residential Schools: 1st Steps of Reconciliation. CBC News - Indigenous. Retrieved from http://www.cbc.ca/news/Indigenous/intergenerational-impacts-of-residential-schools-1st-steps-of-reconciliation-1.3109827–

Dei, G., Hall, J. & Rosenberg, D. (2000). Indigenous Knowledges in a Global Context: Multiple Readings of Our World. Toronto, OISE – University of Toronto Press

Elsey, C. (2013). The Poetics of Land & Identity among British Columbia Indigenous People. Halifax: Fernwood Publishers.

Frampton, K. (1987). Ten Points on an Architecture of Regionalism: A Provisional Polemic. Canizaro, V., Architectural Regionalism: Collected Writings on Place, Identity, Modernity and Tradition. Princeton Architectural Press: New York. 374-385

Heidegger, M. (1954) Building, Dwelling, Thinking from Poetry, Language, Thought. (Translated by Albert Hofstadter). Harper Colophon Books: New York. 1971.

Herman, RDK. (2013). "In the Canoe: Intersections in Space, Time and Becoming." Johnson, J. and Larsen, S. (eds.), *A Deeper Sense of Place: Stories and Journeys of Indigenous-Academic Collaboration* (pp. 55-72). Oregon State University Press: Corvallis

Howard, J. (1996). Powwows as Identity Markers: Traditional or Pan-Indian? Human Organization 55(4): 390-395.

Holsten, J. (1998). "Spaces of Insurgent Citizenship." Sandercock, L., Making the Invisible Visible: A Multicultural Planning History. University of California Press: Berkeley and Los Angeles, 37-56.

James, C. (2001). Varieties of Indigenous Experience: Diasporas, Homelands and Sovereignties. Cambridge: Harvard University Press.

Maracle, L. (2015) Memory Serves: Oratories. Edmonton: West Press.

McMaster, G. (2005). Contributions to Canadian Art by Aboriginal Contemporary Artists. Edited by Newhouse, D., Voyageur, C., and Beavon, D. Hidden in Plain Sight: Contributions of Aboriginal Peoples to Canadian Identity and Culture. University of Toronto Press: Toronto. 140-162.

Smith, L. (2012). Decolonizing Methodologies: Research and Indigenous Peoples, 2nd Edition. Zed Books Ltd. London, UK.

Ward, A. (1996). "The Suppression of the Social in Design: Architecture as War." In T.A. Dutton and L.H. Mann (eds.), Reconstructing Architecture. Minneapolis: University of Minnesota Press, 27-70.

Chapter 24: Always Is: Aboriginal spatial experiences of land and Country

Danièle Hromek – Budawang of the Yuin Nation

Danièle Hromek is a Budawang woman of the Yuin nation. She is a spatial designer and artist, fusing design elements with installations and sculptural form. Her work derives from her cultural and experiential heritage, often considering the urban Aboriginal condition, the Indigenous experience of Country, and contemporary Indigenous identities. Danièle is a lecturer and researcher considering how to Indigenise the built environment by creating spaces to substantially affect Indigenous rights and culture within an institution. Danièle's research contributes an understanding of the Indigenous experience and comprehension of space, and investigates how Aboriginal people occupy, use, narrate, sense, Dream and contest their spaces. It rethinks the values that inform Aboriginal understandings of space through Indigenous spatial knowledge and cultural practice, in doing so considers the sustainability of Indigenous cultures from a spatial perspective. This chapter is based upon one of her PhD chapters.

With Thanks For Supervision and Editorial Support

Benedict Anderson who is a designer, writer and public art maker. Gawaian Bodkin-Andrews of the Bidigal clan of the D'harawal nation, who is a lecturer and researcher.

I write with thanks to countless Indigenous knowledge holders, thinkers, makers and doers. I am especially grateful to my ancestors, who did whatever it took in order that I could be here to write this now. I am here only by standing on their shoulders. I carry their stories (Hromek, Danièle 2017)[1].

Introduction

Aboriginal understandings of space are fused with our knowings of Country, our relationships with land, and our experiences of how those values are embodied through cultural practices, songs and movement, according to our stories, for time immemorial. We are inseparable from the land; our bodies come from and will return to the land, just as our ancestors' bodies have, just as their spirits continue to care for it. In our ways of knowing our spaces, everything is related, unified and carries its own

Law[2], which determines how we act and interact with each other, and always have done so. The fine web of interactivity between people, land, animals, plants, rocks, this blade of grass, that faraway star and everything between has no "hierarchy of privilege", according to Enrique Salmón[3] (2012, p. 27). No one entity, including humans, is placed above or below another, and our differential roles, duties, contexts and places are equally valued.

This chapter privileges Indigenous voices (Rigney, 2006)[4]. These voices are presented here not as a counterpoint or a comparison with western epistemology or understandings of space, but rather on their own terms, and as a part of a project to have Indigenous voices heard, centred and privileged. In so doing, we move away from an either/or binary and we also listen and hear how it is that Indigenous people know, feel and interact with their spaces and lands. In order to reinforce this methodological approach, as well as emphasising Indigenous peoples' diverse connections to their lands, their nations, groups, tribes and clans are acknowledged in my referencing.

The title of this chapter references a maxim used by Aboriginal land rights activists: "always was, always

---

[1] In this chapter I speak from a first-person perspective to ensure my voice is included within the themes covered within the discussion. When using pronouns such as 'we' or 'us', I specifically refer to First Peoples, rather than all people.
[2] Within Aboriginal cultures – and this writing – respect is given to Elders, and as such as a mark of this respect, they are addressed as Aunt and Uncle, with their titles capitalised. Similarly, if referring to ancestors, the term 'Old People' may be used; it is reverentially capitalised to ensure there is no confusion with the term used in everyday vernacular. 'Law', when capitalised, refers to the laws, customs and protocols of the land set out in the Dreaming as a set of rules or guidelines for every entity to follow. 'Lore' is used when referring to knowledge or tradition passed from generation to generation through story, song and other performative expressions.
[3] Enrique Salmón comes from the Rarámuri people of the northern Mexico region of Chihuahua.
[4] Lester-Irabinna Rigney is a Narungga, Kaurna and Ngarrindjeri man.

will be Aboriginal land" and our stories support this phrase. According to Aunty Julie Freeman[5], our connections to our Galamban[6] , or Country, are very ancient, originating from the "absolute beginning of the world […] before we were human beings, when we were other things coming through the world" (Freeman, 2016b). Aunty Julie says our stories are accurate histories of place. They remind us we were here when it was ice, when the first eucalypts bloomed, when other things were forming alongside us, informing our ways of being and thinking. From that ancient beginning, our ancestors have returned to their lands to die, their essences joining their ancestors' essences, to eventually become ours and in turn the essences of future generations. As stated by Aunty Julie,

> The DNA of every grandmother and grandfather from the beginning of the world is here in your Galamban because it was theirs before it was yours and every piece of them is contained in the earth. And singing up the ground and making the dust fly and breathing that in is strengthening you because it is the absolute DNA of everyone you have ever been (Freeman, 2016b).

Through our genetic material we are connected to Country, to other species and to the beginning – and to the creation of Indigenous space.

As with most relationships, Aboriginal connections with land are an ongoing and enduring process of renegotiation, reassessing, reclaiming. These occur on a personal level. Additionally, whilst this chapter discusses shared themes and related ways of knowing, our ways of being as First Peoples are very diverse, and this diversity must be acknowledged and respected. As such, while this chapter discusses Aboriginal connections to spaces, these perspectives come from a diverse range of individual people speaking of their own connections. Largely these are people inhabiting the continent now known as Australia; however, when pertinent, there are references to Indigenous peoples from other lands. Sources include oral narratives as well as written words, delivered from an Indigenous only perspective. Incorporated in the review are the voices of Elders and youngers, academics and people working on Country, peers and heroes. None are privileged above another; rather, they are wrapped together based on themes that make up Indigenous space.

The Indigenous philosophy authored by Dennis Foley[7] interacts via three interrelating worlds; the physical, human and sacred. He says,

> The physical world is the base that is land, the creation. The land is the mother, and we are of the land […]. The land is our food, our culture, our spirit and our identity […]. The human world involves the knowledge, approaches to people, family, rules of behaviour, ceremonies, and their capacity to change. The sacred world is not based entirely in the metaphysical, as some would believe. Its foundation is in healing (both the spiritual and physical wellbeing of all creatures), the lore (the retention and re-enforcement of oral history), care of [C]ountry, the [L]aws and their maintenance (2003, pp. 46-47).

Every entity exists and connects to others in equilibrium according to the Law, all held by Country. These three interacting worlds are interwoven in this chapter across four parts: the first, subtitled *Relationality, Connectivity, Reciprocity,* describes how all entities in land and space are connected, not only physically, but sensorially and experientially. It illustrates how these networks flow into and within each other and how the Aboriginal experience of Country, as well as our identities, are irrevocably intertwined. The second part, *Dreaming Landscape*, discusses how, according to our narratives, our relationships with land and each other originated, resulting in our Laws, custodial responsibilities and kinship structures. At the core of our lands are our sacred spaces, the liminal spaces between the Dreaming[8], the human and physical domains through which the everyday and spiritual, as well as the conceptual and actual, are expressed. The third part, *Singing the Land*, describes the human expression of that Dreaming relationship in which Aboriginal peoples are spatialised and temporalised beings driven by the celestial, earthly and cultural cycles of which they are part. These cycles guide our movements, through which songs, arts, and knowledges map the land. This part includes a discussion of languages and methods of communication, born of the land to facilitate human and

---

[5] Aunty Julie Freeman is a traditional owner of the Wreck Bay Aboriginal Community on the South Coast of New South Wales. Her mother is of the Gurawarl (Wonga pigeon) clan from Botany Bay (Kamay), and her father was a Wandandiandi man of the Yuin nation.
[6] Galamban means homeland, heartland or Country in D'harawal.
[7] Dennis Foley identifies as a Koori, his matrilineal connection is Gai-mariagal of the Guringah language group, and his father is a descendant of the Capertee/Turon River people, of the Wiradjuri.
[8] Whilst there are many words in our languages to describe the Dreaming, there is no direct translation in English. The term has been adopted to describe the creation of the world and human beings, and is often referred to in relation to spirituality and stories. Through Country, our spirituality, identity and heritage originated at a time the Yolŋu people call Wangarr, or Dreaming. Yolŋu Elder Silas Roberts says about the Dreaming, "Aboriginals have a special connection with everything that is natural. Aboriginals see themselves as part of nature. We see all things natural as part of us. All things on Earth we see as part human. This is told through the ideas of [D]reaming. By [D]reaming we mean the belief that long ago these creatures started human society. These creatures, these great creatures, are just as much alive today as they were in the beginning. They are everlasting and will never die. They are always part of the land and nature, as we are" (Neidjie, Davis, & Fox, 1985, p. 13).

nonhuman exchanges carrying messages, stories and memories of Country. The fourth and final part, *Landscape as Monument*, explains the physical inscription, mapping, boundary making and memorialisation embedded into the landscape.

Oliver Costello[9] suggests that Indigenous space has identity and is not empty, and it is important in cultural practice to have an understanding of space. He relates a western definition of space as an empty container to *terra nullius*, land that is empty and can be taken. Whereas, for Indigenous people, in space there are protocols, where ritual and practice are based on spatial aspects and measurements that need to be managed respectfully. Costello says that place is the connection to space and how space is identified (2015b, personal communication, 28 August). Norman Sheehan[10] furthers this, saying, "the space we inhabit cannot be assumed to be the null void that was contrived as the background". He describes beings, objects, and the interactions and relations between them as generating social and natural spaces, and in this sense, "space is alive and has a history and a *feel* that influences all inhabitants […] exercis[ing] a positioning power on us all" (2011, p. 76). Sheehan calls space a living thing with exterior apparent conditions, but also internal hidden processes essential to the life of the space, all sharing relational dimensions. Knowing space as a living entity that holds memory, feelings and relationality provides a framework for understanding core values of space, as well as the cultural practices required to interact in and with space.

According to the Bawaka people[11], Yolŋu ontologies say that knowing and valuing spaces comes from living among them, "learning (hearing, feeling) the language of its soils and winds and birds, and in becoming together" (Bawaka Country et al., 2015b, p. 10). This lived embodiment of space helps us understand the patterns, flows and connections between all entities in the space, as an active knowing of space through everyday life. Thus, writing about an Indigenous experience of space contains challenges as it removes the everyday living within that space, replacing it with static words and static movements over ground. It seems almost cruel that I cannot take you to my Country, introduce you to it, allow you to experience it, breathe in the air and know the scents carried on the breeze, be still within its spaces, and learn directly from the land. Moreover, since colonisation commenced, many of us are no longer able to use our languages. These languages, that were born of our lands and stored within them, have words to describe our lands and relationships with them. English words do not do these relationships justice. Aunty Fran Bodkin[12] says when we use our language words our whole body speaks, and attempting to communicate in English does not give the expression needed. English was not born of this land, so to this land it is effectively a dead language (2016, personal communication, 28 October). Nevertheless, this text has no alternative at this time and in this context but to be in written form and in the English language. Therefore, in my attempts to describe the almost indescribable and purely experiential Indigenous space, I ask your forbearance. My aim is to privilege Indigenous voices as the primary sources of knowing their spaces and in doing so to give an understanding of the narrative, history and knowing of space from an Indigenous perspective. It is not my intention, wish nor right to speak for all Aboriginal people, rather, I gather together the thoughts of some Indigenous peoples about Indigenous space. As a Budawang woman of the Yuin nation and as a spatial designer, I weave my thoughts with theirs as a means of linking them all together.

Relationality, Connectivity, Reciprocity

In the old days before humans came were the eagles, sharks, eels, and ants.
Eagles would keep the skies clean, sharks would keep the seas clean, eels would keep the rivers clean, ants would keep the land clean.
Everything is linked, there are circles.
Interrupt one thing and it carries through the whole system (Bodkin, 2016, personal communication, 28 October).

There is an unbounded interconnectedness "via genealogies contained within a landscape that is really more of a 'storyscape' […] resonant of cosmological and social origins, events, and encounters" (Larsen & Johnson, 2012, p. 10)[13]. When we speak of being related, we are referring not only to our human or kin relatives, it goes beyond this. In Yolŋu terms, it includes "humans and more-than-humans, and how they are connected to each other, how they fit, where their ties and obligations are, where their responses and responsibilities lie" (Bawaka Country et al., 2015b, p. 6).

---

[9] Oliver Costello is a Bundjalung man from northern New South Wales.
[10] Norm Sheehan is a Wiradjuri man born in Mudgee.
[11] Bawaka is an Indigenous homeland on the water of Port Bradshaw in Arnhem Land off the Gulf of Carpentaria in the north of Australia. Research is conducted in collaboration with Indigenous and non-Indigenous people, with Bawaka Country as lead author.
[12] Aunty Fran Bodkin is a descendant of the D'harawal people of the Bidigal clan from South Coast New South Wales. According to Aunty Fran, the Bidigal clan spoke a dialect that could be understood by other clans and were part of a much larger clan (Bidjaigal) which covered the northern section of the Botany Bay area between Cooks River and the high country overlooking the Boora Birra. Unfortunately, the Bidigals suffered pretty horrifically from diseases, and after the massacres there were only five left (2017a, personal communication, 5 December).

For Yolŋu people, spaces are relational, always emerging, being renegotiated and reconsidered in a structured, patterned and meaningful manner. In knowing one's place via the flows of kinship structures, all relationships are acknowledged between human and nonhuman, including songs, land, ceremonies, winds, minerals, animals, tides, rocks and spirits, for "they are components of a whole acting, responding to each other" (Bawaka Country et al., 2015b, p. 7). Each component within the entirety remains distinguishable and diverse, with its own songs, stories, Laws and knowledges.

We are the land. We emerge from the land as part of it and it is part of us. It is "home to our songs and [L]aws that lie in the land; it is our relative; it is our grandmother and grandfather. Our ancestors are alive in the land, and this is in accord with saying that to sell the land is akin to selling one's own mother" (I. Watson, 2009, p. 40)[14].

The land, and thus space, is alive; people are not separate from it, we are bounded to it through reciprocal relationships of care. Animals, and plants, as well as weather, terrain, songs, dances, are kin. They make us who we are, just as we make them who they are (Bawaka Country et al., 2015a). In Bawaka Yolŋu ontology is the notion of co-becoming, in which everything exists in a state of emergence and relationality. Every entity is vital and sapient with its own knowledge and Laws, constituted through relationships that are constantly regenerated. Thus space is the doing, being, knowing and becoming of each entity inhabiting that land (Bawaka Country et al., 2015b).

Knowing the correct place of each entity inhabiting space enables people to relate to them appropriately, for "the world, and all its possible experiences, constitute[s] a social reality, a fabric of life in which everything ha[s] the possibility of intimate knowing relationships because, ultimately, everything [i]s related" (Deloria & Wildcat, 2001, pp. 2-3)[15][16]. Underlying all relationships and holding everything is Country, sentient and ever-knowing.

Country; Sustaining, Maintaining, Sentient

So, Country is known – people sing for it, there are dances known, taught and danced for it, it has its stories that are taught, learned and told. It has its mysteries. It has its rituals. It can be painted, it can be harvested, and one can care for and love it (Dodson, 2007, p. 3)[17].

Country holds everything and the potential for everything. Indigenous space is part of Country and simultaneously has Country in it. It is therefore always full of the everything and the potentiality of Country. It could never have been empty or *terra nullius*. According to Mick Dodson, "We are talking about the whole of the landscape, not just the places on it. [...] All of it is important – we have no wilderness. [...] None of it is vacant or empty, it is all interconnected" (Dodson, 2007, pp. 2-4).

Notably, Country is a lived experience and a heritage, and includes all people who have belonged and will belong to it. For Oliver Costello, Country is holistic. It is the spaces, the places, the relationships, the connections. Country is everything that exists and everything that does not, everything we know and do not know (2015b, personal communication, 28 August).

Expanding on this idea, Kevin O'Brien[18] describes Country as being experienced and understood through the senses and seared into memory (2011). He says,

> Country is an Aboriginal idea. It is an idea that binds groupings of Aboriginal people to the place of their ancestors, past, current and future. It understands that every moment of the land, sea and sky, its particles, its prospects and its prompts, enables life. It is revealed over time by camping in it and guides my way into architecture. There is no disenfranchisement, no censorship and no ownership. Country is a belief. It is my belief (O'Brien, 2012, p. 3).

Brian Martin[19] adds to the discussion by stating that Aboriginal culture is created by the reality of Country, where all things are extracted through memory and continual practice. His philosophical approach sees Country as a grounding of the metaphysical (or theoretical) into the material (or physical). "Country is the basis of Indigenous ideology and it specifically constitutes and is constituted by the relationship between memory, life and culture, which are embedded in land" (2013, p. 187).

Country includes everything within the landscape; land, water and sky, and soars high into the atmosphere, deep into the planet crust and far into the oceans. Country – which incorporates ground, space, site, environment – is aesthetic, environmental, social, spiritual and political. It is geology and geography, landscape and terrain. It writes the ground and imparts the knowledges that abide

---

13 Jay T Johnson is Native American from the Delaware and Cherokee peoples.

14 Irene Watson belongs to the Tanganekald, Meintangk Boandik First Nations Peoples, of the Coorong and the south east of South Australia.

15 Vine Deloria Jr is from the Standing Rock Sioux peoples.

16 Daniel Wildcat is a Yuchi member of the Muscogee Nation of Oklahoma.

17 Michael (Mick) Dodson is a member of the Yawuru people from the Broome area of the southern Kimberley region of Western Australia.

18 Kevin O'Brien is a descendent of the Kaurareg and Meriam people.

19 Brian Martin is of Bundjalung and Muruwari descent.

its care. Cultural connection to Country encompasses narratives and knowledges, incorporating traditions, practices and art, linked to identity, language and community.

Country is inherent rather than owned or earned, we become connected at birth and rights to Country are immediately obtained along with the responsibilities to care for it as we learn through life. This does not change with colonisation; likewise our kin networks never change (Dodson, 2007).

Country is more than just a place marked on a map in a geographical sense. Nor is it passive scenery for humans to play out their lives. Anthony McKnight[20] discusses Country as "decentr[ing] the human authorship privilege of overseer, creator, controller, implementer, and owner" (2015, p. 2). He indicates that Country provides opportunities to reimagine and co-create how we think about and practice knowledge, because Country holds our knowledges in place, as a source for us to connect and reconnect to the land and to ourselves.

While the processes of colonisation do affect Indigenous spaces, Uncle Greg Simms[21] says that Country is unaffectable, only our relationships with Country can be affected. Likewise, affected relationships are also reclaimable and reparable. Uncle Greg speaks of Country as a place to return to for healing, a place of comfort, strength and nourishment. He discusses changes to the land, saying,

> It is still our spirit Country; our spirit still lies there. No matter that they build city on it, it is still a place we can always go back and heal […], it is all changed but it is still Country. You still get healing from that place. Just go back, take off your shoes, walk around on the land to regenerate the soul. Call out the spirits of your ancestors. That is what the Old People taught us. We have got to go home to talk to the Old People, talk to the spirits of our ancestors (Simms, 2015, personal communication, 28 October).

Since Country cannot be divided, while the land may be damaged or traumatised by colonial processes, like a broken arm, it can heal through Country. Thus if one part is removed physically, the songs and stories keep it in place, in memory, and its knowledges remain intact (Burarrwanga et al., 2014)[22].

The Cultural Space of Identity

I will not lose my culture and my tribe to your games like a bird moving from place to place, looking for its camp or to sleep in other places, on other people's land that is not our land. I do not want my people to move from here and die in other places. I don't want this. We don't want this. I am Aboriginal

from mud, red mud. I am black, I am red, I am yellow, and I will not take my people from here to be in these other places. We want to stay on our own land. We have our culture, we have our [L]aw, we have our land rights, we have our painting and carving, we have our stories from our [O]ld [P]eople, not only my people, but everyone, all Dhuwa and Yirritja, we are not making this up (Gumana, 2009, p. 2)[23].

Determined during our deep past, our identity links us to our knowledges, lands and spaces. Residing within us as creative spiritual registers are essences of our ancestral creator beings, linking us perpetually to identity. Culture and identity are not stagnant; they respond to environmental and social changes, and it is through our culture that identity adapts to the future whilst respecting the past. Mary Graham[24] describes our creative and spiritual identities still inhabiting the land (2008, p. 183), a corporeal extension of self, locating us inherently as numerous generations before us who have shared the land.

The shapes and structures of the land give us identification. We evolve physically and psychologically to complement our lands, and thus, according to Marcia Langton[25], our identities are localised. We are associated with being of that land, from that region, in a place, and so are "constituted as spatialised beings" (2002, p. 259).

Supporting this, our narratives reveal we have always had connections to our lands. They tell of the dramatic changes our lands experienced over time, ice ages, volcanoes, colossal floods and the like, yet through this immense time we remained attached to those lands, and adapted with them. Kaleena Smith[26] says culture is change, culture evolves and everything we do today is culture, including ideals from the past, ideals from today, and foreknowledge of future principles. She describes Country as being part of identity, an extension of oneself, like fingernails and hair as part of the same body. Smith reasons that the actions and cultural practices that

---

[20] Anthony McKnight is an Awabakal, Gumaroi, and Yuin man.
[21] Elder Uncle Greg Simms descends from the Gundungurra (water dragon lizard people) of the Blue Mountains and the Gadigal (whale people) of the Dharug nation.
[22] Laklak Burarrwanga, Banbapuy Ganambarr, Djawundil Maymuru, Merrkiyawuy Ganambarr-Stubbs, Ritjilili Ganambarr are all Yolŋu people, from Bawaka in North East Arnhem Land.
[23] Gawirrin Gumana is a leader of the Dhalwangu clan of the Yolŋu people in eastern Arnhem Land.
[24] Mary Graham is a Kombu-merri person and is also affiliated with the Waka Waka group through her mother.
[25] Marcia Langton is a descendant of the Yiman and Bidjara nations of Queensland.
[26] Kaleena Smith is a Wiradjuri/Yorta Yorta woman from the Riverina around Narrandera and near Cummeragunja Mission on the Murray and the Murrumbidgee Rivers.

identify us externally, such as painting ourselves with ochres, using smoke from gum leaves to cleanse, or connecting with our Old People by going back on Country, originate with Country. Likewise, connecting physically back to Country by immersing ourselves in that locality, swimming in the waters, walking barefoot on the land, gazing over vast distances, provides cultural strength to adapt (K. Smith, 2017, personal communication, 5 July).

Oliver Costello says whilst we have continually connected with each other, our identities nonetheless remained diverse. Sharing and passing on knowledge, songs and stories is part of our responsibility, our identity, and our Dreaming (Costello, 2015a, personal communication, 25 November). Through this reciprocal sharing process culture is maintained and restored.

The Kinship Grid

For Aboriginal people, the land is the great teacher; it not only teaches us how to relate to it, but to each other; it suggests a notion of caring for something outside ourselves, something that is in and of nature and that will exist for all time. Every Aboriginal person ha[s] a place at some intersection within the kinship network which extend[s] over the whole of Australia, and every intersection within that grid [i]s anchored, eternally, to some point on the landscape by the relationship to Creator Being ancestors (Graham, 2008, p. 183).

There is an endless reiterating pattern linking people, spaces, and other entities giving the world meaning, order and balance. This may be understood as kinship systems or relationships. For Yolŋu people, Gurrutu[27] , or kinship, "is always emergent; it co-produces a world which is living and interconnected. It maps and co-produces connections between agents and materialities, based on relationships between and across places/spaces and times" (Bawaka Country et al., 2015b, p. 11). They indicate that Country and kin relationships are far more than networks of beings and things; spaces and diverse beings, processes and Dreams, affects and songs emerge relationally.

Bawaka ontologies further explain this as human and nonhuman being connected to the extent of altering each other. They say, "we mean this as a fact, a fact of cells and history influencing each other, becoming each other, changing each other. At Bawaka, the mundane is the spiritual, the emotional is the conceptual. And vice versa" (Bawaka Country et al., 2015b, p. 11). For them, space and place are co-emergent, active and sentient, drawing attention to the dynamic, ongoing, intense webs of living connection.

Thus everything fits and is bounded to make a whole in an intricate perpetual "sacred web" (Graham, 2008, p. 187). Through these interconnecting networks people know their place, roles and responsibilities, for land, other people and nonhumans. It is through our kinship systems that we learn we are not alone in the world; that rock may be our grandfather, that tree may be our sister. Uncle Max Dulumunmun Harrison (2013) describes flora as being tribal, and, along with animals and other nonhuman entities, we are defined by our location in the kinship framework.

Oliver Costello speaks of the kinship structure within the landscape, which incorporates cultural, social and natural constructs. These constructs are the relationships and responsibilities that link us to the land and each other. He says the knowledge to care for the land according to our kin responsibilities is in the land and in us, and through communicating with and listening to Country, Country indicates what it wants and needs (Hong, 2013).

Dreaming Landscape

I am a boorai[28] [or child] of this land
My old ones tell me my spirit
Belongs here
I walk on this land like no other
Following my [D]reaming tracks (Murphy, 2003, p. 55)[29].

In the beginning was Country; in the beginning was the land[30]. At some point, according to Mary Graham (2008, p. 183), immortal ancestral beings, who had been sleeping in a state of potentiality just under the earth's surface, were disturbed and awoke. She describes the land being "like a moonscape, no features, no flora and fauna, just bare open plain" (Graham, 2008, p. 182). Upon awakening, their potentiality transformed into actuality and they arose out of the ground", as very tall and strong beings. They started travelling and interacting with each other, "fighting, dancing, running about, making love, killing" (Graham, 2008, p. 182), and this activity shaped the landscape creating hills, valleys and waterways. Marcia Langton describes the Story[31], or

---

[27] Gurrutu, in Yolŋu, is the complex system of kinship that link individuals and groups to each other and underlies all relationships with Country.

[28] Boorai is the word used by the Wurundjeri people, to describe a baby or child.

[29] Aunty Joy Wandin Murphy is a Senior Wurundjeri Elder of the Kulin alliance in Victoria.

[30] While each group, nation or clan has its own stories about its beginnings their foundations are similar, with the land at their beginning. Brought together here are descriptions from a number of people expressing their understandings of creation, with none being representative of a whole.

Dreaming, beings as "numinous, supernatural beings of power" (2002, p. 257), whose creative energies infuse the land with certain qualities, some dangerous, others protective and nurturing. She says they are "phenomenal, appearing as rainbows, the moon, and the like, and differentiated and speciated by their various characters" (Langton, 2002, p. 254).

During this period, Graham claims, humans were asleep in various embryonic forms. They were awakened by the activity of the ancestral beings, at which time they helped the emergent humans become fully human. They taught them the Laws of custodianship of the land, giving them all the knowledge required to care for the land and have a stable society. Wherever the ancestral beings travelled, they left tracks or traces, and these determined the identity of the people in that location. Thus, every Aboriginal person has some of the essence of those ancestral beings, authorising them to be custodians of that land. The ancestral beings then went back into the land, where they remain in the same eternal sleep from which they were awakened (Graham, 2008). Aunty Julie Freeman likewise speaks of human evolution occurring alongside the evolution of the land,

> Of course we sat here in that fragrant place. Of course we watched and told our children about the perfection of every other living thing in the world and that we are not above that. Those things all have to have a chance to live and survive and help each other […] because they help us also. They give us the secrets of the things that have been in the world from the beginning, when we were not quite anything yet, just observing in a different form the evolution of the world (2016b).

Due to our emergence from the land we actively draw on the potentiality of the land, both physically and spiritually. Our behaviours, beliefs, values, symbols, designs, cultural productions similarly emerged from the land and are inseparable from it (Wildcat, 2001). In their movements through the atmosphere, landscape and waters, the ancestral beings infused the features of the land with their spiritual essences. Irene Watson (2009) describes ruwi[32], or land, as being sung by the ancestral beings. In doing so they sang the names into every feature they shaped, giving responsibilities and authorisation to the peoples and animals living on those lands to care for the lands. With those responsibilities came the Laws, languages, designs, cultural practices and stories. As we are descended from those who hold the essences of the ancestral beings, we are instilled with their characteristics, sharing them with others who are related.

The ancestral beings are tied to particular tracts of Country, and, according to Aileen Moreton-Robinson[33], created the physiographic features, or distinct regions, of the Country associated with their journeys. As they moved across the land, they left behind possessions designating specific sites of significance, creating the world of humans, "being metamorphosed as stone or some other form, disappearing into the territory of another group or into the sky, ground or water. In doing so they leave behind tangible evidence of their presence on earth" (2003, p. 32).

Uncle Max Dulumunmun Harrison[34] (2013) describes the Dreaming as being like a pathway, made up of stories of different events, like initiations and ceremonies, that happen at particular sites. Uncle Max says the river is a journey leading from the mountains to the sea, through the various parts of Yuin Country. The river holds much memory of Yuin culture, a place of sacred walking, with some parts holding particularly powerful significance for Yuin people.

The Dreaming, according to Watson, represents more than an idea of the past, rather a continuing and present time and space. It is an "ever-present place of before, now, and the future, a place that we are constantly returned to" (2009, pp. 36-37). It exists at all times, and is memorised and re-performed through rituals and ceremony. She says, "Nungas[35] believe that we are descended from beings of Kaldowinyeri [or Dreaming] and that they are our ngaitje[37] [or totems] and our spiritual attachment to the land. From our ngaitje, we learn about the interconnectedness of life, that humanity is just a small part of life" (2009, p. 37). Thus, all know their place in the land, their foundations for identity and position, in the present, before birth and beyond death.

----

[31] Story is Aboriginal English for totemic or Dreaming.
[32] Ruwi means land in the language of the Tanganekald peoples.
[33] Aileen Moreton-Robinson is a Geonpul woman from Minjerribah (Stradbroke Island), Quandamooka First Nation (Moreton Bay) in Queensland.
[34] Uncle Max Dulumunmun Harrison is an Elder of the Yuin people from the south coast of New South Wales.
[35] Nungas is a term for Aboriginal peoples in South Australia.
[36] Kaldowinyeri was known to the Tanganekald and Ngarrindjeri peoples as the Dreaming.
[37] Ngaitje means spirit beings or totems in Tanganekald language.

Sacred Geography

This tradition [...] is a body of knowledge about the relationship among particular beings, human and nonhuman, and the places for which they bear particular responsibilities and in which they have particular rights. [...] It is through this knowledge that people write themselves on the land and the land in themselves. Such sacred readings of the landscape through the lens of highly localised bodies of social, ritual, and juridical knowledge is a 'cosmic framework' for interpreting places, binding particular persons and places together in a sacred relationship (Langton, 2002, pp. 255-256).

While all sites across the land, waters and skies are important, some are particularly significant; these may be referred to as special or sacred sites, and are the cultural core of Country. Uncle Max Dulumunmun Harrison describes sacred places as land that has been sung, "it holds the indentation, the singing, the stomping of the feet, the rhythm of the clapsticks [...]. Hundreds and thousands of years of stamping those old black feet as the women and men would be passing through from circle to circle have left their mark" (2013, p. 97). Maintaining ceremony takes us back to the beginning, connecting us to our ancestors, whose spirits, Uncle Max says, are still the guides and guardians of special places. Their spirits have been sung into the land, chanting indenting their sounds into the earth and atmosphere.

According to Uncle Tony Perkins[38], the Old People became 'clever', meaning they were able to access spirit powers through ceremonies carried out in special places. Uncle Tony describes spirit powers as being "in the animals or mountains or different things, and even the things they change into, you know the Old People in them times, when they used to change into different things with their power, different forms" (2010, p. 132).

The Bama[39], or Aboriginal, notion of spirituality is signified by places, and understanding the land from a Bama perspective is predicated on an understanding of the world as a "biography of human and nonhuman presences, some living and mortal, and some spiritual and ever present" (Langton, 2002, p. 265). Langton says spirits reside in specific locations, enlivening them as "powerfully effective, dangerous places to be approached with the protection of the Elders leading the way with their rituals and expressed statements of familiarity and imploration to the spirits" (2002, p. 260). Uncle George Musgrave[40] says it is the responsibility of Elders to "sing out" to ancestors who are the "keepers of life forces – life's fecundity – not only for their own sakes when they enter a [C]ountry or place, but also particularly for the sake of others with them" (cited by Langton, 2002, p. 262). Deceased ancestors never depart from the landscape; the land is full of spiritual presences who are the ancestors of traditional owners who must be spoken to in the appropriate language. "If one does not 'sing out', there are dire consequences. Engaging with a place thus requires engaging with the spiritual presences therein. The aural sense and the power of sound [...] (re)inscribes space" (Langton, 2002, p. 262). Ensuring visitors are correctly announced ensures safe passage through special spaces. The act of singing out, communicating in language, ensures proper respectful etiquette is followed with Country.

Of course spirit presences likewise visit us in our everyday lives; in turn, we feel close to the spirits, and welcome their care and protection. Langton indicates the spirits and memories of our ancestors who have passed continue as affective presences, constantly creating the landscape alongside us. She continues, "deceased ancestors are conceived of as spiritual presences in particular places expressing both a resonating 'spiritual' trace of the once-living persons returning to a Story [or Dreaming] place and as the 'returning' to a place of an ancestor's spiritual force whose source is Story" (2002, p. 254). Mick Dodson extends this idea upwards, saying, "The lightning men and women live in the sky, creative beings have travelled this place we call the sky, and for some of us it is where some of our dead relations now reside" (2007, p. 3).

Garby Elders from Gumbaynggirr Country[41] (cited in Somerville & Perkins, 2010) describe spirits' knowledge being passed on through ceremony, particularly initiation ceremonies, continuing today through songs and stories being told in special places. Places of intensity are known as miirlarl[42] and songs are a part of the language of ceremony through which this knowledge is articulated, holding some of the power of the spirits of place. Stories about spirits in places are "stories of the liminal" (Somerville & Perkins, 2010, p. 131) or threshold spaces, the spaces between human and Dreaming.

---

[38] Uncle Tony Perkins is a Gumbaynggirr Elder, his homeland is on the mid-north coast of New South Wales.

[39] Bama means Aboriginal people in the various languages of the Lakefield and Cliff Island National Parks region.

[40] George Musgrave is a Kuku Thaypan Elder from Cape York in Queensland.

[41] Garby Elders, from Gumbaynggirr Country on the mid north coast of New South Wales, include Tony Perkins in collaboration with Margaret Somerville.

[42] Miirlarl means special or sacred place in Gumbaynggirr language. It often signifies a special place of gathering and ceremony.

Sacred metaphysical connections mark the land with meaning and inform human behaviour, together with the symbols of that place, such as the songs, dances, expressions and designs. Sacred designs are shared through engagement with the spiritual world; human and nonhuman intertwined through common spiritual ancestry (Langton, 2002). According to Langton, "the land is always here, sensual, and experienced in its spirituality" (2002, p. 257) and is written by its spiritual affiliations. She describes the essences and potentials as "pre-existing in the primordial landscape behind the landscape – the sacred" (2002, p. 265). And thus we retrieve the ever-presence of the Dreaming, as our special spaces are perceived simultaneously as mundane and sacred, conceptual and actual, present, past and future.

Law, Lore

Our story is in the land.
It is written in those sacred places.
My children will look after those places,
that's the [L]aw (Neidjie, Bill quoted in Burgess, Johnston, Bowman, & Whitehead, 2005, p. 118)[43].

Our Laws, originating of the land, are complex; they are connected to geography, carry interconnectivity between peoples, and are inseparable from Country. Laws regarding land are not embedded into a written language, rather, they are lived, sung, narrated, practised experientially, stored in the land and passed down generationally. Mussolini Harvey[44] says that Yijan[45], or the Dreaming, made our narnu-Yuwa[46], or Laws. He says, "The Dreamings are our ancestors, no matter if they are fish, birds, men, women, animals, wind or rain. It was these Dreamings that made our Law. All things in our [C]ountry have Law, they have ceremony and song, and they have people who are related to them" (Bradley, 1988, pp. ix-xi). Greg Lehman[47] furthers this idea, saying that the birds give us notice of what is to come, the bush calls us when it is time to burn, the rain punishes our lazy ways. "And always, the great ancestor spirits watch us as they lay sleeping – their bodies forming the ridges, peaks and valleys of the Country all around" (2008, pp. 137-138).

Knowledge, lore and beliefs established during the Dreaming inform the present and future, guiding the lives of all entities sharing the land. Mary Graham describes the Law as an action guide for living, and a guide to understanding reality itself, especially in relation to land. Our land is the Law, and how we treat the land determines our humanness. Our Laws guide our morals, ethics and discipline, and Elders guide us in following the Law. She continues, our Law "doesn't deal with the actions of humans or the events which befall them, but with what makes it possible for people to act purposively, and experience 'events'" (2008, p. 191), rather they are enduring living instructions for the land.

Since the Laws of the land were not written by humans, they cannot be adapted by them or supplanted by other laws. As custodians of the land we are entrusted to follow and pass on the Laws given to us to ensure harmony between all. Our Laws cannot be extinguished as they are embodied in and born from the land, the universal order of all. Law is not imposed, rather, "[L]aw is lived, sung, danced, painted, eaten, walked upon, and loved; [L]aw lives in all things. It is [L]aw that holds the world together as it lives inside and outside of all things. The [L]aw of creation breathes life as we walk through all of its contours and valleys. It holds a continuity as there is no beginning or ending, for the constant cycles of life are held together by [L]aw" (I. Watson, 2002, p. 255).

Apart from being in all things, our Laws also exist between groups like ancient treaties. Watson (2016) indicates that these treaties are embedded in the land, sung across and into the land and across time. She says,

Our voices were once heard in light of the [L]aw. The [L]aw transcends all things, guiding us in the tradition of living a good life, that is, a life that is sustainable and one which enables our grandchildren yet to be born to also experience a good life on earth. The [L]aw is who we are, we are also the [L]aw. We carry it in our lives. The [L]aw is everywhere, we breathe it, we eat it, we sing it, we live it (I. Watson, 1997, p. 39).

Aunty Fran Bodkin describes a space of Law making that exists in the three hills at Yandel'ora[48], or Mount Annan. It is a place of peace, meeting and Law dispensing for people along the eastern side of the continent, where Laws that were common to the eastern peoples were discussed and made in order that those travelling between peoples could do so with knowledge of the Laws they had to obey. Aunty Fran says that this meeting, which occurs about every 19 years, takes place when the three sister stars line up in a straight line in the western sky. Then the peoples start to march from as far north as Cape York and Kakadu, from as far south as South Australia, and from as far west as Hermannsburg, Northern Territory. With the

---

43 Bill Neidjie is a Gagudju Elder from Kakadu in the Northern Territory.
44 Mussolini Harvey is a Yanyuwa Elder from the Gulf of Carpentaria.
45 Yijan means Dreaming in Yanyuwa language.
46 Narnu-Yuwa means Laws in Yanyuwa language.
47 Greg Lehman is a Palawa man descended from the Trawuluwuy people of north east Tasmania.
48 Yandel'ora is the name the D'harawal people gave to Mount Annan. It means 'Place of Peace between Peoples'.

Law hill in the centre, the women gathering on the left and men on the right, Laws have been dispensed on these hills for thousands of generations. This place is the Country of the lyrebird, the only creature allowed to understand and speak all languages[49], the reason this place was chosen to host such meetings (2016, personal communication, 28 October).

The rules of the land exist for all entities. Nonhuman beings follow their own Laws, which weave with our human Laws; their behaviours have been set by the ecology of the planet, and, according to Jim Pura-lia Meenamatla Everett[50], our survival is based upon integrating with the Law. "If you don't show due respect to the water, the water gets sick; your Sister Water is then no good to you or anything else. You formed a responsibility to your Sister Water, that fellow citizen that you should be showing respect to, not to see yourself as superior to her" (2003, pp. 58-59). Law binds us together, to care mutually with each other, for land, for people, for others sharing spaces with us.

Custodial Economy

Those who arrived in our Ancestors' time did not understand that the bush they saw around them was not a wilderness, but a culturally managed landscape; that life in all its shapes watched them anxiously from the ground, the water, the sky; and that there was not a single grain of sand beneath their feet that was not part of a thinking, breathing, loving land. In their language, the British described and catalogued the land as an object, not grandmother, grandfather, mother, father, sister, brother and family (Kwaymullina, 2008, p. 11)[51].

Our Laws inform us how to maintain balance via our kinship care networks, manage the land sustainably, and use it appropriately, ensuring we leave it healthy for those coming after us, human and nonhuman. Through knowing and experiencing Country, ethics of care and responsibility emerge. Understanding every action and movement impacts others in the kinship web, ensures that we act responsibly towards Country. Bandak Marika et al[52]. relate this to the ancestral beings' travels, saying, "The paths they took on their journeys and their resting places in the land, rivers and sea require our ongoing care and protection" (Marika et al., 2012, p. 132), thus it is our role to perform rites that ensure the land is correctly tended. Cultural practices, such as burning, arts or crafts, dance, or song, are part of lore and part of our role to keep Country healthy and balanced, for not only ourselves but those yet to be born.

According to our Law, land is held in common, and we are only momentary custodians. Within the wider community, we as common custodians have responsibilities and rights to ensure a broader action of care and balance of the land's resources is maintained. Aunty Julie Freeman furthers this notion, saying, "we have never wandered around the landscape aimlessly [...] but were given by Miryyal[53], [a creator being], traps of Country for ourselves and our descendants after us" (2016b). Whilst our lands are held in common and we work cooperatively, individual people are responsible through our kinship systems for sustaining particular animals, trees, tracts of land or waters. Uncle Bruce Pascoe[54] (2014, p. 138) calls our system a "jigsawed mutualism" in which people have rights and responsibilities for particular pieces of the jigsaw, and are constrained to operate that piece so it adds to, rather than detracts from, our neighbours' pieces and the "epic integrity of the land".

Our custodial responsibilities require us to maintain Country using land management techniques, fire, preservation of water sources, land and sea cultivation, seed selection and plant distribution, as described by Uncle Bruce (2014). Through these actions we shape and sustain the animal and plant life of the continent. Resources are shared through trade and cultural relationships, and sufficient food is available for all. Uncle Bruce calls this sharing economy "more than a commodity; it [i]s a civilising glue" (2014, p. 137).

Our sustainable land management techniques work within our Laws and our ecosystems. Victor Steffensen[55] describes how Aboriginal people evolve like the land; different ecosystems and species evolve in different places, requiring diverse cultural practises, techniques and methodologies to manage their landscapes (Steffensen, 2016, personal communication, 22-26 August). For instance, fire is essential to our cultural practices. We burn the land to keep it healthy, maintain campgrounds and pathways and tend resources. Burning keeps some plants and ecosystems safe and encourages

---

[49] According to Aunty Fran, in the story of the lyrebird, everybody once spoke the same language, but events resulted in the punishment that all different peoples would speak their own language, and only the lyrebird was allowed to understand and speak all languages – even today the lyrebird can speak the language of the camera or the rifle, or the cat and dog fight (Bodkin, 2017b, personal communication, 14 October).

[50] Jim Pura-lia Meenamatla Everett is from the Plangermairreenner clan of the Ben Lomond tribe, north-eastern Tasmania.

[51] Ambelin Kwaymullina belongs to the Palkyu people from the Pilbara in the north west of Western Australia.

[52] Banduk Marika, Banul Munyarryun, Buwathay Munyarryun, Napunda Marawil, Wanyubi Marika are Yolŋu and come from the Laynhapuy Homelands in north-east Arnhem Land in the Northern Territory.

[53] Miryyal means the creator in Dhurga language.

[54] Uncle Bruce Pascoe is a Bunurong, Yuin and Tasmanian Aboriginal man.

[55] Victor Steffensen is descended from the Tagalaka people of far north Queensland.

others to renew. Burning looks after Country, revitalising our stories and people. Fire also sends messages, warning of impending events or advice of movement, aids both current and future hunting, clearing tracts of land to foster animal visitation and of course we use fire to cook, keep warm, provide light. Smoking ceremonies welcome and cleanse us (Costello, 2016). Costello says that cultural fire is about "leadership, empowerment and cultural practice. It creates a pathway for recognition and to rebuild cultural frameworks that exist in the landscape, when clans, families and larger language groups act together to look after [C]ountry" (2016, p. 144).

While custodial ownership of Country may not exist in a monetary or transactional sense, the land belongs to us, and we belong to it. Irene Watson explains that ownership of land is not considered as material; rather, it is understood in terms of values such as knowledge, relationships, resolution of a problem, or ceremony in relation to that land. Since we hold both obligations and rights, our "relationship to land combines traditional ownership and custodianship and is difficult to translate" (2009, p. 38). Furthermore, Uncle Bob Randall[56] says that the land owns us (Global Oneness Project LLC, 2015), and thus caring for the land is equivalent to caring for our own bodies. "It is an act of self-preservation and self-protection, and it engages a deep knowledge of our interdependency" (I. Watson, 2009, p. 41). In this sense, just as we cannot sell ourselves or our relatives, we cannot sell Country, as our connections lie deeper than a commodity that can be bought or sold.

Land cultivation occurs in ways such that many groups of people and other entities, present and future, are considered. For instance, trees are planted to recognise sites of significance in the knowledge that descendants will be visiting that location for many years to come, and will need sustenance there. Certainly we are not passive in the harvesting of the resources of the land; Shane Carriage[57] describes the land as nurturing us physically and mentally, feeding us and keeping us alive. He calls the land our economy – even if that economic structure has changed through colonisation (NSW Aboriginal Land Council, 2015).

Through our kinship network, all plants have meaning, so if a tree needs to be cut, Ephram Bani indicates an Elder should come and talk to it. "We do not just get rid of it; that's how big the attachment is. We have harvest ceremonies for the fruits that we can eat. We have to say to the trees 'Please bear for us so we can survive'" (Bani, 2003, pp. 88-89)[58]. Aunty Fran Bodkin says that Aboriginal people "encourage plants to grow"

(2016, personal communication, 28 October); this gentle practice of interacting with flora respects their Laws of how and when they need to be nurtured, where they need to be to flourish and how Country needs to be sustained.

Singing the Land

When our creator emerged from the ocean and stepped onto our land he left his footprints forever embedded in the landscape of my homelands, Djugan Country on the Kimberly coast of Western Australia. The creator brought with him our Law and culture, through songs he gave my people our identity, taught us the boundaries of our land and the rules we must live by. From Djugan Country he travelled north to other tribes leaving a trail, a path of knowledge, a web of songs. These songs stretch from Djugan Country thousands of kilometres into the Northern Territory and beyond. Our songlines have been passed down through the generations and connect us to other tribes along the songline trail (Ozies, Cornel in Torres, 2016)[59].

Songlines link sites to people, landscape and ecosystems, to sky, water and languages. They connect Countries and groups, creating lines of knowing, interchange and movement, often across vast distances. Jakelin Troy[60] tells of our ancestors using epic songs that record how our Countries and peoples were shaped when they travelled and interacted with each other to create the landscape. Songlines are "shared histories and knowledges that track our ancestral creators and connect the living to the spirit world and all those who have gone before us" (2016).

Songlines follow a trail, a path of knowledge, carrying a web of songs. Uncle Max Dulumunmun Harrison describes songlines as an important part of our mental and spiritual structure, lines of energy running between places, animals and people. They energise and galvanise, enabling communication between entities and generating spiritual strength (2013). People and place are sung into being whenever ceremony is performed; within the ritual, landscape and water,

---

[56] Uncle Bob Randall is a Yankunytjatjara Elder from the Central Desert region.
[57] Shane Carriage is from the Dhurga language group on the South Coast of New South Wales.
[58] Ephram Bani is from Mabuiag Island in the Torres Strait Islands.
[59] Cornel Ozies is descended from the Djugun people in the Kimberly Western Australia.
[60] Jakelin Troy is a Ngarigu woman whose country is the Snowy Mountains of NSW.
[61] Lorraine Muller is a Murri woman, born on Kalkadoon Country, raised in the Torres Strait and lives on Girramay Country in North Queensland.
[62] Burriwee (Ju Ju) Wilson comes from the Miriwung-Gajerrong group of the Kimberley region of Western Australia.

plants and animals are sung into being in specific places, connected through songlines (Somerville & Perkins, 2010).

Also known as storylines, stories also travel along these tracks, often encased in art, song or dance (Muller, 2014)[61]. Ju Ju Wilson[62] (2016) says that stories lie in the Country, and it is the spirit in the Country that gives people song. Knowing the songs means you know the Country. Singing the songs of Country keeps Country strong and nurtured.

Trade routes follow them, used to trade not only products of the land, but also intellectual property and technologies. Cornel Ozies describes songlines as a library of information. He says, "They are many things: a road map, a bible, our history […] [they] guide the way we live and give us our unique cultural identities" (Mandybur, 2016). Furthering this idea, Francis Jupurrurla Kelly[63] says "Country holds our story forever like an archive. Travelling through Country, the songs reveal themselves. They are embedded in Country" (Mandybur, 2016).

Songlines form walking paths that link events that happen at particular landmarks, noting animals and plants living there. These are thus marked out forever in the landscape, seascape and skyscape, to be followed as our ancestors did, creating a knowing and mapping of Country through song, story and lore. In Gumbaynggirr Country they tell the story of Birrugan, a powerful warrior and cleverman, and his travels and battles that form many landmarks. This story links Gumbaynggirr Country with its neighbours, extending into the night sky to become the Southern Cross. Birrugan's story is symbolised in the diamond patterns of the linking trails and on carved trees that mark special places (Somerville & Perkins, 2010). Uncle Greg Simms speaks of another songline running from the Queensland border all the way down to the Victorian border. People travel this route, staying with family members along the way – coastal people with coastal people, mountain people with mountain people – all connected via the songline (2015, personal communication, 28 October). My own ancestors followed this songline from their homes in Yuin Country north to family connections in Gumbaynggirr Country, where they felt their children would be safer from colonisers.

Songlines remain a means for connecting with Country and each other, irrespective of colonisation. "Modern songlines […] now tell political stories and keep us connected in our struggles for recognition and sovereignty" (Troy, 2016). Bawaka people speak of connections enduring, despite damage to the material aspects of the land through mining. They say,

Now, many trees and some Country have been removed. Those trees aren't there anymore but Yolŋu still sing them, Yolŋu still keep them alive remembering them. Like a young person who took their own life, or an ant crushed thoughtlessly under a human foot, their gurrutu [or kinship systems] still holds them. These are the present absences of gurrutu (2015b, p. 12).

Knowing Country as sentient land, and singing its presence even when physical alterations have occurred, maintains connections to land and other peoples.

The Language of Place

I listen and hear those words a hundred years away
that is my Grandmother's Mother's [C]ountry
It seeps down through blood and memory
and soaks
into the ground (J. Watson & Martin-Chew, 2009, p. 141)[64].

Our languages were born of the ground, and thus explain the experiences of Country perfectly. Aunty Julie Freeman says that language is unique and specific to Country and landscapes, as it expresses the most intimate things that no one else other than those who evolved to that particular Galamban, or Country, knows. Each entity with which we share the land has words and language that accurately describe their evolution because while they were forming so were we (Freeman, 2016b).

Aunty Julie furthers this concept, describing languages as a living entity, like the wind, associated not only with the direction in which it flows, but also with the emotional attachments it carries, sickness and health, anger and quietness. She says, "Language is not just the word – it's the concept that goes behind the word and its relationship to landscape. […] Languages reflect their own worldviews, they reflect their own landscapes and their own beliefs" (2016a, p. 131).

Using the stability of our languages as evidence for our long connections to specific lands, Uncle Bruce Pascoe says the ageless stability of our languages is "proof of their existence over millennia, and their intimate linguistic connections to a specific landscape is proof that they have remained in that place since the language was developed" (2007, p. 114). Uncle Bruce states that the truth about Country is embedded in languages, and knowing our languages enables us to live respectfully and knowledgeably with the land.

---

[63] Francis Jupurrurla Kelly is a Warlpiri man, Warlpiri Country is located in the Northern Territory.
[64] Judy Watson is a descendant of the Waanyi people of north west Queensland.
[65] Uncle Stan Grant Senior is an Elder of the Wiradjuri people of inland New South Wales.

According to the Garby Elders, who work to bring the Gumbaynggirr language home, language belongs to Country (Somerville & Perkins, 2010). Uncle Stan Grant Senior[65] supports this, saying that language does not belong to people, it belongs to the land you live on. He indicates that many Old People were multilingual, and the etiquette of travel when going to another's Country was to speak the language of that Country, or risk being disrespectful to the land and people (Tan, 2016).

Holding knowledge is a collective responsibility, and "story knowledge is held collectively, shared between generations, between men and women, and resides in [C]ountry" (Somerville & Perkins, 2010, p. 162). Knowledge about language and story is knowledge about Country; and knowledge about Country is stored in language, story and connection to place. While language is the underlying basis of connection between people and place, it is the stories that hold the meaning of language.

Temporality, Ephemerality

The way that Bama perceive landscapes is thus rather like the way that someone with a reasonable astronomical knowledge in Western culture perceives the night sky resplendent with twinkling stars. As one looks at the stars, there is the simultaneous sense of perceiving something that is present, the view itself sensed visually at that time, and of perceiving things that are past, the stars whose deaths many thousands of light years ago are perceived as the twinkling radiances in the black depths of space. And again at the same time, there is the knowledge behind these perceptions, that we can only know these things because of our understandings of time as past-present-future. The future is implicated in our understanding of the past and the present. These temporalities are inscribed in our being as fields of experience, memorialised as the landscapes we know. Experiences are sensual topographies of time and space not simply inscribed and affirmed through physically imposed anthropogenic marks, but through the marks of socio-ontological order and understanding (Langton, 2002, p. 265).

Time is grounded in land, waters and skies, and based on seasonal and cosmological cycles, and our evolution remains intrinsically linked with land and time. As such, our temporalities are fluid in nature, dependent on events recurring in particular places, making them contemporaneous with the present and oriented towards an awareness of flow and ambience (Larsen & Johnson, 2012). Seasons as cycles, visibly and ephemerally, impact land, air and water, communicating when and how events may occur.

Thus the land is the indicator for human and nonhuman movement, which is tied to responsibilities to the land as well as other people and their needs to avail themselves of the products of the land. Uncle Max Dulumunmun Harrison describes the seasons in Yuin Country as indicators for events that relate to products of the land being available at that time; particular blossoms indicate which fish are travelling at that time; specific colours in the bark of mountain trees designate when it is time to move from mountain to coast. He says, "When we go to take our food from plants or trees, we have to shake that tree three times. If the plant or the trees don't release their crops, then they are not going to give us anything at all" (2013, p. 57), at which point it is time to move on. Time and thus space are vibrant, perpetual and familiar companions. The relationships with Country tell us when and what we do.

It is the mullet, as part of Country, along with the other messengers who tell us when it is the right time to hunt. And if it is the right time, if the animals, the plants, the winds, the sunsets, the clouds, tell us that they are ready to be hunted or harvested and if we do not attend to the messages, we fail to harvest yam or hunt fish, that is disrespectful. That is not to care for and nourish Country, not to take our part as one being alongside others, not to contribute to keeping Country balanced (Bawaka Country et al., 2015a, p. 275).

As indicated by Bawaka Country et al, our kinship systems suggest a view of space that is dynamic and ever moving towards an emergent future, sustained via practices and knowings of the past. "Gurrutu thus makes sense of relational spatial production through multiple dimensions […] temporality, like spatiality, is contextual, knowing/knowable and affecting/able to be affected. […] In Bawaka, messages are generated through material shifts in Country, which both mark time's passage and reproduce times past and future through the evocation of knowledges and practices" (2015b, p. 12).

Linda Tuhiwai Smith[66] (2012) introduces the experiential quality that links time and space. She says that the Māori word for space and time is the same, and everything is understood through spatial relationships in the environment. There is no single direction of travel or progress, be it through space or time, young to old; rather a cyclical, environmental, ongoing living of spaces and times. Sharing our stories using oral methods of transmission over repeating generations of peoples, makes us spatially and temporally entwined peoples, as Marcia Langton identifies us (2002). Likewise, following our ancestors' corresponding movements and returning to special places situates us as spatialised and temporalised beings.

---

[66] Linda Tuhiwai Smith is a Māori academic who affiliates to the Ngāti Awa and Ngāti Porou iwi.

Furthering this concept, Brian Martin says the situated experience of Country gives us a more objective view of the world as an ontological experience. He says, "In Indigenous culture there is no division between the real and the ideological or split between memory and temporality" (2013, p. 193). In linking memory with time, space is also connected; Country is always; the Dreaming is at every time.

Understanding time through repeating cycles of the cosmos enables a longer view of life sequences, with humans decentred from the patterns and ephemeral flows binding all entities. Noel Nannup[67] describes star stories told by his mother, which indicate that as the world turns, star patterns pass overhead signalling the time of year. Certain stars or groups of stars are connected to particular Dreaming tracks, which in turn are connected to significant places on the land (2008). This suggests that our space, held by Country, may be "understood as more than living with(in) the physical landscape, it has a certain mobility; it is embodied and thus travels […] and it reaches out to incorporate distant stars and space" (Bawaka Country et al., 2015b, p. 11).

Time is intrinsically linked to space, as spatial movements through Country are determined by occurrences in time. Songlines are embodied time and space, where time and space is sung, storied and embodied through movement. Furthermore, space is united in time due to our ways of learning, which are cyclical. Of course, we do not learn Country in a classroom, we learn Country in Country, in the spaces of Country through time. We learn by being shown over and over, listening to the same stories repeatedly over our lifetimes, being with Elders and knowledge holders in Country – and thus the recurring temporal experience-based learning continues. Miriam Rose Ungunmerr[68] (1993) explains this through dadirri[69], inner deep listening and quiet, non-obtrusive observation and hearing without ears. She says, "Through the years we have listened to the stories. In our Aboriginal way, we learn to listen from our earliest days. We could not live good and useful lives unless we listened" (Ungunmerr, 1993, p. 35). Judy Atkinson[70] furthers this, saying, "Listening invites responsibility to get the story – the information – right. However, listening over extended periods of time also brings the knowledge that the story changes over time" (Atkinson, 2002, p. 18). Relating this to Country, the importance of time in regard to space is evident; observing deeply the messages of Country as they come to us, waiting for them to be ready in space, in the right space at the right time. We are not the authors of nor authority on time, nor indeed space, it is an immeasurable cyclical continuum of which we are one part. In this way time becomes and is space.

Reading the Terrain

Everything at Bawaka has and tells a story. Everything communicates, through its own language and its own Law (Burarrwanga et al., 2014).

Each entity in space speaks its own language, communicating and sending messages to each other and humans. We are only one part of Country, and being able to read the stories and hear the lessons and requests being sent by others in space is the responsibility of people as custodians. In Yolŋu ontology, "animals, rocks, winds, tides, emotions, spirits, songs and humans speak. They all have language and knowledge and Law. They all send messages; communicate with each other" (Bawaka Country et al., 2015a, p. 270). According to Bawaka people, it is their role to ask Country to welcome ngapaki[71], or westerners, so the land, tides, currents, plants, animals, winds, rocks, songs, emotions and Dreams recognise them. While these entities might not all communicate as humans do, they do create and they do communicate, they all tell stories. They leave signs in their own written languages, give knowledge and meaning in their own ways of being and communicating (Bawaka Country et al., 2015a; Burarrwanga et al., 2014). While we cannot possibly read the language of every entity in a space, it is our responsibility to listen to the messages, engage with their subtleties and respect their diversity.

In telling the stories and singing the songs of Country, dancing up the land and holding ceremony, we send messages to the other entities sharing our spaces as they read us also. According to Yolŋu people, what humans do is attended by many others, and to hear the messages of Country, we must take great care to the world (Bawaka Country et al., 2015a; Bawaka Country et al., 2015b). They continue,

---

[67] Noel Nannup is a Nyungar/Indjarbandi man connected to the south-west and north-west areas of Western Australia.
[68] Miriam-Rose Ungunmerr is an Elder from Nauiyu (Daly River) from the of the Ngan'gityemerri language group.
[69] Judy Atkinson indicates that while the word dadirri belongs to the language of the Ngangikurungkurr people of the Daly River area, the activity or practice of dadirri has its equivalent in many other Indigenous groups. She says, "The Gamilaraay have the words winangar (listening) and gurri (deep), so winangargurri has a similar meaning to dadirri (Judy Knox, of Tamworth Gamilaraay, 1998). Aboriginal peoples of Central Queensland talk of yimban yiar a (listening to [E]lders), which has similar meanings and behavioural responsibilities to dadirri (Milton Lawton, Rockhampton, 1998)" (Atkinson, 2002, p. 15).
[70] Judy Atkinson is of the Jiman people of the Upper Dawson in Central West Queensland, and the Bundjalung of Northern NSW.
[71] Ngapaki means western in Yolŋu language.
[72] Wärrkarr is the white sand lily in Yolŋu.

When the wärrkarr[72] [or white sand lily] is in flower, we know it is time to hunt stingray. You know the sweat you felt when you sat drinking tea on the sand earlier this evening? That sweat tells you that the fruits are ripening. We know that when it is hot there will be good fruits to eat. The thirst we feel in our bodies is linked with the trees that give the fruit. We know and the tree knows. We feel these messages in our body, and our body sends messages to the fruits and the animals. In our heart and our soul we feel the season unfolding. The fruits will be ready when we go out on Country, when we need them. These messages are part of our very being (Bawaka Country et al., 2015a, p. 275).

Deep ties between people, land and others sharing spaces enable a reading of and communication with one another, through observation, awareness and respect. Uncle Max Dulumunmun Harrison tells the story of his Uncles and father chanting, calling in Koorah Koo-rie[73], the wind spirit, and slapping the surface of the sea water with their sticks, a message to the dolphins to herd the fish to be hunted in the shallows. He says, "These old men were masters of communicating and getting in touch with the spirit of the dolphins. They never went out in a boat and trained the dolphins to do this; they did this through connection of spirit, telepathically" (2013, p. 53). Uncle Max also describes the songs trees sing. He says that a tree, from its leaves to its roots, records everything that passes around it or connects through it, telling about the health of our environment. By reading the messages the trees pass to us we can know the wellbeing of the land. Trees also indicate important places; Uncle Max says, "Angophoras, they are old female trees. If you look at a tribe of angophoras that's sprouted out from some rocks, you will see they are so huge and how they twist and turn and are embracing everything. Once you start looking at those old grannies, as we call them, then you know 'Whoa, there's a women's place somewhere round here', because they are used as a signpost" (2013, p. 141).

Reading the messages of Country requires awareness of the connections around you, being open, alert and conscious that people are not at the centre of all. Oliver Costello supports this, describing the intangible spirit of Country, which can be sensed when read respectfully. Land and memory operate side by side, a simultaneous collective connectedness, and thus the memory of land becomes tangibly visible on the landscape despite changes occurring. Costello says that through memory the land can respond, remember ecosystems, repopulate displaced species, re-establish itself. It is our role to listen to the messages of the land, read what the land is teaching, support Country, in doing so stories emerge and re-emerge, the memories of place rematerialise (2015a, personal communication, 25 November).

Landscape as Monument

The ochre is a story painted on the body. It's a connection. It makes you strong when you dance, it's part of the land because the ochre comes from the land, so it represents you being part of it. [...] There's a connection with the song and paint (Bin Saaban, Brian in Torres, 2016)[74].

Spaces remind people of culture and identity, of origin and narrative. Terrains become memory and experience. Land becomes both tangible and intangible monument, inscribed into the senses. For Gumbaynggirr people, the bend of the river literally is Birrugan's knee, recording where the giant man fell when killed in the Dreaming. Irrespective of changes to the material structure of the place, visiting that river bend is a reminder of the associated story and the origin (Somerville & Perkins, 2010). We remember narratives in an embodied sense by smearing our bodies with the paint of the land – ochre – and telling the story through dance.

Marcia Langton adds to the discussion, describing landscape as monument in terms of the land being marked, known and memorialised phenomenologically through the senses. She describes sites as being "inscribed through metaphysical relationships and are experienced through relationships with the emplaced *Story* [or Dreaming] Beings who gave rise to the original clan ancestors" (2002, p. 255). As such, not only are people's rights marked by ancestral connections, but cultural memories become inscribed in places, accessed "through engagement and an inscription of the senses" (Langton, 2002, p. 254).

The landscape is the material embodiment of narratives embedded into the creation of a site, a monument and physical reminder of connections to sites and ancestors. Uncle Greg Simms tells the story of why the cliff faces in the Blue Mountains are bare. He says that in the Dreaming, the Rainbow Serpent came down the valley from Lithgow, making the winding rivers. Following behind was Gurangatch[75], a giant part-serpent part-fish, and as it swam behind the Serpent it splashed its tail along the surface of the water. As the water sprayed out up onto the cliff faces it washed them clean of trees and plants, as they remain today (2016, personal communication, 14 December). This story endures embedded in the

---

[73] Koorah Koo-rie is the name of a wind spirit in Yuin language.
[74] Brian Bin Saaban is a Djugun Law boss in Western Australia.
[75] Gurangatch is a giant Dreaming spirit that is part-serpent part-fish who was responsible for creation in the Gundungurra nations around the Blue Mountains in New South Wales.

landscape, a visible memory of the formation of the land.

Similarly, Aunty Fran Bodkin describes how in her family, when a girl child was born, a native frangipani tree was planted (2016, personal communication, 28 October), thus signifying the continuation of peoples and culture, marking a personal moment as physical monument in the land.

Ground as Cartography

Representations of people, spirits, and landscapes are symbols in a rich variety of rites, from the merely petitionary to the profoundly cosmological. The cultural map through which the landscape is reinscribed with the cultural memories, regulations, and logic of the Elders is marked and memorialised through social experience (Langton, 2002, p. 256).

Mapping is a process of both tangibly and intangibly writing into the land; the map "extends from the community into the landscape through inscriptions on trees and rocks, drawings on the ground, or dance and ceremony" (Pearce & Louis, 2008, pp. 110-111)[76]. Our mappings accentuate the lived experience of spaces, and thus our maps are phenomenologically spatialised (Pearce & Louis, 2008). Habitual movement over ground maps the land, whilst knowing the stories and songs of the land enables travel.

Correspondingly, the land becomes a navigational instrument to those who read and know it, with certain landmarks enabling movement in the appropriate direction. Uncle Jack Campbell[77] describes Didthul, or Pigeon House Mountain, as a navigation landmark for the Yuin people. He says the mountain not only directs people where to fish but is also a ceremonial 'high test', or initiation, site for the Djirringany people and that knowledgeable men are needed to operate its many ceremonial sites (1974). Tangibly, Didthul appears as the breasts of a woman, Mother Earth nurturing us, physically and mentally.

In Yolŋu ontologies, gurrutu, or kinship systems, explain an emplaced and distinctive space that incorporates all time, thus reiterating "an ontogenetic form of cartography [a form of mapping concerned with the origin and development], a continual mapping of not only space but the particular combinations of practice, materiality, temporality and conceptualisation" (Bawaka Country et al., 2015b, p. 11). This means of mapping forms the foundations for living in a space in which humans are only one part, and in which the relationality between all parts is vital.

Place names carry narratives, meanings and interrelationships, and identify events or geographic features. Jakelin Troy discusses the names of places or topographical features like mountains or rivers. She says the naming of rivers is noteworthy, as the whole waterway may not be named, rather each bend or waterhole is designated. She says, "The river is deeply significant all the way along because different parts of it are known for being good fishing spots or [...] spots where [...] ancestral figures have had some contact with the landscape" (Giakoumelos, 2012). Oliver Costello further explains that different groups may have different names for sites based on their responsibilities and authority for that location, as well as cultural structure and language (2015a, personal communication, 25 November).

Delineation, Demarcation

It took me weeks to find out the problem was the boundaries of the land claim. Kartiya [or white people] asked the Old People, 'where is your Country?' and kartiya just drew a straight line on the map. Kurtal [his grandfather's Country] was outside the boundary. Spider [his grandfather] can't understand what the confusion is all about. It's his Country and always has been his Country. In his mind, he never lost it in the first place. The problem is the whitefella's rules. It's written on paper, and it always changes. The blackfella Law is written in the stars, the ground and countryside, and it never changes (Lawford, Tom in Ma, 2016)[78].

Spatial demarcation or boundary making comes from geographic features in the landscape; a bend in a river, a range of mountains, or even "the rain shadow, trees, and rocks, as well as fabricated markers" (I. Watson, 2009, p. 37). Likewise, songlines do not travel in straight lines across the land, nor do absolute boundaries exist. Jim Pura-lia Meenamatla Everett claims that ground and territory cannot be fought over, as the land, not humans, creates our boundaries. Nor may we try to change those boundaries as everything we need is in them. Everett describes the Law in relation to boundaries thus, "The [L]aw is to sit and wait at that land boundary. Sit and wait, and after a while the right person would come out and talk with you to see what your business was. If they were happy they would bring you in. The same protocol existed between all Aboriginal people" (2003, p. 58).

Aunty Fran Bodkin furthers this understanding of boundary delineation by describing how sea level changes reformed spatial demarcations for the Bidigal clan and neighbours. She says, "as the seas rose we all moved further westward following our environment which also moved, then, as the sea levels fell, we moved eastwards, again following our familiar food sources. That

---

[76] Renee Pualani Louis is a Hawaiian woman.
[77] Kartiya means white person in Wangkajunga language.
[78] Tom Lawford is a Wangkajunga man who lives in Fitzroy Crossing.

is why we say we belonged to the land, we did not own it" (2017a, personal communication, 5 December).

Edges are defined through knowing Country, walking and experiencing the land, camping in the landscape, rather than lines on a map. According to Uncle Tony Perkins, straight lines on a map are problematic as they do not conform to Country as understood through "the delicate negotiations with others involved in boundary work" (Somerville & Perkins, 2010, p. 195). Movement outside of boundaries is undertaken through knowledge of languages, totems and spiritual awareness, and is passed down through generations by way of Law.

Knowing the boundaries of Country is not only important to maintain harmony with neighbours and maintain respectful protocol, it also signifies identity. For Gumbaynggirr people, their sense of their Country's boundaries is constructed from the inside, from the centre of their being. Identities are an "intertwining of self, people and place" (Somerville & Perkins, 2010, p. 191).

Uncle Max Dulumunmun Harrison says that language is key to understanding demarcations. "Some people think language is just talking, here and there, but it is much more. It represents a border and it holds culture and [L]aw" (2013, p. 136). He says taking language outside its boundaries is disrespectful as it removes it from its homeland and creation spaces. Respecting boundaries ensures safe movement and, according to Uncle Max, similar limits exist between people and the animal world, for instance, the boundaries set by sharks in the oceans.

Interstitial spaces that are shared between many groups are often places of gathering or meeting, mutually accessed, used and cared for. According to Irene Watson, some areas are shared, others restricted, some require permission to travel across or hunt in to avoid conflict (2009). Similarly, liminal spaces, often between Countries, mark the thresholds between peoples via monuments within the terrain, visible for all who can read the land.

Designed Land

Indigenous spaces have been designed. Our spaces are culturally designed by the community in accordance with what the land needs and wants. Through our connections to our homelands, to one another and to other beings inhabiting spaces, we have planned the function of particular zones of land based on the meanings and stories embedded in those tracts, as laid out by our ancestral beings and predecessors. Our lands are designed through caring for Country activities, including spending time on Country, cultural burning, gathering food

and medicines, taking part in ceremony, creating art and designs, and protecting special sites. Performing caring for Country actions and maintaining knowledge systems ensures the land, and in turn people and ecosystems, remain healthy.

The design of land occurs physically, conceptually, sensorially, spiritually and intergenerationally; we learn from our Elders, who learned from their Elders how to know and read the land. Mussolini Harvey describes our design process thus, "In our ceremonies we wear marks on our bodies, they come from the Dreaming too, we carry the design that the Dreamings gave to us. When we wear that Dreaming mark we are carrying the [C]ountry, we are keeping the Dreaming held up, we are keeping the [C]ountry and the Dreaming alive" (Bradley, 1988, pp. ix-xi). Marking our bodies with the design of the land using ochre at times of ceremony is a direct embodiment of the land; a corporeal representation of our relationships, kinships and Country. Designing the land also happens at more mundane moments, when walking the land and feeling feet connecting with ground, reading the landscape to burn at exactly the right time and location, drawing a marker in the sand or on a tree.

Cultivating the earth using our subtle encouraging techniques designs ecosystems, and acknowledges that future generations will continue to nurture the ground. In designing the land with our descendants in mind, we design sustainably, using proven ancestral techniques. Designing the land in partnership with Country ensures all beings are considered and cared for.

Conclusion

As spatial designers in collaboration with Country, we maintain a reciprocal relationship with ourselves, with the land and with previous generations unbroken over thousands of years of inhabitation. Guided by our ancestors we have created spaces of identity and kinship, known to us via our lore and Laws. Our ways of reading, singing and speaking Country are determined by our ephemeral and temporal understandings of who we are within the landscape we occupy, as a part of rather than separate to it. As custodians of the land, our Laws have guided us in how to care for Country realising sustainable co-existence. We maintain our diversity as First Peoples, remaining continually and respectfully interconnected with each other, the land and all entities inhabiting the land. Our maps, boundaries and monuments do not occur as documents, instead they exist in the appearances of terrain and formations, based on those determined by our Dreaming ancestors. We are designers of land. This is how our Indigenous spaces always were and always will be.

References

Atkinson, J. (2002). Trauma trails, recreating song lines: the transgenerational effects of trauma in indigenous Australia. North Melbourne, Victoria, Australia: Spinifex Press.

Bani, E. (2003). The Sea. In P. McConchie (Ed.), Elders. Cambridge, UK: The University of Cambridge.

Bawaka Country, Wright, S., Suchet-Pearson, S., Lloyd, K., Burarrwanga, L., Ganambarr, R., . . . Maymuru, D. (2015a). Working with and learning from Country: decentring human author-ity. Cultural Geographies, 22(2), 269–283.

Bawaka Country, Wright, S., Suchet-Pearson, S., Lloyd, K., Burarrwanga, L., Ganambarr, R., . . . Sweeney, J. (2015b). Co-becoming Bawaka: Towards a relational understanding of place/space. Progress in Human Geography, June 30, 1-20.

Bodkin, F. (2016, 28 October 2016) Personal Communication on 28 October 2016/Interviewer: D. Hromek.

Bodkin, F. (2017a, 5 December 2017). [Personal Communication on 5 December 2017].

Bodkin, F. (2017b, 14 October 2017). [Personal Communication on 14 October 2017].

Bradley, H. (1988). Yanyuwa Country: The Yanyuwa people of Borroloola tell the history of their land. Richmond Victoria: Greenhouse Publications.

Burarrwanga, L., Ganambarr, B., Maymuru, D., Lloyd, K., Ganambarr-Stubbs, M., Ganambarr, R., . . . Wright, S. (2014). Welcome to my Country: seeing the true beauty of life in Bawaka. September 15. Retrieved from https://theconversation.com/welcome-to-my-country-seeing-the-true-beauty-of-life-in-bawaka-31378

Burgess, C. P., Johnston, F. H., Bowman, D. M. J. S., & Whitehead, P. J. (2005). Healthy Country: Healthy People? Exploring the health benefits of Indigenous natural resource management. Australian and New Zealand Journal of Public Health, 29(2), 117-122.

Campell, J. (1974, February) Howard Creamer interviews Jack Campbell and Percy Mumbler in February 1974, Reference CREAMER_H02 009539/Interviewer: H. Creamer. AIATSIS.

Costello, O. (2015a, 25 November 2015) Personal Communication on 25 November 2015/Interviewer: D. Hromek.

Costello, O. (2015b, 28 August 2015) Personal Communication on 28 August 2015/Interviewer: D. Hromek.

Costello, O. (2016). Country needs community: Oliver Costello on cultural fire. In E. Pike (Ed.), Jonathan Jones: barrangal dyara (skin and bones). Botany, New South Wales, Australia: Kaldor Public Art Projects.

Deloria, V., & Wildcat, D. (2001). Place and Power: Indian Education in America. Golden, Colorado, USA: Fulcrum Publishing.

Dodson, M. (2007). Indigenous Protected Areas in Australia. Paper presented at the International Expert Group Meeting on Indigenous Peoples and Protection of the Environment, Khabarovsk, Russian Federation.

Everett, J. P.-I. M. (2003). Lore, Law. In P. McConchie (Ed.), Elders. Cambridge, UK: The University of Cambridge.

Foley, D. (2003). Indigenous Epistemology and Indigenous Standpoint Theory. Social Alternatives, 22(1 Summer), 44-52.

Freeman, J. (2016a). Objects are connections to traditions: Aunty Julie Freeman on landscape and language. In E. Pike (Ed.), Jonathan Jones: barrangal dyara (skin and bones). Botany, New South Wales, Australia: Kaldor Public Art Projects.

Freeman, J. (2016b). Spot Fire 1 - Reading country - Aunty Julie Freeman.   Retrieved from https://vimeo.com/170559810

Giakoumelos, P. (2012). Search for Indigenous Place Name Meanings. 31 October. Retrieved from http://www.sbs.com.au/news/article/2012/10/31/search-indigenous-place-name-meanings

Global Oneness Project LLC. (2015). The Land Owns Us. Inverness, California, USA.

Graham, M. (2008). Some Thoughts about the Philosophical Underpinnings of Aboriginal Worldviews. Australian Humanities Review(45 November).

Gumana, G. (2009). Statement from Dr Gawirrin Gumana AO. Indigenous Law Bulletin, 7(12 May/June).

Harrison, M. D., & McConchie, P. (2013). My People's Dreaming : an Aboriginal Elder speaks on life, land, spirit and forgiveness. Sydney, Australia: HarperCollins Publishers.

Hong, V. (2013). Paddocks Alight - Traditional Burning In The Lachlan, video recording.   Retrieved from https://vimeo.com/72953714

Kwaymullina, A. (2008). Introduction: A Land of Many Countries. In S. Morgan, T. Mia, & B. Kwaymullina (Eds.), Heartsick for Country: stories of love, spirit and creation (pp. 5-20). North Fremantle, Western Australia, Australia: Fremantle Press.

Langton, M. (2002). The Edge of the Sacred, the Edge of Death: Sensual Inscriptions. In B. David & M. Wilson (Eds.), Inscribed landscapes: Marking and making place (pp. 253-269). Hawaii, HI, USA: University of Hawaii Press.

Larsen, S. C., & Johnson, J. T. (2012). In between worlds: place, experience, and research in Indigenous geography. Journal of Cultural Geography, 29(1 (February)), 1-13.

Lehman, G. (2008). A Snake and a Seal. In S. Morgan, T. Mia, & B. Kwaymullina (Eds.), Heartsick for Country: stories of love, spirit and creation (pp. 131-142). North Fremantle, Western Australia, Australia: Fremantle Press.

Ma, N. (Writer). (2016). Putuparri and The Rainmakers: NITV.

Mandybur, J. (2016, 13 June). Landmark documentary series Songlines On Screen Retrieved from http://www.sbs.com.au/nitv/songlines-on-screen/article/2016/04/29/landmark-documentary-series-songlines-screen-coming-soon?cid=inbody:songlines-of-my-country-belonging-to-land-is-a-universal-right-that-shouldnt-be-denied

Marika, B., Munyarryun, B., Munyarryun, B., Marawili, N., Marika, W., & Kerins, S. (2012). Ranger djäma? Manymak! In J. Altman & S. Kerins (Eds.), People on Country: vital landscapes Indigenous futures. Sydney, New South Wales, Australia: The Federation Press.

Martin, B. (2013). Immaterial Land. In E. Barrett & B. Bolt (Eds.), Carnal knowledge: towards a 'new materialism' through the arts (pp. 185-204). London, England: I. B. Tauris.

McKnight, A. (2015). Preservice teachers' learning with Yuin Country: becoming respectful teachers in Aboriginal education. Asia-Pacific Journal of Teacher Education, 12 July 2015, 1-15.

Moreton-Robinson, A. (2003). I Still Call Australia Home: Indigenous Belonging and Place in a White Postcolonizing Society. In S. Ahmed, C. Castaneda, A.-M. Fortier, & M. Sheller (Eds.), Uprootings/Regroundings : Questions of Home and Migration (pp. 23-40). New York, NY, USA: Berg Publishers.

Muller, L. (2014). A Theory for Indigenous Australian Health and Human Service Work. Crows Nest, NSW, Australia: Allen & Unwin.

Murphy, J. W. (2003). Family. In P. McConchie (Ed.), Elders. Cambridge, UK: The University of Cambridge.

Nannup, N. (2008). Caring for Everything. In S. Morgan, T. Mia, & B. Kwaymullina (Eds.), Heartsick for Country: stories of love, spirit and creation (pp. 101-114). North Fremantle, Western Australia, Australia: Fremantle Press.

Neidjie, B., Davis, S., & Fox, A. (1985). Australia's Kakadu Man Bill Neidjie. Queanbeyan, New South Wales, Australia: Mybrood.

NSW Aboriginal Land Council. (2015, 29 March). The Journey So Far - Ulladulla Local Aboriginal Land Council.   Retrieved from https://youtu.be/nF6Q5FMPT0k

O'Brien, K. (2011). In pursuit of an architecture of realism. Monument, 101(March), n/a.

O'Brien, K. (2012). For architecture and country.

Pascoe, B. (2007). Convincing Ground: Learning to fall in love with your country: Aboriginal studies press.

Pascoe, B. (2014). Dark Emu: Black seeds agriculture or accident? Broome, WA, Australia: Magabala Books Aboriginal Corporation.

Pearce, M. W., & Louis, R. P. (2008). Mapping Indigenous Depth of Place. American Indian Culture and Research Journal, 32(3), 107-126.

Rigney, L.-I. (2006). Indigenist Research and Aboriginal Australia. In J. E. Kunnie & I. G. Nomalungelo (Eds.), Indigenous Peoples' Wisdom and Power: Affirming Our Knowledge Through Narratives. Farnham, Surry, UK: Ashgate Publishing Limited.

Salmón, E. (2012). Eating the Landscape: American Indian Stories of Food, Identity, and Resilience. Tucson, Arizona, USA: University of Arizona Press.

Sheehan, N. W. (2011). Indigenous Knowledge and Respectful Design: An Evidence-Based Approach. DesignIssues, 27(4 Autumn), 68-80.

Simms, G. (2015, 28 October 2015) Personal Communication on 28 October 2015/Interviewer: D. Hromek.

Simms, G. (2016, 14 December 2016) Personal Communication on 14 December 2016/Interviewer: D. Hromek.

Smith, K. (2017, 7 July 2017) Personal Communication on 5 July 2017/Interviewer: D. Hromek.

Smith, L. T. (2012). Decolonizing Methodologies: Research and Indigenous Peoples (2nd edition ed.). London, United Kingdom: Zed Books Ltd.

Somerville, M., & Perkins, T. (2010). Singing the Coast. Canberra, ACT: Aboriginal Studies Press.

Steffensen, V. (2016, August 22-26). [Personal Communication at Indigenous Fire Workshop 2016].

Tan, M. (2016, September 1, 2016). Yamandhu marang? Language does not belong to people, it belongs to country. The Guardian, p. n.p. Retrieved from https://www.theguardian.com/culture/2016/sep/01/yamandhu-marang-language-does-not-belong-to-people-it-belongs-to-country

Torres, M. (Writer). (2016). Footprints, Songlines. Australia: NITV.

Troy, J. (2016). Songlines of my Country: belonging to land is a universal right that shouldn't be denied. 5 July. Retrieved from http://www.sbs.com.au/nitv/article/2016/07/05/songlines-my-country-belonging-land-universal-right-shouldnt-be-denied

Ungunmerr, M. R. (1993). Dadirri: Listening to One Another. In J. Hendricks & G. Hefferan (Eds.), A Spirituality of Catholic Aborigines and the Struggle for Justice (pp. 34–37). Brisbane, Queensland, Australia: Aboriginal and Torres Strait Islander Apostolate, Catholic Archdiocese of Brisbane.

Watson, I. (1997). Indigenous Peoples' Law-Ways: Survival Against the Colonial State. Australian Feminist Law Journal, 8(1), 39-58.

Watson, I. (2002). Buried Alive. Law and Critique, 13, 253-269.

Watson, I. (2009). Sovereign Spaces, Caring for Country, and the Homeless Position of Aboriginal Peoples. South Atlantic Quarterly, 108(1 (Winter)), 27-51.

Watson, I. (2016). Prof Irene Watson. Let's Talk. Australia: 98.9FM.com.au.

Watson, J., & Martin-Chew, L. (2009). Judy Watson : blood language. Carlton, Victoria, Australia: Melbourne University Publishing.

Wildcat, D. (2001). Understanding the Crisis in American Education. In V. Deloria & D. Wildcat (Eds.), Power and Place: Indian Education in America. Golden, Colorado, USA: Fulcrum Publishing.

Wilson, J. J. (Writer). (2016). Goorrandalng: Brolga Dreaming, Songlines. Australia: NITV.

Chapter 25: 'Kohanga Rehua' – Restoring the last earth floor Māori meeting house in Aotearoa New Zealand

Rau Hoskins – Ngāti Hau, Ngā Puhi

Rau has over 25 years experience working with Māori community-based design projects and has for the past 20 years specialized in the design of Māori educational institutions in the upper North Island. In 1997, Rau completed his Master's degree in architecture, culminating in a thesis that focused on the re-emerging role of the Māori architect in relation to the design of Kura Kaupapa Māori. He has also worked extensively as an urban and cultural design consultant, as well as in iwi liaison capacities on a range of large public projects. Rau teaches part-time at the Unitec Department of Architecture and, with colleague Carin Wilson, has been active in researching both traditional and hybrid Māori dwelling construction techniques. He presented the 13-part TV series "Whare Māori," which won the AFTA for best information programme at the 2011 Aotearoa Film and Television Awards.

Introduction

The Whanganui River runs 290 kilometres from its source on Mt. Tongariro in the central North Island to meet the sea at the city of Whanganui on the west coast. The river is regarded as a Tūpuna Awa (ancestor) by the Te Āti Haunui-a-Pāpārangi Iwi (tribe) and is central to their lives as a source of food, a single highway and spiritual mentor (Waitangi Tribunal, 1999).

Kōhanga Rehua marae is located on the right bank of the Whanganui river diagonally opposite the Pipiriki township and consists of a set of remnant structures from a once, much larger kāinga (small settlement). This set of structures includes the Kōhanga Rehua earth floor wharepuni (meeting and sleeping house) which is believed to be the last full size earth floor wharepuni in Aotearoa.

Both the marae and wharepuni take their name from the nearby Kōhanga Rehua fortified pā (hill fort) which sits immediately to the south-west of the marae and acted as a defensive position for the hapū (kinship group) into the mid 1800s and again when occupied as a military redoubt by colonial troops from 1865-66 (Waitangi Tribunal,1999).

Like many Whanganui River kāinga on the right bank, Kōhanga Rehua was largely abandoned by World War II with only sporadic visits and occupations by whānau (family) members up until the commencement of restoration activities in 2014.

Background

Following a visit to the marae in 2011 to film an episode of the Whare Māori Television series (NZ on Screen, Scottie Productions [2011] I remained in contact with descendants of the marae Don Robinson and Adrian Pucher along with Dean Whiting of Heritage New Zealand Pouhere Taonga and, together in 2014, we commenced a comprehensive restoration and rebuilding project for the Kōhanga Rehua wharepuni and associated facilities to enable the marae to become fully functional again.

Te Hononga

The project so far has involved over 100 2nd, 3rd and 4th year architecture students from Te Hononga o Whaihanga Ki Wairaka (Te Hononga) at the Unitec Architecture Pathway (Department) in Auckland. The students have worked alongside and under the guidance of descendants of the marae, myself (Rau Hoskins) and Carin Wilson from Te Hononga along with Heritage New Zealand conservation experts Dean Whiting and Jim Schuster. Te Hononga students hail from all parts of the globe with up to half of each cohort being born overseas. Former Te Hononga student, conservation carpenter and architecture graduate Brent Withers has also become a key team member and has attended all 11 workshops in both a tutoring and specialist carpentry role.

Figure 1. Kōhanga Rehua Wharepuni, April 2016, Source: Author

Te Hononga – The centre for Māori Architecture and Appropriate Technologies have been offering real world Māori community studio design projects at Unitec New Zealand since 1999. The centre has three main objectives:

• To engage in Māori community based project work
• To engage in, promote and support academic research in the field of Māori Architecture
• To provide holistic support for Māori students within the Architecture Pathway.

Te Hononga was established as a response to perceived shortcomings in architectural education in Aotearoa where up until the early 1990s Māori students and, by extension Māori communities, were poorly served by the Eurocentric programmes on offer at the University of Auckland and Victoria University of Wellington, relying on a few culturally sensitive non-Māori lecturers being available to provide some academic support. Māori architecture was barely acknowledged as a valid architectural focus (Hoskins, 1997).

In 1992 the Whaihanga Māori student support unit and studio strand was established by myself (Ngāpuhi) and

Saul Roberts (Tainui) (then new architecture graduates), at the University of Auckland School of Architecture and was followed in 1993 with the appointment of the first full time Māori lecturer in architecture Mike Barns.

While Whaihanga continued to offer Māori studio projects and some Māori student support until the late 1990s, the focus for innovation in Māori architectural education effectively shifted to Unitec soon after the architecture course was established in 1994. This included the appointment of Derek Kawiti (Ngāti Hine) as a full-time lecturer, the establishment of Te Rūnanga o Whaihanga as an external Māori advisory group in 1996, my appointment in a part time capacity and the formation of Te Hononga in 1999. In 2001, designer and artist Carin Wilson (Ngāti Awa) was also appointed in a part time capacity to support the wider activities of Te Hononga.

The primary focus of Te Hononga is to engage in integrated design studio projects drawn from the Māori community. These are real-world projects centred on architecture but extended to include issues of sustainability, the revival of traditional Māori construction

Figure 2. Kōhanga Rehua Marae clearing (central) 2017 with Whanganui River, Source: Author

methods, resource management, planning, and artistic expression. All projects have a "hands on" building component and the Centre collaborates with hapū and whānau (extended Māori families) to support built environment outcomes, the development of both traditional Māori and contemporary building skills and the cementing of long term working relationships.

Te Hononga has been pivotal to the establishment of, and maintains a close association with, Ngā Aho, the National Māori Design Professionals network incorporated in 2009 (Ngā Aho Website, n.d.). Ngā Aho seeks to nurture the development of Māori designers (including many Te Hononga graduates) and Māori community built environment aspirations in Aotearoa. From 2016 it has broadened its focus to build relationships with Indigenous architects and design professionals worldwide. This commenced with *I Te Timatanga*, the inaugural International Indigenous Design Conference held at Whakapara marae (Northland) in February 2016 (I Te Timatanga - Ngā Aho website, n.d.)

Over time Te Hononga has developed expertise in articulating a local language to guide students through an investigative approach to cultural landscapes, living patterns, identifying sustainable solutions, discovering appropriate materials and evaluating construction solutions while engaging in experiential opportunities.

Critical to the Te Hononga approach is to engage students (both Māori and non-Māori) directly with Māori communities and their built environment aspirations broadening their cultural learning opportunities "well beyond the lecture room." While Te Hononga has undertaken over a dozen real world Māori community design and build projects, the Kōhanga Rehua marae redevelopment is its most ambitious to date and the project has benefited greatly from the multi year approach.

Heritage Issues

As an historic site that has been occupied for several hundred years, Kōhanga Rehua comes under the

Figure 3. Kōhanga Rehua Wharepuni 2014, Source: Author

auspices of the Heritage New Zealand Pouhere Taonga Act 2014 which sets out archaeological controls for such sites (Parliamentary Counsels Office, n.d.)

Heritage New Zealand Pouhere Taonga is an autonomous Crown Entity that works to promote the identification, protection, preservation, and conservation of the historical and cultural heritage of New Zealand.

The organisation is governed by a Board, and assisted by the Māori Heritage Council, whose purpose and functions include developing Māori programmes for the identification and conservation of places of significance to Māori (Sec 27 (1)(b) HNZPT Act 2014). As part of their Māori programme, Heritage New Zealand has been working with marae communities since the 1970s on the conservation and restoration of their marae buildings.

Heritage New Zealand has been working with the whānau of Kōhanga Rehua since 2004, when Dean Whiting, Manager of the Māori Built Heritage Programme, worked with conservation architect Chris

Cochran to prepare a conservation plan for the buildings on site (Cochran, 2005).

History of the Whanganui river and Kōhanga Rehua marae

The three remnant buildings and central marae ātea (ceremonial forecourt in front of the wharepuni) which now form Kōhanga Rehua marae exist as a small remnant of the much larger Pipiriki settlement which formerly occupied both sides of the river. In 1843 the recorded population was 296 (Taylor, 1843) and up until the 1890s most of the Pipiriki population lived on the right bank of the river in a linear arrangement of three neighbouring kāinga, with Rangiāhua to the north, Te Pōti in the centre and Kōhanga Rehua to the south.

Introduced European diseases and warfare in the mid 1860s drastically reduced the population at Pipiriki until a gradual return from the mid 1870s. In 1881 former Pipiriki residents returned from the village of Parihaka in

Figure 4. Kōhanga Rehua wharepuni in its original location prior to the 1904 flood, Source: Alexander Turnball Library, Ref. 1/1-021768-G

Figure 5. Pipiriki (Rangiāhua) Village: Photograph taken by Alfred Burton, ca 1885, Source: Alexander Turnball Library, Ref. F61469 1/2

Figure 6. Ihaka Rerekura (far left) and others outside Kōhanga Rehua Wharepuni in 1910 (in its current location) with Pātaka to left (Source: Robinson Whānau)

the neighbouring Taranaki area. Parihaka was a centre of passive resistance to European colonisation under the leadership of the prophets Te Whiti o Rongomai and Tohu Kakahi and had from the mid 1860s become a haven for Māori from around the North Island who had become dispossessed from their lands and for those who were attracted to their new religious teachings which focussed on non-violent resistance to the surveying and fencing of newly confiscated Taranaki lands (Scott, 1975). It is well known that there was a strong connection between the middle and upper Whanganui river hapū (Young, 1998) and Parihaka and that many hapū members returned to the river from Parihaka in the 1880s following its invasion by government troops in 1881 (Butler, 1887).

Burton Brothers photographs from 1885 (pictured below) show the Rangiāhua end of the linear Pipiriki right bank settlement with a series of pātaka (storehouses), domestic dwellings and wharepuni flanked by wheatfields which had by that time become a staple trade commodity and food source for hapū on the Whanganui River. Interestingly at this time some corrugated iron roofed dwellings are beginning to appear including on some pataka.

In this period, each wharepuni was the domain of an individual rangatira (chief) as it was the responsibility of each rangatira to both welcome and host visitors, hence a larger capacity wharepuni was required. Such wharepuni were named after important ancestors, events or local landmarks (as with Kōhanga Rehua) and also received levels of carved and later painted decoration not applied to common dwellings.

With the advent of the Alexander Hatrick & Company Steam boat ferry, tourism activity from the 1890s and later the Whanganui River road built in the 1930s (Young, 1999) the population of Pipiriki progressively shifted to the left bank and today Kōhanga Rehua marae provides the only built presence on the right bank. In contrast Pipiriki township on the left bank consists of over 60 dwellings with a 2013 census population of 149 (NZ Census, 2013).

While the Whanganui River road and resulting urbanisation undoubtedly contributed to the loss of population at Kōhanga Rehua, the impact of flooding was another important reason why the settlement on the right bank was finally abandoned. The land on the right bank was lower-lying than that on the left bank and therefore more vulnerable to flooding. Oral sources (Robinson, 2016) supported by photographic records claim that the Kōhanga Rehua wharepuni was relocated to its present position some time between 1904 and 1910, and shifted back from the river edge Te Pōti kāinga to its present

Figure 7. The Wharepuni, 2015 Source: Author

location in order to reduce the risk of flooding. In 1891, flooding caused families to temporarily leave the right bank settlement, with many returning in 1901. However, there were further problems in 1904 when the river rose to about 18 metres above its average height (Cochran, 2005). Oral evidence indicates that most people had moved permanently from the right bank by the 1920s and that Te Pōti kāinga was last occupied in the late 1930s (Robinson, 2015).

Kōhanga Rehua Restoration

Kōhanga Rehua wharepuni follows the traditional form of Whanganui River wharepuni with its central door and windows either side and a single window in the centre of the back (south) wall which appears to have been added later. The wharepuni measures 9.4m long (including the mahau or porch) x 5.4m wide with walls being 1.3m high and the height to the underside of the Tāhuhu (ridge board) being 3.525m.

The wharepuni represents a hybrid Māori / European construction approach consisting of pit sawn timber wall frames fixed directly to timber piles, timber rafters with collar ties, timber weather boards and a corrugated iron roof. The decorative elements include hand planed poupou (wall posts), rafters and tāhuhu (ridge board).

The restoration and rebuilding process has generally followed the 2005 conservation report completed by Chris Cochran with Rebecca O'Brien and Dean Whiting (Cochran, 2005) and has comprised a series of 11 three to seven day working bee visits with participants living in at this remote location which has no road access or any reticulated services. All personnel, food, equipment, and materials are jet boated or canoed to the site with the assistance of a local operator with family connections to the marae. Student involvement (20-35 students per visit) has been invaluable in terms of the physical labour requirements of the exercises, particularly carrying materials up the river bank and along the 100m bush track to the marae site. Tents have generally been used for

Figure 8. New raupō (bullrush) insulation inserted into rear / south wall (February 2015) Source: Author

Figure 9. Interior of Kōhanga Rehua with levelled and compacted earth floor (December 2017), Source: Author

Figure 10. PVC membrane roof dining structure with kitchen lockup to rear, Source: Author

Figure 11. Plywood kitchen lockup with brick fireplace pre-levelling, Source: Author

Figure 12. Re-levelled fireplace with new brickwork to chimney (November 2017), Source: Author

Figure 13. Rain water collection tower and tanks located in bush to rear (October 2016), Source: Author

Figure 14. Plywood bathroom complex with composting toilet (November 2017) Source, Author

accommodation up until Kohanga Rehua has become fully habitable for sleeping and each visit has become progressively more comfortable as cooking, dining, water collection and toilet facilties have been designed and installed.

As part of this process the Kōhanga Rehua wharepuni has been brought back from the brink with the whare being:

1. Fully repiled with heart tōtara timber piles recycled from fence posts
2. New 100x100mm bottom plates inserted
3. All rotted stud base timbers mortice and tenon jointed to bottom plates
4. New raupo (swamp reed) wall insulation installed
5. New tōtara south wall frame inserted
6. Replacement tōtara weather boards fixed to south and side walls,
7. New tōtara maihi (front and rear barge boards) and amo (front wall end posts)
8. Replacement tōtara rafters and purlins
9. Repacement tōtara diagonal wall linings
10. New colorsteel corrugated iron roof

Care has been taken to replace all rotted timbers with equivalent or superior native timbers such as tōtara (Podocarpus tōtara) for all exterior and structural applications and matai for replacement interior linings.

Additionally all timber jointing techniques were replicated from existing elements with students learning how to create mortice and tenon connections for all of the replacement structural elements.

Earth floor treatments

With the Kōhanga Rehua earth floor being such a unique feature, much attention has been given to the levelling and sealing of the earth to ensure a long term dust free surface. While the descendants were unaware of the earlier treatments we knew from our knowledge of other smaller domestic whare (earth floor houses) that a shiny almost burnished surface was achievable.

Coincidentally a large flood in June 2015 caused damage to the Te Paku o te Rangi wharepuni at Pūtiki Marae at the bottom of the Whanganui River. When the damaged timber floor was removed the original earth floor was revealed to be in remarkable condition and a local whānau member was then able to recall personally coating the surface up until the 1970s with shark liver oil sourced from wider whānau contacts in Waitara in the neighbouring Taranaki region (Whiting, 2015). While

Figure 15. Unidentified Māori Group at Pipiriki, 1885, (Note: Two traditional Pātaka on the left), Source: Burton Brothers, Alexander Turnbull Library, Ref F46788 1/2

more difficult to source today, shark liver oil remains the preferred long term option for sealing the floor with boiled linseed oil being a possible fall back option.

Painted interior decoration

While Kōhanga Rehua is an uncarved house typical of many late 19th Century wharepuni on the Whanganui River, a unique feature are the Victorian landscape polychrome oil paintings applied to the upper portions of the poupou (interior wall posts). These paintings consist of a series of river scenes and local flora and fauna such as tui birds, pikiararoa (New Zealand Clematis), karaka berries and rata flowers. While the painter is unknown the artist appears to have had some formal training with the scenes providing snap shot records of life on the Whanganui river at the time of painting. The paintings are in remarkably good condition for their age, partly owing to a top layer of varnish (Cochran, 2005) and will be restored under the guidance of Dean Whiting who is a specialist in conserving Māori painted decoration.

Apart from the photographic evidence, one of the clues to date of the origins of Kōhanga Rehua wharepuni is the painted figure on the pane (underside of the porch section of the tāhuhu (ridge board) which features a male holding a whalebone patu (hand weapon) and wearing what appears to be three huia feathers in his hair. Huia feathers were popular as hair adornments in Māori society in the late 18th century and generally denoted chiefly ancestry.

According to descendants this pane figure represents Te Kaioroto (also known as Hōri Pātene) a chief from Pipiriki who was killed in the battle of Katikara in Taranaki on the 4th of June 1863 while fighting colonial troops alongside his Taranaki relatives (Young, 1998 p. 55). It appears that this tāhuhu figure has been painted in memory of Te Kaioroto in the decade following his death giving us the estimated 1880s date of construction for Kōhanga Rehua.

Integration of new appropriate technology marae facilities

Today the three key facilities required for all types of marae are a wharepuni for meetings and to sleep guests, a wharekai and kitchen to support cooking and dining and ablutions facilities comprising toilets and showers.

With these facilities along with the marae ātea (ceremonial courtyard in front of the meeting house) any type of gathering can be accommodated (Hoskins, 2012).

Given the isolated location, lack of reticulated services and intermittent, mainly summer use proposed, a unique set of supporting facilities have been designed and built at Kōhanga Rehua to compliment the restored 19th century buildings as follows.

Membrane roof Dining structure

While all functioning marae in Aotearoa now have enclosed dining halls as core facilities, the requirement at Kōhanga Rehua is somewhat different where the need is really about providing multipurpose communal shelter from both the sun and rain. A cost effective and easily transported solution arrived at, is the earth floor PVC membrane roof dining structure designed, prefabricated and erected in 2015. The portal frame elements and purlins were all made from CNC plywood sheets, pre-cut at Unitec in Auckland and trucked to Pipiriki before being jet boated across the river and assembled on site. The 80m2 heat welded PVC UV resistant membrane roof was donated free of charge (by a company specialising in PVC advertising hoardings) and provides for a range of other functions including tool and gear storage as well as being particularly useful as a sheltered work location mainly for cutting timber.

Kitchen lockup

The Kitchen lockup is designed as a robust, functional and secure place to store and prepare food that can be locked up and remain vermin proof over the winter months when visits to the marae are rare. The lockup consists of a 2.4m wide x 3.6m deep north facing kitchen with a corner entry and preparation benches to all sides and three large plywood awning windows which are operated by second hand gas struts sourced from vehicle wreckers in Auckland.

The southern section of the lockup is separated from the kitchen area by an internal wall and is dedicated to the storage of tools and fuel and is separately accessed by double doors. A small mezzanine floor has been created above the tool store area and, while large enough for a small sleeping space, is currently used for additional storage.

The lockup also includes an outdoor dishwashing area with stainless steel sink bench to the west side which receives cover from the plywood awning window above when open.

The kitchen lockup is made from plywood and LVL timber framing supplied free of charge through sponsorship from Juken New Zealand

Fireplace Relevelling

A remnant brick fireplace from a long demolished cottage to the east of the marae ātea belonging to Ihaka Rerekura became a focus for another minor restoration project in 2016 and 2017 with a team of four students researching and proposing a levelling technique along with designing and building a social, dining deck area with an open fire as a central focus.

The fireplace had progressively leaned to the east from being close to level at our initial visit in 2014 and by October 2016 was in danger of collapsing. The levelling technique proposed was adapted from the approach taken for the Leaning Tower of Pisa from 1993-97 (Daily Mail, 2013) with the chimney fully braced and a careful excavation of the soil on the west side allowing the chimney to gradually come back to a near level position over the last three days of our October 2016 visit.

A recycled hardwood deck was built to the front of the chimney and the area is now used as communal dining space for smaller groups as well as the telling of "fireside stories" in the evenings. In November 2017 a wet back hot water heating system was integrated into the fire place with a small tank stand and 135l hot water cylinder to the east of the fire place. The chimney section was also rebricked and the system now provides convenient hot water for dishwashing purposes negating the need to continually heat water on the gas hobs.

Rain water tower

While it has been possible to utilise a well, located near the cottage for cooking, washing and drinking water, by early summer the well is normally dry so a key project for the October 2016 visit was to design and build a water collection tower at the western end of the site. This location sits approximately 3m higher than the kitchen lockup floor level which has the most need for a year round water supply. This is a simple mono pitch roof structure (with tanks located in the bush area to the south) which also provides for an additional shelter to the marae western camping area and private solar showering location to the rear.

LED lighting system

While cooking and water heating at the marae is via LPG gas bottles, one of the main requirements for the marae is a safe, reliable and low energy lighting solution. As part of the October 2016 studio exercise students were asked to research, design, and source the necessary components for an LED lighting system. The students were able to obtain a second hand photo voltaic / solar panel, two deep cell batteries and LED light fittings and installed the system during the week long working bee. The system now provides good lighting levels to the kitchen lockup, dining, and bathroom areas. It is intended that this system will eventually be extended to the cottage and possibly even into Kōhanga Rehua wharepuni.

Bioloo composting toilet

While for the first two years the only toilet facilities available for the working bees was an old long drop with corrugated iron surround, in 2016 a 50 person capacity Bioloo composting toilet was sourced from the supplier in Rotorua and installed in a plywood bathroom complex that also includes a shower and hand basin. The bathroom complex is located to the east of the marae ātea in regenerating native forest and also includes a north facing roof to receive future solar photovoltaic and hot water panels.

The Bioloo consists of a self-contained ventilated polyethylene tank with a custom designed throne and 200mm vent pipe capped with a wind cowling. Te Hononga has previously installed similar composting toilets for projects on Rangitoto Island (2009) and at Waihihi (2011) and were confident that the system would also work well at Kōhanga Rehua in providing an odour free and environmentally friendly solution.

In addition to the Bioloo a second hand Department of Conservation (DOC) fibreglass longdrop toilet cubicle compliments the Bioloo and is located near the marae entry, primarily for the use of visitors prior to their arrival at the marae. Both toilets are back vented which both evaporates fluids and prevents odours.

Pātaka restoration

Pātaka are raised timber store houses which were common on marae and within kāinga up until the early 1900s where food, tools, weapons and valuables were stored to keep them safe, away from both rodents and people. While most pātaka were used to store dried or preserved foods, some were used to house and protect taonga or treasured items (Phillips,1952). At Rangiahua, (the northern part of the right bank Pipiriki settlement) photographic records show a large number of pātaka which are either dedicated to separate storage types or allocated to individual rangatira (chiefs).

The pātaka at Kōhanga Rehua sits to the south-east of the wharepuni and was oriented to face North keeping the interior warm and dry as well as acknowledging the marae ātea as a significant communal building. A porch at the front of the pātaka was generally used to deposit various articles of value. Pātaka played an important role on all marae and kāinga on the Whanganui River with the need to store seasonally harvested food for year long consumption.

With restoration of Kōhanga Rehua wharepuni nearing completion, in 2016 a dedicated student team began to research Whanganui River pātaka styles and with the assistance of Dean Whiting (Heritage New Zealand) completed a conservation plan for the pātaka (Te Hononga, 2016).

In consultation with the whānau it was agreed to relocate the pātaka to sit forward and closer to the wharepuni and to better address the marae ātea. This was also a desirable approach given the poor state of the existing pātaka foundations and sub floor elements with new tōtara piles, bearers and floor joists installed at the proposed new site without the need to touch the existing pātaka structure. The pātaka was then in 2017 lifted by hand onto the new floor structure and new weatherboards, flooring, and ceiling sarking elements installed along with a new rear window.

Original pātaka standing on marae are rare in Aotearoa today and this one gives special significance to Kōhanga Rehua marae. This particular pātaka demonstrates a hybrid European and Māori construction approach with the use of rusticated weatherboard cladding, tongue and groove flooring, timber trusses and a corrugated iron roof. As evident in the Burton Brothers photo (see Figure 15), kāinga often had multiple pātaka for various uses, ordinary pātaka for food storage and carved or ornamented pātaka for garments, weapon storage and other valuable possessions.

This pātaka appears to be of the common variety and would likely have stored food such as dried eels and piharau (lamprey), freshwater mussels, flour, and preserved kererū or wood pigeons.

Changing attitudes to Marae restoration

Over the last 30 years a number of restoration approaches for Kōhanga Rehua have been considered. One of the options discussed was to relocate the wharepuni to the left bank of the river to sit at Paraweka Marae alongside the other marae buildings (Cochran, 2005) This approach has been followed in several other locations further down the Whanganui river at Koroniti / Otukopiri Marae where Poutama wharepuni was moved from Karatia in 1967 (Waitangi Tribunal, 1999) and at Parikino Marae where two wharepuni (Wharewhiti and Te Aroha) were moved across the river when the entire marae was relocated to the left bank (Beaglehole, 2015)

While this approach has ensured that these ancestral whare have been saved and are now well utilised it has involved abandoning the previous kāinga sites on the right bank. This was the primary source of resistance from many of the whānau involved to following this approach at Kōhanga Rehua. They did not want to lose their ancestral connection to their kāinga which also includes an historic urupā (cemetery) at the eastern base of Kōhanga Rehua Pā (Robinson, 2014).

The traditional Māori approach to an obviously ageing whare was to treat it as an ancestor that had lived its life and could now be taken away and buried. This practice acknowledges the original karakia (incantations) that were given to imbue the trees with their purpose in coming together to form a whare as tane whakapiripiri (the collective embodiment of the forest god) and with that purpose now over, karakia were again performed to end the life of the whare and consign it to burial. This practice still occurs occasionally today. For example, the Rangihouhiri II wharenui in Whakatāne was taken down and buried after three years of hui, wānanga and consultation in 2000 (Rangihouhiri II Home, 2017).

Notwithstanding this, it is now increasingly likely that marae whānau will seek to restore older wharepuni in order to maintain a spiritual connection to those ancestors who have gone before them. In this way Māori, particularly those who have been disconnected from their ancestral homes, are progressively adopting more western attitudes to the conservation of marae buildings as part of on an ongoing cultural renaissance.

Additionally, the complexity and cost of whare restoration has become a significant barrier to these exercises with specialised conservation assessment and carpentry skills being extremely rare within Māori communities. While Heritage New Zealand have a small team of Māori Pouarahi or experts who can support these processes, (Heritage New Zealand, 2017) the exercises need to be initiated and led by the marae communities themselves. Until 2016 specialist heritage building conservation courses were not available in New Zealand with individuals needing to

travel to Australia to complete such post graduate qualifications. The University of Auckland has since established a Masters in Heritage Conservation course which has operated as of 2016 (University of Auckland, 2016). It is hoped that a new generation of Māori heritage professionals will now be able to both receive their training and apply their skills to much needed marae restoration projects here in Aotearoa.

Funding for such restoration exercises is also limited being primarily provided on a contestable basis through the Marae Heritage and Facilities fund administered by the Department of Internal Affairs Lottery grants board (Department of Internal Affairs, 2017).

Future use of Kōhanga Rehua Marae

The primary challenge for Kōanga Rehua remains its isolation with road access to this part of the right bank of the Whanganui river unlikely to ever be available and jet boat access being relatively expensive even with "whānau rates" generally applying. A flying fox has been discussed as a partial access solution similar to the one further down the river at Koroniti. However, there are significant logistical and cost issues associated with such a solution. Increasingly two person canoes have provided an efficient means of transporting both small groups of people and equipment to and from Kōhanga Rehua and it is anticipated that this waka (Māori canoe) tradition will remain a permanent feature of the marae experience.

While the relative inaccessibility of the marae remains as a barrier to high usage, its isolation can also be seen as an advantage for both whānau and outside visitors who appreciate the opportunity to connect with both the natural and cultural setting and disconnect from the outside world.

Tira Hoe Waka

The Tira Hoe Waka is a 12 day long 240 kilometre annual iwi (tribal) pilgrimage down the Whanganui River from the town of Taumarunui (where the river becomes navigable) to the city of Whanganui and allows descendants of the river (Āti Haunui-a-Pāpārangi) to come together to learn oral histories of the river and reconnect with ancestral kāinga and each other. The Tira Hoe Waka commenced in 1989 and attracts around 120 paddlers using both six and two person canoes. The Tira commences on the 5th of January each year and marae stayed at in alternate years ensuring that all have turns to be hosts and to tell their own stories. One of the main intended uses for Kōhanga Rehua

Figure 17. Kōhanga Rehua with local whānau and Te Hononga Staff and students November 2017, Source: Author

marae is for it to be made available for the Tira Hoe Waka itinerary where it is likely it will alternate with the nearby Paraweka Marae on the left bank of the river in the Pipiriki township. In this way Kōhanga Rehua will proudly resume its place as one of the "living marae" of the river.

Apart from the Tira Hoe Waka and wider whānau use, it is likely that the marae will be attractive for wānanga (intensive live-in Māori knowledge sharing exercises) which rely on a degree of isolation to ensure the focus of participants. Such wānanga could be based on Whanganui reo (language) whakapapa (genealogy) and tikanga (custom) or even for wider groups who would appreciate this unique and historic off-grid marae environment.

Conclusion

The Kōhanga Rehua wharepuni restoration and wider marae redevelopment exercise has demonstrated the value of collaborative working relationships forged between marae whānau, tertiary Māori architecture education and Māori Heritage professionals in bringing significant marae buildings and, in this case, an entire marae back to life.

Here while the Kōhanga Rehua whānau have provided the critical impetus for the project and ongoing resources, the enthusiasm, good will and combined "muscle" of a committed student cohort has been essential for this project, as has been the skilled and culturally sensitive support of Māori Heritage New Zealand professionals.

Figure 16. Pātaka in 2014 prior to restoration, Source: Author

This restoration exercise has involved a deep appreciation of the cultural significance of Kōhanga Rehua marae and a correspondingly sensitive approach to the design and construction of a set of support structures and systems which are uniquely suited to this isolated river environment in being practical, low cost, appropriate technology and environmentally sustainable.

Finally, this project demonstrates an evolving collaborative approach to marae redevelopment processes that recognises the cultural and spiritual values embodied in such ancestral buildings that are still capable of being given new life and, in so doing, allowing descendants to reforge critical ties to ancestral kāinga.

References

Beaglehole, D. (2015), "Whanganui places – River settlements," Te Ara – *the Encyclopedia of New Zealand* Retrieved 2017, December 11 from http://www.TeAra.govt.nz/en/whanganui-places/page-6.

Butler, W.J. (1887). *Letter to Under-Secretary*, Native Department, 18 May 1887, AJHR, 1887.G-1, p 14.

Cochran, C. (2005). *Rangiahua Wharenui, Te Poti Marae, Pipiriki Conservation Report*.

Daily Mail Australia (2013, October 28) Italian landmark loses 2.5cm of its famous tilt after £25m salvage project, Retrieved 2017, February 24 from http://www.dailymail.co.uk/news/article-2478295/STRAIGHTENING-Tower-Pisa-Italian-leaning-landmark-loses-2-5cm-tilt.html#ixzz52XqxR3dO

Department of Internal Affairs (2017) Lottery grants, Retrieved 2017, February 16 from http://www.communitymatters.govt.nz/Funding-and-grants---Lottery-grants---Lottery-Marae-Heritage-and-Facilities

Heritage New Zealand website (n.d.) Māori Heritage, Retrieved 2017, November 20 from http://www.heritage.org.nz/protecting-heritage/maori-heritage

Parliamentary Counsel Office (n.d.) Heritage New Zealand Pou Here Taonga Act 2014, Retrieved 2017, February 20 fromhttp://www.legislation.govt.nz/act/public/2014/0026/26.0/DLM4005414.html

Hoskins, R. (2012). "Māori Cultural Sustainability in the 21st Century, Changing Patterns of Marae Development and Use in Aotearoa / New Zealand in House Rauru, Master Piece of the Māori." *Journal of the Hamburg Museum of Ethnology*, Neue Folge 44, Page 354.

Hoskins, R. (1997). "Te Puawaitanga o te Kaihoahoa whare Māori me ngā Kura kaupapa Māori." Masters Thesis, University of Auckland.

Ngā Aho (n.d.) HomepageRetrieved 2017, September 15 from http://www.ngaaho.maori.nz/index.php?m=20

NZ on Screen, Scottie Productions (2011) Whare Māori Retrieved 2017, September 15 from https://www.nzonscreen.com/title/whare-maori-2011/series

Phillips, William J. (1952), *Māori Houses and Food Stores*. Wellington Dominion Museum Monograph No. 8 / R. E. Owen, Government Printer Wellington.

Rangihouhiri II, (2017) *Te Rangihouhiri II Marae Facebook page*, Retrieved 2017, December 10 from https://www.facebook.com/pg/Rangihouhiri/about/

Scott, D. 1975 *Ask That Mountain: The Story of Parihaka*. Raupo Publishing, New Zealand.

Taylor, R. (1843) "Native population of Wanganui river 1843" Journal Taylor MS, Papers 254, Vol. 3) (Table I, Fig. 2)

Te Hononga (2016). *Te Pōti Marae Pātaka Conservation Report*. Student output, Auckland University of Technology, Auckland, New Zealand.

University of Auckland (2016). Masters of Heritage Conservation, Retrieved 2017, February 16 from https://www.auckland.ac.nz/en/study/study-options/find-a-study-option/master-of-heritage-conservation.html

Young, D. (1998). *Woven By Water*. Huia Publishers, Wellington.

Waitangi Tribunal (1999). *The Whanganui River Report*. WAI 167 Waitangi Tribunal Report 1999. GP Publications.

I te Timatanga – Ngā Aho (n.d.) *I te Timatanga Symposium*, Retrieved 2017, December 20 from http://www.ngaaho.maori.nz/project.php?project_id=215&m=10)

Oral Sources

Robinson, Don. (multiple discussions 2014-17).

Whiting, Dean (July 2015).

Hei Whakakapi

The Provenance of Our Voices: Indigeneity and Architecture

A recent International Indigenous Architecture and Design Symposium in Ottawa in May 2017 was the impetus for this book. Having been part of a day of powerful presentations from Indigenous architects and designers, discussions at the post-conference dinner turned to publication. The overwhelming verdict was that it was time that Indigenous voices on architecture and design were heard. And, how rich would those voices be were they to come from ngā hau e wha (the four winds) and include authors from Indigenous communities, architectural practice and academia offering a diversity of Indigenous perspectives on architecture and design.

These conversations were also prompted by concerns over a lack of existing scholarship on Indigeneity, architecture, and design led by Indigenous people. We acknowledge the good work many non-Indigenous academics and practitioners have undertaken to support and bolster architecture and Indigeneity. However, now it is time for Indigenous academics and practitioners to lead the theory building and practice with respect to Indigenous placemaking, architecture and design. We call on non-Indigenous academics and practitioners to support this effort to forefront Indigenous voices. This book then, is a figurative request to "move over" and asks for a rethinking of who controls Indigeneity and architecture scholarship and how we might deliver leadership into the hands of Indigenous Peoples in regenerative ways.

Diverse Contests

As noted earlier, the authors involved in this book are all Indigenous hailing from a range of mobs, nations, and tribes. We have academics, housing advocates, secondary school students, architects, artists, Elders, urbanists, planners and policy people's voices included here. Some speak of having lost cultural roots and knowledge due to the impact of colonisation, whilst others who are deeply rooted in Indigenous settings,

speak with a stronger understanding of traditional values and practice. Given this diversity of background and experience the book offers different views – sometimes convergent, sometimes divergent.

There are numerous contests represented here. Some work to recover and conserve the traditional, others seek to carve out new Indigenous architectural methodologies and outcomes. Some reject the commodification of Indigeneity with respect to architecture whilst others see the value of capital processes for promulgating Indigenous identities in the architecture and design of our towns and cities.

As much as there are connections through the work, there remains a spectrum of opinions. Whatever the perspective, it is clear that all of us have experienced the impact of colonisation in one way or another. The effects of invasion, genocide and colonisation have left us all affected by our past, present and futures. We sit at the nexus, trying to manage multiple worlds. All of us are working in different, or similar ways to assert the importance of Indigeneity in the architecture and design of the communities, neighbourhoods, towns and cities in which we live and play.

This book is a mere beginning to this dialogue. As noted earlier, the authorship of this book has formed a publishing collective – *Our Voices Publishing Collective* which will continue to promulgate Indigenous voices. We look forward to broadening our author base and welcoming new authors to join us in future publications.

Acknowledgements

Enabling such a book requires commitment and belief in the project from a number of people. Firstly, we want to acknowledge ORO Editions, the publisher who believed in and backed the project with funding and ongoing support. We knew that this kind of book would need a publisher who understood Indigenous communities and the implications this had for the style and nature of writing on architecture and design. Our initial conversations with Gordon Goff of ORO Editions immediately drew us to this publisher. Gordon's own connection with his Cherokee heritage, his wife's First Nations heritage, their work with Indigenous Hawaiian communities and the promotion of the project as a collaborative endeavour that would allow us as the editors and authors to define the nature of the book all formed part of our desire to work with ORO Editions.

In addition to the publisher contribution, funding was also secured from the University of Sydney, Australia; Unitec, Auckland, NZ; Victoria University of Wellington, NZ; and, the AASA – Australasian Association of Schools of Architecture for the project. We would like to wholeheartedly thank these institutions for their generous support of the book. Without it this book would not have been possible.

Finally, we would like to thank all the authors, and associated voices conveyed within the book, for the time, energy and brain power offered up to create a truly unique collection of ideas, theories, analyses and reflections.

Rebecca, Kevin and Patrick